Common Wealth

ALSO BY JEFFREY D. SACHS

The End of Poverty

Common Wealth

ECONOMICS FOR A CROWDED PLANET

Jeffrey D. Sachs

ALLEN LANE
an imprint of
PENGUIN BOOKS

ALLEN LANE

Published by the Penguin Group

Penguin Books Ltd, 80 Strand, London WC2R ORL, England

Penguin Group (USA) Inc., 375 Hudson Street, New York, New York 10014, USA

Penguin Group (Canada), 90 Eglinton Avenue East, Suite 700, Toronto, Ontario, Canada M4P 2Y3
(a division of Pearson Penguin Canada Inc.)

Penguin Ireland, 25 St Stephen's Green, Dublin 2, Ireland (a division of Penguin Books Ltd)

Penguin Group (Australia), 250 Camberwell Road, Camberwell, Victoria 3124, Australia
(a division of Pearson Australia Group Pty Ltd)

Penguin Books India Pvt Ltd, 11 Community Centre, Panchsheel Park, New Delhi – 110 017, India

Penguin Group (NZ), 67 Apollo Drive, Rosedale, North Shore 0632, New Zealand
(a division of Pearson New Zealand Ltd)

Penguin Books (South Africa) (Pty) Ltd, 24 Sturdee Avenue, Rosebank, Johannesburg 2196, South Africa

Penguin Books Ltd, Registered Offices: 80 Strand, London WC2R ORL, England

www.penguin.com

First published in the United States of America by The Penguin Press,
a member of Penguin Group (USA) Inc. 2008
First published in Great Britain by Allen Lane 2008

1

Printed in Great Britain by Clays Ltd, St Ives plc

A CIP catalogue record for this book is available from the British Library

978-0-713-99919-8

www.greenpenguin.co.uk

Mixed Sources
Product group from well-managed
forests and other controlled sources
www.fsc.org Cert no. SA-COC-1592
© 1996 Forest Stewardship Council
FSC

Penguin Books is committed to a sustainable future
for our business, our readers and our planet.
The book in your hands is made from paper
certified by the Forest Stewardship Council.

For Lisa, Adam, and Hannah,
my three best reasons for hope

Contents

Foreword

DRAWING FROM HIS UNEXCELLED EXPERIENCE and knowledge, Jeffrey D. Sachs has written a state of the world report of immediate and enormous practical value. *Common Wealth: Economics for a Crowded Planet* delivers what the title promises: a crystal-clear analysis, a synthesis, a reference work, a field manual, a guidebook, a forecast, and an executive summary of recommendations fundamental to human welfare. It says to those responsible for Earth's 6.6 billion people: Just look at the numbers. The world has changed radically in the past several decades; it is going to change more, faster and faster. In spite of all we have accomplished through science and technology— indeed *because* of it—we will soon run out of margin. Now is the time to grasp exactly what is happening. The evidence is compelling: we need to redesign our social and economic policies before we wreck this planet. At stake is humankind's one shot at a permanently bright future.

Modern humanity was born, so to speak, about ten thousand years ago with the invention of agriculture and the villages and political hierarchies that soon followed. Up to that point our species had perfected hunter technology enough to wipe out a large part of Earth's largest mammals and birds—the megafauna—but it left most of the vegetated land surface and all of the oceans intact. The economic history that followed can be summarized very succinctly as follows: people used every means they could devise to convert the resources of Earth into wealth. The result was steady population growth accompanied by expansion in geographic range, sustained until virtually every habitable parcel of land was occupied, to as much a level of density as technology and disease resistance permitted. By 1500 the exponential form of the surge was obvious. By 2000 it had produced a global population dangerously close to the limit of Earth's available resources. The key trait of human economic advance has always been exponential growth: that is, with each increase, that same amount of increase is next attained sooner. The simple command humanity has followed is biological in nature: *be fruitful and multiply—in every way try to be exponential.* More precisely, the growth is logistic: it is exponential until it slows and tapers off because of restraints imposed by the environment.

As the large mass of data summarized in *Common Wealth* shows with sobering clarity, we have arrived at a narrow window of opportunity. Humanity has consumed or transformed enough of Earth's irreplaceable resources to be in better shape than ever before. We are smart enough and now, one hopes, well informed enough to achieve self-understanding as a unified species. If we choose sustainable development, we can secure our gains while averting disasters that appear increasingly imminent.

Please look at the numbers, then, in *Common Wealth*. Extrapolate a bit. We still can correct the course, but we do not have much time left to do it.

Almost all of the crises that afflict the world economy are ultimately environmental in origin: they prominently include climatic change, pollution, water shortage, defaunation, decline of arable soil, depletion of marine fisheries, tightening of petroleum sources, persistent pockets of severe poverty, the threat of pandemics, and a dangerous disparity of resource appropriation within and between nations.

Unfortunately, while each of these problems is understood to some degree by decision makers, they typically continue to be addressed as separate issues. Yet the world has little chance to solve any one, Sachs shows, until we understand how all of them connect by cause and effect. We will be wise to look upon ourselves as a species and devise more realistic and pragmatic approaches to all the problems as a whole.

Why has our leadership—political, business, and media—been so slow to put the pieces together? I believe the answer is that while the facts presented by Sachs picture reality, and are not very difficult to grasp, we all operate by a worldview distorted by the residues of hereditary human nature. We exist in a bizarre combination of Stone Age emotions, medieval beliefs, and godlike techology. That, in a nutshell, is how we have lurched into the early twenty-first century. We so enjoy the *Star Wars* movie series because it represents us, and our inborn archetypes, projected into the future.

I believe that good citizenship, national and global, will be well served if every educated person masters the illustrations in *Common Wealth* and reads what Jeffrey Sachs has to say about how to interpret and apply the information they contain. The presentation in this book should further be taken as a strong argument for better education in science and statistics in our schools. The subject is basic and universal. It transcends our many differences in religion and political ideology.

EDWARD O. WILSON

Pellegrino University Research Professor Emeritus at Harvard University and Honorary Curator in Entomology at the Museum of Comparative Zoology

PART ONE

New Economics for the Twenty-first Century

Chapter 1

Common Challenges, Common Wealth

THE TWENTY-FIRST CENTURY WILL OVERTURN many of our basic assumptions about economic life. The twentieth century saw the end of European dominance of global politics and economics. The twenty-first century will see the end of American dominance. New powers, including China, India, and Brazil, will continue to grow and will make their voices increasingly heard on the world stage. Yet the changes will be even deeper than a rebalancing of economics and politics among different parts of the world. The challenges of sustainable development—protecting the environment, stabilizing the world's population, narrowing the gaps between rich and poor, and ending extreme poverty—will take center stage. Global cooperation will have to come to the fore. The very idea of competing nation-states that scramble for markets, power, and resources will become passé. The idea that the United States can bully or attack its way to security has proved to be misguided and self-defeating. The world has become much too crowded and dangerous for more "great games" in the Middle East or anywhere else.

The defining challenge of the twenty-first century will be to face the reality that humanity shares a *common fate on a crowded planet*. That common fate will require new forms of global cooperation, a fundamental point of blinding simplicity that many world leaders have yet to understand or embrace. For the past two hundred years, technology and demography have consistently run ahead of deeper social understanding. Industrialization and science have created a pace of change unprecedented in human history. Philosophers, politicians, artists, and economists must scramble constantly to catch up with contemporaneous social conditions. Our social philosophies, as a result, consistently lag behind present realities.

In the last seventy-five years most successful countries gradually came to understand that their own citizens share a common fate, requiring the active role of government to ensure that every citizen has the chance and means (through public education, public health, and basic infrastructure) to participate productively within the society, and to curb society's dangerous encroachments on the physical environment. This activist philosophy, which holds that the self-organizing forces of a market economy should be guided by overarching principles of social justice and environmental stewardship, has not yet been extended robustly to global society.

In the twenty-first century our global society will flourish or perish according to our ability to find common ground across the world on a set of shared objectives and on the practical means to achieve them. The pressures of scarce energy resources, growing environmental stresses, a rising global population, legal and illegal mass migration, shifting economic power, and vast inequalities of income are too great to be left to naked market forces and untrammeled geopolitical competition among nations. A clash of civilizations could well result from the rising tensions, and it could truly be our last and utterly devastating clash. To find our way peacefully through these difficulties, we will have to learn, on a global scale, the same core lessons that successful societies have gradually and grudgingly learned within their own national borders.

It has not been easy to forge cooperation even within national boundaries. In the first century of industrialization, England and other early industrializing countries were characterized by harsh social conditions in which individuals and families were largely left to scramble in the new industrial age. Charles Dickens and Friedrich Engels left a lasting testimony to the harshness of the times. Gradually and fitfully, the early industrializing societies began to understand that they could not simply leave their own poor to wallow in deprivation, disease, and hunger without courting crime, instability, and disease for all. Gradually, and with enormous political strife, social insurance and transfer schemes for the poor became tools of social peace and prosperity during the period from roughly 1880 onward. Around half a century ago, many nations began to recognize that their air, water, and land resources also had to be managed more intensively for the common good of their citizens in an industrial age. The poorest parts of town could not be the dumping ground of toxic wastes without jeopardizing the rich neighborhoods as well. Heavy industry was despoiling the air and the water. Industrial pollution in one region could be carried by winds, rains, and rivers hundreds of miles downstream to destroy forests, lakes, wetlands, and water reservoirs.

The forging of nationwide commitments was hardest in societies like the United States, which are divided by race, religion, ethnicity, class, and the native born versus immigrants. Social-welfare systems proved to be most effective and popular in ethnically homogenous societies, such as Scandinavia, where people believed that their tax payments were "helping their own." The United States, racially and ethnically the most divided of all the high-income countries, is also the only high-income country without national health insurance. Even within national borders of divided societies, human beings have a hard time believing that they share responsibilities and fates with those across the income, religious, and perhaps especially, racial divide.

Yet now the recognition that we share responsibilities and fates across the social divide will need to be extended internationally so that the world as a whole takes care to ensure sustainable development in all regions of the world. No part of the world can be abandoned to extreme poverty, or used as a dumping ground for the toxic, without jeopardizing and diminishing all the rest. It might seem that such global cooperation will prove to be utopian. The prevailing unilateralism of the United States will seem for many people to be an inevitable feature of world politics in which politicians are voted in or out of office by their own populations rather than by a global electorate. A major theme of this book, however, is that global cooperation in many fields has been enormously successful in the past, in large part because well-informed national electorates support global cooperation when they understand that it is in their own enlightened self-interest and vital for the well-being of their children and children's children. Our challenge is not so much to invent global cooperation as it is to rejuvenate, modernize, and extend it.

AVOIDING THE CLIFF

The world can certainly save itself, but only if we recognize accurately the dangers that humanity confronts together. For that, we will have to pause from our relentless competition in order to survey the common challenges we face. The world's current ecological, demographic, and economic trajectory is unsustainable, meaning that if we continue with "business as usual" we will hit social and ecological crises with calamitous results. We face four causes for such potential crises:

- Human pressures on the Earth's ecosystems and climate, unless miti-gated substantially, will cause dangerous climate change, massive species extinctions, and the destruction of vital life-support functions.

- The world's population continues to rise at a dangerously rapid pace, especially in the regions least able to absorb a rising population.

- One sixth of the world remains trapped in extreme poverty unrelieved by global economic growth, and the poverty trap poses tragic hardships for the poor themselves and great risks for the rest of the world.

- We are paralyzed in the very process of global problem solving, weighed down by cynicism, defeatism, and outdated institutions.

These problems will not solve themselves. A world of untrammeled market forces and competing nation-states offers no automatic solutions to the har-rowing and increasing difficulties. Ecological conditions will be worsened, not improved, by the rapid economic growth that is under way in most of the world unless that growth is channeled by active public policies into resource-saving (or sustainable) technologies. The transition from high to low fertil-ity (birth) rates, necessary for lower population growth, requires concerted public action to help guide private and voluntary fertility choices. Market forces alone will not overcome poverty traps. And the failures of global prob-lem solving mean that we are failing to adopt even straightforward and sen-sible solutions lying right before our eyes.

By looking ahead, husbanding resources more sensibly, and maximizing the gains attainable from science and technology, we can find a path to pros-perity that can spread to all regions of the world in the coming decades. Global prosperity need not be limited by dwindling natural resources; the world economy need not become an us-versus-them struggle for survival. The dire threats can be averted if we cooperate effectively. We can, indeed, se-cure four goals in the coming decades:

- Sustainable systems of energy, land, and resource use that avert the most dangerous trends of climate change, species extinction, and de-struction of ecosystems

- Stabilization of the world population at eight billion or below by 2050 through a voluntary reduction of fertility rates

- The end of extreme poverty by 2025 and improved economic security within the rich countries as well

- A new approach to global problem solving based on cooperation among nations and the dynamism and creativity of the nongovernmental sector

Attaining these goals on a global scale may seem impossible. Yet there is nothing inherent in global politics, technology, or the sheer availability of resources on the planet to prevent us from doing so. The barriers are in our limited capacity to cooperate, not in our stars. We need agreements at the global level and attitudes throughout the world that are compatible with meeting our global challenges.

GLOBALIZATION WITHOUT TRUST

Despite the urgent need for increased global cooperation, such cooperation has been slipping away in recent years. Technological advances in transport, communication, and information have brought us closer together than ever economically. Market forces harnessed to those technologies have created a global division of labor of unsurpassed complexity and productivity and played a major role in lifting hundreds of millions of people out of extreme poverty. Yet even as the global economy has become more intertwined, global society has seemed to become more divided, acrimonious, and fearful. Fleets of jumbo jets ply the skies of our interconnected global economy, yet our fear of terrorism is so great that we are rationed in the toothpaste and shampoo that we can carry onto the planes.

The paradox of a unified global economy and divided global society poses the single greatest threat to the planet because it makes impossible the cooperation needed to address the remaining challenges. A clash of civilizations, if we survived one, would undo all that humanity has built and would cast a shadow for generations to come. We've actually been there before. The first great wave of globalization in the nineteenth century ended up in the blood-drenched trenches of Europe in World War I. It is especially sobering to realize that before August 1914, globalization and the march of science seemed assured, as they seem to many today. A best seller of the day, *Europe's Optical*

Illusion (by Norman Angell, 1909), had correctly emphasized that war as a tool of European policy was passé because no country could possibly benefit from outright conflict. Yet distrust and failed European institutions brought war just the same, with cataclysmic effects that reverberated for the rest of the century. The war itself was unmatched in ferocity and death. And in its wake emerged bolshevism, the 1919 flu epidemic, the Great Depression, the rise of Hitler, the Chinese civil war, the Holocaust, and consequences that extend till now. The world was truly torn asunder in 1914. In many ways, it still has not fully healed.

It may seem impossible to conceive of such a cataclysm today, yet the widening arc of war and vituperation, often pitting U.S. foreign policy against global public opinion, reminds us daily of a growing threat to global peace. Today's worry is not only the violence itself but also the messianic fervor with which various combatants are waging their battles. President George W. Bush, Osama bin Laden, and the suicide bombers all claim God's guidance as they launch their attacks against their foes. The world edges closer to catastrophe. In future years the rising power of China and India could further wound U.S. pride and self-confidence, and further ratchet up global tensions.

LEARNING FROM THE PAST

For young people around the world, "history" is 9/11 and the Iraq War, a world of violence, terror, and division. History is the United States rejecting the Kyoto Protocol, trying to eliminate the Millennium Development Goals from international agreements, scrimping on foreign aid, and declaring, "You are either with us or against us." For increasing numbers of Americans, and most people around the world, this has been a time of dismay and growing fear. Yet there is another and longer history dating back to the end of World War II, which can give us much guidance and hope. After World War II, despite the perils of the Cold War, world leaders stirred to face common challenges of the environment, population, poverty, and weapons of mass destruction. They invented new forms of global cooperation, such as the United Nations, and global campaigns to eradicate smallpox, immunize children, spread literacy and family planning, and embark on global environmental protection. They proved, despite the odds and cynicism, that global cooperation could deliver the goods.

The Cold War nearly went hot in October 1962 when the Soviet Union positioned offensive nuclear weapons in Cuba, in part in response to a failed CIA-led invasion of Cuba the year before, the so-called Bay of Pigs invasion. After the United States and the Soviet Union reached the brink of nuclear Armageddon, the Soviets removed the weapons, as part of a secret agreement in which the United States would also remove its tactical nuclear weapons based in Turkey. The world trembled. Many Americans believed that war with the Soviet Union was inevitable, just as some Americans today believe that war with Islamic fundamentalism is inevitable. John Kennedy, in the finest hour of the American presidency after World War II, believed otherwise and helped to lead Americans, Soviets, and the world back from the brink by finding a new path of cooperation, starting with a partial nuclear test ban.

Having nearly been pushed to nuclear war by CIA covert operations, followed by Soviet nuclear provocation, and then by hotheaded U.S. generals eager to launch a first strike against Cuba in response to the Soviet nuclear missile placement, Kennedy was deeply shaken by the ease with which the world had slid toward an apocalypse and by the fragility of life itself.

Courageously, in his famous Peace Address at American University in June 1963, Kennedy urged a global quest to find solutions to human-made problems.

> Too many of us think [that peace] is impossible. Too many think it is unreal. But that is a dangerous, defeatist belief. It leads to the conclusion that war is inevitable, that mankind is doomed, that we are gripped by forces we cannot control. We need not accept that view. Our problems are man-made; therefore, they can be solved by man. And man can be as big as he wants. No problem of human destiny is beyond human beings. Man's reason and spirit have often solved the seemingly unsolvable, and we believe they can do it again. I am not referring to the absolute, infinite concept of universal peace and goodwill of which some fantasies and fanatics dream. I do not deny the value of hopes and dreams, but we merely invite discouragement and incredulity by making that our only and immediate goal.
>
> Let us focus instead on a more practical, more attainable peace, based not on a sudden revolution in human nature but on a gradual evolution in human institutions—on a series of concrete actions and effective agreements which are in the interest of all concerned. There is no single, simple key to this peace; no grand or magic formula to be adopted by one or

two powers. Genuine peace must be the product of many nations, the sum of many acts. It must be dynamic, not static, changing to meet the challenge of each new generation. For peace is a process—a way of solving problems.

Having come right to the edge of global destruction, and having peered over the edge, Kennedy, as had no other person on the planet at the time, mustered the eloquence to make vivid our precarious position and common fate:

> So, let us not be blind to our differences—but let us also direct attention to our common interests and to means by which those differences can be resolved. And if we cannot end now our differences, at least we can help make the world safe for diversity. For, in the final analysis, our most basic common link is that we all inhabit this planet. We all breathe the same air. We all cherish our children's future. And we are all mortal.

Kennedy's speech, which first and foremost called on Americans to believe in the very possibility of cooperation with a seemingly implacable enemy, changed history. The Soviet leader Nikita Khrushchev called it the finest statement by an American president since Franklin Roosevelt and declared his intention to negotiate a nuclear test ban with Kennedy. Six weeks later the Partial Test Ban Treaty was signed in Moscow, and the Soviet Union and the United States established a modus vivendi that eventually led to the end of the Cold War itself and the reemergence of Russia and fourteen other former Soviet republics as sovereign nations.

There have long been two faces of U.S. foreign policy. Since the United States became a great global power after World War II, U.S. foreign policy has veered between the visionary cooperation of Kennedy's Partial Test Ban Treaty and the reckless unilateralism of the CIA-sponsored invasion of Cuba that preceded it. Great acts of U.S. cooperative leadership include the establishment of the UN, the IMF and World Bank, the promotion of an open global trading system, the Marshall Plan to fund European reconstruction, the eradication of smallpox, the promotion of nuclear arms control, and the elimination of ozone-depleting chemicals. Notorious acts of U.S. unilateralism include the CIA-led overthrows of several governments (Iran, Guyana, Guatemala, South Vietnam, Chile), the assassinations of countless foreign officials, and several disastrous unilateral acts of war (in Central America,

Vietnam, Cambodia, Laos, and Iraq). The United States has thrown elections through secret CIA financing, put foreign leaders on CIA payrolls, and supported violent leaders who then came back to haunt the United States in a notorious boomerang or "blowback" effect (including Saddam Hussein and Osama bin Laden, both once on the CIA payroll). As a recent and shocking history of the CIA terms it, militant and covert unilateralism is a "legacy of ashes."

The Bush administration's unilateralism therefore has deep roots in one facet of American foreign policy, but its crudeness and violence are unprecedented. Like the earlier excesses during the Cold War era, the Bush administration's excesses are rooted in a perverse belief system in which American goodness can and must be defended against foreign evil by violent, covert, and dishonest means. Both the Cold War and today's war against Islamic fundamentalism are born of a messianism that sees the world in black and white, and lacks the basic insight that all parts of the world, including the Islamic world, inhabit the same planet and breathe the same air. Indeed, as deeply ecologically stressed parts of the world, the Islamic drylands of the Sahel of Africa (just south of the Sahara), the Middle East, and Central Asia have a greater stake in international cooperation on the environmental challenges and extreme poverty than just about any other part of the world. Yet the United States has completely failed to recognize our common links with these regions, and instead has carried on an utterly destructive war on peoples and societies that we barely understand.

MODEST INVESTMENTS
TO SAVE THE WORLD

A group of global public investments, undertaken by the nations of the world, is needed in order to avert the greatest risks facing the world. The costs of these investments—to fight climate change, loss of biodiversity, rapid population growth, and extreme poverty—will not be large, especially if the costs are shared equitably among the world's nations. The challenge lies not so much in the heroic efforts needed to avert catastrophe, but in the current difficulty of getting the world to agree on even modest efforts. We don't need to break the bank, we only need common goodwill.

As we will discuss, the conversion of our global energy system, which now threatens devastating climate change, into a sustainable energy system in which climate change is brought under control, would likely cost well under 1 percent of annual world income. The adoption of a bold population policy to slow the runaway population growth in the poorest countries would cost less than one tenth of 1 percent of the annual income of rich countries. And the end of extreme poverty would also require less than 1 percent of the annual income of the rich world to finance the crucial investments needed in the poorest countries to extricate them from the poverty trap (and even that modest transfer to the poor would be temporary, perhaps lasting only until 2025). Yet despite the huge imbalance between the modest costs of action and huge consequences of inaction, the world remains paralyzed. The types of steps needed to avert the worst outcomes are clear to many specialists, though not to the public. The main problem, I shall suggest time and again, is not the absence of reasonable and low-cost solutions, but the difficulty of implementing global cooperation to put those solutions in place.

OUR MILLENNIUM PROMISES

The greatest economic and political challenges of our time—the sustainability of the environment, the stabilization of the world's population, and the end of extreme poverty—have certainly not escaped worldwide notice. In the past twenty years, world leaders on occasion have groped for ways to cope with these challenges. In fact, they've achieved some important successes and with considerable public support. A framework of shared global commitments has actually been adopted that can provide a foothold for a sustainable future. The challenge is to turn those fragile—and as yet unfulfilled—global commitments into real solutions.

The new global scaffolding emerged during the decade 1992–2002, spurred in part by the awe-inspiring arrival of the new millennium. The Rio Earth Summit in 1992 brought us three crucial environmental treaties. The first was the United Nations Framework Convention on Climate Change (UNFCCC) to address the newly recognized and harrowing threats of man-made climate change. The second was the Convention on Biological Diversity (CBD) to address the growing evidence of massive and planetwide species extinction at the hands of human activity. The third was the United Nations Convention to Combat Desertification (UNCCD) to put the world's policy focus on the drylands—areas such as Darfur and Somalia—which face hardships in food production and human health unrivaled in other ecological settings.

The new millennium also brought with it new global commitments to fight extreme poverty, hunger, and disease. In 1994, 179 governments came together in Cairo for the International Conference on Population and Development (ICPD) to build on earlier global progress in reducing mortality and fertility rates around the world. The governments adopted the ICPD Plan of Action, which emphasized the vital links of population-related policies (related to fertility, mortality, sexual and reproductive health services, education, gender equity, and more) with sustainable development. The Plan of Action, in addition to calling for universal primary education and steep reductions in infant and child mortality, put emphasis on "ensuring universal access by 2015 to reproductive health care, including family planning, assisted childbirth and prevention of sexually transmitted infections including HIV/AIDS."

The global commitment to fighting extreme poverty in all its forms was deepened and sharpened at the United Nations in September 2000, when the world's leaders adopted the Millennium Declaration, which expressed the goals of the world on the eve of the new millennium. These commitments included eight Millennium Development Goals (MDGs), adopted as specific, time-bound objectives to improve the conditions of the poorest of the poor by the year 2015 in the areas of income, hunger, disease control, education, and environmental sustainability. The MDGs were subsequently given financial impetus in the Monterrey Consensus of 2002 and at several summits of the so-called G8, the eight richest large economies.

Taken together, the Rio treaties, the Plan of Action on Population and Development, and the Millennium Development Goals can be called our Millennium Promises for sustainable development. They are the promises that our generation made to itself and to future generations at the start of the new millennium. As a group, these treaties and commitments are broad reaching, inclusive, and inspiring. The scaffolding is impressive. If successfully implemented, the agreements will put the world on a trajectory of sustainable development. Yet these Millennium Promises might also do little more than join history's cruel dustbin of failed aspirations. Turning large goals into real results on the ground is always challenging. So too is the cooperation needed to achieve them, but never more so than when the goals are global.

Most dangerously, the fragile scaffolding is shaken daily by the realities of global conflict. The new millennium, which began on January 1, 2001, had not yet seen one year before the world was thrust into great fear and discord by 9/11. The attack was harrowing, but the U.S. response was even more consequential. The Bush administration launched a new "war on terror" that crowded out all other aspirations. Even before 9/11, the United States had thumbed its nose at the Kyoto Protocol, which implements the UN Framework Convention on Climate Change. The Millennium Development Goals were met with stony silence and scorn within the corridors of the White House. And the administration launched initiatives for new nuclear weapons, seeming to challenge the rest of the world to a new arms race. Violent conflicts opened across the Middle East. The Oslo peace process between Israel and Palestine was shut down. The shared goals of sustainable development were nearly brushed aside in the process. Yet a single-minded pursuit of a war on terror was doomed to fail, undermining global cooperation, addressing symptoms rather than causes, and draining attention and resources away from the fundamental challenges of the new world economy.

A NEW APPROACH TO DEVELOPMENT PRACTICE

In addition to the problems of achieving global cooperation, we also neglect highly effective and low-cost solutions because our very methods of research and governance are not well suited to the challenges of sustainable development. Scientific research proceeds in intellectual silos that make far too little contact with one another; research in the physical sciences, biology, engineering, economics, and public health is rarely intertwined, even though we must solve problems of complex systems in which all of these disciplines play a role. The problems just refuse to arrive in the neat categories of academic departments.

Moreover, the problems can only be solved through an interactive approach that combines general principles with the details of a specific setting. Academic studies too often begin and end on the basis of general principles without due regard for ground-level complexities. The challenge of ending extreme poverty in Mali, or combating desertification in Darfur, or reducing population growth in India, or overcoming economic isolation in Afghanistan, is akin to the challenge that a medical doctor faces in treating a patient. A successful clinician needs to understand both the general principles of physiology and disease control and the unique circumstances of the patient, including her symptoms, lab tests, medical history, and family circumstances. In *The End of Poverty* I called for a new "clinical economics" that combines theory and practice, general principles, and specific context. Thirty years ago, in two beautiful books, MIT professor Donald Schön wrote in a related way about "reflexive practice," meaning the combination of general training and specific problem solving. More generally, we need a new clinical approach to sustainable development, and new methods of training the next generation of development leaders.

My professional home, at The Earth Institute at Columbia University, is an unalloyed gift and joy in the opportunity to engage in complex problem solving and clinical economics. The Earth Institute brings together physical scientists, ecologists, engineers, economists, political scientists, management experts, public health specialists, and medical doctors in an extraordinarily exciting and fruitful common search for solutions to the global challenges of sustainable development. Much of the scientific information in the pages that follow comes from the extraordinary research and teaching of my colleagues. I hope that as an economist I have been able to do at least some justice to the richness and wondrous insights of the partner disciplines. This book is written with my profound admiration for and gratitude to my colleagues.

Chapter 2

Our Crowded Planet

WE HAVE REACHED THE BEGINNING of the twenty-first century with a very crowded planet: 6.6 billion people living in an interconnected global economy producing an astounding $60 trillion of output each year. Human beings fill every ecological niche on the planet, from the icy tundras to the tropical rain forests to the deserts. In some locations, societies have outstripped the carrying capacity of the land, at least with the technologies they deploy, resulting in chronic hunger, environmental degradation, and a large-scale exodus of desperate populations. We are, in short, in one another's faces as never before, crowded into an interconnected society of global trade, migration and ideas, but also risks of pandemic diseases, terror, refugee movements, and conflict.

The world is in fact experiencing several simultaneous transformations that offer the prospect of shared prosperity or devastating crises depending on how we respond as a global society. Here are six Earth-changing trends, unprecedented in human history.

First, the process of sustained economic growth has now reached most of the world, so that humanity on average is rapidly getting richer in terms of income per person. Moreover, the gap in average income per person between the rich world, centered in the North Atlantic (Europe and the United States), and much of the developing world is narrowing fast.

Second, the world's population will continue to rise, thereby amplifying the overall growth of the global economy. Not only are we each producing more output on average, but there will be many more of us by midcentury. The scale of the world's economic production is therefore likely to be several times that of today.

Third, the rise in income will be greatest in Asia, home to more than half of the world's population. As a result, the world will not only be much richer by 2050 but will have its economic center of gravity in Asia.

Fourth, the way people live is changing fundamentally as well, from rural roots that stretch back to the beginning of humanity to a global urban civilization. We crossed the midway point between urban and rural in 2008, on a one-way path to an urban-based society.

Fifth, the overall impact of human activity on the physical environment is producing multiple environmental crises as never before in history. The environmental crises we face cannot be compared with the past because never before in history has the magnitude of human economic activity been large enough to change fundamental natural processes on the global scale, including the climate itself.

Sixth, the gap between the richest and the poorest is widening to proportions simply unimaginable for most people. This is not contradictory to the idea that on average the poor are getting richer. Most are, but the bottom billion people on the planet are stuck in a poverty trap, which has prevented them from experiencing sustained economic growth. The center of the crisis is in sub-Saharan Africa. This is also the site of the fastest population growth, meaning that the population bulge is occurring in the part of the world that at this point is least able to generate jobs.

This chapter discusses these six aspects of our crowded planet, with a view to global problem solving. The first part of the chapter lays out the six trends. The second part of the chapter discusses the strategy of sustainable development. The final part of the chapter discusses the challenge of global cooperation, because any viable strategy to achieve sustainable development must be a global strategy, with shared participation among the world's countries.

SIX TRENDS THAT WILL SHAPE THIS CENTURY

The Age of Convergence

The planet has filled up with people and economic activity much faster than we have realized. The world's population has risen by more than 4 billion people since 1950, from 2.5 billion to 6.6 billion today. Sub-Saharan Africa's population has more than quadrupled, from 180 million to around 820 million. So too has the population of western Asia, which includes the Middle East, Turkey, and the Caucasus region, from 51 million in 1950 to around 220 million in 2007. And the global economy, which provides a rough indication of human pressures on the Earth's environment, has of course soared even faster, because population growth has been accompanied by a steep rise in income per person. A rough estimate suggests that the gross world product, the sum of the gross domestic products of every nation in the world, has risen by a remarkable eight times since 1950.

A crucial economic point is that there is a lot more economic growth to come, not only because the global population will continue to rise, but more important, because income per person will continue to rise, especially in today's poorer countries. The good news is that most of the world, including large parts that remain poor today, has unlocked the mysteries of sustained economic growth. What was once the formula of success of a small part of the world—Europe, the United States, Japan, and a handful of other places—is now the prize of Brazil, China, India, and other vast populations. Rapid economic growth and the spread of prosperity are on the way. This spread of prosperity is fueled by globalization—the networks of trade, finance, production, technology, and migration—which creates deep interlinkages across the world, and which helps to spread the technologies that underpin productivity and economic development.

Economists use the concept of convergence to describe the processes by which the poorer countries catch up with the richer countries. Convergence occurs when the per capita income in poorer regions rises more rapidly in percentage terms than the per capita income of the richer regions, so that the ratio of per capita incomes of the poorer regions to the richer regions rises toward one, that is, toward the same standard of living. As Brazil, China, and India achieve market-based economic growth based on globalization, they are able not only to raise living standards but to narrow the per capita income gap with the rich countries. Through their competitive exports, these countries earn the foreign exchange to purchase state-of-the-art technologies, for example, in communications and information technology. The rapid uptake of technology leads to a similarly rapid growth of national income, and also improves the competitiveness of the economy in world markets. A virtuous circle of rapid economic growth is created, based on rapid technological upgrading paid for through the rapid growth of exports. This is a wonderful process, making available to billions of people the wonders of modern science and technology. Most of the world is now part of this convergence club, as economists call the countries that have successfully integrated into global markets, and thereby achieve economic growth at a convergent rate (that is, economic growth that is faster than that in the rich countries).

How fast is future economic convergence likely to be? A useful rule of thumb is the following: the poorer the country, the faster its economic growth in comparison with the leader, as long as the preconditions for convergence are met (that is, as long as countries are not stuck in the poverty trap). Today's technological leader, the United States, sustains average annual growth in per capita income of around 1.7 percent, with a per capita income level of around $40,000 per year. The growth of a "follower," or lagging country, depends on the gap in income with the United States. At $20,000, or half of the U.S. per capita income level, growth will exceed the U.S. rate by around 1.5 percentage points per year, so that growth will be around 3.2 percent per year (= 1.7 + 1.5). At $10,000, or half of U.S. per capita income, another 1.5 percentage points per year can be added, so that growth will be around 4.7 percent per year (= 1.7 + 1.5 + 1.5). The overall pattern is shown in Figure 2.1. The horizontal axis shows the income level of the laggard country as a pro-

Figure 2.1: Annual Growth Rates from 1990 to 2005 vs. Income Level in 1990

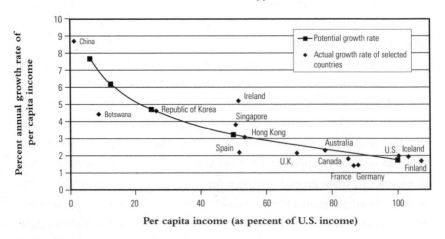

Source: Calculated using data from World Bank (2007)

portion of U.S. per capita income as of 1990. The vertical axis measures the growth rate, and the solid curve shows the growth rate expected on the basis of convergence. The poorer the country, the faster is the growth that it will tend to achieve.

The figure also adds some dark points for per capita growth during 1990–2005 for a selection of fast-growing countries in each income range. We see a group of poor countries with exceptional growth, a group of middle-income countries with rapid growth somewhat less than the growth of the poor countries, and a cluster of rich countries with modest yet positive growth. These fast growers in each income class illustrate how convergence is achieved when other obstacles (especially due to geography, infrastructure, and politics) are overcome. Most poor countries fall far short of their potential for convergence because of notable liabilities regarding their baseline levels of infrastructure, health, education, or governance. Some of the poorest countries don't grow at all because they are stuck in a poverty trap.

More and more countries are joining the convergence club. Literacy has spread to almost all of the world's populations. Electrification and roads have come to the villages of India and China and dozens of other low-income countries. Information technology, starting with the ubiquitous cell phone, and now extending to wireless Internet, is reaching the most remote areas of the world. National aspirations to join the global economy are nearly universal. Sovereignty is the rule rather than the exception in vast regions of the world that until two generations back were under colonial rule. There is, in short, no reason why nearly all of the world will not be part of the convergence club in the first part of the twenty-first century. This would imply the acceleration of total world growth in the coming years, and such a trend is evident in the past half century.

It is instructive to apply the convergence framework to the future development of per capita income in different parts of the world. Suppose that all parts of the world join the convergence club, and thereby have the chance to narrow their income level gaps with the high-income countries. Let's then run the clock forward to 2050, assuming that U.S. economic growth remains at its historical average (1.7 percent per annum) while the rest of the world achieves economic growth in proportion to the income gap with the United States. The poorest countries grow most rapidly, and then slow toward 1.7 percent per annum as they close the income gap with the United States. As a result of these assumptions, global income per person is projected to follow the path shown

Figure 2.2(a): The Convergence of Global Income
per Capita through 2050

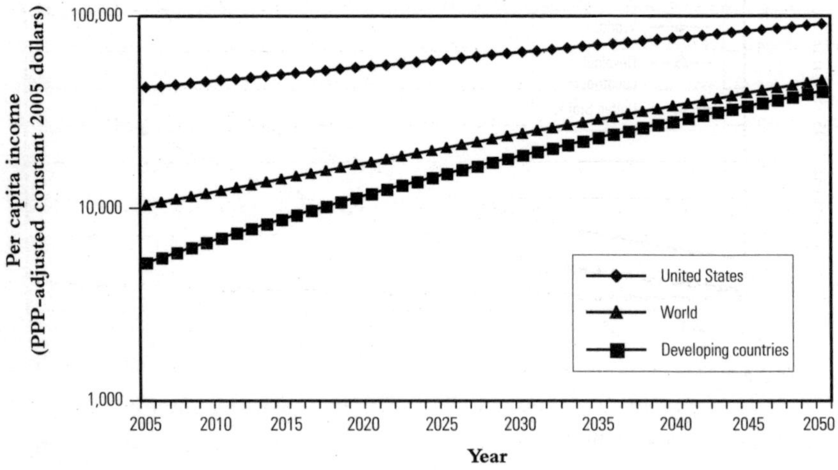

Source: Calculated using data from World Bank (2007)
Note: Vertical axis on logarithmic scale. Income is measured in purchasing power parity (PPP)
to adjust for difference in price levels across countries.

in Figure 2.2(a), where we show the world average, the U.S. curve, and the path for today's developing countries. World per capita income grows by 4.5 times between 2005 and 2050 in this simple model. By 2050, today's developing countries would have an average income of $40,000 per person, roughly equal to U.S. income in 2005, and the United States would have a projected 2050 level of $90,000. Of course, this scenario is highly optimistic in that it assumes the world avoids any prolonged crisis, that the United States grows at the historical average, and that all other countries achieve convergent growth.

More People and Higher Incomes

Not only will most of the world be richer, but there will be a lot more people around enjoying those higher incomes. The world's population continues to grow rapidly, even though the proportional rate of population growth (each year's increase relative to the size of the global population) has declined. The United Nations Population Division makes several forecasts of the world's population based on different assumptions about the average number of births per woman (the fertility rate). The medium forecast, deemed to be the most likely, envisions that the global population will rise from 6.6 billion in 2007 to

Figure 2.2(b): World Product through 2050

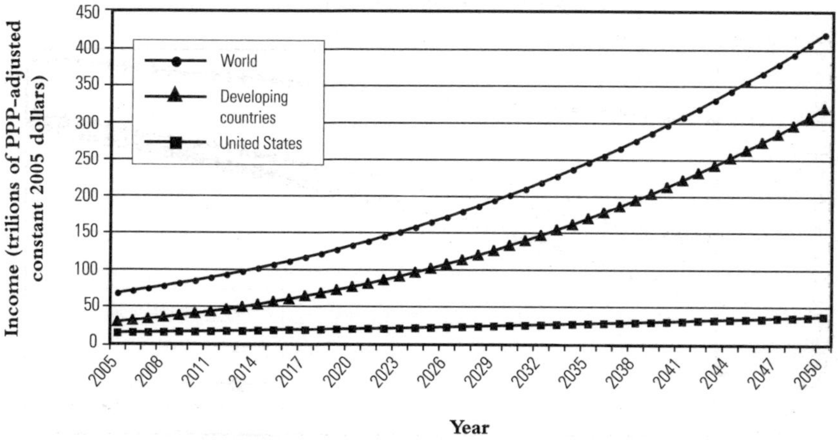

Source: Calculated using data from World Bank (2007)

9.2 billion in 2050. This is not as large as the population increase over the past half century, but it is still a whopping 2.6 billion people to be added to an already crowded planet. Indeed, I will argue at some length that this is too many people to absorb safely, especially since most of the population increase is going to occur in today's poorest countries. We should be aiming, as we've noted earlier, to stabilize the world's population at 8 billion by midcentury.

The total magnitude of economic activity on the planet is calculated by multiplying the average income per person by the number of people. In our convergence scenario the world's average income per person rises by around fourfold between 2005 and 2050. In the medium-fertility forecast of the UN, the world's population rises by around 40 percent, or a factor of 1.4 times. Therefore, the gross world product rises, in this scenario, by 6.3 times, from around $67 trillion in 2005 to around $420 trillion in 2050, as shown in Figure 2.2(b). With a 2050 population at 8 billion rather than 9.2 billion, and the same per capita income, the global world product would reach around $365 trillion rather than $420 trillion. Either way, there is a lot of pent-up economic growth in the world today, which will result from technological catch-up.

Let me emphasize, once again, that these scenarios are highly optimistic but convey the underlying power of convergence, the dominant force at play in the world economy in our era. The overall lesson is that the world economy will be bigger, much bigger, by 2050, even if we can't say precisely by how much. That economic growth can be monumentally good for human well-being if we can manage the side effects, especially vis-à-vis the environment.

The Asian Century

Rapid catch-up growth in Asia will bring about a historic shift in the center of gravity of the world economy. Since 1800, the North Atlantic economies have been the world's dominant economies and political powers. The cataclysms of World War I, the Great Depression, and World War II did not shake the dominance of the North Atlantic economies, though they did shift the balance of geopolitical influence away from Europe, especially the British Empire, to the United States. Now, after many centuries, the unquestioned economic and geopolitical dominance of the North Atlantic will end. The American century will end sometime in the second quarter of the twenty-first century, when Asia becomes the center of gravity of the world economy, in the sense of producing more than half of the world's income (Figure 2.3). The end of the American century will *not* be the result of any collapse of America's well-being but rather the rise of Asia's economic power.

In the long haul it is natural that Asia should be the center of gravity of

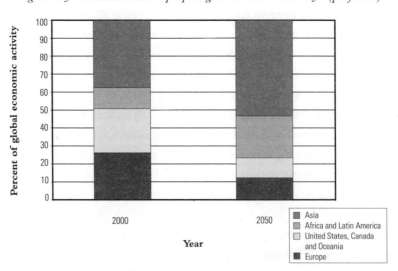

Figure 2.3: Economic Activity by Region in 2000 and 2050 (projected)

Source: Calculated using data from Maddison (2001)

the world economy, since it is the center of gravity of the global population. In 1820, Asia constituted perhaps 56 percent of the world economy. With the onset of industrialization in Europe and North America, Asia's share declined to 28 percent by 1900. With Asia's turmoil between 1900 and 1970, the share declined further, to reach a low point of around 18 percent of the world's output in 1950. Then began the great convergence. Asia's share of world income recovered to around 23 percent in 1970 and to 38 percent by 2000. According to the convergence scenario, Asia's share of global income would rise to around 49 percent by 2025 and to around 54 percent by 2050.

History has shown that profound geopolitical frictions, even bloodshed, can accompany the changing fortunes of leading powers. The rise of Germany and Japan in the early twentieth century gave rise to lethal rivalries and armaments races with the leading powers, Great Britain and the United States. Geopolitical jealousies flared. Militarists and demagogues in Germany and Japan argued that their place in the sun was being blocked by the United Kingdom and the United States, and that war was the only solution. And in the leading countries, politicians often took provocative steps—for example, the harsh terms after World War I against Germany—which ended up fanning the flames.

In our day, America's continued assertions of preeminence in global power could cause dangerous frictions with China, India, and other rising regional powers. And if America's assertions of power are again carried to unrealistic extremes, as in the unprovoked war in Iraq, the regional and global reactions are likely to be swift and severe. The belief among U.S. neoconservatives that the United States is the world's sole superpower and can therefore have its way is passé and will become even less true in the coming decades. Such unrealistic views would no doubt trigger similarly unrealistic nationalism within China and India. Power is already diffusing widely in the twenty-first century. A new kind of global politics must take shape, built not on U.S. or Chinese preeminence, but on global cooperation across regions. Despite the reveries and fantasies of some, the age of empire is over, and certainly the age of a U.S. empire. We are now in the age of convergence.

The Urban Century

The economic shift from the North Atlantic to the Pacific and Indian oceans is not the only fundamental change ahead. For the first time in human history, most of the world's population will live in urban centers rather than villages. From the origin of the species through the birth of agriculture and right up to 2007, most of the world's people have been residents of rural communities rather than towns and cities. In prehistory the world was, of course, entirely rural. Cities arose with the end of the last ice age and the rise of agriculture some ten thousand years ago. The essence of city life is a non-agricultural community that obtains most of its food by trading with the countryside, or that extracts food from the countryside in a coercive manner (taxation, slaveholding, tribute, or the like). When agricultural productivity is low—so that the typical farm family basically feeds itself, with only a small surplus to trade with urban dwellers—most of the population must be engaged in food production in order to subsist. It is only when agricultural productivity is very high—so that a farm family can feed many urban residents—that a significant share of the population can reside in urban areas and be engaged in manufacturing and services. (Some manufacturing and services can take place in rural areas as well, but in general, such activities benefit from the density of urban life. Thus, rurality is largely but not entirely synonymous with agriculture, and urbanism is largely but not entirely synonymous with manufacturing and services.) Thus, until the rise of agricultural productivity in the eighteenth century in the North Atlantic (England, Holland, Flanders), almost all regions of the world at all times were 90 percent or more rural, with a mere sliver of the population living in the cities.

The rise of scientific farming—including modern seed varieties, chemical fertilizers, modern irrigation, mechanization, and innovations in farm management (crop rotations, tillage, pest control, and more)—has enabled a decling share of the world's population to feed all the rest and, therefore, has enabled a rising share of the world to live in cities. From less than 10 percent in 1800, the urban share rose to around 13 percent in 1900, 29 percent in 1950, 47 percent in 2000, and 50 percent in 2007. High-productivity farming has gone hand-in-hand with overall economic development, so the high-income world has also been the first to urbanize, reaching 50 percent urban by around 1950 and 75 percent urban today. The low-income world will reach 50 percent urban only around 2017, compared with around 44 percent today. Yet urbanization has risen steadily in virtually all parts of the world as crop production per hectare and, more important, crop production per farm family have continued to rise over time. In the United States, with its enormous output per farmer (due both to high productivity per land area and large area per farm),

farm families constitute just 1 percent of the population and are able to feed the other 99 percent.

In 2008, the historic, and presumably irreversible, halfway mark was reached when half the world was urban and half rural. By 2030, based on current (and admittedly uncertain) trends, the world might be 60 percent urban and just 40 percent rural. Indeed, the UN projects that *all* of the 1.7 billion population increase between now and 2030 (in the medium-fertility forecast) will take place not only in the developing world but in the *cities* of the developing world.

The rising rates of urbanization can have countless benefits for the world, including the low-income countries. From the earliest days of civilization, cities have been the site of technological advancement, science, and productivity advancement due to specialization and the division of labor. Thus, agricultural productivity not only frees labor to work in cities but helps to unleash the technological advances that are part and parcel of urban life. The high population densities of urban settlements have other benefits as well, including much lower costs per person than in rural areas of providing roads, power, clinics, and schools to the population.

Yet urban life raises its own host of challenges, many of them of profound significance for sustainable development. In the worst cases, rural populations migrate into urban areas not because of rising farm productivity or the lure of urban jobs but out of desperation and hunger in the countryside. Urban slums then complement rural desperation. Hunger itself is urbanized, and young, unemployed men on the prowl may create urban settings of violence and insecurity. A rural crisis can thereby become an urban nightmare.

Even if such crises are avoided by adequate urban job creation, rising farm productivity, and slowing population growth rates in rural areas, urbanization can pose many additional challenges. The enormous densities of urban populations mean that pollutants, too, are heavily concentrated, far above the power of nature to disperse the pollutants through harmless flows into waterways and the atmosphere. Therefore, unless pollution is controlled through appropriate technologies and policies, cities can become sites of untold ecological destruction. Also, by bringing millions of people into proximity, cities have long been host to infectious diseases that depend on large populations of susceptible individuals to sustain the long-term transmission of the disease. Moreover, the rising populations of large cities will be vulnerable to other natural hazards, including floods, landslides, and earthquakes. This is especially the case because the world's cities have been heavily concentrated along the coastlines to take advantage of access to global trade, fisheries, and the amenities of coastal life. My colleagues at The Earth Institute have calculated that roughly 10 percent of the world's population lives in low-lying coastal zones (within one hundred kilometers of the coast and at less than ten meters above sea level), though such areas constitute a mere 2.2 percent of the Earth's land area. This implies, of course, that such low-lying coastal settlements are roughly five times more densely populated than the average land area on the planet. Of the people living in low-lying coastal zones, about 60 percent are in coastal cities. As the Earth's climate changes in future decades, rising sea levels and increasingly intense tropical storms will threaten these coastal settlements around the world. The New Orleans tragedy of Hurricane Katrina could be replayed many times.

And if these worries are not enough, we are discovering that the modern style of urban (and suburban) living has itself become an unanticipated health hazard. Today's urban citizens tend to walk less, eat more, and eat more unhealthy foods than ever before. With blinding speed, still not recognized in most of the world, populations are moving rapidly from one kind of malnutrition—a shortfall of calories, proteins, and micronutrients—to another kind of malnutrition—an excess of calories, harmful fats (especially industrially synthesized transfats), and sedentary lifestyles shaped by the automobile and the television set. The result is a global epidemic of obesity, cardiovascular disease, and adult-onset diabetes, the devastating lifestyle disease of the modern urban age. We shouldn't be entirely shocked. Each new scale of human settlement, from forager group to village to city, has entailed new diseases, though in the past they were infectious diseases. As in the past, we will learn to adjust to the new dangers, but a time lag could impose unnecessary suffering.

All this means that the science of urban ecology—linking human activity with the physical environment of urban areas—will be a crucial scientific and policy discipline. It is one that at least currently is in short supply, since architects, city planners, ecologists, public health specialists, and environmental engineers still operate largely in disconnected disciplines rather than as partners in the quest for sustainable urban development. Moreover, the developing world in particular suffers a greater shortage, just as it does in other crucial areas of public management.

The Environmental Challenge

We are learning fast that the growth of the world economy is not a complete joy. The scale of human economic activity—rising eight times since 1950, and possibly another six times by 2050—is causing environmental destruction on a scale that was impossible at any earlier stage of human history. Economic activity is based heavily on the utilization of natural resources and physical flows such as rainfall, river flow, and of course photosynthesis for our food supply. Yet with the incredible increase of populations and incomes per person, virtually every major ecosystem in the world is now under threat from human activities. The ocean fisheries are being depleted of fish and corals. The scarcity of freshwater for drinking and irrigation is likely to affect hundreds of millions, perhaps billions, of people in the coming decades unless it is much better managed. Climate change will render large parts of the world unfit for agriculture unless we are able to mitigate the man-made climate trends as well as adapt successfully to them. Human destruction of the habitat of other species is leading to a massive extinction of plants and animals. We are causing this in the face of evidence that a decline in biological diversity may render many parts of the world less hospitable, less resilient, and less productive for human beings as well.

It is useful to decompose the human impact on the environment (I) into three parts: the total population (P), income per person (A), and the environmental impact per dollar of income (T). We use the letter T to signify the level of technology. When T is high, the kind of technology being used imposes a high environmental burden (for example, extensive use of land or high emissions of greenhouse gases) per unit of GNP. The total human impact on the environment is equal to the product of population, per capita income, and technology, so that: $I = P \times A \times T$. This is sometimes called the I-PAT (pronounced EYE-pat) equation.

Clearly, the I-PAT relationship signals that a dramatic rise in population and income per person, as we've experienced since 1950 and will experience again till 2050, has a similarly dramatic impact on the environment, unless technology changes in a way to protect the environmental impact. It is useful for us to turn T on its head, and use the letter S to signify the income that is produced per unit of environmental impact. The letter S in this case signifies sustainable technology. A high value of S means that it is possible to produce a high income per unit of environmental impact. The higher the S, the lower is the human impact on natural systems. The equation becomes $I = P \times A \div S$.

Now we can restate the environmental conundrum as follows: The world's population is on a business-as-usual track to rise by roughly 40 percent by 2050, and the world's income per person is on a business-as-usual track to rise perhaps fourfold. Thus, $P \times A$, or total world income, is on track to rise roughly sixfold. The human impact on the environment, I, with an unchanged set of technologies, would also therefore be sixfold. Since the human impact on the environment today is already unsustainable, a sixfold increase in impact would be devastating and would almost surely feed back to block the rise in world income. In other words, we would never achieve the targeted economic growth because it would be frustrated by environmental catastrophe. Many environmentalists say that we are indeed doomed to lower economic growth as a result, and that in fact the best we can do is to manage an orderly and equitable reduction of per capita income. This school of thought holds that global convergence can only be achieved by reducing the income of the rich countries while making room for some modest rise in income of the poor countries. Convergence, in this view, requires that incomes fall at the top and rise at the bottom.

The alternative strategy is to offset the much-desired rise in A with a stabilization of P and a rise in S, meaning that the world adopts sustainable technologies that have low environmental impact per unit of income. Rather than focusing, as some environmentalists do, on reducing the income and consumption of the rich world, we should focus much more on raising S, the sustainability of the world's technologies. There are many examples of high-S technologies, which we will discuss in the coming chapters, including new forms of renewable energy, the capture and storage of carbon dioxide emitted from coal-burning power plants, sustainable fish farming, drip irrigation to maximize the crop output per unit of water input, and improved seed varieties that produce higher agricultural output on a given amount of farmland. In ways such as these, the world can sustain a rising global income without environmental catastrophe.

The Poorest Billion and the Poverty Trap

The last dominant characteristic of our time, and a major threat for the future, is the fact that the convergence club is not yet complete. There are still large regions of the world, with roughly one billion people, that have not un-leashed convergent economic growth. These regions are, by definition, falling further and further behind the world's leaders. In 1820, the richest country in the world, the United Kingdom, had an average income per person that was roughly three times greater than that of the poorest region, sub-Saharan Africa. By 2005, the richest country in the world, the United States, had a per capita income that was roughly twenty times larger than that of the poorest region, still sub-Saharan Africa. For the past generation, sub-Saharan Africa has failed to achieve a rise in income per person.

The growing gap is dangerous in countless ways. It is dangerous for the poor first and foremost, as millions die each year of their extreme poverty. The poorest people are undernourished, without access to safe drinking water, and without reliable access to basic health services. Life expectancy in sub-Saharan Africa is forty-seven years, and less than forty years in several countries, com-pared with seventy-nine years in the high-income countries. The poorest countries, for reasons we shall see, have the highest fertility rates and the most rapid population growth rate. Much of the expected 2.6 billion rise in global population by 2050 will come from the poorest countries, the places least able to absorb the increase. The poorest countries are the most unstable po-litically, and the most prone to violence and conflict, often to conflicts that spill over national and regional borders, thereby involving the rest of the world. And the poor, in their desperation to stay alive, are often contributing to massive local environmental degradation by depleting soils of nutrients, overfishing lakes and rivers, and clearing forests to make way for new farm-land to absorb a rising population.

The poverty trap is self-reinforcing, not self-correcting. Therefore, over-coming the poverty trap requires special policies and global efforts. There is nothing inevitable about Africa, or any other region, remaining stuck in ex-treme poverty, yet it will take conscious public efforts in addition to the blind forces of the marketplace to end the poverty trap.

THE STRATEGY OF SUSTAINABLE DEVELOPMENT

Sustainable development means prosperity that is globally shared and envi-ronmentally sustainable. In practice, sustainable development will require three fundamental changes in our business-as-usual global trajectory. First, we will have to develop and adopt on a global scale, and in a short period of time, the sustainable (high-S) technologies that can allow us to combine high levels of prosperity with lower environmental impacts. Second, we will have to stabilize the global population, and especially the population in the poorest countries, in order to combine economic prosperity with environmental sustainability. And third, we will have to help the poorest countries escape from the poverty trap. These three basic goals—environmental sustainability, population stabilization, and ending extreme poverty—are of course the essence of the Millennium Promises.

Market forces alone cannot solve these problems. First, market forces alone will not guarantee that the world's scientists and engineers direct their efforts to the development of high-S technologies. Many important technologies will have a huge social benefit for sustainable development but will not produce private-market profitability, so private businesses won't invest in research and development (R & D) to discover and develop them. Second, even when sustainable technologies have been discovered and developed, market forces alone may not guarantee their widespread adoption. We often need special incentives, in addition to market forces, to spur the adoption of sustainable technologies. Third, market forces alone do not guarantee an appropriate pattern of population change within a single country or at the global level. Population policies of various sorts are needed to supplement free-market forces. Fourth, market forces do not guarantee that all parts of the world can meet their basic needs, much less get on a path of convergent growth. Markets leave one billion or more people behind, and the numbers could rise tragically in the future unless we take corrective action.

The Development of Sustainable Technologies

Markets alone will not develop the sustainable technologies that we will need for the twenty-first century. Scientific discovery in general, on which sustainable technologies depend, is a public good that is underprovided by market forces. This is because scientific knowledge is a nonrival good that can be used by anybody without lessening its availability for everybody else. With apples and oranges, more for you means less for me, but you and I can utilize scientific knowledge such as $E = mc^2$ or the structure of DNA without diminishing the availability of the same knowledge for anybody else. Indeed, knowledge works most powerfully when it is widely shared, thereby giving a common base for understanding, action, and development of technological systems. Therefore, science works partly because the worldwide community of scientists makes its discoveries known quickly and freely through peer-reviewed publications, rather than keeping them private and secret. The scientists do not directly capture much, if any, of the economic benefits of their discoveries, nor should they if that knowledge is to have maximum beneficial impact.

Since scientific discovery should remain publicly available, nonmarket means must be used to support the financial investment of resources into scientific discovery. In the past, monarchs were the patrons of scientists. They funded basic science or gave prizes for scientific discovery. Today science must be supported by governments and by philanthropists who give grants to universities and to scientific research centers, both public and private. Private foundations offer awards that also spur effort, most famously, the Nobel Prize. The need for public and philanthropic funding is widely recognized in the United States, even if it is not fully understood by free-market ideologues. It is why the United States, the paragon of free markets, spends upward of $100 billion per year of federal budgetary funds on research and development. Sadly, much of that is squandered, with little benefit, on military R & D for weapons systems, but the federal government still manages to spend $30 billion per year on biomedical research at the National Institutes of Health. Without that effort, the progress of biomedical science would be far behind where it is today, and our life expectancy and well-being would be much lower as well. This public investment in biomedical knowledge has repaid us many times over.

We will need a comparable global commitment to fund R & D for sustainable technologies, including clean energy, drought-resistant seed varieties, environmentally sound fish farming, vaccines for tropical diseases, improved remote monitoring and conservation of biodiversity, and much more. To every dimension of sustainable development there is a crucial technological need, which must be underpinned by investments in basic science. And in every case there is an important need for public finance to spur the new technologies that can enable us to achieve simultaneously the objectives of high global incomes, the end of extreme poverty, the stabilization of the global population, and environmental sustainability.

There is also an important role for a patent system alongside public spending on science. A patent is an exclusive right granted to the patent holder for use of a novel and useful invention, usually for twenty years from the time of filing. Under U.S. and European patent law, abstract ideas—mathematical algorithms, natural phenomena, and laws of nature—are in principle not patentable, though the boundaries between scientific principles and patentable inventions are sometimes murky and controversial. The prospect of winning a patent serves as an important market-based incentive for inventors to develop intellectual property in the first place, and this is the main reason for a patent system. In essence, the patent holder gets to charge monopoly prices during the life of the patent. To mitigate the potential harms of granting such a monopoly, the patent applicant is required to disclose how to make and use the invention so that others can benefit from the advance of knowledge, subject to the exclusivity given to the patent holder.

The policy challenge is to set the right balance between freely available scientific information, which has to be financed by public-sector and philanthropic sources, and privately owned technology, which can be stimulated by the prospect of a patent. This policy challenge is complex, and if done well, leads to a complex and subtle mix of institutions devoted to R & D. These institutions are called innovation systems, and they include the public budget, government research laboratories, private businesses that undertake R & D, academic institutions, government foundations (such as the U.S. National Science Foundation), nongovernmental foundations, individual philanthropists, professional scientific associations such as the U.S. National Academy of Sciences, and more.

When R & D is aimed mainly for general scientific knowledge, the needs of the poor, the global commons, or rapid social uptake, public financing is advantageous compared with reliance on patents. When R & D is targeted mainly for the rich or private use or gradual uptake, the patent-based incentives are relatively advantageous. In general, a healthy innovation system will use a mix of public financing and patents. For global sustainable development, the mix of public financing and private incentives should be harmonized globally to ensure that the needs of the poor and the global commons are properly addressed and financed by shared contributions of the world's governments.

Even when the patent system is clearly useful for sustainable development, such as helping to spur the development of new medicines, steps can be taken to reduce the harmful side effects of the temporary monopoly. For example, in the case of antiretroviral medicines to fight HIV/AIDS, the patent-holding drug companies agreed to sell products at a reduced or nonprofit basis in the poorest countries, while making patent-protected profits in the high-income markets, an approach called tiered pricing or market segmentation. In this way, the patents in the high-income markets offered incentives for continued R & D, without denying the benefits of the resulting new medicines to the poor.

The Adoption of Sustainable Technologies

It is one thing to develop new high-S technology and quite another to have it adopted on a widespread basis and in a timely manner. The central challenge is to create incentives for firms and households to adopt environmentally sustainable technologies instead of the unsustainable technologies that they now deploy. In many contexts, a high-S technology exists but is more expensive than an environmentally damaging low-S technology. The extra cost of adopting the sustainable technology may be small relative to the large benefit to society of reducing the environmental harm, but the market prices don't send that signal, since the environmental harm is not reflected in market prices and therefore in the incentives facing businesses and households. In those cases, we say that the environmental harms are "externalities," meaning that environmental costs are felt by society but are external to the narrow profit-and-loss calculations of individual businesses and the budget choices of individual households.

Consider a classic example from recent decades. Atmospheric scientists and ecologists began to realize in the late 1960s that sulfur dioxide emitted from coal-burning power plants was mixing with rainfall to produce sulfuric acid. Forests downwind of these factories were being destroyed by the resulting acid rain. Smokestack scrubbers can remove the sulfur dioxide from the flue gas by mixing the gas with lime to produce calcium sulfate, thereby preventing the acid rain. The flue gas desulfurization represents an added cost for the factory, but a cost that is much less than the benefit of saving the forests. The problem is that in a free and unregulated market, each profit-maximizing power plant lacks the incentive to buy a scrubber. Despite the large social benefits, the firm itself would reduce its profits by investing in the scrubber. A public policy to correct the market prices is needed to give the power plants the incentive to buy the smokestack scrubbers.

Four types of policies can be used to align private incentives and society's environmental interests. The simplest is a tax on the environmental harm, in this case a tax on sulfur emissions. In the economics jargon, this "internalizes" the externality. Assuming the tax per ton of sulfur emission is high enough, equal to the high social cost to the forests of an incremental ton of emissions, each factory will buy the scrubber in order to avoid the tax. A second mechanism, the one actually adopted by the U.S. government under the 1990 amendments to the Clean Air Act to fight acid rain, is the issuance of a limited number of permits for sulfur emissions. A company is allowed to emit a certain quantity of sulfur dioxides only if it owns the equivalent number of permits. The permit is tradable and therefore has a market price. If the market value of the permit is higher than the cost of adding a scrubber (and thereby avoiding the emission), the company sells its permit and buys a scrubber. The permit price thereby gives a market-type incentive equivalent to the emissions tax. A third mechanism is an industry performance standard, which in this case might require that all power plants as of a given future date must, by law, dramatically reduce sulfur dioxide emissions. This is the approach that Europe followed under its 1994 Sulphur Emissions Reduction Protocol. The protocol specifies that by 2004 all major combustion sources should reach specified emissions limits. The treaty also says that the parties "may, in addition, apply economic instruments to encourage the adoption of cost-effective approaches to the reduction of sulphur emissions."

A fourth mechanism is zoning, according to which any of these environmental measures (taxes, tradable permits, or performance standards) is applied in certain spatial zones but not in others. The zoning is designed to allow plants to emit more gases where the effects on populations or ecosystems are likely to be small, and to limit the emissions where the damages are likely to be large. The zoning will be designed, for example, to steer polluting industries away from densely populated areas or from especially vulnerable ecosystems. Zoning, or some kind of spatially based policy, is crucial when the social costs of environmental impacts depend strongly on where those impacts occur. In that case, intuitively, the social costs that need to be internalized cannot be captured by a single tax rate, or a single price of a tradable permit, or a single industrial standard.

A pollutant such as sulfur dioxide is an obvious case where private interests and social interests diverge unless market forces are corrected by public policy. Yet there are many other circumstances, some very subtle, where private interests and society's environmental interests are likely to diverge, and thereby to require some corrections to the market forces. The most important of these today, without doubt, is the emission of carbon dioxide by fossil fuel users. Carbon dioxide is the most important greenhouse gas now changing the Earth's climate system. It is not a typical pollutant, because carbon dioxide is harmless and odorless, and doesn't bother anybody except for the fact that it could devastate the planet in coming decades! It requires a market correction, just like sulfur dioxide. Yet the manner for making that correction is much more complex, given the global scale of the problem and the extent to which fossil fuel use is at the core of the modern economy. The challenge is discussed in Chapter 4.

Sustainable Harvesting of Natural Systems

Another major category of human activity that requires the correction of market forces involves the intensity with which society uses natural capital. Human societies tap into innumerable Earth processes that are termed ecosystem services. These processes include the natural growth of forests, which provide fuel wood, construction materials, and more; the hydrological (water) cycle, which is used for irrigation, safe drinking water, industrial production, and more; the growth of fish populations, which are harvested for fish consumption; the regrowth of grasses that feed grazing livestock; the natural fixation of nitrogen in the soils of croplands, which support food production; and countless more. When ecosystems are harvested faster than they can regenerate or recharge, the underlying resources (forest, freshwater, fish, pastureland, soil nutrients) are depleted, sometimes to complete collapse. Under many circumstances, untrammeled market forces will lead relentlessly to collapse rather than to a sustainable rate of resource use.

The risk is greatest if the resource is an unmanaged commons, or open-access resource. The classic example, which gives rise to the term *commons*, is an open-access pastureland, freely available to all who would like to graze their livestock on it. An example of the global commons is the ocean floor beyond national borders, where fishing fleets are free to destroy natural ecosystems as they drag their trawls on the ocean bottom. In these cases, the market incentive is for each individual or business to harvest the resource in question to the point where the market value of the product is equal to the cost of harvesting that extra (marginal) unit. If a ton of fish caught in the trawls is worth $1,000, fishermen will expand their fishing activities as long as the cost of catching the additional ton is less than or equal to the $1,000 of market value. If the value of logging an open forest stand is $1,000 per ton of logs, the forest will be cut as long as the cost of logging the additional ton of trees is less than or equal to $1,000. The rate of harvesting (fishing, logging, or grazing) can dramatically exceed the natural regrowth rate of the natural population of fish, trees, or grasses. In this case, the commons will be depleted. This recognition that an open-access resource will give rise to rapid depletion was famously termed the "tragedy of the commons" by Garrett Hardin in 1968.

Just as with pollution control, there are many mechanisms to limit the rate of harvesting to a sustainable level.

One method is to introduce tradable permits for harvesting, akin to the tradable permits for pollution emissions. The most efficient fishing fleets, which stand to make the highest profits on fishing, will buy more permits. The total catch will be limited to the sustainable yield by design. Many countries, including Australia, New Zealand, Iceland, Canada, and Namibia, use such systems, alternatively called individual transferable quotas or individual fishing quotas. The United States has used a variety of quota systems, including an assignment of fishing rights to individual companies on the West Coast and limits on days at sea on the East Coast. A similar mechanism can apply to logging, grazing, hunting, or comparable uses of a renewable resource. As we might expect, these systems have often languished under intense political conflict over the allocation of the rights.

Another common recommendation is to privatize the commons, a process known as enclosure when it is applied to grazing land. Say the grassland is owned by a rancher with an interest in avoiding overgrazing, since she wants to maximize profit in the long term. The rancher will keep the size of her herd to a sustainable level, compatible with harvesting the grassland at the same rate as its natural regrowth. An open-access tree stand or forest that suffers from excess logging can similarly be stabilized if the commons is privatized. Privatization of the commons may prove to be unwise because of equity considerations, the risk that scarce resources will end up in a few powerful and rich hands while the rest of society is driven to penury. Privatization can also be destructive ecologically, for example, if enclosing the rangeland into small private farm units would impede the vital migratory path of the natural fauna. In many cases of the commons today—the oceans, the atmosphere, land areas of high biodiversity—privatization is barred by practical or ecological considerations.

In these cases, the commons must still be converted from an open-access resource to a common property resource, not a privately owned system. One proven option is community-based management, in which the community, through a local political process, agrees on how to allocate resource use within the community. The community-based organization may decide, for example, on the number of livestock each household is allowed to maintain in the pastures. The entire community, and future generations as well, can benefit compared to living with an open-access status quo. Community-based management of forests, grasslands, water, fisheries, and other common-pool resources has proved to be enormously successful in many contexts and many societies. A fascinating recent success story comes from a pastoralist community in Bayinhushu, Inner Mongolia, which was suffering massive loss of pastureland from overgrazing and soil erosion. In an initiative sponsored by the Chinese Academy of Sciences, the villagers successfully cooperated to reduce herd sizes, reserve part of the common lands for growing animal feed, and seed new grasses. The result was the restoration of degraded pasturelands and a rise in village incomes.

Overcoming the Importance of the Market

Even when natural resources are properly managed, either through private ownership, permits, or community agreement, social choices might still lead to depletion rather than sustainable management. Consider the following illustration: A lake is filled with a rare fish species that has a market value as food. If the lake is owned as a public commons, and is freely accessible for fishing, the result will be a rapid depletion of the fish population if the costs of fishing are low enough. Now suppose instead that the lake is privately owned (or communally managed) to maximize the economic value of the lake. Will the owner (or community organization) guard against depletion today in order to reap the benefits of selling fish in the future? Certainly the owner will calculate whether it is advantageous to catch more fish today and sell them now, or to catch fewer fish today in order to sell more in the future. Since money in the pocket today is worth more than the same amount in the future (because money today can be invested at the market interest rate and thereby grow over time), the decision will be to keep the fish in the lake only if the market value of the fish stock is expected to increase more rapidly than the rate of interest. If the price of the fish per ton is expected to remain unchanged, and if the fish is a slow-growing species, then the value of the fish in the lake will grow less rapidly than the rate of interest. The profit-maximizing owner will deplete the fish stock and perhaps drive a rare species to extinction, rather than wait to sell more fish in the future. Private (or community) ownership alone will not save the species.

Two subtle issues are at work in this example. The first is that the market price of a species will generally *not* reflect the species' societal value as part of Earth's biodiversity. Market prices do not reflect the value that society puts on avoiding the extinction of other species, only the direct consumption value of those species (for food, aphrodisiacs, pets, hunting trophies, or ornaments). Second, the rate of interest diminishes the incentive of the resource owner to harvest the resource at a sustainable rate. If the value of the resource is likely to grow more slowly than the market rate of interest, the blaring market signal is to deplete the resource now and pocket the money! Since the market rate of interest depends ultimately on the saving decisions and preferences of the current generation alone, without any voice of the future generations, the market rate of interest can give the signal to deplete the resource at the expense of future generations. When the current generation is impatient, that is, it places a high value on current consumption relative to future consumption, the market interest rate will tend to be high and the market signal transmitted to each individual resource owner will be to deplete the resources under the owner's control. In essence, there is a tyranny of the present over the future.

As expected from the theory, slower-growing animals and plants are especially endangered today. Consider as an example one major category: slow-growing megafish. Their slow growth makes them a "poor investment" even in managed fisheries, and their large size makes them an easy prey. A new megafishes project has identified a number of species that are endangered (Chinese paddlefish, Mekong giant catfish, Tanganyika lates, and the pallid sturgeon, among others). Large land animals are in similarly desperate straits.

Once again, public policy can intervene to align private interests with sustainable development and, specifically, with the interests of later generations unrepresented in the market today. The overharvesting of a natural forest or a rare species can be banned by setting aside protected land or marine areas, and by banning hunting, fishing, or trading of particular species. Both methods are widely used, though imperfectly, and both still fall to the onslaught of illegal harvesting and free-market ideologies. The Convention on International Trade in Endangered Species of Wild Fauna and Flora (CITES), adopted in 1963, is the preeminent international trade treaty to protect endangered species by regulating and in some cases banning trade in endangered species. The treaty agrees on a hierarchy of endangered species: (1) those that are threatened with extinction and therefore banned for trade except in exceptional circumstances; (2) those that are endangered and therefore regulated; and (3) those that are protected in at least one country, a country that asks for cooperation from the other signatories. There are now 172 members of the convention, and these members agree on the classification of species and the follow-up actions.

Toward a Sustainable Population

Controlling population growth on our planet is the second great challenge of sustainable development. However, there is also a tyranny of the present when it comes to population growth. Parents often have many children in order to ensure the parents' old-age security, a decision that may well come at the expense of the children's own well-being. After all, an impoverished family cannot really provide for the nutritional, health, and educational needs of six or seven children, yet impoverished parents may have that many children for their own benefit, a subtle form of exploitation of future generations by today's generation. Similarly, in places where land ownership is communal and land is redistributed according to family size, each family might well overproduce children because it expects the community to transfer land to it as a result. If natural resources (such as trees for fuel wood) are held communally, this, too, can result in a choice of excessive family size. Each family will not take into account the social costs of added children to the sustainability of the commons.

A household's decision on fertility also depends on widespread cultural norms, on the availability of contraception in public health facilities, on the educational opportunities and costs for children, and on many other matters that are determined by public policy. All of this is to say that the decentralized decision making of individual households can easily lead to excessive population growth, at rates that jeopardize the physical environment and the well-being of the children (and later generations). On the other hand, public policies designed to promote a voluntary reduction of fertility rates can have an enormous effect, benefiting both present and future generations.

Ending the Poverty Trap

Ending the trap of extreme poverty is the third great challenge of sustainable development. The central solution to ending extreme poverty is to empower the poor with improved technology so that they can become productive members of the world economy. The central problem is that the extreme poor are unable to purchase those very technologies on their own. They lack their own savings and they also lack the creditworthiness to borrow. The result is the poverty trap, in which extreme poverty keeps vital, even life-saving, technology out of the reach of the poor, and the lack of that technology keeps the poor unproductive and condemns them to continued poverty. The trap can be broken if public financing provides the poor with the technologies that they need but cannot afford. The technology raises their productivity; this increases their income, allows for savings and investment, and thus breaks the trap.

We will describe four priority areas where improved technologies are already widely used around the world but not by the extreme poor: high-yield agriculture (including improved seed varieties, chemical fertilizers, and small-scale irrigation), educational technologies (as basic as classrooms and sanitary facilities for girls, but also connectivity for distance learning), health care technologies of all sorts, and modern infrastructure (all-weather roads, rehabilitated rail lines, electricity, safe drinking water, sanitation, telecoms, and the Internet). If the poor can be empowered with these technologies, they will experience a significant rise in productivity and thereby be enabled to join the process of convergent economic growth.

Foreign assistance can be the key in this process. If well targeted toward the crucial needs—in agriculture, health, education, and infrastructure—foreign aid can provide the breakthrough financing to enable the poor to escape from poverty. Such success has occurred many times in the past, for example, in the international support for countries to fight diseases such as smallpox and measles, or to raise agricultural production through the adoption of high-yield seed varieties. We will describe at length some of these earlier successes and how the lessons from them can be usefully applied in our own time.

Will We Run Out of Resources?

Even with the best of intentions, it might seem futile to plan for a richer world with shared prosperity. After all, many key resources are necessarily depleting, with no prospect for regrowth within the time span of society. Fossil fuels, for example, were laid down hundreds of millions of years ago by the deposition of organic matter that gradually was converted into coal, oil, gas, and other fossil fuels. As we use the oil, it is running out. Perhaps there are just a few decades left until we've exhausted the world's oil stocks. This seems the stuff of nightmares, the assured collapse of our fossil fuel civilization. Similarly, in some places we are running out of "fossil" groundwater, meaning water in deep underground aquifers that is being pumped to the surface for human uses at rates vastly greater than the aquifers' natural recharge through rainwater that infiltrates into the aquifer. Are we doomed, or more precisely, is the future doomed?

Even in the face of some resource depletion, future generations can be spared a collapse of living standards. First, as we run out of one resource, say, oil, we can shift to other resources in more plentiful supply. Perhaps both are depletable, but by shifting from one to the next, we postpone the ultimate reckoning. Second, we can shift from the depleting resource (say, oil again) to a renewable resource, such as solar power. Third, we can economize on the use of the depleting resource, for example, by investing in better insulation in order to use less home heating oil.

There has been much consternation about "peak" oil, the idea that the world may be nearing the peak of total oil production and, therefore, faces a decline of oil reserves and oil production in future decades because we have discovered and already developed most or all of the world's great oil fields. The common assumption is that peak oil, if true, is a disaster: the world hitting a brick wall of oil supply just as the developing world is ramping up its demand for it. Yet the consequences would not be nearly as dire as some have suggested. We might run out of conventional petroleum in a few decades, but we have centuries left of coal and other nonconventional fossil fuels, such as tar sands and oil shale. This may seem like slight consolation, since it is hard to put coal into the gas tank. Yet chemists know precisely how to do that, using an industrial process known as Fischer-Tropsch liquefaction, which converts coal into liquid hydrocarbons such as gasoline at relatively low cost. In the long run, we need to be more concerned about the total supply of fossil fuels than with the supply of oil alone, since the fossil fuels are reasonably changeable from one to the other through known industrial processes.

The best evidence regarding the total fossil fuel supply is that we have enough for this century, even with substantial economic growth, but we will have to rely increasingly on coal and nonconventional fossil fuels. In the most authoritative recent estimate, Hans-Holger Rogner reaches the following crucial conclusion:

> The global fossil fuel resource base is abundant and is estimated at approximately 5000 Gtoe (billion tons of oil equivalent). Compared to current global primary energy use of some 10 Gtoe per year, this amount is certainly sufficient to fuel the world economy through the twenty-first century, even in the case of drastic growth in global energy demand.

The challenge for this century will not be in the limited availability of fossil fuels, but in their safe ecological use and in the timely investments needed to ensure that the right kinds of fuels are available at the right times and places (such as the conversion from coal to liquids). For the twenty-second century and onward, there is a reasonable chance that we will need to convert massively to alternative technologies, such as solar power or nuclear power.

Fortunately, the long-term prospects for solar power are very good. The total solar radiation that reaches the Earth is about ten thousand times greater than our current commercial energy use. By harnessing that solar power, we could eventually dispense altogether with our reliance on fossil fuels. We already harness solar power in many forms: solar panels to produce electricity, the direct solar heating of water, wind power (which itself is the conversion of solar radiation into the movement of air molecules), hydroelectric power (remembering that the hydrological cycle is powered by solar radiation), and, of course, biofuels (using the products of photosynthesis). Currently, the cost of these various kinds of solar power tends to exceed most applications of fossil-fuel-based energy. With improved technologies, however, solar power will eventually compete favorably with fossil fuel power, and thereby provide a backstop technology to ensure the world's long-term energy future.

With other threatened resources (groundwater, fish, tropical forests, soil nutrients, farmland), there are usually many ways to use man-made capital to economize on the depletable natural resource under stress. Ocean fisheries can be made sustainable, for example, by the introduction of fish farms to replace open-sea fishing. The ocean is spared at the expense of increased land use (both for the fish farm and for the land to produce the fish meal). The development of high-yield seed varieties allows for a reduction of land under cultivation while still producing the same amount of food. Drought-resistant seed varieties can facilitate the reduction of water use. And the list goes on.

None of these possibilities ensures that such sustainable technologies will be adopted smoothly and at a scale necessary to avoid massive ecological and economic disruptions. Coal can be converted to liquid fuels, for example, but it can only be converted at a large scale if significant investments in Fischer-Tropsch industrial units are made in advance. Sustainable development may be achievable in theory but not reached in practice if public policies and market forces do not lead to the needed investments.

We can summarize in the following way: the world is facing enormous ecological and environmental problems, but running out of natural resources is not the right way to describe the threat. Earth has the energy, land, biodiversity, and water resources needed to feed humanity and support long-term economic prosperity for all. The problem is that markets might not lead to their wise and sustainable use. There is no economic imperative that will condemn us to deplete our vital resource base, but neither is there an invisible hand that will prevent us from doing so. The choice will be ours to make through public policy and global cooperation.

Resource Scramble or Systematic Innovation?

Despite the vast stores of energy, including nonconventional fossil fuels, solar power, geothermal power, nuclear power, and more, there is a pervasive fear of an imminent energy crisis resulting from the depletion of oil. The scramble of powerful countries to control Middle East oil or newly discovered reserves in other parts of the world, such as West Africa and the Arctic, has surely intensified, while investments in alternative and sustainable energy sources have been woefully insufficient. This is an example of a vicious cycle of distrust. The world could adopt a cooperative approach to develop sustainable energy supplies, with sustainability in the dual sense of low greenhouse gas emissions and long-term, low-cost availability. Alternatively, we can scramble for the depleting conventional oil and gas resources. The scramble, very much under way today, reduces global cooperation, spills over into violence and risks great power confrontations, and makes even more distant the good-faith cooperation to pool R & D and investments to develop alternative fuels and alternative ways to use nonconventional fossil fuels.

The Bush administration has been more consumed by the scramble rather than by cooperative global investments in a long-term future. The administration's outlook has been dominated by the oil industry, not by a broader perspective on sustainable energy potential or global sustainable development more generally. The Iraq War has its roots in the misapplied quest of the Bush administration for U.S. energy security, though the war has only deepened the insecurity. Yet the U.S. fixation on Middle East oil goes back more than half a century to the CIA-backed coup that overthrew the prime minister of Iran in 1953 and a seemingly endless series of CIA and military misadventures since then. Hundreds of billions of dollars have been spent in military efforts to ensure the security (for the United States) of Middle East oil fields, swamping the funds that have been applied to developing long-term energy alternatives. Panic has consistently superseded good judgment and a long-term cooperative perspective.

Reinvigorating Global Cooperation

From time to time since World War II the world has cooperated on the central challenges of living together on this small planet. The American neoconservatives who have fantasized about U.S. unilateral dominance have ridiculed those who believe in global cooperation, but the truth is that when global cooperation has been tried, it has paid off brilliantly.

- Foreign aid has contributed to the economic development of Asia and Latin America through the Green Revolution of increased agricultural productivity; the control of infectious diseases, such as smallpox; the vast rise of literacy and school attendance; and much more.

- Foreign aid and global agreements have facilitated the dramatic, indeed revolutionary, dissemination of modern methods of contraception and family planning, leading to a crucial voluntary drop of fertility rates in most of the world.

- Global cooperation has produced major advances in global environmental control, most successfully in heading off the destruction of the layer of stratospheric ozone, and has established frameworks for dealing with climate change, biodiversity, and desertification.

- Global cooperation has dramatically slowed the proliferation of nuclear weapons and encouraged several dozen countries to abandon their quest for such weapons.

These are global achievements of historic proportions. Yet the roots of these successes are almost forgotten today by unilateralist or free-market ideologues in the United States, obscured by a heavy dose of reactionary ideology and rhetoric that claim, against the facts, that such progress was ordained by market forces alone and was not the result of the massive collective actions and financial backing that went into these efforts.

The New York University economist William Easterly played to the Washington right wing in recent years when he waved a red flag against foreign aid, charging that it was $2.3 trillion down the drain in the past fifty years. It is a false charge, but it was eagerly and gratefully received by cynical U.S. politicians who would like to be absolved from spending even 70 cents in budgetary outlays for each $100 of U.S. national income, the agreed on but unfulfilled global target for official development aid, to improve the lot of the world's poor.

The charge is phony in two ways. The first is the claim itself that aid has failed. While that headline claim is eagerly embraced, even Easterly admits the contrary, but his admission is buried in the middle of his book, where he acknowledges that

> Foreign aid likely contributed to some notable successes on a global scale, such as dramatic improvement in health and education indicators in poor countries. Life expectancy in the typical poor country has risen from forty-eight years to sixty-eight years over the past four decades. Forty years ago, 131 out of every 1,000 babies born in poor countries died before reaching their first birthday. Today, 36 out of very 1,000 babies die before their first birthday.

Moreover, Easterly's insinuations about aid failures, exaggerated as they are, are also completely Washington focused. Aid from Japan, for example, which played an important role in building the basic infrastructure and technological capacity that enabled Southeast Asia to attract Japanese private investment and to become industrial exporters in the 1960s and onward, is simply not evident in his account. More generally, as we will note in Chapters 9 and 10, today's successful emerging markets, such as Korea, Taiwan, China, and India, have *all* been the beneficiaries of important external assistance.

The second fallacy is the implication that $2.3 trillion is so gargantuan as to prove obviously, and without further calculation, that aid has been a massive waste on a global scale. I dare say that most people before making the calculation would have a hard time knowing whether the sum is actually gargantuan or not. It is not easy to judge, since it signifies *all* aid to *all* countries from *all* donors over a fifty-year period! That's a hard sum to contemplate accurately. A little calculation puts the figure in perspective. There were, on average, three billion people in low-income countries during the fifty years, so averaging the aid by person per year tells us that the average aid recipient received the grand sum of $15 each year (Figure 2.4). Recognizing the enormous worldwide gains in literacy, life expectancy, disease control, reduced poverty, reduced fertility, school attendance, HIV treatments, and so on, one would think that aid outlays of $15 per person per year have surely been among the greatest bargains on the planet. Another way to judge the modest magnitude of aid is to realize that it is currently around 0.3 percent of the income of the donor countries, meaning 30 cents in aid per $100 of income. In the United States, it stands at just 17 cents per $100 of national income, that is, 0.17 percent.

Put $2.3 trillion in comparison with U.S. military spending during the same period, which totaled $17 trillion, nearly eight times the aid levels. And we can note that the Iraq War cost $500 billion in direct outlays by the middle of 2007 and about the same amount in indirect costs (for example, the costs of medical and long-lasting disability care for veterans). The Vietnam War cost at least $500 billion in today's dollars. Suddenly $2.3 trillion over a fifty-year period for the entire world of development—health, water, disease, literacy, family planning, roads, power, courts, democracy, famine, and other emergency relief—is not so self-evidently extravagant.

The truth is that Easterly's heated attacks don't undermine the case for aid, but usefully remind us that aid can be wasted. He and I certainly do agree that much aid has been wasted, especially aid that has gone for U.S. political purposes with little regard for a true developmental impact (for example, aid to support U.S. foreign policies vis-à-vis the Cold War, the Israel-Palestine conflict, and the war on terror), or aid to pay the salaries of high-priced U.S. and European consultants, or expensive shipments of U.S. food to satisfy farm-state senators, when aid to raise Africa's own food production would have provided vastly less expensive and longer-lasting benefits. Indeed, I strongly applaud Easterly's conclusion at the end of his long diatribe against aid, when he finally gets around to his own positive recommendations:

*Figure 2.4: Official Development Assistance from All Donors to
All Developing Countries, per Person in Developing Countries*

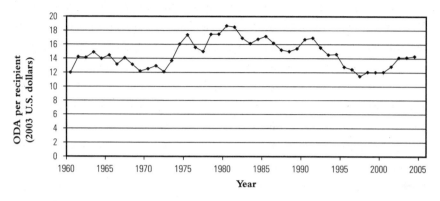

Source: Calculated using data from OECD (2007)

Put the focus back where it belongs: get the poorest people in the world
such obvious goods as the vaccines, the antibiotics, the food supplements,
the improved seeds, the fertilizer, the roads, the boreholes, the water pipes,
the textbooks, and the nurses. This is not making the poor dependent on
handouts; it is giving the poorest people the health, nutrition, education,
and other inputs that raise the payoff to their own efforts to better their
lives. (Just like a National Science Foundation fellowship to get a Ph.D.
once increased the payoff to my own efforts to pursue a career.)

This is a good list, and it includes the kinds of investments being supported
by the Millennium Village Project described in Chapter 10.

Fortunately, much of the critical groundwork for renewed global cooperation is in place. In each area of concern we are starting from a track record
of success, not failure, but we are facing harder problems and in recent years
a flagging of wills and memory. Here's a quick rundown of some of the key
challenges.

Environment

Progress has been made in many middle-income and rich countries in the
control of local pollution and even cross-border pollution across neighbors.
Dirty air and water have been controlled in much of the world. Gasoline is
now unleaded. Smokestack scrubbers reduce sulfur dioxide. Catalytic con-

verters reduce urban smog. Even the tough challenge of stratospheric ozone depletion has been contained. But the crowded planet and burgeoning populations are leading to environmental devastation in other areas still not controlled: species extinction, global climate change, desertification, and the massive destruction of natural habitats.

Population

Fertility rates have declined below 4 children per woman on average in almost every country outside of tropical Africa (the exceptions in 2005 are Guatemala, 4.3; Lao PDR, 4.5; Maldives, 4.0; Pakistan, 4.1; Solomon Islands, 4.0; the West Bank and Gaza, 4.6; and Yemen, 5.9), but they are still above 4 in thirty-five out of forty-six tropical African countries (with the exceptions mainly in countries with small populations). Population control is arriving late to the most difficult places, the regions with massive illiteracy, lack of health care, high child mortality, and typically, low social conditions for women.

Extreme Poverty, Hunger, and Disease

The world has seen an astounding reduction in extreme poverty since the beginning of the Industrial Revolution. Before 1800, perhaps 85 percent of the world's population lived in what we would consider today to be extreme poverty. By 1950, this had reached the 50 percent mark as shown in Figure 2.5. Since then, extreme poverty has continued to decline to below 25 percent in 1992 and to just 15 percent today. The challenge now is that extreme poverty is concentrated in the toughest places: landlocked, tropical, drought-prone, malaria-ridden, and off the world's main trade routes. It is no accident that today's poorest places have been the last to catch the wave of globalization. They have the most difficulty in getting on the ladder of development.

THE CHALLENGE OF GLOBAL COOPERATION

To solve the remaining dire problems of environmental degradation, population growth, and extreme poverty, we will need to create a new model of twenty-first-century cooperation, one that builds on past successes and over-

Figure 2.5: Global Poverty from 1820 to 1992

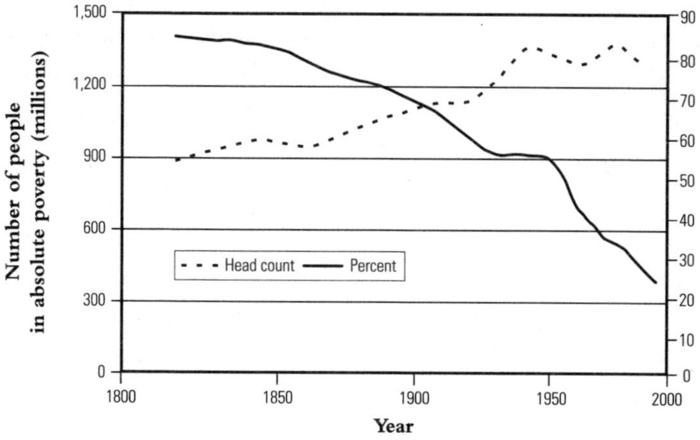

Source: Bourguignon and Morrisson (2001)

comes today's widespread pessimism and lack of leadership. This century's global cooperation won't be led by any single country. It will be based on global agreements and international law, first and foremost as contained in the treaties and agreements that constitute the Millennium Promises. Financial contributions and ideas will have to come from many quarters, not only the rich countries but also a host of emerging markets and emerging powers, including Brazil, China, India, South Africa, and Nigeria, among others. Such multipolar cooperation is time-consuming and often contentious. Solutions will be complicated; the problems of sustainable development inevitably cut across several areas of professional expertise, making it hard for any single ministry—or academic department, for that matter—to address the issues adequately. A sound climate change strategy must be informed by climate science, environmental engineering, energy systems, economics, ecology, hydrology, agronomics (plant breeding), infectious disease control, business, and finance. Solutions for African poverty require strategies that simulataneously tackle disease control, agricultural modernization, ecological conservation, fertility control, the upgrading of infrastructure, and a host of other components. Governments will need to be restructured for such twenty-first-century problems.

The new global cooperation will also include an increased role for businesses and civil-society organizations. Modern businesses, especially the vast multinational companies, are the repositories of the most advanced technologies on the planet and the most sophisticated management methods for large-scale delivery of goods and services. There are no solutions to the problems of poverty, population, and environment without the active engagement of the private sector, and especially the large multinational companies. Yet the main objective of such companies is to earn profits rather than to meet social needs. The two are definitely not incompatible, but they are not the same. It will take hard work to bring together the leaders of business, government, and nongovernmental organizations to ensure that private-sector incentives and societal needs are harmonized.

The role of the global citizenry will also be crucial in ensuring that governments abide by the commitments they have undertaken in the name of their citizens. The temptation of any individual government to shirk its global obligations is ever present. Global cooperation is sustainable only if such shirking is punished, most important, by a loss of reputation throughout the world. Governments can be shamed into doing the right thing but only if the global citizenry is paying attention, understands the stakes, cares about the outcomes, and has the organizational heft to take on the shirkers. When governments fail to follow through, they need to know that global public opinion will raise the costs of shirking. Many NGOs are now playing that role effectively, monitoring governments for follow-through on promises of aid, environmental management, clean governance, the fight against disease, and commitments in the fight against poverty. The remarkable social networking strategies now being deployed will strengthen this crucial role of global citizenry.

All of this will require financial help from the rich-world governments, at levels that have long been promised but not delivered. The good news is that official development assistance (ODA) as a share of donor-country income is beginning to rise again after a long downslide. The ratio of ODA to donor income reached its nadir in the late 1990s, falling from around 0.5 percent in the early 1960s to roughly 0.35 percent in the 1980s and to a mere 0.22 percent in 1997. This was contrary to the long-standing pledge made in 1970 and reiterated countless times thereafter to achieve 0.7 percent of GNP in official development assistance. In 2002, the donor countries again committed to make concrete efforts to reach 0.7. In 2005, the European Union (but not the United States) set a timetable to do so by the year 2015. The major donors are on the record promising a doubling of aid to Africa (an extra $25 billion per year) by the year 2010, but as of 2007 have not delivered a sustained increase above the 2004 levels. There is still time to make good on the promises, but the clock is running and millions of lives are lost each year by this neglect.

PART TWO

Environmental Sustainability

Chapter 3

The Anthropocene

THE WORLD'S ABILITY TO COMBINE long-term economic growth with environmental health is heavily debated. Yet one thing is certain: *the current trajectory of human activity is not sustainable.* If we simply do what we are doing on the planet with unchanged technology—but on a much larger scale as China, India, and other large population centers experience rapid economic growth—the environmental underpinnings of global well-being will collapse. The limits of the environment itself will defeat our global aspirations for prosperity. Yet if we channel a modest part of our growing resources and knowledge into high-S technologies, the result can be very different.

NATURE'S SERVICES AND THE HUMAN POPULATION

To succeed, we'll have to break some bad and long-standing habits. Our species' natural history is not merely one of human migration and population growth. Our deepest pattern, in fact, has been the *appropriation* of the Earth's natural systems for human use, often at great and unwitting cost to other species and to the long-term well-being of human society itself. Nature provides us with the stuff of life—food, water, fuels, fibers—and human society has worked relentlessly to harness nature's services to support a rising human population and rising levels of consumption per person, but typically unaware of the long-term consequences. In fact, those consequences were generally manageable until recently, as the world became exceedingly crowded with human beings and their high-intensity activity.

Our species, Homo sapiens, has been around now for around a hundred thousand years. For the first ninety thousand or so years of human existence, the human population was limited by the ability of small bands of humans to hunt and gather their foodstuffs within complex ecological systems. The carrying capacity of each environment differed. Human populations varied in number and density depending on the underlying productivity of the local ecology and the competition with other species, whether in deserts, mountains, riverbanks, coastal estuaries, or the countless other locales of human existence. Human numbers were probably not far different from what would be expected of mammals of our size, around one to two humans per square kilometer, higher in settings of great productivity, such as the banks of rivers and estuaries, where fishing was easy and plentiful, and smaller in settings of low productivity, such as desert margins. On a global scale, hunter-gatherers might have totaled ten million in number at the start of the Neolithic era ten thousand years ago.

Even in this early phase of human existence (indeed, even before modern humans emerged), our ancestors began to alter the landscape to tilt the advantage toward human needs at the expense of other species. There is evidence that humans, and even protohumans, used fire to alter their landscapes in order to convert forests to grasslands and to facilitate hunting. These earliest steps of our species foretold the pattern that brings us to the ecological challenge of the twenty-first century.

The decisive breakthrough in human populations came not with fire, but with the invention of agriculture, around ten thousand years ago. The shift to agriculture represented a qualitative change in the natural order, one whose consequences are still being played out. In an agricultural system, the land is cleared of natural communities of plants and animals so that the solar energy can be appropriated by human beings in a more direct manner. Photosynthesis is directed toward foodstuffs directly consumed by humans, or foodstuffs consumed by domesticated animals that are directly consumed by humans. Agriculture was truly something new and revolutionary. The balance between humans and the rest of the biosphere was decisively altered.

Human populations soared after the onset of agriculture, both because our species was able to increase its density wherever it was located and because agriculture opened the opportunity for a massive expansion of the range of human habitats. Now it was possible to cut down a forest with the intention of planting a crop and expanding human settlements. For the past ten thousand years, deforestation has been the policy of choice of human societies for increasing the human carrying capacity of the local environment. The result was a rise in the human population of perhaps more than an order of magnitude from the onset of agriculture to the beginning of the first millennium in AD 1, when the human population is estimated to have been around 230 million in total.

In the earliest days of agriculture, this bulging population was most heavily concentrated in the great river systems of Asia and the Nile in Egypt. Those riverine ecologies offered a full suite of ecosystem services for human survival: ample solar radiation, water for irrigation and household use, trees for fuel wood and construction, nutrient-rich soils with soil nutrients replenished by the silt carried downriver from the erosion of mountains upstream, and river-based transport. One can fairly say that the Himalayan/Tibetan mountain ranges support Asia's vast population potential by enabling the river-based societies of the Indus, Ganges, Brahmaputra, Ayeyarwaddy, Mekong, Yangtze, Yellow, Salween, and other rivers. The Tigris and the Euphrates in modern-day Turkey and Iraq, and the Nile, made possible the ancient civilizations of the Near East.

Our species has proven to be remarkably versatile, finding a niche in virtually every ecological zone on the planet, from the tropics to the tundra, the lowlands to the mountain peaks, the drylands to the rain forests. Everywhere, population densities grew to the extent that basic human needs could be met by the local resource base. And with improving technologies, the ecological base was molded and reshaped by society. Mountain slopes were terraced. Natural grasses were replaced by edible grasses, notably wheat, rice, and maize. Low-yielding seeds were very gradually displaced by higher-yielding seeds, so over generations the physical appearance of the original crops changed to become unrecognizable from the distant ancestors. Woodlands were cleared for pasture, and the wildlife population was systematically replaced by domesticated animals.

That, at least, is what happened in the lucky cases. In other circumstances, human societies devoured the natural environment to the point of collapse. One of the most striking cases is the arrival of humans in the Americas at the end of the Ice Age, around thirteen thousand years ago. Small bands of migrating hunter-gatherers crossed the land bridge between Asia and North America to find a continent with vast stocks of large land mammals, including horses, mammoths, and bison. The hunter-gatherers went to work, and within two thousand years had hunted the large animals to extinction. The result was disastrous for the future history of the descendants of these populations. Horses, had they not been driven to extinction, would have provided the indigenous Americans with motive power for plows, transport, water wells, and the like, but they were gone before these technological possibilities were recognized. Other large North American mammals might have been domesticated for agriculture.

For the next ten millennia or so, the North American indigenous populations were bereft of animal power and farm animals. Indeed, the only domesticated large animals in all of the Americas were the llamas and alpacas of the Andes, animals that were unfit for adaptation to societies at lower elevations. Native Americans paid a fearsome price for the early extinctions. When horses were eventually reintroduced to the Americas, the reintroduction was by Spanish conquerors who mobilized the horse power for military conquest over the unfortunate indigenous populations.

THE FITFUL RISE OF HUMAN POPULATIONS

By the standards of the past two centuries, the increase of human populations from AD 1 to the Industrial Revolution at the start of the nineteenth century was exceedingly gradual and fitful. Over roughly 1,800 years, the population increased approximately fourfold, from around 230 million estimated as of AD 1 to 1 billion, first reached in 1830. In the subsequent 175 years, the global population has risen sixfold, from 1 billion to 6.5 billion, in 2005. In the preindustrial era, societies learned gradually to master the local environment—crop choices, water control, soil management, domestication of animals, mining of minerals, land clearing for pasture and fuel wood—in order to support larger populations. Each opening of new trade routes, such as the silk road from China to Europe during the Roman Empire or the sea routes from Europe to the Americas at the time of Columbus, gave opportunity for another step increase in human populations because increased productivity came along with increased trade. Trade allowed the exchange of crops, animals, technologies, and, of course, human populations. Wheat and horses were introduced by Europeans into the Americas. Potatoes were brought from the Andes to be grown in Europe, and maize was brought from Mesoamerica to become a staple crop throughout Europe and Africa. The banana tree, similarly, was carried from Southeast Asia to Africa, where it would become the main food crop for large parts of Africa. The list of such exchanges is vast.

In addition to the exchange of crops, other crucial technologies supported the expansion of the human population. Better plows after about AD 1000 allowed Europeans to settle the heavy soils of Northern Europe, which centuries earlier had posed a barrier to the expansion of the Roman Empire. Better axes allowed the felling of thick forests. Newly applied crop rotations, such as rotating nitrogen-fixing legumes and alfalfa with grass crops, allowed the restoration of nitrogen in soils and thereby a higher average crop yield. Other advances included improved irrigation, transport, water power, wind power, cookstoves, and cloth making.

Human populations tended to expand to the carrying capacity of each ecological niche. The introduction of a new crop that allowed for higher food production would soon enough induce a rise in population through some combination of in-migration and natural population increase. The natural population increase would result from both rising birth rates and falling death rates. Better nutrition would increase child survival. Rising household wealth would make possible an earlier age of marriage in the community and a higher proportion of children with enough wealth to take a spouse and start a new household.

With favorable food conditions, human populations could expand fairly rapidly. But the ascent of human populations was repeatedly checked by two forces. The first was infectious disease. The second was the natural limits on food output in traditional farm systems. Both of these limitations meant that the long-term rise of human populations was both limited by and subject to repeated crises.

The question of disease requires our most careful attention, especially in an age of AIDS, avian flu, Ebola, and other emerging diseases. Growing populations throughout history have been repeatedly set back by devastating epidemics. "New" diseases have hit human populations for at least three reasons. First, diseases have been carried from one population to another when two formerly separated societies are brought together through conquest and trade. The "virgin" population, being exposed to the disease for the first time, can be devastated. It seems likely, for example, that the opening of silk route trade between the Roman Empire and the Han dynasty of China also carried disease to Europe, with devastating consequences for the Roman Empire's population. The increased Asian-European trade of the fourteenth century made possible by the harsh peace imposed by the Mongols also occasioned the introduction of bubonic plague into Europe, which caused several catastrophic epidemics, including the Black Death of 1347–51. The Spanish conquests of the Americas after Columbus's voyages brought smallpox, measles, and other Old World diseases to the New World, contributing to the catastrophic collapse of the indigenous populations.

Second, diseases may require a minimum threshold of population size or density to support ongoing transmission of the disease. Therefore, a rise in human population size or density can expose the population to a disease that previously could not be sustained in the population. The advent of agriculture, for example, resulted in the transmission of countless diseases that require higher human densities than occur in hunter-gatherer societies. Malaria is an example of a massive killer that probably took on its modern killer form around five thousand years ago with the introduction of settled farming in Africa. Until settled agriculture, hunter-gatherer communities in Africa were too small and sparsely settled to support the sustained transmission of malaria. Urban life similarly supports the spread of numerous diseases, such as measles, that require higher population densities than occur in agricultural settlements. Therefore, throughout history, when societies achieved breakthroughs in farming that enabled the growth of an urban population, the initial spread of urbanization was often set back by bouts of infectious diseases.

Third, shifting patterns of human settlements bring societies into new contacts with animal species that harbor infectious diseases that can then mutate and jump to human populations. The result can be a zoonotic disease, meaning an infectious disease transferred from an animal population to the human population. The AIDS epidemic is such a zoonosis. Careful genetic reconstruction of the history of AIDS suggests that the human immunodeficiency virus (HIV), which causes AIDS, is a mutation of a simian immunodeficiency virus (SIV) carried by chimpanzees. SIV does not harm the chimpanzees, but HIV, of course, has killed more than twenty-five million humans. It seems likely that HIV emerged sometime around 1930 in West Africa, when an African chimpanzee hunter or an eater of bush meat was inadvertently exposed to SIV, which in turn mutated to enable human-to-human transmission.

In the end, none of the calamitous epidemics fully extinguished human populations, except perhaps in local areas, and societies often bounced back in a relatively brief span. The Renaissance of Europe followed the Black Death by a few decades, and some historians have even surmised that the much-reduced human population densities in Europe, and the attendant disruptions of medieval life, actually favored the onset of creativity of the Renaissance. One long-term reason for the survival of the human species has been evolutionary adjustments in the human population in the face of the new diseases, because natural selection favors genetic traits that are protective against the diseases. Pathogens similarly have evolved in some cases to become less lethal over time. Societal responses, such as more effective methods of quarantine, perhaps also played some role in protecting human populations even before the age of modern medicine. For whatever reason, some of history's worst killers, such as bubonic plague, largely disappeared from the scene without any clear and decisive societal countermeasures that can fully explain the disappearance.

Given all that can go wrong with human life—crop failures, war, epidemic diseases—it is no surprise that the underlying long-term trend of global population increase was punctuated by repeated disasters, including the Black Death, the decimation of indigenous American populations after 1492, the flu epidemic after World War I that killed twenty to forty million people, and the AIDS pandemic today. Climate shocks, such as the "little ice age" after 1600, similarly led to hunger, disease, and bouts of population decline. Through it all, the long-term ascent of the human population continued, as societies around the world gradually took control of local ecosystems and gradually improved their abilities to grow food, clear forests, harness wind and water, and squeeze out the habitats of other species. Yet after a long, gradual, and rocky ascent, all was to change with the onset of the modern era.

THE INDUSTRIAL TAKEOFF

Nothing in human history really prepared humanity or the Earth for what came after 1800. The gradual rise of the human population, from perhaps ten million in 8000 BC to five hundred million in AD 1800, was followed by an explosion of human population shown in Figure 3.1 that has changed everything about us and the natural environment. As of 1800, give or take a few decades, we entered the age of the Anthropocene, when human activity became the dominant driver of the natural environment.

Starting around 1800 the traditional limits on the human population gave way to unprecedented new technologies. Before then, humanity had lived on the contemporaneous energy of the sun, mainly in the forms of food, fuel wood, fibers, and a modest capture of wind and water power. Since 1800, humanity has lived on the treasure trove of hoarded solar power that is packaged in fossil fuels. Until 1800, when not beset by epidemics, the human population was limited in number by the ability to grow food and to provision other basic needs (cooking fuels, animal traction, water, shelter). After 1800, those same limits could be surmounted by coal, oil, and natural gas. Those fossil fuels were the results of photosynthesis eons ago, perhaps 300 to 350 million years in the past, when plant and animal material had become buried in the Earth's crust, separated from humanity until miners began to dig up the stuff at the start of the industrial age. After humans harnessed those fuels, the traditional limits on food, water, transport, and shelter all gave way to the new fossil-fuel-driven technologies.

While the Industrial Revolution encompasses a vast range of ingenious technological breakthroughs that have transformed every dimension of life, the steam engine was the pivotal initiator of the revolution and the very emblem of it. This is because the mobilization of a new and vast energy resource—coal—was the key step in every other industrial process. Coal made possible factory production (for example, the textile industry), heavy indus-

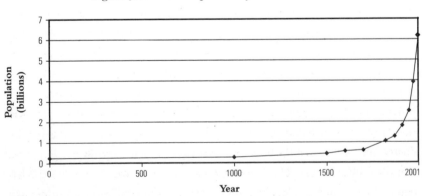

Figure 3.1: World Population from AD *1 to 2001*

Source: Data from Maddison (2001)

try (steel production), transport (railroads, ocean freight), and chemical processing, which solved huge problems in provisioning human society. Food could be carried vast distances, hinterlands such as the Argentine pampas could be opened up for meat and grain production, perishables could be refrigerated, water could be pumped at huge scales and distances, and on and on. With the scientific breakthroughs related to electrification at the end of the nineteenth century, fossil fuels (and hydroelectric power) could be harnessed for still larger areas of human sustenance and well-being. And with the invention of the internal combustion engine, another fossil fuel, petroleum, could provide the decisive motive power of the twentieth century.

Interestingly, all of the unprecedented industrial might that was assembled and mobilized in the Industrial Revolution could not overcome certain barriers to human survival and population growth. By the end of the nineteenth century, food production was still hampered by a basic agronomic constraint. Even though it was now possible to open up vast lands around the globe, ship farming equipment and food across oceans, harness water for irrigation on unprecedented scales, harvest crops with an efficiency unachievable in the past, and process agricultural outputs such as cotton with industrial scale and speed, the soil nutrients needed to grow crops were still constraining the supply of foodstuffs for the world's population. Industrialization had eased the constraint a bit by allowing large-scale ocean transport of Chile's natural nitrate deposits to supply chemical fertilizers for Europe's farms. Yet the nitrates were too limited in scale and too constrained by costs of production to solve the nutrient challenge. At the end of the nineteenth century, a leading British chemist, Sir William Crookes, predicted that the shortfall of nitrogen in the soils would lead to massive hunger in the face of the world's booming population unless new ways were found to harness Earth's nitrogen.

Fossil fuel once again came to the rescue. Between 1908 and 1914, a group of industrial scientists, led by Fritz Haber and Carl Bosch, developed a way to use energy (natural gas and to a lesser extent hydropower) to convert atmospheric nitrogen (N_2) into nitrogen-based compounds, such as urea, which provide nutrients to plants. The invention of the Haber-Bosch process for synthesizing nitrogen-based chemical fertilizers not only created a vast global industry but also created the biological possibility of a massive expansion of the world's food supplies. The limiting factor of soil nitrogen had been overcome. Energy, and specifically fossil fuel, had set free the human population. Technology historian Vaclav Smil estimates that the Haber-Bosch process

stands behind 80 percent of the increase of cereal production in the twentieth century.

The most important result was an explosion of human population, which
on average was also better fed. Despite two world wars, ongoing epidemic diseases, massive dislocations of populations, and other checks to population increase, the world's population rose fourfold in the twentieth century, from 1.5
billion to around 6 billion. Moreover, the industrial age had raised human
productivity to unimaginable levels. The takeoff of population was matched
by a simultaneous takeoff in average economic production per person, as
shown in Figure 3.2(a). Just as with population, global and seemingly insu-
perable constraints to human productivity were unlocked in the industrial age. The dramatic increase in population and productivity meant, of
course, that total economic activity on the planet was exploding, as seen in
Figure 3.2 (b).

THE ANTHROPOCENE

Two centuries into the Industrial Revolution, human society is now confronting the vast benefits, but also the massive risks, of these spectacular technological successes. We have become so adept at clearing the ecological playing
field to satisfy human desires that we are often shoving the rest of life right
off the stage. Some of the effects are easily understood. Vast tracts of trees dis-

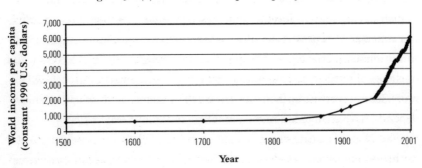

Figure 3.2(a): World Income per Capita from 1500 to 2001

Source: Data from Maddison (2001)

Figure 3.2(b): World Income from 1500 to 2001

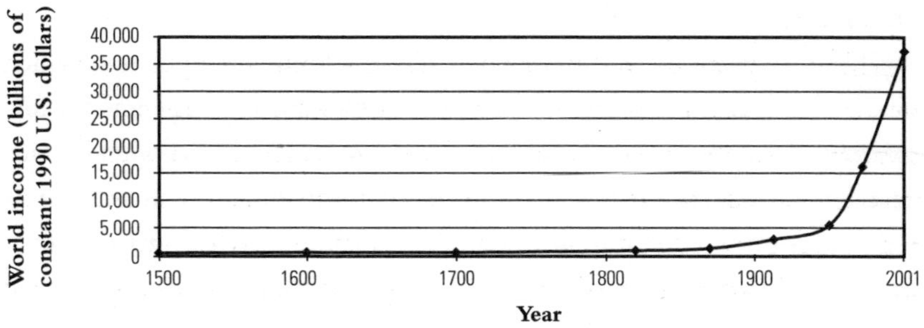

Source: Calculated using data from Maddison (2001)

appear when we clear forestlands to grow crops and graze livestock; ocean fisheries are fished to near depletion when high-powered fishing fleets prowl the seas on a massive scale. Some of the effects are much less clear, making it difficult to see the links between our actions and their effects on the planet. Obscure atmospheric chemistry causes the burning of fossil fuels to have as one side effect the derangement of the Earth's climate systems. Man-made climate change is not a sin of humanity, or even a result we could have easily predicted and avoided; it is, rather, an accident of chemistry, specifically, the accident that carbon dioxide has greenhouse climate effects (described in detail in Chapter 4). This accident is so novel and has come upon us so recently that global society has been caught largely unawares as to how it should respond.

A tenfold increase in human population since 1750 and a similar increase in production per person on the planet mean that human society's level of economic activity is perhaps one hundred times what it was at the start of the industrial era. That hundredfold increase corresponds to the surge in activities aimed at commandeering the Earth's physical processes for human consumption: land clearing and crop production, energy use, fish harvests, use of chemical fertilizers, dams and diversions of rivers, road construction, and more. It's not surprising, then, that the Earth's systems, on which our existence depends, have changed in many untoward and unexpected ways.

The Nobel laureate chemist Paul Crutzen dubbed the modern era the Anthropocene, a human-dominated Earth, because the scale of our human activities is now so large that it has thrown every fundamental, life-sustaining system on Earth off kilter. The great Stanford University ecologist Peter Vitousek and his colleagues have cataloged with great sophistication the extent to which humans now dominate natural systems. One of their famous summaries, shown in Figure 3.3, is worth pondering with care. It tells the amazing story of how humankind now appropriates the vital resources of the Earth's ecosystems on the planet and leaves the rest of life to fend for itself on an ever-narrower ledge of survival. Vitousek and colleagues look at seven dimensions of the Earth's natural systems to show the extent of human appropriation. Consider each from left to right in the figure. Each bar offers a powerful indicator of the extent to which humankind has come to dominate some aspect of key ecological processes.

Land Transformation

Land clearing for agriculture, both crops and pasture, is not a new phenomenon of the industrial or capitalist age. It is as old as humanity itself. We clear land mainly to harness the planet's photosynthetic output for our own use, as cropland and pastureland, and to a much smaller extent to make way for our houses, roads, parking lots, stadiums, and other appurtenances of human settlement. In a world of vast forests and no less than one hundred million square kilometers of land, up to *50 percent of the Earth's photosynthetic potential* is directly appropriated for human use. Land that is cleared now is either increasingly inhospitable or home to precious and unique stocks of biological diversity, such as the tropical rain forests that have been

Figure 3.3: Human Dominance or Alteration of Several Major Components of the Earth System

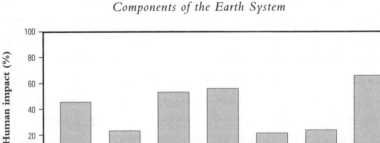

Source: Vitousek et al (1997)

falling under the ax in recent decades. We are, in short, running out of space to clear. Humans will continue to press against the land constraint as the human population expands and as increasingly richer populations seek more meat in their diets (which requires vast land areas for the grasses and crops to feed the livestock). Yet these land pressures now threaten pervasive extinctions of other species, whose habitats are being eliminated by relentless human encroachment.

Carbon Dioxide (CO₂) Concentration

Carbon dioxide is a naturally occurring trace gas in the Earth's atmosphere. For hundreds of thousands of years before the industrial age, the level of CO_2 in the atmosphere was on the order of 280 molecules per million molecules of air. (This is typically denoted as 280 parts per million, or ppm.) Carbon dioxide has a complicated natural cycle. On an annual timescale, trees absorb atmospheric carbon dioxide in photosynthesis in order to produce carbohydrates, while animal decomposers digest the carbohydrates (for example, in fallen leaves) and return the CO_2 to the air. On geologic timescales, CO_2 is emitted into the atmosphere by volcanoes and reabsorbed from the air by the oceans and the Earth's crust. Yet now, in the industrial age, CO_2 is being released into the air in vast quantities by the burning of fossil fuels, which combines the carbon (C) in the fuels with atmospheric oxygen, (O_2), to result in CO_2 plus the release of energy (and lots of it!). As Figure 3.3 shows, humans have significantly interfered in the carbon cycle, to the extent that around one quarter of all carbon dioxide now in the atmosphere is the result of recent human activity. Compared to 280 ppm in the preindustrial age, the atmospheric concentration of carbon dioxide today is 380 ppm. The increase of 100 ppm has resulted from deforestation and the burning of fossil fuels. The outcome, we now know with near certainty, is that human activity is decisively changing the climate, since CO_2 traps heat from the sun, warms the planet, and alters countless ecological processes (including rainfall, extreme storms, crop productivity, disease transmission, and much more).

Water Use

Photosynthesis, for food production and more generally, needs water along with soil nutrients, seeds, and sunlight. Humans also need water daily for personal use (drinking and sanitation) and for industrial processes. Water for agricultural use predominates, accounting for approximately twice the use of water for all other purposes combined. Just as there is a natural carbon dioxide cycle, so too is there a natural water (hydrological) cycle. Solar radiation heats the Earth and causes evaporation of water from land and water bodies, and the transpiration of water through the leaves of plants. The combined evapotranspiration turns to clouds, rainfall, and a return of water to the land and the sea. Some of the water falling on the land is directly evaporated or transpired, while some runs off to the oceans in river flows. Similarly, some of the water vapor that evaporates from the oceans returns in rainfall directly over the oceans, while some is transported by wind over land, where the rainfall occurs.

Humans have dramatically interfered in the hydrological cycle, mainly to ensure adequate water for human food production. As shown in Figure 3.3, up to 60 percent of accessible river runoff is now appropriated for human use through dams, irrigation systems, and other water diversion activities. The commandeering of the freshwater flow is now so high that many of the world's great rivers—including the Ganges in India, the Yellow in China, and the Rio Grande between the United States and Mexico—no longer reach the sea. Moreover, further damming of rivers will often create a zero-sum struggle in which greater upstream users deprive both humans and natural ecosystems located downstream of the water that they need for survival. More generally, human activity is likely to contribute to severe water crises in the coming years. Groundwater (that is, water in underground aquifers) is being taken out of the ground for irrigation much faster than it is being replenished naturally. Water tables are falling rapidly, and irrigation wells are running dry in many places, notably in China and India. Wetlands are being drained for economic development, especially for farms and urban expansion, with adverse consequences for ecological processes and biodiversity. And, of course, major waterways are being massively polluted.

Nitrogen Fixation

Nitrogen dominates the Earth's atmosphere, composing 78 percent of the molecules. Nitrogen is also vital for all living organisms, since it is the basic element in protein. Yet the form of nitrogen in the atmosphere, N_2, is not directly available to plants or animals for use in biological processes. The triple bond that holds the two nitrogen atoms together is too strong to be broken in most metabolic processes. Some biological "specialists" in nitrogen, mainly certain kinds of bacteria, are able to use energy to convert the N_2 into various nitrogen-based compounds (nitrates, ammonia, and so forth) which can then be absorbed biologically and used by other plants and animals to build proteins and contribute to biological functions. Lightning, too, can split the N_2 molecule and deposit nitrates and ammonia naturally on Earth.

The process of converting atmospheric nitrogen to active nitrogen is called nitrogen fixation. The problem today is that the natural fixation processes are too slow to provide the vast stores of nitrogen needed to grow food crops sufficient to feed the 6.6 billion people on the planet, much less the 7 to 9 billion the world will have by midcentury. That's where the Haber-Bosch process came in at the start of the twentieth century. And in addition to chemical fertilizers, farmers also abet the natural cycle by planting leguminous crops such as alfalfa and soybeans, which have root systems that contain nitrogen-fixing bacteria. As Figure 3.3 indicates, the amount of nitrogen fixed by chemical fertilizers and human crop choice is now around 60 percent of the Earth's total nitrogen fixation. Nitrogen-based fertilizers are vital for feeding the planet, but when used in excess, as is the case in many parts of the world, the costs can be very high. Human interventions in the nitrogen cycle are also polluting rivers and streams with excess flows of nitrates, ammonia, and other nitrogen-based chemicals. The results are poisoned drinking water and widespread destruction of estuaries and river ways fed by water flowing through large agricultural regions.

Plant Invasions

From the earliest days of agriculture, humans have been transporting seeds, plants, and animals from some locations on the planet to others. Very often the introduction of new species into a new locale has been deliberate, as when potatoes were introduced into Europe from the Andes. Sometimes the introduction of species is inadvertent, as when hyacinths invaded Lake Victoria and nearly choked the lake by depriving it of vast areas of sunlight. Humans have long been rearranging the Earth's ecology with little understanding of side effects and unanticipated consequences. Some introduced species act as devastating weeds, taking over an ecosystem that lacks proper defenses. Pests and pathogens easily cross from one location to another. Bacteria and other infectious agents can be carried in the bilges of ships. As Vitousek and coauthors note, "On many islands, more than half of the plant species are non-indigenous, and in many continental areas the figure is 20% or more." Vitousek and coauthors illustrate this in Figure 3.3 through the example of Canada, where an estimated 20 percent or so of plant species have been introduced from elsewhere by human activities. In general, the consequences of such introduced species are complex, typically unpredictable, and sometimes devastating to native species and to the functioning of the local ecosystems.

Bird Extinctions

Ecologists warn us that we are now in the Earth's sixth great extinction episode. Plants and animals are apparently going extinct at a rate that is between one hundred and one thousand times the natural rate of extinction before human dominance of the Earth's ecosystems. The five earlier episodes were caused by massive natural disruptions of the Earth's ecological processes, including collisions with asteroids, changes to the Earth's climate through geological processes such as volcanic eruptions, and changes in the characteristics of the Earth's orbit. The current episode of mass extinctions is the only one in which one species has pushed the others over the cliff. As shown in Figure 3.3, it is estimated that perhaps a quarter of all of the Earth's species of birds have been driven to extinction by human activities over the past two millennia. We should not be entirely surprised, though we should bemoan and curb our own destructiveness. Human activity is, after all, devoted quite explicitly to ensuring that habitat, water supply, nutrient flows, and introduced species all serve human needs rather than the needs of other species.

Marine Fisheries

Traditional hunter-gatherer societies, including those before the age of agriculture and the tiny numbers of such tribes that survive today, hunted with bows, arrows, and poisoned darts. In the industrial age, the global fishing industry constitutes the main hunting and gathering activity. Fishing fleets scour the seas and the seabeds for valuable marine life, with little to no responsibility for replenishing what they take. The result has been compared to hunters and gatherers with machine guns. The natural prey is simply no match for the incredible power and technology of modern fishing fleets, complete with fishnets that stretch for miles and satellite-based tracking of open-sea schools of fish. As a recent study shows, perhaps two thirds or more of the world's major marine fisheries are "fully exploited, overexploited, or depleted."

RISING PRESSURES

Today's rates of economic activity, if they were to be maintained at current rates into the future with current technologies, would be environmentally unsustainable. Yet both population and income per capita are rising rapidly. The pressures on the ecological systems are intensifying, and development and dissemination of sustainable technologies are far too slow. If we do little more than scale up what we are consuming today, we will drive many of the planet's ecosystems, and countless species, to the point of collapse.

The most famous early doomsday prediction came in 1798 from the Reverend Thomas Malthus, who noted that populations tend to rise geometrically (in compounded multiples) while food production only rises arithmetically (in added increments). Populations would be held in check mainly by misery. Gains in productivity, Malthus opined, would be quickly swallowed up by further population growth, which would drive temporary advances in living standards back down to subsistence. Thus, for Malthus, humankind was condemned to wipe out any temporary gain in living standards through excess population growth. This Malthusian gloom has remained a constant source of debate and controversy.

Certainly Malthus failed to anticipate the industrial age, with its geometric advances in productivity that kept well ahead of geometric advances in population. Since that notorious failure of doomsaying, some economists have become inveterate optimists, reassuring themselves, the public, and the politicians that improvements in technology will invariably come along to save the day. They have sought to banish Malthus to the scrap heap of faulty predictions. And they could be right yet again—but certainly not if we navigate these risks on autopilot.

The optimists have two huge points in their favor. The first is the likelihood that the global population will stabilize in this century. Malthus certainly could not anticipate the rise of modern contraception and the ready uptake of contraception in most societies in the world. The second cause for optimism is that technological advancement continues to be rapid and is probably accelerating. The revolutions in computing, data management, ecological science, spatial modeling, materials science (including nanotechnology), and other areas of knowledge all suggest that technologies, at least potentially, can rescue us and the planet yet again. The science and technology can be harnessed. The harder question is whether we will be well enough organized, and cooperative enough on a global scale, to seize the chance.

Yet we must not be complacent. The global population continues to rise rapidly, as does the average economic activity per person. And just as important, the severe pressures from massive human appropriation of ecosystem services—land, water, carbon dioxide, nitrogen, and the rest—would be challenging enough if they were occurring in just one of the areas, but they are now occurring *simultaneously* on every front. Take virtually any habitat on the planet, and we find that the nonhuman species in it are under unprecedented stress for multiple reasons. Their habitats are being overtaken by cropland, pollution, overhunting and overharvesting, invasive species, and new pests and pathogens. And when disastrous thresholds are reached, such as the mass die-off of amphibian species in many parts of the world, there are so many specific culprits that a single cause cannot be established. The massive threats to species survival are not due to land clearing or water stress or pollution or invasive species alone, but to all of them combined, with interacting and amplifying effects. Will coral reefs survive the twenty-first century, and if not, what will do them in? Global warming will raise ocean temperatures and lead to massive coral bleaching, in which the corals expel the microalgal organisms that give the corals their dazzling colors, and often die. The reefs will be threatened by overfishing in and around them, by pollution, by increased tropical storm intensities, by direct destruction by tourists, and by ocean acidification due to the rising concentration of carbon dioxide in the air and ocean surface water. Already coral reefs around the world are seriously degraded, and the multiple causes of degradation are intensifying.

A recent study of degradation along coasts and estuaries adds more evidence showing how environmental degradation results from multiple assaults rather than a single factor. The degradation of these coastal areas is massive and unmistakable. As summarized by the study:

Reconstructed time lines, causes, and consequences of change in 12 once diverse and productive estuaries and coastal seas worldwide show similar patterns: Human impacts have depleted >90% of formerly important species, destroyed >65% of seagrass and wetland habitat, degraded water quality, and accelerated species invasions.

The specific findings on impacts, however, are just as important:

> Our results indicate that human impacts do not act in isolation. In 45% of species depletion and 42% of extinctions, multiple human impacts were involved, commonly, exploitation [harvesting] and habitat loss. Such synergistic effects have been significant for terrestrial extinctions and estuarine depletions.

Just as multiple human impacts are typically implicated in serious degradation, multiple interventions are typically required to restore a degraded ecosystem. To "run the movie backward" and recover lost ecosystem services, it is rarely enough to remove just one source of human pressure:

> Although 22% of [ecosystem] recoveries resulted from mitigation of a single human impact, mostly exploitation, 78% resulted from reduction of at least two impacts, mostly habitat protection and restricted exploitation but also pollution.

But, alas, some degradation is extremely difficult, if not impossible, to reverse. Of course, species extinction is beyond repair (at least with current technology). More generally, the study found that while conservation efforts have had some positive effects in the coasts and estuaries, they "have so far failed to restore former ecosystem structure and function."

CHINA AND THE GLOBAL ENVIRONMENT

China's economic rise, while improving the well-being of hundreds of millions of people, exemplifies the kind of global stresses that will be pervasive in the coming decades. It is unfair in a way to single out China for following in the well-trodden path of the rich countries, being no more or less guilty of environmental harm, but the scale and rapidity of China's economic ascent make the country's global environmental impact especially vivid. China is already causing massive global change, and much more is to come.

China is currently adding the equivalent of two 500-megawatt coal-fired plants per week, equivalent in a year to the total capacity of the UK power grid. The effects on global climate change are huge. The International Energy Agency estimates that China has surpassed the United States in annual emissions of carbon dioxide from fossil fuel use and therefore will be the single largest contributor to human-made climate change in future years. China's global environmental effects also include massive dust storms due to large-scale land degradation, air pollution, and the introduction of new infectious diseases, such as SARS.

China's demand for raw materials from around the world is already vast and growing rapidly, with enormous environmental and economic consequences, including the following:

- The possible consequences of massive imports of soybeans from Brazil, largely for animal feed in response to a boom in meat consumption, include large-scale deforestation in the Amazon to make way for increased soybean production.

- The possible consequences of massive imports of tropical hardwoods from Southeast Asia, and increasingly from Africa, to support the boom in residential and commercial construction include large-scale deforestation throughout Southeast Asia and parts of Africa.

- Massive imports of oil from the Middle East and the Caspian Sea contribute to the rapid rise in global energy prices and have possible knock-on effects, such as land clearing for corn-based ethanol to substitute for high-cost petroleum.

- The consequences of massive imports, both legal and illegal, of exotic animal products, often for traditional delicacies or aphrodisiacs, could include the extinction of several megafauna in Africa and Asia.

Now consider the fact that the overall Chinese economy is doubling in size every seven to ten years, so that its formidable level of consumption is bound to increase. As of 2003, just to give one example, there were around 24 million motor vehicles, roughly 18 per 1,000 population. In the United States, there are roughly 250 million motor vehicles, or roughly 800 per 1,000 population. China's annual production is now soaring, up to around 7 million per year as of 2006 compared with just 2 million in the year 2000. If China reaches even half of today's U.S. motor vehicle density by 2050, that would mean roughly 560 million Chinese vehicles on the road! The *increase* is twice the total current stock of U.S. vehicles. Even if the fleet were to get twice the miles per gallon that U.S. vehicles get today, its oil use (and carbon emissions) would roughly equal that of the entire U.S. transport sector today. This is, of course, not a forecast, but only another illustration of the size of the energy-and-climate volcano on which the world is perched.

Similarly startling calculations can be made with regard to China's growing food demands (especially the increase in meat consumption), electricity use, water requirements, and more. These calculations do not mean that China's growth—or global growth, for that matter, of which China's is but a part—is incompatible with global environmental sustainability, but only that it is incompatible unless there is a deep and widespread uptake of sustainable technologies: new ways to produce electricity, power cars and other transport, grow food, utilize freshwater resources, and the like.

ABRUPT ENVIRONMENTAL CHANGE

Yet another reason for worry is that enormous environmental changes can be triggered by relatively small underlying events called forcings, whether the forcings are human induced or natural. Small forcings can set off monumental changes if they trigger follow-up changes that amplify the original forcing, and if these further changes set off yet more changes that also push in the same direction. A kind of chain reaction takes place in which the full impact is vastly greater than the original forcing.

Consider as a pertinent example the most monumental of the Earth's environmental changes: the movement into and out of ice ages during the past couple million years. The timing of the rise and retreat of the ice ages, in cycles of roughly forty-one thousand years, is linked to subtle changes in the Earth's orbit, especially the tilt of the Earth's axis of spin and also the shape of the orbit around the sun. These orbital changes set off the physical processes that give rise to the ice ages as well as their subsequent retreat. Scientists say that the ice ages are paced by the orbital changes. The orbital fluctuations affect the amount of incoming solar radiation over land and water, and therefore the temperature of the planet. But here's an interesting twist: it is possible to calculate rather precisely the changes in solar radiation that accompany a change in the orbit. These changes can explain the direction but not the magnitude of the changes in the Earth's temperature and therefore of the cycles of glacial buildup and retreat.

What is happening, scientists have realized, is that the small changes in the incoming solar radiation trigger other changes in the Earth's climate system, which then amplify the initial solar forcing. The change in the orbit gets the process started, but it turns out not to be the most important effect in the end. Two such feedback effects seem to be most important. First, when the orbital pattern starts to warm the Earth, some of the ice begins to melt. When the sun's rays hit ice, those rays are mostly reflected back into space. When the sun's rays hit seawater or land cover instead of ice (because the ice has now melted), the sun's rays are no longer reflected into space but are absorbed by the Earth and thereby further warm the planet. The initial warming due to the change in the orbit gives rise to further warming due to the change in the Earth's surface from ice cover to seawater and land cover. The extent to which the Earth reflects solar radiation rather than absorbs it is called the Earth's albedo.

In scientific jargon, we can say that the warming due to the orbital change gives rise to a positive feedback that results from a decline in the Earth's albedo, meaning that a warmer planet absorbs more incoming radiation and reflects less radiation back to space. A second feedback involves carbon dioxide. As the orbital change warms the ocean, some of the carbon dioxide dissolved in the ocean water is bubbled into the air, like the release of carbon dioxide from warm soda water. The carbon dioxide released from the oceans is a greenhouse gas, which further warms the planet.

The point is that a small initial change in temperature due to the Earth's orbit has given rise to a very large change in the Earth's temperature due to two amplifying feedbacks: the albedo and the release of carbon dioxide from the oceans. A small forcing can thereby produce a very large outcome, indeed nothing less than the onset or retreat of an ice age! Ecological systems are replete with such positive feedbacks, contributing to the possibility of large changes in Earth processes. And though it was orbital change that triggered the positive feedbacks of albedo and the ocean releases of CO_2 during the epoch of the ice ages, it could well be human forcings that do the same now.

There is another important ecological phenomenon closely related to positive feedbacks: threshold effects. Thresholds abound in nature. A slight rise in temperature can lead to death, to the failure of a crop, to the transmission of an epidemic disease, or to a massive rise in sea level as the result of melt-ing ice sheets. An increase in the use of vaccines in a population from, say, 50 percent of the population to 70 percent, can cause an epidemic to disappear altogether. A slight drop in an animal population can set in motion a process of eventual extinction of the population.

When a natural system is characterized by thresholds combined with pos-itive feedbacks, it is also likely to be characterized by abrupt changes, mean-ing a dramatic change that occurs when the system crosses a threshold and then sets off a chain reaction of positive feedbacks. One of the most famous mechanisms has been studied extensively by my colleague Wallace Broecker, the dean of the science of abrupt climate change. This is the sudden alteration in the pattern of the "ocean conveyor belt," which carries vast quantities of ocean water in a global circulation. An important example is the so-called Younger Dryas event, which began around 12,800 years ago, as the Earth was gradually exiting from the most recent Ice Age. The Earth's gradual warming, Broecker explains, led to the melting of a giant glacier in North America, which then burst into a torrential flood, emptying an enormous flood of meltwater into the Atlantic Ocean. The sudden flooding of freshwater into the North Atlantic in turn changed the pattern of heat circulation in the ocean, and this in turn allowed the rapid formation of ice sheets in the North Atlantic. As the ice sheets formed, further positive feedbacks of rising albedo reduced the temperature even further, allowing a spread of the ice sheets. The end result was an astounding temperature drop of around 5 to 10 degrees Fahrenheit in just a few decades. Thus, after a long period of gradual warm-ing as the Earth left the Ice Age, there was a sudden abrupt cooling, which per-sisted for about one thousand years.

As humanity pushes against ecological limits, we are bound to be sur-prised by the consequences, including abrupt ones. Or as Broecker puts it, hu-manity is recklessly "poking the beast" of nature, which may well shrug off a few pokes initially but then respond violently to human provocations. In an age of AIDS, species extinctions, sudden extreme weather events, and more, we are becoming used to the fact that nature under stress can pack some mighty, unanticipated blows. With ecological systems being threatened with multiple human forcings (human impacts) at levels never before experienced, we must expect severe and unanticipated consequences. Climate systems are vulnerable to sharp and sudden shifts in conditions as thresholds are passed. Temperature increases from global warming may have little effect up to a point, but a small increment can lead to devastating results (for example, by passing through the threshold at which the great ice sheets of Greenland and Antarctica disintegrate, or by triggering the threshold for an epidemic disease such as malaria or dengue fever). A decline in species abundance might be discomfiting but still not a disaster—until the species is driven down to a threshold level below which it cannot survive. And the consequences of one change, such as a rise in temperature, might be modest unless an ecosystem is already under stress for other reasons as well.

Another likelihood is that we will be confronted with a continuing explosion of new infectious diseases, diseases that seemingly come out of nowhere and suddenly pose phenomenal risks for the entire world. Recent examples include AIDS, SARS, avian flu, and the Nipah virus (transmitted from pigs to humans). These emerging diseases have several interconnected causes, all linked to the increasing pressure of human activity on ecosystems. The diseases typically involve the transfer of pathogens from an animal reservoir to a human reservoir based on more intensive human-animal contacts (for example, through land clearing or hunting of bush meat), changed animal habitats (including intensive animal rearing in feedlots and other industrial settings, or altered animal migratory patterns due to climate change), and invasive species and pathogens transported by plane, ship, or human migration. They may also involve the mutation of drug-resistant forms of existing pathogens. Once these diseases spread to the human population, their ongoing transmission tends to be facilitiated by high population densities and extensive movements of human populations, bringing infected and susceptible populations into contact. The very real risks of abrupt changes and sudden appearances of new killer diseases must make us take note and rethink our often heedless approach to human-induced change on the global scale. All of the scientific evidence is shouting to us that "so far, so good" can no longer be our guide on a crowded planet. Prudence, a scientific regard for the Earth's interconnected systems, and a shared commitment to look ahead are the real lessons of abrupt change.

THE PARADOX OF ENRICHMENT

The ultimate irony is that humanity's vital success in appropriating the Earth's services could also prove to be its downfall. It is perfectly possible that we will end up choking on a very good thing. Just as our post–Ice Age forebearers in North America drove the megafauna to extinction, leaving them bereft of animal power and animal husbandry for the following millennia, our age might well carry the transitory successes of industrialization to the point of global ecological collapse.

Such overshooting is not humanity's fate but it is our potential, and it has been our repeated history at a local scale. As Jared Diamond has powerfully recounted in his important study *Collapse*, there is nothing automatic about a society managing the transition to sustainability. As Diamond notes: "Thus, human societies and smaller groups may make disastrous decisions for a whole sequence of reasons: failure to anticipate a problem, failure to perceive it once it has arisen, failure to attempt to solve it after it has been perceived, and failure to succeed in attempts to solve it."

We must keep remembering that complex global problems can be solved by collective global goal setting, reliance on scientific evidence, mobilization of technology, and most crucially, thinking ahead. We will have to appreciate, with urgency, that the ecological challenges will not solve themselves in a "self-organizing" manner. Markets, we have emphasized, won't do the job by themselves. Social norms do not suffice. Governments are often cruelly short-sighted. Sustainability has to be a choice, a choice of a global society that thinks ahead and acts in unaccustomed harmony.

Chapter 4

Global Solutions to Climate Change

IN RECENT YEARS THE EARTH'S CLIMATE has been buffeted by extremes. Eleven of the twelve hottest years worldwide on record occurred during 1995 to 2006. The frequency of droughts has risen significantly around the world, and the same is true of extreme hurricanes like Katrina. Regions have been hit by extraordinary heat waves, such as the one in Europe that killed around thirty thousand people in 2003. There is no doubt that the Earth is warming and the climate is changing. A consensus exists among scientists that these changes are human induced, or anthropogenic. Anthropogenic climate change is the greatest of all environmental risks, since large-scale climate change would disrupt every ecosystem and impose catastrophic hardships on many parts of the world. The risks are growing markedly as we delay launching strong measures in response. The reason for hope is that powerful technologies will likely be available to enable us to mitigate the climate shocks at a very modest cost, much lower than the costs of inaction. But these technological opportunities will be small consolation if we keep closing our eyes to the dangers. Markets alone, on a business-as-usual path, will not carry us to safety.

THE GREENHOUSE GAS EFFECT

Carbon dioxide (CO_2), water vapor, methane, nitrous oxide, and a few other gases are called greenhouse gases, and their increasing concentration in the atmosphere is the cause of anthropogenic climate change. The greenhouse effect occurs because these specific gases act like a greenhouse: they let solar radiation into the planet, but then trap the resulting heat. Specifically, the greenhouse gases are transparent to incoming ultraviolet (short wavelength) radiation from the sun, which passes through the atmosphere and hits the Earth. The Earth is warmed by this radiation, and in response radiates infrared (long wavelength) energy back into space. That is where the greenhouse gases come into play. These atmospheric gases absorb some of the outgoing infrared radiation, trapping the heat energy in the atmosphere and thereby warming the Earth.

This greenhouse effect is an essential part of the Earth's geological history and of life itself. A blanket of CO_2, water vapor, and other greenhouse gases in the atmosphere has existed for billions of years and has made the Earth habitable for life by raising its temperature by roughly 59 degrees Fahrenheit above that which would prevail without these gases. Simply put, human life could not exist without the greenhouse gases. The remarkable fact of the Anthropocene is that human beings are now causing a major increase in the concentration of greenhouse gases. We are changing a fundamental part of the Earth's physical system. Whenever we burn fossil fuels such as gasoline, jet fuel, heating oil, coal, and natural gas, CO_2 is emitted into the atmosphere and the greenhouse effect is increased.

The basic chemistry is straightforward. A fossil fuel is made up of carbon and hydrogen in varying proportions. Coal is mostly carbon, with a bit of hydrogen (and other elements as impurities). Petroleum is mainly CH_2, that is, two hydrogen atoms to each carbon atom. Natural gas is CH_4. When a fossil fuel is burned, the C combines with oxygen (O_2) to make CO_2 and the hydrogen combines with oxygen to produce water, H_2O. Part of the resulting carbon dioxide remains in the atmosphere. Deforestation has roughly the same effect as burning fossil fuels, because it converts the carbon in trees and plants into atmospheric CO_2, most directly when fire is used to convert forestland into farmland and pastureland.

CO_2 is not the only greenhouse gas affected by human activity, though it is by far the most important of the anthropogenic changes. Water vapor is another greenhouse gas on the rise, as a natural positive feedback caused by the rise of CO_2. Warmer air holds more water vapor, and water vapor itself is a greenhouse gas and, therefore, warms the world still more. The implication is that the warming caused by a human-induced rise of CO_2 is greatly amplified by the rise of water vapor in the atmosphere. Methane (CH_4) and nitrous oxide (N_2O) are two additional important greenhouse gases strongly influenced by human activity. Methane emissions are caused mainly by bacteria that digest carbon compounds and produce methane in three key locations:

rice paddies under water; the stomachs of livestock, which emit the methane both in burps and from the other end (roughly in a two-to-one ratio); and landfills. Thus, the great expansion of livestock production on the planet due to rising populations and living standards has led to large increases in atmospheric methane concentration. Methane is also released from coal seams and oil and gas fields, and during the burning of biomass. Nitrous oxide results from human use of nitrogen-based fertilizer. A group of chemical gases known as fluorinated gases (specifically, sulfur hexafluorides, HFCs, and PFCs) are the other three man-made greenhouse gases. While the control of all of these greenhouse gases will be important, the control of CO_2 is the most important and will be my focus in this chapter.

Since the start of the fossil fuel era, human combustion of fossil fuels and clearing of forests have increased the concentration of CO_2 in the atmosphere from 280 ppm to 380 ppm today. Figure 4.1 depicts the Keeling curve, which shows the upward trend of CO_2 concentrations in the past four decades as a result of fossil fuel use and deforestation. Starting more than forty years ago,

Figure 4.1: Atmospheric Carbon Dioxide

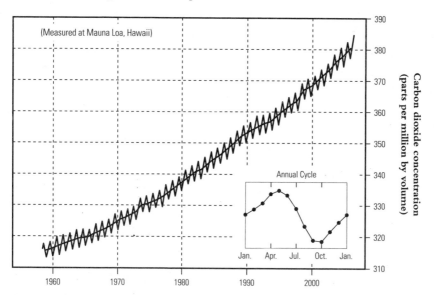

Source: Image created by Robert A. Rohde, Global Warming Art Project,
http://www.globalwarmingart.com/wiki/Image:Mauna_Loa_Carbon_Dioxide_png
Note: The smoothed line is the annual average.

the scientist Ralph Keeling has made a wonderful contribution to our knowledge by measuring the concentration of CO_2 in the air above the Hawaiian mountain of Mauna Loa. The idea was to find a remote place where local industry wouldn't distort the global measurements. The Keeling curve is remarkable because it records the annual up-and-down cycles of carbon dioxide as well as the long-term upward trend. The annual up-and-down cycle has been called the breathing of the Earth. Each spring in the Northern Hemisphere, where most of the Earth's landmass and trees are located, the forests and other land plants increase in mass by absorbing carbon dioxide from the air in the process of photosynthesis. During the fall months, in contrast, the dead trees and leaves are decomposed, and carbon dioxide is released back into the atmosphere. In addition to that annual cycle, so stunningly vivid in the figure, there is the amazing upward trend. The Keeling curve shows that the overall trend in the carbon concentration (the smoothed line) has been a rise since 1960 from around 315 ppm to 380 ppm today. In the preindustrial era, before 1820, the CO_2 concentration was unchanging at 280 ppm.

Along with the increasing CO_2 and other greenhouse gases have come higher global temperatures. The meteorological record shows that the Earth has already experienced an average 0.8 degree centigrade (or 1.4 degrees

Figure 4.2: Global Average Near-Surface Temperatures from 1850 to 2005

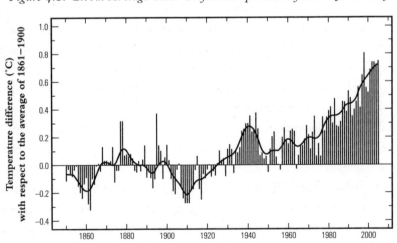

Source: Stern (2006)
Note: The individual annual averages are shown as bars and the dark line is the smoothed trend.

Fahrenheit) increase in average temperature since 1850, as illustrated in Figure 4.2, resulting mainly from the rise in CO_2 from 280 ppm to 380 ppm. What is not widely realized is that even if there were no further rise in CO_2 above today's concentration of 380 ppm, there would still be a further rise in the Earth's average temperature of around 0.5 degrees centigrade. This is because the oceans have not yet fully warmed in response to today's concentration of 380 ppm of CO_2. Land temperatures increase faster in response to the rise in greenhouse gases, while ocean temperatures increase with a much longer lag, a phenomenon known as thermal inertia. As the oceans warm gradually in response to the CO_2 increases that have already occurred, the land will also continue to warm. The warming is not uniform over the planet. Higher latitudes (toward the North and South poles) tend to warm more than areas at the equator. This is partly because warming leads to greater changes in albedo at high latitudes (for example, because of the melting of ice), which then causes the sun's radiation to be absorbed by the Earth's surface to a greater extent.

THE IMPACTS OF CLIMATE CHANGE

These effects of greenhouse gases are often summarized as "global warming," but that is far too simple a description. Changing greenhouse gas concentrations in the atmosphere will change not only temperatures but also many other aspects of the Earth's chemical, climate, and biological processes. The precise scale of these effects is uncertain, but it is clear that they will operate globally and will affect society deeply, especially if we simply continue on our present course. There are significant uncertainties regarding the scale of effects associated with any particular time path of atmospheric CO_2 concentration, especially because of various possible positive feedback effects that could dramatically multiply the initial forcings of human-made emissions. It is clear, however, that the rise in greenhouse gases will raise land and ocean surface temperatures, with innumerable complex effects on other aspects of climate, including rainfall, storms, ocean circulation, wind patterns, and more. These multiple and complex effects have recently been surveyed in two important studies, the *Stern Review on Climate Change* and the *Intergovernmental Panel on Climate Change Fourth Assessment Round*, and can be summarized as follows.

Rising Ocean Levels

Ocean levels are likely to rise for two reasons: thermal expansion of seawater as the ocean warms and melting and disintegration of the great ice sheets of Greenland and Antarctica. Rising ocean levels will submerge coastal areas, lead to higher sea surges during storms, and cause saline infiltration of coastal groundwater aquifers. Some small islands may well be completely submerged.

Habitat Destruction

Changes in the climate and chemistry of various habitats are likely to provoke large-scale extinctions of vulnerable species with limited habitat ranges or limited mobility in the face of changing climates. Polar bears and alpine species (living in the mountains) may be the first to go, since they will have no place to escape to as temperatures increase. Detailed studies show that millions of species, large and small, known and unknown, will be threatened with extinction.

Increased Disease Transmission

Many infectious diseases are regulated by climate, including average temperature and precipitation. The climate effects are often complex and often interact. A decline in rainfall, for example, can intensify certain vector-borne diseases by pushing animal species into more limited watering and breeding areas. The geographic range in which diseases are transmitted may be expanded because of higher temperatures. Malaria, for example, is now expanding into highland areas of Africa, where previously the temperatures were too low to enable transmission of the disease.

Changes in Agricultural Productivity

Higher temperatures, shifting growing seasons, changing species composition, and altered rainfall patterns could locally modify agricultural productivity. Some places may experience a rise in productivity (for example, higher-latitude environments as a result of longer growing seasons and perhaps an effect known as carbon fertilization), but others, particularly in the warm and dry regions of the world, are likely to experience significant declines. In some regions, the adverse effects are likely to be substantial. Climate change, moreover, may interact with increased air pollution to result in even larger declines in crop productivity.

Changes in Water Availability

Climate change will lead to systematic changes in rainfall, evaporation, and river flow. The changes in rainfall patterns will be complex and are still too hard to model with reliability. It is known, however, that evapotranspiration (the sum of evaporation and transpiration of water through the leaves of plants) will increase with temperature, so that in hot environments, rising temperatures will make rainwater less available for human use and crop production before it evaporates. Rising temperatures will also accelerate the melting of glaciers and snow in the high mountains. Hundreds of millions of people downstream of mountains depend on snowmelt and glacier melt for their water in the spring and summer, and climate change will greatly threaten these vast areas of Asia and the Americas. For some decades, the communities will be threatened by flooding caused by rapid glacier melting, but after that the risk will switch abruptly to water scarcity when the glaciers disappear altogether. Snowmelt will come earlier in the spring and not be available during the dry summer months when crops require water for irrigation.

Increased Natural Hazards

It is generally expected that extreme weather events are likely to intensify as a result of warmer temperatures. While the overall frequency of hurricanes might not change, the energy released in hurricanes seems to be increasing, and therefore the frequency of major hurricanes seems to be on the rise. Flooding and droughts are both likely to increase in some parts of the planet.

Changes in Ocean Chemistry

Rising CO_2 levels will acidify the surface waters of the ocean. The resulting changes in ocean chemistry will stunt or kill corals, shellfish, and some microscopic plankton that build their bodies with calcium carbonate. The overall consequences for all marine life—fish, corals, mollusks, and more—and, therefore, for human life could be profound.

IN A FEW PLACES, the overall changes might be positive, especially in some of the colder high-latitude regions. There are, however, three overriding conclusions reached by every study of these issues. First, the negative effects are likely to be large and severe. Even if there are some climate change

winners, there will be hundreds of millions, or billions, of climate change losers. Second, negative effects outweigh the positive effects. It's not only that climate losers will outnumber the winners but also that the losses of the losers
will outweigh the winnings of the winners. Third, the negative consequences,
both in gross and net terms (weighing the benefits as well), will be tremen-
dously amplified the more the average temperature increases.

THRESHOLDS AND ABRUPT
CLIMATE CHANGE

The global costs of going from the preindustrial baseline temperature to 1 degree centigrade above the preindustrial average will be modest. The next 1 degree (that is, up to 2 degrees above the preindustrial baseline) will be much
more costly. Indeed, each incremental 1-degree increase will be very costly. It's
just like a fever. Going from 98.6 degrees Fahrenheit to 99.6 is unpleasant.
Another degree is debilitating. Each additional degree of fever is even more
threatening. A 6-degree increase, to 104.6 degrees, can be fatal. So too as we
change the Earth's temperature, seemingly slight changes can cause dangerous,
abrupt, and uncharted change.

One of the reasons for this nonlinear effect is that natural systems and
human systems will hit certain temperature thresholds. For example, if the
Earth warms enough, the ice sheets in Greenland and Antarctica will break
apart through melting and ice quakes, and the resulting flow of water and ice
from the land to the oceans will raise the sea level and displace hundreds of
millions of people living in low-lying coastal areas. When temperatures rise
beyond a certain point, food crop yields could plummet because seeds will no
longer germinate. Similarly, diseases such as malaria could be transmitted to
regions where the disease is currently nonexistent. Above certain temperatures
soil moisture will evaporate so rapidly that semiarid lands will be converted
into deserts, unable to support farming. The survival range of many species
is tightly limited by temperature, so an increase in temperature beyond a certain threshold will push those species to extinction. And so it will go, on
and on.

CLIMATE SENSITIVITY TO GREENHOUSE GASES

One of the key characteristics of the climate system is the response of the average temperature to a given change in the greenhouse gas concentrations. Scientists describe this as the "climate sensitivity" and focus on the degrees centigrade by which the Earth will warm for a doubling of CO_2 from 280 ppm in the preindustrial era to 560 ppm. The doubling of CO_2 is not only a convenient and easily understood unit of account but is also the scale of man-made change that we can expect by 2050 if we don't head off the carbon emissions earlier.

To measure the climate sensitivity, scientists can use at least two main tools. The first is the climate record itself, dating back hundreds of thousands of years. Ingenious methods have been developed by climatologists to uncover the Earth's ancient temperature history together with the accompanying CO_2 concentrations. Among them is the use of subtle isotopic measurements from ice samples, rock formations, and other bits of geological evidence. The second is the use of computer models of the Earth's climate system to predict how large the greenhouse effect should be based on basic scientific principles. There are around twenty large-scale climate models used by scientific groups around the world. These models are constantly being examined and compared to learn what is robust in our scientific knowledge and what is more uncertain. The range of climate sensitivity is now judged to be 2 to 4.5 degrees centigrade for a doubling of CO_2, with the best estimate 3 degrees centigrade (5.4 degrees Fahrenheit).

CO_2, we have noted, is not the only greenhouse gas. Each of the greenhouse gases has its own distinctive effect on global warming. The full story of the other greenhouse gases is complex, and society will have to attend to all of the greenhouse gases, not merely carbon dioxide. Yet CO_2 is the most important of the gases because the anthropogenic emissions of CO_2 are large and rapidly rising, the effects on the climate are enormous (especially taking into account the presumed positive feedback of higher water vapor in the atmosphere), and the anthropogenic increases in CO_2 in the atmosphere will tend to persist for centuries, while the buildup of some other greenhouse gases can be reversed in a much shorter time period if and when emissions of those gases are brought under control.

GREENHOUSE GAS TRAJECTORIES

There are three key dimensions to take into account when looking at greenhouse gas emissions. The first is the flow of emissions, which is the amount of the gas that is emitted per year. The second is the net uptake of those emissions into the atmosphere. When carbon dioxide is emitted, some is taken up by the land in the form of plant matter and carbon dioxide in the soils, and some is dissolved in the ocean. Roughly one half of the emissions currently ends up in the atmosphere. The third dimension that is crucial, indeed the one that determines the greenhouse effect, is the concentration of greenhouse gases in the atmosphere. When we track all of these together—the emissions, the uptake in the atmosphere versus land and ocean, and the concentration in the atmosphere—we speak of a "greenhouse gas budget."

Consider the carbon dioxide budget. Roughly 36 billion tons (or gigatons) of carbon dioxide are now emitted annually, as of 2007. Of these, about half, or 17 billion tons, goes into the atmosphere, with the rest absorbed in the natural "sinks" of land and ocean. The annual rise of 17 billion tons translates into a rising concentration of carbon dioxide in the atmosphere. Each additional 7.8 billion tons is equivalent to one part per million in the atmosphere, so that an extra 17 tons each year is equivalent to a rise of roughly two parts per million. Assuming that we can make an estimate of the annual emissions in the future, based on projections of fossil fuel use and deforestation, and then calculate the share of those emissions that go into the atmosphere, we can trace out a future scenario of carbon dioxide concentrations in the atmosphere. Then, knowing the climate sensitivity, it is possible to determine a range of temperature increases that corresponds to the trajectory of carbon emissions.

If the world were to continue at its *current* rate of emissions, which is causing an annual rise of roughly 2 ppm, the carbon concentration would rise from 380 ppm today to 560 ppm (a doubling of the preindustrial CO_2) in ninety years, or by the end of the twenty-first century. The doubling of CO_2 is often judged to be the outer limit of risk for society. Beyond that level of

CO_2 the damages of climate change may prove to be uncontrollably high. Yet the business-as-usual path is much worse than this because we are on a steeply rising slope of emissions due to the rapid economic growth of China, India, and much of the rest of the convergent world economy. If we take into account that rapid growth, it is likely that we will reach a doubling of CO_2 not by 2100, but by around 2050!

There is a major added headache. The standard calculations assume that the share of emissions that is taken up by the sinks of land and ocean and the share that reaches the atmosphere will remain relatively constant over time. Yet there are feedback effects on the greenhouse gas budgets that could be phenomenally important. For example, as the Earth warms, the icy tundra in the far Northern Hemisphere will start to thaw. As the tundra ice melts, it is possible that vast amounts of carbon and methane will be released from the soils, leading to a massive positive feedback effect. Similarly, the warming of the oceans could release vast amounts of CO_2 and methane now dissolved in the water or trapped in deep-sea ice formations (known as methane hydrates). It is possible that temperate-zone forests and soils will become better sinks for the CO_2 (thereby becoming a negative feedback), but it is also possible that a warming of the midlatitude forests and soils will lead to a release of CO_2, in which case the forests and soils will become positive feedbacks. Even more subtle effects add to the uncertainty—and to the risks. Increased storminess and winds might change ocean patterns and reduce the ability of the oceans to absorb CO_2 from the atmosphere. Recent evidence suggests that increased tropospheric ozone (in the lower atmosphere), which results from human-induced emissions of nitrous oxides, methane, and carbon monoxide, could damage plants and crop yields, and thereby significantly reduce the uptake of carbon dioxide on land.

The main conclusion, however, is clear enough and remains robust—as complicated as the analysis becomes. The world is on a trajectory of steeply increasing greenhouse gases, which are likely to lead to a doubling of the preindustrial concentration of CO_2 in a matter of a few decades. Moreover, the rise could be even faster than expected if one or more of the positive feedbacks kick in. And we know from the paleoclimate record that such positive feedbacks abound, even if we are not sure which ones are most likely in our time.

AVOIDING DANGEROUS
ANTHROPOGENIC INTERFERENCE

The UN Framework Convention on Climate Change (UNFCCC) set the right standard for global action. The treaty is clear and compelling. It starts by "acknowledging that change in the Earth's climate and its adverse effects are a common concern of humankind." It then recognizes the scientific underpinning of the challenge:

> [H]uman activities have been substantially increasing the atmospheric concentrations of greenhouse gases, that these increases enhance the natural greenhouse effect, and that this will result on average in additional warming of the Earth's surface and atmosphere and may adversely affect natural ecosystems and humankind.

The treaty then sets the basic objective as follows: "to achieve stabilization of greenhouse gas concentrations in the atmosphere at a level that would prevent dangerous anthropogenic interference with the climate system." Wisely, the goal is to stabilize greenhouse gas concentrations rather than merely to slow their increase. Only by stabilizing the concentrations of greenhouse gases can we avoid passing climate thresholds of great risk to humanity and the Earth's ecosystems. The key is to translate this goal into quantitative targets and the targets into economic and other policies that can achieve them.

Of course, there is inherent ambiguity in the UNFCCC objective, which the treaty makers left to further debate and decision. When the treaty says "dangerous," we must ask, "Dangerous for whom?" The hardest-hit places in the world? Or the average impact? Or the impact on each and every signatory to the treaty? Do we mean dangerous just for humans, or dangerous for other species as well, such as polar bears, which might be driven to extinction? Do we require that the danger be certain or only likely, and if likely, with what probability? These and related issues have recently been explored in a brilliant analysis by my colleague James Hansen and several coauthors. Hansen's conclusion is that the world is even closer to dangerous anthropogenic interference than we realize.

Hansen uses climate modeling and the paleoclimate record to argue that we face several potential thresholds of dangerous risk, including breakup of the ice sheets in Greenland and Antarctica, which could lead to massive rises in sea level with profound costs for human settlements along the coasts around the world; an increase in extreme weather events; and the extinction of species due to the shift in habitat range. The prevailing view among European policy makers and many scientists has been that an increase of 2 degrees centigrade above the Earth's mean temperature of the preindustrial era would be a threshold of danger, with climate models implying that CO_2 should therefore be stabilized below "$2 \times CO_2$," meaning below twice the preindustrial level. Since the preindustrial level is 280 ppm, the recommendation is to prevent CO_2 from reaching 560 ppm, in the range of 450 to 460 ppm.

Hansen takes a more stringent view, since he finds evidence "that added global warming of more than 1 degree centigrade above the level in 2000 has effects that may be highly disruptive." If so, the target for stabilization would have to be far more stringent than $2 \times CO_2$, and Hansen indeed suggests preventing CO_2 from exceeding 450 ppm. One major part of his argument is that the ice sheets of Greenland and Antarctica may be much less stable than is conventionally presumed. Traditional models of the ice sheets have envisioned that these great sheets would melt gradually and from the top. New research suggests that the ice sheets could actually break apart and slide into the ocean through more complex and accelerated forms of collapse. For example, the Antarctic ice sheet is buttressed in part by underwater ice shelves that could weaken as a result of a warming ocean, which in turn could "lead to rapid ice sheet shrinkage or collapse." Also, the melting water at the top of the ice sheets can percolate through crevasses in the ice to the bottom of the sheet, where the ice sits on the land surface, and could thereby lubricate a slide of the ice sheet into the sea. These events, which would be a sudden collapse rather than a gradual melting, could raise ocean levels by several meters, with huge effects around the world.

The challenge of picking the right target for 2040 or 2050 cannot be definitively settled now, since the scientific evidence remains uncertain. Prudence points to a lower-end stabilization goal, yet the economic costs of greenhouse gas stabilization could multiply enormously if the target is set arbitrarily low. The global consensus remains closer to a long-term target of between 450 and 560 ppm, but Hansen's warnings are having a powerful effect worldwide in causing scientists and policy makers to rethink their assumptions, and perhaps to revise the targets to a much more stringent and climatically prudent level.

CARBON MANAGEMENT

Whatever the precise target, we have now arrived at the nub of the problem. The world faces a novel challenge that it didn't know existed a generation ago, and for many of us, even a few years ago. The problem can be called carbon management. The world must manage the global carbon budget so that the atmospheric concentration of carbon dioxide remains at safe levels, especially so that we avoid dangerous thresholds that could have devastating effects on human societies and ecosystems. To manage our carbon budget, we must have a good look at its precise components, and then home in on the areas that are most effectively controlled by human activity.

The bad news about the carbon budget is that every one of us on the planet participates in the carbon cycle, by driving, using electricity produced by fossil fuels, eating food, using fuel wood, and a thousand and one other actions. It often seems too complicated to get one's arms around, especially if

Table 4.1: Total Carbon Dioxide Emissions in 2007
(in gigatons and percent of total)

	G T	%
Total	36	100
Fossil fuels	29	81
of which: electrictiy	11.5	32
industry	8	22
transportation	6.5	18
residential	2	6
commercial	1	3
Deforestation	7	19

Source: Author's estimates based on fossil fuel emission estimates for 2005 from International Energy Agency (2007), extrapolated to 2007 assuming that all categories increase by 2.3 percent per annum during 2005–7. Deforestation is estimated to be 7 GT per year, based on World Resouces Institute (2007) for the year 2000. Note that industry includes emissions from cement due to direct materials transformation as well as fossil fuel use.

each of us is to adjust our own carbon budget (or carbon footprint, as our carbon-related actions are sometimes called). Yet we can simplify the picture by realizing that the vast bulk of carbon emissions is due to a small number of activities. Table 4.1 provides a useful breakdown.

To manage the carbon budget, we don't need to change everything about our society, but we do need to face head-on six important activities:

- We must slow or stop deforestation.

- We must reduce emissions from electricity production.

- We must reduce emissions from automobiles.

- We must clean up industrial processes in a few major sectors (especially steel, cement, refineries, and petrochemicals).

- We must economize on electricity use through more efficient motors, appliances, lighting, insulation, and other electrical demands.

- We must convert point-source emissions in buildings (such as furnaces) into electricity-based systems powered by low-emission electricity.

These are big challenges to be sure, but they are each manageable. Indeed, with modest economic incentives, big reductions in emissions can be achieved.

Let's briefly consider some of the technological options. Deforestation, interestingly, is one of the easiest of all of the processes to slow or stop. Most deforestation that takes place has little economic value. Forest is cleared to make new pastures, say in the Amazon, but these are lands of low agricultural quality and end up being abandoned shortly after clearing. With modest economic incentives, such as a payment to the local community to preserve the forest rather than turn it into pastures, it is possible to overcome the weak economic incentives that now lead to deforestation.

The challenge of reducing emissions from electricity generation is much more complicated, but that, too, is a solvable problem. There are three major avenues to reduced emissions from the power sectors: greater efficiency in the use of electricity (more usable output per kilowatt-hour), a greater proportion of electricity generation with nonfossil fuel sources of energy (including wind, solar, hydro, geothermal, biofuels, and nuclear), and special engineering processes to capture the carbon dioxide from fossil fuel electricity plants and to safely store it, using a technology known as carbon capture and sequestration (CCS).

The expert assessments of these options agree on several broad conclusions. First, much greater energy efficiency is possible, with more consumer awareness and more government R & D support. Second, energy efficiency will not be sufficient by itself to reduce carbon emissions. The world economy might grow sixfold by 2050. Even if efficiency allows us to keep the rise of electricity usage to half of that, we would still face a tripling of global electricity use by 2050! Third, renewable and other nonfossil fuel energy sources (such as nuclear) can play an important but also limited role in reducing carbon emissions from power generation from now to 2050. Fourth, many kinds of fossil fuels, especially coal, will remain inexpensive, plentiful, and in widespread use. Fifth, the option of carbon capture and sequestration will be very important, assuming that the CCS technologies prove to be as cost-effective as engineers now predict. If CCS proves feasible, this technology will allow the world to continue to use low-cost fossil fuels such as coal in a manner that does not wreck the climate.

If we look to the best engineering predictions, the cost of reducing carbon emissions from electricity production, relative to the current business-as-usual trajectory, is likely to be around $10 to $50 per ton of CO_2, which translates into a modest and manageable 1 cent to 5 cents per kilowatt hour. In places especially favored by wind or solar power or where the geology is favorable for carbon sequestration, the costs will be lower. In some other places, the costs could be higher. The overall cost levels will depend on public investments we make in R & D needed to take these basic technologies from paper to practice. The greater the early investments in R & D are, the lower the eventual costs per ton of avoided carbon dioxide will be. All in all, the costs are likely to be moderate if we think and plan ahead.

With regard to automobile emissions, we have all recently become aware of the potentially enormous increase in miles per gallon from the new hybrid technology that combines the use of gasoline with battery power. That technology is already roughly doubling the miles per gallon of some car models (depending on driving patterns). Another doubling of miles per gallon on top of that is becoming feasible if the hybrid can be plugged into the power grid as well. The idea is that a car would depend mainly on battery power for the first forty or so miles each day and carry a reserve of gasoline for when the battery runs low or when peak power is needed. The car would be recharged in the evening by plugging it into a wall socket at a time of day when the electricity grid is off-peak and therefore available to recharge tens of millions of cars. In this way an automobile could soon reliably get one hundred miles per gallon of gasoline rather than the twenty-five miles per gallon or so it gets today. This kind of plug-in hybrid technology is nearly at hand, and depends mainly on some further improvements in battery technology. Of course, the net benefit of such a move will depend enormously on the mix of technologies used to produce the electricity that recharges the hybrid each night. If we were to merely shift the automobile from gasoline to electricity produced by standard coal-fired power plants, the benefits wouldn't be large. The trick will be to shift from gasoline to electricity produced by renewable sources or by power plants that capture and sequester their carbon emissions.

The plug-in hybrid option will likely be available shortly, and if combined with clean electricity, it will avoid emissions at very low cost. Taking into account all of the changes from conventional engines to plug-in hybrids (for example, the extra costs of batteries, the costs of clean electricity production and transmission, and so on) is not a straightforward calculation, but it is likely that plug-in hybrids would avoid carbon dioxide emissions at a cost below \$25 per ton of avoided emissions. In fact, the fuel economies could well pay for themselves if the battery costs are kept low enough. I should also mention that other automobile technologies, such as low-weight construction materials, or the use of biofuels (if produced in an ecologically and economically sound manner), can also significantly improve mileage and thereby reduce carbon dioxide emissions per mile at low cost or net saving. So too can a shift to more convenient public transport and greater reliance on bicycling and walking. There are, in short, many options for large-scale and low-cost solutions to reducing emissions from automobiles.

Industrial solutions also exist. A few industrial sectors—steel, cement, refineries, petrochemicals—produce the preponderance of carbon emissions by industry. These industries have good options for low-cost avoidance of carbon emissions. Like power plants, the bigger factories are likely to be able, at low cost, to capture and sequester their carbon dioxide and connect their own pipelines from the factories to the CO_2 pipelines used by power plants. Many factories can also convert from burning coal and oil on site to using electricity from the grid, which is beneficial as long as the grid electricity is produced in a low-carbon manner. The factories can also convert from fossil fuels to on-site low-carbon alternatives, such as solar power and hydrogen fuel cells (which are beneficial as long as the hydrogen is produced in a low-emission process). The combinations and permutations are endless. The chances for low-cost carbon reduction are therefore plentiful.

Another area ripe for powerful results is green building, that is, designing homes and commercial buildings to reduce the on-site use of fossil fuels and to economize on energy use more generally. Green buildings are designed to tap more effectively into solar radiation (both direct sunlight and solar panels), recycle waste and water, use better insulating materials, and harvest rainwater. Furnaces and boilers on the premises can be converted to electricity-driven units connected to the power grid, providing a net carbon reduction if the electricity is produced by a low-carbon method.

MORE ON CARBON CAPTURE AND SEQUESTRATION

The most important energy question facing us is not whether fossil fuels are soon to run out—the answer is no, not in this century—but whether we can use fossil fuels safely. If we are forced to scale back sharply our use of fossil fuels, the economic consequences could be very high, even choking off economic development in some poor regions of the world. It is important, therefore, that we do all that we can to develop and harness technologies that can capture and safely store the carbon dioxide produced when fossil fuels are burned.

The basic idea of carbon capture and sequestration is already proved. It is possible to collect the CO_2 from the exhaust gases of a power plant and to put it into a pipeline and pump it down into geological storage sites. The entire process is illustrated in Figure 4.3 (see insert). Capture refers to the process of collecting the CO_2 at the point of electricity generation—petrochemical plant, cement factory, and so on—and sequestration to its geological disposal. The hardest part of the challenge is to find storage options that are large enough and safe enough to accommodate billions of tons of CO_2 each year. Although engineers know how to store carbon and are doing so currently on a small scale, large-scale storage is still unproved. The most feasible options for storage are injecting the carbon dioxide into underground reservoirs, such as abandoned oil wells; geological formations (such as basalt formations) in which the CO_2 will react with minerals to form a stable solid (such as magnesium carbonate); areas below the ocean floor where the CO_2 would take on a solid form and sink; or underground saline aquifers, which are areas of trapped saline water that can hold vast stores of CO_2.

As for capture itself, there are two lines of thought. The standard idea is that CO_2 should be captured at its source—the power plants, cement kilns, and steel furnaces—before it is emitted into the atmosphere. A fascinating alternative, which could prove to be a breakthrough technology, would be to capture CO_2 directly from the air through special chemical processes and then sequester the captured CO_2. Most engineers have assumed that the capture of CO_2 at power plants and other large industrial facilities would be much less costly than the capture of CO_2 from the air, since the power plant creates an exhaust gas of high CO_2 concentration from which it is relatively inexpensive to extract the CO_2 and send it on its way to a pipeline and ultimate geological storage. On the other hand, my visionary colleague Klaus Lackner and others have pointed out that direct capture of CO_2 from the air would have huge advantages. The first would be to offset the CO_2 emissions from sources that can't easily control their own emissions at the source, for example, airplanes. Second, the air capture could take place close to geological deposits that are especially desirable for carbon sequestration, and thereby avoid the need for expensive pipelines or other means of transporting CO_2 from power plants to the sites of ultimate disposal and storage. Third, and crucially, air capture would allow humanity to *reverse* a previous rise of CO_2 by capturing and sequestering more carbon dioxide than is being emitted in any period! Put differently, the best that can be achieved at a power plant is to stop new emissions. With air capture, we could put into reverse what we've done up to that point.

Since the CCS options are so important for the continued safe use of fossil fuels, it is crucial to promote an aggressive agenda of research, development, and demonstration to prove those technologies. The Intergovernmental Panel on Climate Change issued an important background study of CCS in 2006, suggesting that with close-to-proved technologies, the added costs of carbon capture and sequestration above a standard coal-fired plant would be modest, on the order of 1 to 3 cents per kilowatt-hour (KwH) of electricity. This translates roughly into $10 to $30 per avoided ton of carbon dioxide. The best options seem to be two new designs of power plants known respectively as integrated gasification combined cycle (IGCC) and oxyfuel combustion. These technologies are highly promising but not yet proved in practice. In addition to the challenge of power-plant design, the other big question for CCS involves the feasibility of long-term and large-scale underground storage of the CO_2. Which kinds of geological deposits will be safe, secure, and reasonably low cost as sites for sequestration? This is a high-priority area for assessment by geologists, engineers, and economists.

SUBSTITUTES FOR FOSSIL FUELS

We can reasonably expect nonfossil energy sources to provide a meaningful and growing fraction of the world's energy supply. While fossil fuels will likely predominate for some decades more, in the longer term, nonfossil alternatives are likely to come to preeminence. Wind, hydroelectricity, ocean waves, biofuels, and geothermal energy will likely be extremely competitive in certain regions, but each of these is limited in some way. They depend on favorable local conditions and are generally not applicable as global solutions by themselves. The bulk of the large-scale nonfossil fuel alternatives are likely to come from nuclear power and solar energy. The constraints on nuclear energy will be primarily security related, centering on fears of nuclear proliferation. They will also be environmental and political because of concerns about nuclear waste disposal. Solar energy, potentially the largest, safest, and longest-lasting energy source, is currently too expensive, but it is reasonable to assume that large-scale R & D over the coming decades will make it a viable and very attractive alternative energy source at the grand scale. Happily, incoming solar radiation represents about ten thousand times our society's use of commercial energy. There is a vast amount of solar energy to harvest, and we've hardly begun heading down that path.

One of the many potential forms of solar power is biofuels, which are produced through photosynthesis. There is currently a boom in enthusiasm for biofuels, most notably for ethanol derived from crops such as sugarcane, as in Brazil, and maize, as in the U.S. Midwest. While there is merit in the cane-to-ethanol production in Brazil, there is considerably less merit in the maize-to-ethanol boomlet, which is driven more by farm interests than good energy policy. There are two problems. The first is that Midwestern corn is actually extremely energy intensive, indeed fossil-fuel intensive, once the full life cycle of the crop is taken into account, from the needed fertilizer input (produced with natural gas), to the transport of the input and output, to the processing into ethanol. In other words, the net carbon reduction involved is slight, or even nonexistent according to some calculations. The second problem is the direct competition of corn-based ethanol and other biofuels with food crops. The amount of farmland that would have to be converted to supply a significant proportion of America's driving needs through ethanol would be huge. As one analyst has summarized: "Anything but a marginal contribution from biofuel would pose a serious threat to both food security and the natural resource base of land, soil, and water." The best hope for more than a marginal contribution would be biofuels derived from inedible grasses (such as switchgrass) and woody plants on lands that are not appropriate for food crops. Such technologies, including so-called cellosic ethanol, may well arrive soon, but they do not yet exist on a commercial basis.

AN EXAMPLE OF LOW-COST CARBON MANAGEMENT

By adopting a number of practical low-carbon technologies, it is possible to bring the climate change problem under control at modest cost, indeed a far lower cost than the horrendous climate risks we will face with business as usual. The evidence is strong and corroborated by a number of studies that show that concerted action, begun now and carried out over the course of several decades, could avoid the doubling of CO_2 at a cost of less than 1 percent per year of world income. The longer we wait, the higher will be the likely costs, since we would have to carry out even more radical changes in basic energy and transport infrastructure in a shorter period of time.

Even though we can't guess now which of the technologies will win in the end (and the choice may well entail technologies not even mentioned or known at this point), it is worth illustrating our options by looking at one simple low-cost strategy for moving to a low-carbon economy. In a study published in 2005, Klaus Lackner and I studied the adoption of two core, scalable, and low-cost technologies: hybrid automobiles and carbon capture and sequestration. The purpose of the study was to illustrate how, using just two low-emission technologies and without inventing anything dramatically new, we could avoid a doubling of atmospheric CO_2. In fact, the study is already behind the times, since we considered regular hybrids, offering twice the miles per gallon of conventional cars, rather than plug-in hybrids, which may well soon offer four times the miles per gallon.

First, we supposed a world in which the entire fleet of automobiles changed over gradually so that by 2026 all the world's automobiles would be gas-electric hybrids. We found that that alone would reduce the predicted atmospheric CO_2 concentration in 2050 from 554 ppm to 534 ppm. The costs are negligible, at least in our model, because the added costs of the hybrid battery, assumed to be $3,000 per vehicle, would be offset by the savings in fuel costs. Alternatively, we supposed that carbon capture and sequestration would be phased in at every major fossil-fueled power plant between 2006 and 2036. Under those assumptions, we found that the atmospheric CO_2 concentration would be around 508 ppm in 2050, instead of the predicted 554 ppm. Combining the phase-in of gas-electric hybrids with the CCS-reduced concentrations even further, to 488 ppm. And if we assumed that major fossil-fueled industrial facilities outside the power sector would be outfitted with CCS as well, then the CO_2 concentrations would drop even further, to 468 ppm by 2050. We assumed that the cost of CCS would be 1 to 3 cents per KwH, and we estimated that at that cost, the conversion of the power and industrial sectors to CCS could be undertaken at much less than 1 percent of gross world product (GWP), perhaps as little as 0.1 to 0.3 percent of GWP per year as of 2050! The costs would be a tiny fraction of the benefits of heading off ecological disaster.

This combination of policies—large-scale CCS at power plants and major industrial facilities plus a large-scale shift to hybrids (or, still better, plug-in hybrids)—can provide a solid low-cost foundation for avoiding the doubling of the carbon dioxide concentration up to the year 2050. Yet it will not be enough, and many other low-cost options abound. We also should slow or stop tropical deforestation; promote aggressive development of alternative noncarbon energy sources, especially solar power; and support the shift from point-source emissions such as furnaces in homes and boilers in factories to reliance on electricity produced by low-emission power plants.

Moving from this very specific scenario to a quick "back-of-the-envelope" calculation of costs confirms that the overall global cost of achieving emissions control is likely to be much less than 1 percent of annual world income as of midcentury. Let us suppose that by 2050 the world economy grows six times, from roughly $60 trillion in 2005 to $420 trillion in 2050. Suppose that improved energy efficiency keeps the overall growth of global energy use at three times today's rate, compared with the sixfold increase of the world economy. With today's technologies and energy mix, annual carbon dioxide emissions from fossil fuel use would also rise three times, from twenty-nine billion tons (shown in Table 4.1) to eighty-seven billion tons. Now suppose that the new mix of technologies allows the world to avoid at least two thirds of these emissions at a cost of $30 per ton, a reasonable scenario. That would mean avoiding fifty-eight billion tons per year of emissions at a total cost of $1.74 trillion (= 58 billion × $30) per year. Suppose also that we can avoid the current annual rate of deforestation (that is, seven billion tons of CO_2) at a price of $10 per ton of avoided emissions, or $70 billion per year. These assumptions suggest, at a cost of roughly $1.8 trillion per year, that the world could keep its total emissions in 2050 at roughly twenty-nine billion tons. That is a large cost in absolute terms, but compared with a $420 trillion per year global economy in 2050, it is a mere 0.4 percent of annual world income. A level of emissions of twenty-nine billion tons by midcentury (compared with thirty-six billion tons in 2007) would be compatible with a long-term avoidance of a doubling of CO_2 as long as emissions continue to decline after 2050 through further progress in technology. The costs could be even lower than supposed here.

CREATING MARKET INCENTIVES

The climate risks of business as usual are dire. The costs of mitigation—limiting carbon emissions—are manageable. Yet even the lowest-cost steps are unlikely to be taken on their own. Each individual emitter, whether a power plant, industrial facility, homeowner, or car driver, has no incentive to spend the extra sums required to sequester carbon or adopt low-carbon technologies if the new technologies are costlier than high-carbon technologies. Similarly, scientists and engineers have little incentive to undertake the science and engineering of low-carbon energy systems under conditions in which the atmosphere is treated like a global commons, and emissions of carbon dioxide (and other greenhouse gases) are made without market penalty.

We have noted the core areas where public policy is needed to augment market forces. The first is in basic climate science. We must continue, and indeed greatly increase, the public financing of scientific efforts such as the

Intergovernmental Panel on Climate Change, which assesses the published scientific research on climate issues for the global public and policy community. Similarly, there is an urgent need to increase funding for climate science in the poorest countries to help those countries understand how to adapt to climate changes already under way and to changes that are likely to occur in the years ahead. Science is also needed to enable those countries to participate effectively in global mitigation efforts, for example, by reducing the rate of deforestation and by adopting low-carbon energy strategies in the course of economic development.

The second area where public policy is needed is in the development of new scalable alternatives to carbon emissions. The most urgent is a global effort to prove, and if successful, to disseminate, CCS technologies. If CCS works, then we can combine continued large-scale fossil fuel use with reduced emissions. Other large-scale scientific and engineering efforts are also needed regarding solar, nuclear, biofuel, geothermal, wind, and other alternative energy sources.

Yet these efforts will lead nowhere in terms of widespread adoption unless additional incentives are put in place. There must be a cost, in one form or another, of choosing a high-carbon technology over a low-carbon technology. We have noted the many ways that such a cost can be imposed. Most directly, the world (or individual nations) might agree to industry standards, for example, that every power plant built after a target date must emit no more than a specified level of CO_2 per KWh of electricity produced. The plant would be free to select a nonfossil fuel energy supply (for example, hydro, wind, solar, or nuclear) or to use a CCS approach. Mileage standards could be imposed on automobiles in the same manner. An alternative would be to tax carbon dioxide emissions and to subsidize any CCS activities. Such a tax could be easily collected by taxing the underlying carbon-based fuel and then offering a subsidy per ton of CO_2 that is sequestered. A certification process would be needed to verify the sequestration. Yet another mechanism, as we've discussed, would be a tradable permit system. This, too, would impose a cost per unit of CO_2 emissions equal to the price of a permit for that amount of emissions. The main problem with such a system is that it is very cumbersome, requires extensive monitoring and auditing, and also requires a system for allocations of the valuable permits, possibly leading to favoritism and even corruption. I believe that after a considerable debate on these alternatives, the world will ultimately agree to phase in a set of industrial standards (for power, automobiles, cement, steel, and other key sectors) augmented by a gradually rising tax on carbon emissions, a subsidy for sequestration, and perhaps some limited use of a tradable permit system.

It is worth noting that revenues from a carbon tax or from auctioning carbon permits could be used to finance public goods or perhaps to offset other distortionary taxes.

LIVING WITH CLIMATE CHANGE

Climate change is already upon us, and it will get worse. The planet will continue to warm even without any further emissions, and further emissions are certainly on the way. Many countries have already begun to experience the consequences of climate change: more droughts (as in the U.S. Southwest, the African Sahel, and Australia), heat waves (notably in Europe), rising tropical storm intensity (as with Hurricane Katrina), a widening transmission belt for malaria, and more. Countries need to invest in adaptation to climate change alongside their criticial investments in mitigating emissions. Adaptation and mitigation are not alternatives. Both are needed.

Adaptation will be required in several spheres of life. Coastal regions will have to protect themselves against rising sea levels and more intense storms and storm surges. This will involve physical infrastructure and disaster preparedness. Highland tropical regions, which are currently too elevated to experience malaria transmission (because of cooler temperatures), must protect themselves against the epidemics that could arise. Farmers everywhere will require new seeds that are adapted to the changing climate; they must be more heat resistant, for example, or able to withstand torrential rains in the equatorial regions and more droughts and water stress in the semiarid regions. Climate uncertainties will require new forms of insurance, but they will also put strain on traditional insurance contracts that may have been priced according to out-of-date assumptions.

In the worst cases, such as those described in Chapter 5, water stress may render some regions no longer farmable, and perhaps no longer even livable. Environmental refugees could destabilize nations and global politics as desperate people, especially in rural areas, crowd into cities or across national borders. Such problems are bound to arise. They will be vastly more manageable to the extent that we also manage global cooperation on climate mitigation, population policies, and poverty reduction, and to the extent that special international funding is available to poor countries to manage the adaptation process. Moreover, a new science and profession of climate change adaptation must be encouraged, given the scale of the change and dislocation that lie ahead.

A STRATEGY FOR GLOBAL CLIMATE COOPERATION

We have seen that climate change is a truly global problem: Every country shares some responsibility, albeit to a widely varying degree, for the rise in CO_2 emissions, retrospectively (bringing us from the preindustrial 280 ppm to 380 ppm today) as well as prospectively. No part of the world will be spared the consequences of global warming. This truly global problem requires a global action plan. Of course, there is nothing new in this insight. The UN Framework Convention on Climate Change (UNFCCC) was adopted in 1992 by the world's governments for exactly this purpose. President George H. W. Bush adopted the treaty on behalf of the United States, and the U.S. Senate duly ratified it shortly after, in 1994, agreeing to the treaty's objective to stabilize greenhouse gas concentrations to avoid dangerous anthropogenic interference in the climate system.

The problem is not the framework or purpose but the implementation. The UNFCCC needs a protocol for action, and the first of such protocols was the Kyoto Protocol, adopted in 1997 to prevail until 2012. The Kyoto Protocol divided the world between high-income (Annex I) and developing (non–Annex I) signatories of the UN Framework Convention. The rich countries are required by the protocol to reduce their greenhouse gas emissions by at least 5 percent during the commitment period 2008–12, compared with the baseline of 1990. The poor countries are not bound by any obligations, but they have some opportunities under the protocol to receive payments for voluntarily adopted emission-reducing projects.

The Kyoto commitments were very modest (a 5 percent reduction) and short term (till 2012). At best, the treaty formed a very early step to set the world on a carbon management trajectory. Even so, the protocol generated a political firestorm in the United States. The so-called Byrd-Hagel Senate Resolution, passed 95–0 in 1997 in the lead-up to the final round of negotiations on the Kyoto Protocol, held that " . . . the disparity of treatment between Annex I Parties and Developing Countries and the level of required emission reductions, could result in serious harm to the United States economy." The resolution thereby made it the sense of the Senate that the United States should reject any new commitments that did not also limit the developing countries. The resolution exemplifies the declining sense of global responsibility felt by U.S. politicians, because it conveniently and even self-righteously puts aside the small detail that the United States, with just 5 percent of the world's population, accounts for one quarter of the world's emissions! Here is the United States, far and away the biggest contributor to greenhouse gas emissions, indignantly telling poor countries bearing the consequences in famines, droughts, increased malaria transmission, and more that the United States will not even start on emissions control because the developing countries are not yet bound to do so.

In the end, the Kyoto Protocol was adopted by the rest of the world, with the United States refusing to ratify it. President Clinton never sent it to the Senate for ratification (fearing immediate defeat), and President George W. Bush rejected it out of hand at the start of his administration. Strangely, though, President Bush went much further than that, even denying until 2007 the climate science his father had endorsed fifteen years earlier. The prevarication on this issue was reckless. It went far beyond mere dissatisfaction with specific elements of the protocol, and it marked an inexcusable assault on evidence and science itself. The world recoiled at the Bush administration's brazen neglect of the risks of climate change. Most Americans did as well after they experienced the climate disaster of Hurricane Katrina.

We are now in a new era. Climate change is upon us, and the scientific consensus is strong. After heat waves, droughts, powerful hurricanes, and more, the world's public knows all of this too. The world's leading climate scientists, organized under the auspices of the UN's Intergovernmental Panel on Climate Change (IPCC), in their Fourth Assessment Report, have recently brought us up to date on the scientific consensus, and the message is stark: the risks are enormous and time is running out. The Kyoto Protocol has accomplished one major advance: the start of a market price on carbon emissions, in the form of tradable carbon permits, albeit only in Europe. We must now move beyond Kyoto, which, in any event, expires shortly. Even to reach a new global agreement by 2012 will require diplomatic agreement by 2009–10 to give time for countries to ratify a new protocol.

There is a practical way ahead. Since the spring of 2005, The Earth Institute at Columbia University has sponsored the Global Roundtable on Climate Change (GROCC), which brings together leaders from business, government, universities, and international organizations. The GROCC has developed and adopted a concrete plan of action (GROCC Consensus Statement on Climate Change) to address the climate change problem, one that has won assent from leading businesses, scientists, and organizations around the world. The GROCC's starting point is that there is a scientific consensus that global warming is real and that it is caused by greenhouse gas emissions and primarily by our consumption of fossil fuels. The GROCC proposes a three-pronged solution to address global warming: mitigation; adaptation; and research, development, and demonstration (RD & D) of new technologies.

Mitigation

At the core of the GROCC's consensus statement is the importance of setting a global target to stabilize atmospheric concentrations of carbon dioxide over the coming century, including midcentury interim targets for CO_2 concentrations and rates of emission. Unlike Kyoto, which focused only on emissions targets, the new protocol would embrace a limit on overall greenhouse gas concentrations as well. As discussed earlier, mitigation efforts will involve increased energy efficiency, carbon capture and sequestration, development of nonfossil technologies, green buildings, hybrid cars, and other promising technologies. These will be spurred by putting a price on carbon emissions, implemented through a combination of emission taxes and tradable permits as well as by industry standards in key emitting sectors. While the world will have to agree on shared targets and a division of responsibilities among individual countries, it is likely that the countries will keep flexibility in choices over specific policies to achieve targets. Instead of one grand scheme, there will be many variations of policy.

Adaptation

Since global warming is already under way, and will get worse before it is stabilized, we must also prepare for and adapt to the impacts of climate change. Many of the impacts will fall most heavily on the poorest and most vulnerable communities and in developing countries with the least ability to adapt. Technical and financial assistance will be needed by particularly vulnerable, low-income, developing countries to meet their mounting adaptation needs (that is, to protect society and the economy against droughts, floods, extreme weather events, and climate-related disease transmission). Mitigation and adaptation efforts need to be part of a coherent dual strategy. As the GROCC puts it, "Effective climate adaptation will require stronger efforts within international climate agreements as well among development agencies, the private sector, and non-governmental organizations."

RD & D

Governments will need to support, through direct funding or incentives for the private sector, major increases in research, development, and demonstration (RD & D) of advanced noncarbon energy technologies. Funding currently is just a few billion dollars per year. Worldwide RD & D needs are probably closer to $30 billion per year at the minimum (comparable, for example, to what the United States spends on health research in the National Institutes of Health). Targets for increased RD & D should include technologies such as solar photovoltaic cells, solar thermal, geothermal, tidal, wave, and nuclear energy; carbon capture and sequestration; improved land management; and sustainable transportation. Special demonstration programs and other kinds of public policies that support innovation should be adopted so that promising new technologies and practices can reach the market quickly. Such programs will be of special importance in the rapidly industrializing developing countries, where most of the growth in emissions will be coming from. The highest demonstration priority, without question, is a series of CCS projects in the United States, India, China, Russia, and Australia, the world's heavy coal-using economies. If CCS works, we will have much clearer sailing toward global action. If CCS proves highly costly and unreliable, our options will be much worse and we'll have to redouble our efforts and creativity.

WHO WILL PAY?

Having a global road map for action is the critical first step. The next step is figuring out who will pay for the plan. The issue is especially important when considering the developing countries. Soon the developing world, with roughly five sixths of the world's population, will be emitting more carbon dioxide in total than the industrialized world, though still much less on a per capita basis. The world cannot reach a viable solution for reducing carbon emissions without including the developing countries. Yet because of their limited resources, the developing nations cannot afford to pay for mitigation, adaptation, and RD & D on their own. They will necessarily require support from the developed countries, which will remain the much larger emitters of greenhouse gases per person.

There are many reasons why the developed countries should help finance the developing countries' efforts to limit and adapt to climate change. First, it is in their best interest to do so. A solution that excludes the developing world would be no solution at all. If the developed countries wish to protect themselves from the negative effects of climate change, they had better help the developing countries protect themselves as well. Second, the developed countries are responsible for the preponderance of global carbon dioxide emissions since the start of the industrial era. Most important, however, cost must not be used as an excuse to postpone action. The longer we wait, the more expensive and dire the problem will end up being.

The issue of cost sharing will be highly charged and could cause negotiations to drag on for years. But the costs should not be exaggerated, nor should we wait for a perfect standard of fairness and efficiency, since no such standard exists. It would be one thing if the costs were huge—say, several percent of the GNP in high-emitting countries. But the good news, emphasized earlier, is that the global costs of keeping carbon dioxide concentrations below a long-term doubling of preindustrial CO_2 (or even much less) are likely to be considerably below 1 percent of the world's annual income. Yes, there will be a fight over allocating costs, but it need not be a huge battle.

LESSONS FROM OZONE DEPLETION

Although the prospect of reaching a global agreement on such a complex issue, which involves a resource (the atmosphere) shared by every nation on the planet and strikes at the very core of our global economic system, is daunting, it is not impossible. Climate change is certainly a solvable problem. Indeed, we have addressed a similar, if far more focused, challenge in the past, with tremendous success. The progress in controlling the depletion of stratospheric ozone provides important lessons for us now.

In the mid-1970s, three brilliant atmospheric scientists—Paul Crutzen (originator of the concept of the Anthropocene), Sherwood Rowling, and Mario Molina—published a series of papers putting forward the idea that a class of chemicals known as chlorofluorocarbons (CFCs) was endangering humanity through their effects on stratospheric ozone. When the CFCs were carried by air circulation into the upper atmosphere, the ultraviolet radiation of the sun dissociated the chlorine atoms from the CFC molecules, and the chlorine atoms then attacked the ozone. Since ozone protects us from ultraviolet radiation by absorbing the incoming solar UV rays, the depletion of the stratospheric ozone layer posed a grave health hazard to humanity as well as a danger to crops and marine phytoplankton.

After the first studies of ozone depletion by Crutzen, Rowling, and Molina, scientists began to debate the new and still controversial findings about CFCs. The first reaction from businesses that relied heavily on CFCs was to attack the new findings. The chairman of DuPont, the world's leading maker of CFCs for refrigeration and aerosol sprays, famously described the theory as "a science fiction tale . . . a load of rubbish . . . utter nonsense." Very soon afterward, though, further scientific research confirmed the initial findings, and a scientific consensus emerged. The public rallied behind the issue, galvanized in particular by the shocking picture, taken in space by a NASA satellite in 1985, of the visibly gaping hole in the ozone layer above Antarctica. It is important that a safe alternative to CFCs was developed and adopted by industry leaders, which made the prospect of abandoning the harmful chemicals more palatable to industry. Finally, the world adopted a global framework for action under the auspices of the United Nations.

In 1985, the world took its first steps in the Vienna Convention on the Protection of the Ozone Layer, a framework convention analogous to the UNFCCC. By 1987, the first operational steps were taken in the Montreal Protocol, analogous to the Kyoto Protocol on climate change. The Montreal Protocol began phasing out the use of CFCs in industrialized countries, while giving poorer countries extra time to phase them out as well. When DuPont realized that it could eliminate CFCs through the use of other chemical compounds, it signaled the U.S. government to support even tighter standards, and these tighter standards were adopted in the 1990 London Amendments to the Montreal Protocol.

The world quickly, indeed almost painlessly, headed off a major man-made threat. Solving the climate change problem will demand the same four steps: scientific consensus, public awareness, the development of alternative technologies, and a global framework for action. We have come far in each area. The scientific consensus is strong. The public awareness has risen dramatically because of the onset of actual climate change, not merely its prediction for the future. New and exciting low-emission technologies are in the R & D stage, though not yet in widespread use. Finally, there is a global framework, the UN Framework Convention on Climate Change, a first step in the Kyoto Protocol, and a growing determination to move forward to much stronger implementation. If the Vienna Convention is like the UN Framework Convention on Climate Change, and the Montreal Protocol is analogous to the Kyoto Protocol, we now need a post-Kyoto global agreement, the climate version of the London Amendments to the Montreal Agreement. Unlike the very limited and flawed Kyoto Protocol, a successful international agreement on climate change will have to recognize the increasingly important role of the developing world, both as contributors to the problem and as leaders in solving it.

Chapter 5

Securing Our Water Needs

THE CHALLENGE OF SECURING SAFE and plentiful water for all regions of the world will prove to be one of our most daunting tasks. Water stress is already a grim fact in many regions, and climate change will disrupt the water cycle on a global scale. The impacts on global society, and especially the poor, can be devastating. Without drinking water there is no survival beyond a few days. Without water for crops, there is no food. Without clean water, there is pervasive disease, especially killer infectious diseases that claim millions of children's lives each year. Without readily accessible water, available in convenient locations, if not pumped directly to the household, there is drudgery in the world's impoverished villages for women and girls, who often spend hours each day walking many miles to fetch the household's water supply. And without secure water—for crops, livestock, and human use—there is conflict.

Water is characterized (appropriately enough) by pervasive spillover effects, to use the economic jargon. Water use by one group or region affects the water availability and security of others. This is sometimes called hydrological interdependence. When one group withdraws some river flow for irrigation, the impact may well be reduced availability of water downstream. An upstream dam may wreak havoc on downstream communities. Often the interdependence is more insidious, hidden underground in the flow of groundwater. When a community drills boreholes for irrigation, the consequences can easily be a reduction in the flow of water to other neighboring wells or even far downstream. A tradition of first come, first serve to the use of water can lead to massive losses for all—one of the greatest manifestations of the tragedy of the commons. Yet simply privatizing water without strong protections for the poor can end up denying the weakest part of the population the access to safe water it needs to stay alive. Privatization of water rights may be contrary to basic ecological good management as well, for example, through overexploitation of groundwater.

By far the largest demands on water by society are for agriculture. Some 70 percent or more of surface water use (for example, from rivers) is for agriculture, with roughly 20 percent for industry and 10 percent for household use. In most places, even arid environments, ensuring water for household use is not usually a problem of sheer availability but rather of the limitations of physical investment in wells, pumps, pipes, and the like. Water availability becomes more of a problem when we turn to the larger-scale uses: industrial production and especially agriculture. In those cases, the volume of water used may be very large relative to environmental capacities. The resulting water stress could limit the sustainability or scale of agriculture, or it could result in severe environmental degradation if society persists in heavy water use despite the ecological threats.

A considerable amount of water use, especially the pumping of groundwater, is akin to mining a depleting resource. Deep groundwater is sometimes a fossil remnant of ancient lakes. These underground aquifers may be tapped, but the discharge of water by the community will not be compensated for by a recharge of the deep aquifers through the infiltration of rainwater back to the aquifer. And like a rich vein of ore, the drying up of the aquifer may be rather sudden. An aquifer might deliver a reliable flow of water for years or decades, only to run dry suddenly at some point, resulting in desperation of the population, and even large-scale migrations of populations away from the region.

Human societies have grappled with water stress, and therefore with water regulation, since their beginnings, yet the *scale* of water stress is new. This is also the result of large-scale pollution, which is poisoning much of the freshwater that would otherwise be available. The world took an early stab at global cooperation regarding extreme water stress in the world's drylands by adopting the United Nations Convention to Combat Desertification in 1992. The treaty sets an organizational framework for action, but it has not delivered on the needs because it has been mostly ignored by the powerful nations. We will turn to the great potential of the treaty, and how to revive it, after we look first at the nature of water stress and the kinds of technological and economic approaches we can adopt in response.

THE HYDROLOGICAL CYCLE

All of life and all ecological processes are conditioned by the circulation of water on the planet. As is well known, salt water in the oceans covers three fourths of the Earth's surface, and salt water accounts for 97.25 percent of the Earth's water. Of the 2.75 percent that is freshwater, roughly three quarters is locked in glaciers, sea ice, and the ice sheets of Greenland and Antarctica. Most of the rest is in freshwater lakes, with a much smaller amount of freshwater in rivers, wetlands, and the atmosphere. A full breakdown is in Table 5.1.

Human life, and ecosystems generally, depend vitally on freshwater, and especially on the flows of freshwater from the land and sea to the atmosphere into precipitation (rainfall) and back to the land and sea in the hydrological cycle. From ancient times, human societies have grown up along rivers and other locations from which they could tap into freshwater supplies for food production and other uses. In recent decades, with the ad-

Table 5.1: Volume of Water Stored in the Water Cycle's Reservoirs

RESERVOIR	VOLUME OF WATER (MILLIONS OF KM³)	PERCENT OF TOTAL
Oceans	1,370	97.25
Freshwater	38.71	2.75
of which: Ice caps and glaciers	29	2.05
Groundwater	9.5	0.68
Lakes	0.125	0.01
Soil moisture	0.065	0.005
Atmosphere	0.013	0.001
Streams and rivers	0.0017	0.0001
Biosphere	0.0006	0.00004

Source: http://www.physicalgeography.net/fundamentals/8b.html

vent of diesel and electrical power for pumping, there has been considerable tapping of groundwater as well, most remarkably, and alas, unsustainably, in Asia.

The hydrological cycle is crucial for all that follows. Water evaporates from land and mainly from the oceans and is carried into the atmosphere by convective currents. As the water vapor rises and cools, it condenses, until it returns to Earth as precipitation. A considerable amount of the ocean water that evaporates is transported by wind currents over the land, where it is precipitated as rainfall. This ocean-to-land transport is balanced by an equal flow of water from the land to the sea, mainly as surface runoff in rivers. Some of the precipitation over the land infiltrates into the ground and then moves to the sea as flows of groundwater.

There is a huge variation in the amount of freshwater flows in different parts of the planet. Some places receive several meters of rainfall per year while other places receive almost no rainfall at all. Some human settlements are close to year-round rivers, or can easily tap groundwater, while other places are far from rivers and have no practical way to dig wells to tap groundwater. Precipitation is year round and most intense at the equator, in a global band that is characterized by rain forests sustained by year-round heavy precipitation. As one moves away from the equator, but still in the tropics, both north and south, the year-round rainfall becomes seasonal instead, with the tropical rainy season corresponding with the summer months. During the hot summer months, intense solar radiation leads to heavy evaporation of surface water, which is then carried into the upper atmosphere by convective currents and returned to Earth as precipitation. These tropical regions have an alternating climate of wet summers and dry winters, sometimes called a savanna climate because of the savanna or grassland vegetation that results.

As one moves still farther northward, to the outer edges of the tropics and into the subtropics (around 20 to 30 degrees latitude north and south), we come to the Earth's desert regions, including the Sahara, the Gobi, much of the Middle East, the Mexican-California desert in the Northern Hemisphere, and the Kalahari and Australian deserts in the Southern Hemisphere. These are regions that catch the down current of dry air that has been lifted by convection closer to the equator. In its rising phase, the air has shed its water as rainfall over the equator. By the time the air descends in the subtropics, the air is dry, and the result is a high-pressure zone of descending dry air, with persistent arid conditions. Moving still farther toward the poles, in the mid-to-high latitudes of the temperate regions, where the United States, Europe, Japan, and China are located, the precipitation patterns are more complex and depend on the intricate interactions of cold air masses from the poles and warm air masses from the tropics. In general, the precipitation is year-round and more plentiful than in the savanna regions or the arid regions.

Of course, local precipitation conditions are determined by much more than latitude. The location of a landmass near the coast versus the interior of continents, in the highlands versus the lowlands, or on the windward versus the leeward side of mountain ranges has enormous effects on the location of rainfall and the location of surface runoff in rivers, which carry the water back from land to the sea. Proximity to cold, upwelling waters along the coast, as in Peru and Chile, can lead to local desert conditions. The underlying geology of the landmass, and the human uses of the landmass, also determine how and when the water runs off, whether it runs off on the surface, after infiltration into the ground, or whether it evaporates before reaching the sea, perhaps from a man-made reservoir behind a dam.

WATER AND ECONOMIC DEVELOPMENT

What we can say in general is that the precipitation and runoff patterns have shaped the Earth's ecosystems and determined the places suitable for human habitation. The ideal location for growing food is a region with plentiful and (ideally) year-round freshwater, easy access to irrigation (for example, from a river or groundwater that is easily tapped by shallow wells), good soils rich with nutrients, a flat land surface that resists soil loss and land erosion, a climate of moderate temperatures, and safety from extreme weather events such as hurricanes. The situation is still better for habitation and economic activity if the region is relatively safe from tropical diseases (for example, malaria) and is accessible to ocean- and river-based navigation. Such regions, alas, are certainly not the norm. They characterize some parts of the United States, much of Western Europe, and parts of temperate-zone Asia (China, Japan, Korea) and Oceania. Many other locales have significant advantages in water, soils, and the like, but they face other challenges, such as a heavy tropical disease burden or other natural hazards. Other places have adequate water and climate but poor underlying soils.

From the perspective of water availability, the midlatitude and high-latitude temperate zones, and the equatorial rain forest regions, have a big advantage relative to the much more arid subtropics and desert regions. Ecologists define the dryland regions as those in which the rainfall is low compared with the rate of "potential evapotranspiration" (that is, the rate of evapotranspiration that occurs when water is actually present). The drylands include four subcategories in degrees of increasing aridity: dry subhumid, semiarid, arid, and hyperarid. We see in Figure 5.1 (see insert) that the drylands include much of Africa other than around the equator, all of the Middle East, most of South Asia and Central Asia, and parts of Mexico, the Andes, Argentina, and northeast Brazil. Some arid lands, such as Egypt and Pakistan, can still support intensive agriculture because they have access to river-based irrigation (the Nile and Indus, in these cases) or access to deep fossil aquifers (where the aquifers contain water that collected thousands of years ago in geologic sites that are not replenished by rainfall because they are too deep or lie below impermeable barriers). In total, the drylands cover roughly 41 percent of the Earth's land area and support 35 percent of the world's population.

The adequacy of water supply is determined not only by the average amount of water available in a year but also by the variability and predictability of the rainfall. The African savanna, and even more the African Sahel, is characterized not only by low levels of rainfall, relative to potential evapotranspiration, but also by extreme variability of rainfall. Drought risk is very high; in many years the rains fail entirely, without enough precipitation to produce a crop. My colleagues Casey Brown and Upmanu Lall have found that the variability of water availability is strongly and negatively related to per capita income. Countries with high rainfall variability tend to be poorer, and low variability (higher predictability) is associated with greater economic prosperity. Brown and Lall's findings highlight the need for better storage of water during the rainy season and adequate irrigation during the dry season in countries with high rainfall variability.

In humid and subhumid tropical regions with plentiful rainfall and low-cost irrigation, the dominant staple crop tends to be rice, a highly coveted grain. In subhumid locations where irrigation is unavailable, rain-fed maize and upland (rain-fed) rice tend to replace irrigation-based rice as the dominant staple crops. In yet drier lands, farmers shift to more drought-resistant crop varieties such as sorghum and millet, as well as tubers such as cassava.

In the driest habitable lands, farming of food crops becomes impossible altogether, and pastoralism (meaning animal husbandry on pastureland) becomes predominant. The African Sahel, the Horn of Africa, and much of the Middle East and arid Central Asia are home to pastoralist communities raising camels, goats, sheep, and cattle, and often moving between pasturelands to follow the brief seasonal rains that replenish the pastureland grasses. The seasonal movement of pastoral communities is known as transhumance and constitutes one of the most difficult and precarious lifestyles on the planet today.

The very poorest of the poor are found in regions with low average water availability per person, high variability of rainfall, lack of irrigation, and low water storage capacity (for example, no dams, reservoirs, year-round rivers, or predictable runoff from snowmelt and glaciers). This description fits the African savanna and Sahel. These regions have almost no irrigation and lack year-round river runoff. When the rains fail, which they do with increasing frequency because of anthropogenic climate change, the crops, the livestock, and then the people die. It is not surprising that all ten of the countries ranked as having the lowest human development are water-stressed countries with extensive dryland populations: Niger, Sierra Leone, Mali, Burkina Faso, Guinea-Bissau, Central African Republic, Chad, Ethiopia, Burundi, and Mozambique. In the pastoralist Horn of Africa, the water situation is so dire that violence is pervasive in Sudan, Chad, northern Uganda, Ethiopia, and Somalia. Pastoralists and farmers battle for the little water that remains, and water refugees, who flee drought-stricken areas, often trigger violent conflicts as they arrive in communities already suffering from poverty and water stress.

THE EXPANDING WATER CRISIS

Much of the world today is already in a water crisis, and the crisis will grow. Societies around the world are using more water than ever before, at increasing rates, while paying too little attention to the future consequences of that consumption. As we have seen with other sustainability challenges, growing populations and the unsustainable mining of natural resources (in this case, the depletion of groundwater and the continued damming of rivers) will intersect with climate change to make this crisis all the more urgent.

In many parts of the world we have exceeded sustainable limits on the withdrawals of water from groundwater aquifers and from rivers. The overuse of groundwater, at a rate much faster than the aquifers are recharged, is a pervasive problem, including in some of the most populous parts of the world. The main factor in groundwater use is the usual suspect: irrigation. Farmers around the world, from the High Plains of the United States to the Gangetic Plain of northern India to Australia, have been sinking millions of bore wells and pumping water out of once plentiful groundwater aquifers at an astounding rate. Though bore wells were an essential part of the Green Revolution, particularly in India, the indiscriminate use of and unregulated access to groundwater resources is putting entire aquifers in peril. The overpumping of groundwater not only leads to the disappearance of the resource, it also has further harmful consequences. It can lead to land subsidence—literally a collapse of the land above the aquifers—a phenomenon that is increasingly frequent in major cities such as Beijing. It can also lead to the contamination of those aquifers with salt water, the salination and poisoning of soils, and collapse of aquifers that reduces their storage capacity.

Building dams has been a popular way to collect and divert water for industrial and agricultural use and hydroelectric power since the early twentieth century. According to one estimate, there are forty-five thousand large dams in the world today, and up to eight hundred thousand smaller dams! Dams have often been seen as magic bullets for regional development, as in the cases of the Hoover Dam, the Aswan Dam on the Nile, and the recent controversial Three Gorges Dam in China. The attractiveness of dams is easy to understand. In one fell swoop, major dams seem to offer multiple vital services: hydroelectricity, irrigation water, storage water for protection against droughts, and downstream flood control.

By now, for good or ill, most of the world's major river systems have already been dammed. There is simply no way—even if desirable—to achieve massive increase in abstraction through new dams or similar engineering projects. As the United Nations Development Program recently reported:

An estimated 1.4 billion people now live in river basin areas that are "closed," in that water use exceeds the minimum recharge levels, or near closure. Such basins cover more than 15 percent of the world's land surface. Among the more prominent examples:

- In North China, an estimated quarter of the flow of the Yellow River is needed to maintain the environment. Human withdrawal currently leaves less than 10%. During the 1990s the river ran dry at its lower reaches every year and for a record 226 days in 1997, when it was dry for 600 kilometers inland . . .

- In Australia's Murray-Darling Basin irrigated agriculture uses almost 80% of available water flows. With estimated environmental requirements of about 30%, the result is extensive environmental destruction, including salinity, nutrient pollution and the loss of floodplains and wetlands.

- The Orange River in southern Africa is the site of growing environmental stress. The upstream reaches of the basin have been so modified and regulated that the combined reservoir storage in the basin exceeds annual flows.

Moreover, the complex ecological costs of dams are only now coming into clearer view. The vast proliferation of dams in the twentieth century has fragmented rivers, destroyed wetlands, taken up huge swaths of land, reduced the fertility of floodplains by trapping silt, and led to tremendous water loss through evaporation from reservoirs. Dams and other diversions of river flows have also been responsible for two disturbing and disruptive phenomena: the disappearance of lakes and inland seas, and the interruption of rivers such that they no longer reach the sea. The famous Rio Grande River in the southern United States and northern Mexico has been dammed and its waters diverted so extensively that for several months a year it no longer flows into the Gulf of Mexico. The Yellow River, as mentioned earlier, is being dried up as a result of irrigation and urban use, and this is contributing to the birth of a new dust bowl in what was once China's great agricultural heartland. Similarly, great infrastructure follies have created major catastrophes for inland seas: the Aral Sea in the former Soviet Union was drained entirely to create a giant, water-guzzling cotton-producing region that straddles several Central Asian republics. The Hadejia-Nguru wetlands on Lake Chad in Nigeria have been drying out at a rapid rate. The wetlands used to support close to a million people who lived from its plentiful fish stocks and off the fertile land created by its floods. After an ill-fated irrigation and dam-building scheme, the wetlands are dry and hundreds of thousands of livelihoods have been lost.

Another recurring problem with projects that tamper with river flows, beyond the direct environmental consequences, is that they tend to create zero-sum situations. Downstream areas are often heavily and negatively affected by the upstream projects. Building a dam or diverting a river upstream deprives those downstream of various ecosystem services. Those situations are serious enough when the river flows only within one country, but open confrontation can result when the river flows through several countries. Around the world, water is emerging as a potential source of interstate conflict. For dozens of countries, much or all of the nation's water supply originates in other countries. Bangladesh, for example, depends on India for 91 percent of its water flows. The Occupied Palestine Territory, where per capita access to water is one of the lowest in the world, is the site of tremendous water inequality. The Israeli population, which is not quite twice the size of the Palestinian population, uses 7.5 times more water than the Palestinians, with Israelis in control of the rivers and groundwater aquifers.

In addition to groundwater depletion and the excessive use of river flows, the third problem is pervasive water pollution. A major source of pollution is nitrogen and ammonia from chemical fertilizers, which enter the groundwater or rivers. There has been a quite shocking increase in nitrogen transport in many rivers compared with so-called predisturbance levels, that is, before synthetic fertilizer came into wide use. The increase is especially remarkable in Europe, North America, and large parts of East and Southeast Asia. Human waste is another major source of pollution, with 85 to 95 percent of sewage in developing countries being discharged untreated into rivers and coastal waters. The consequences of the transmission of waterborne diseases are large. Industrial waste, heavy metals in particular, and other chemical substances, such as phosphates found in soaps and detergents and pesticides used in agriculture, are also major pollutants with negative effects on water quality, the environment, and human health.

Though the rich countries have reduced heavy-metal contamination through regulation and safe disposal practices, rapidly industrializing countries such as India and China are still polluting at dangerous rates. China has recently experienced one pollution calamity after another in its major rivers.

In 2005, the Songhua River in the northeast became heavily polluted with benzene after an industrial explosion. In 2006, the Yellow River ran red after a large discharge of industrial dyes near the industrial city of Lanzhou. In several cases, the polluters are local industries, but in many other cases they are major multinational companies that have fled tighter regulations at home and are skirting the law and ethical obligations in the host country.

CLIMATE CHANGE AND WATER STRESS

The stresses on the world's water resources are already enormous, and man-made climate change will exacerbate these difficulties profoundly. While there are huge unknowns in the precise consequences of man-made climate change on the hydrological cycle, a few things are clear. First, warmer temperatures will intensify the cycles of evaporation and precipitation. There will be more rainfall on average, but in shorter and more intense episodes. There will be more evapotranspiration at higher temperatures, and storms will increase in intensity.

Some more detailed conclusions are as follows:

- The drylands will tend to become even drier.

- The wet equatorial areas will become even wetter and more subject to floods and other extreme events.

- The populous regions with water supplies dependent on annual snowmelt and long-term glacier melt will lose water security with the disappearance of the glaciers and the elimination of the buffering effect of mountain snow.

- The frequency of droughts will rise significantly.

- Drier and more variable conditions combined with higher temperatures will lead to lower and more variable crop yields.

Recent studies have confirmed the human influence on precipitation patterns in the twentieth century: a wetter equatorial band and high-latitude zone, and a drier subtropical zone. Another recent study has found that the proportion of land area suffering from very dry conditions rose from 15 percent in 1970 to around 30 percent at the start of the twenty-first century.

One robust conclusion is that climate change will adversely affect the world's regions dependent on snowmelt and glacier melt. The lives of hundreds of millions of people, especially in South Asia and East Asia, depend on regular snowmelt from major mountain ranges in the dry spring and summer months. Much of the Indian subcontinent, 250 million people in China, and inhabitants of cities near the Andes all depend on such water flows. Higher temperatures will lead to more rapidly melting snow, and thus to more frequent floods and faster-flowing rivers. The water flow will come earlier in the spring and there will be water shortages during the summer months. Ironically, many regions will experience massive flooding in the coming decades due to glacier melt, which will then be followed by extreme water scarcity once the glaciers have disappeared several decades from now.

WATER DANGER ZONES

It is useful to focus on several regions primed for water trouble in the coming years, so that we can take preventative and remedial action. These are the areas in particular that are mining the groundwater, living on temporary glacier melt, and experiencing declining precipitation as a result of long-term climate change. In many cases, declining water availability is exacerbated by rising populations, extreme poverty, ethnic divisions, and other political cleavages that make problem solving especially complicated. Here are some of the most challenging regions:

The Sahel
Rainfall has been declining sharply in much of the Sahel: down by one quarter to one half during the past thirty years compared with the first part of the twentieth century. The drying seems to be related to long-term, human-induced warming of the surface waters of the Indian Ocean as well to global air pollution that is, apparently, affecting the location of the tropical rains. The Sahel's troubles are a combination of water stress, rapid population growth, and extreme poverty.

The Horn of Africa

This region, including Ethiopia, Sudan, Eritrea, Somalia, and parts of Kenya, is a hotbed of instability, with decreasing precipitation intersecting the multifaceted demographic, environmental, economic, and agricultural crises of pastoralism. Grasslands are overgrazed and destroyed by drought. Tribal, ethnic, and religious strife intensifies as communities struggle for the dwindling supplies of drinking water, arable land, and grassland for livestock.

Israel-Palestine

The ongoing battle between Israel and Arab Palestine is aggravated by a deepening water crisis. The waters of the Jordan River, long disproportionately appropriated by Israel, are being used unsustainably to the point that the Dead Sea, at the terminus of the Jordan River, is disappearing because the diminishing inflow of river water does not replace evaporation from the Dead Sea. Groundwater aquifers are being depleted. The Gaza Strip is among the most water-stressed, high-density settlements on the planet. Because of overuse of the groundwater, Gaza's aquifers are becoming dangerously salty. And through all of this, the Palestinian population is continuing to soar, so pressures on the environment are bound to increase.

The Middle East, Pakistan, and Central Asia

The entire band of drylands stretching from the Arabian Peninsula through Iraq and Iran to Pakistan and the steppes of Central Asia is burdened by rising populations and long-term declines in precipitation. The oil-rich principalities are relying increasingly on desalination, the conversion of seawater into freshwater. This solution is far too expensive for poor states, such as Yemen, and landlocked states, such as Afghanistan.

The Indo-Gangetic Plains

India's Green Revolution was based on a powerful combination of high-yield, dwarf-variety wheat; irrigation; and fertilizer. Small holder farms (that is, farmers with small farms) irrigated their fields by sinking boreholes to tap the groundwater. Green Revolution technology enabled India to escape from seemingly endless cycles of famine and to break out of the poverty trap. Yet now a water crisis is intersecting with India's rising population. The twenty million or so boreholes that pump irrigation water to India's farmlands (up from ten thousand in 1960) are depleting the groundwater aquifers, with declines of the water table from 100 to 150 meters in some places. A similar crisis is affecting the Indus valley in Pakistan. Water that now flows from glaciers in the Himalayas will cease in a few decades, when those glaciers have completely melted and disappeared. And there is massive water pollution to boot, with only about 10 percent of wastewater from industrial and municipal uses treated before it is discharged into lakes, rivers, and the sea. There is no immediate solution in sight.

The North China Plain

China north of the Yangtze River is dry and getting drier at the same time that groundwater aquifers are being depleted. Too much water is being taken from the Yellow River, which no longer reaches the sea. And as too much water is taken from the underground aquifers, the urban land above those aquifers is actually sinking, causing serious structural damage to homes, commercial buildings, and urban infrastructure.

The U.S. Southwest

The semiarid U.S. Southwest is becoming more arid and has the potential to become a dust bowl within years or decades. The paleoclimate record as well as large-scale climate models point robustly to further human-induced drying ahead. Till now, much of the region's rising population has been supported by abstracting river flow, for example, from the Colorado River. Yet the region has reached limits in the amount of water abstraction from the rivers and will have to promote far more "crop per drop" solutions, and perhaps a significant substitution away from agriculture in the coming years. The same problems, with even less ability to respond, occur across the border in northern Mexico.

Murray-Darling Basin

This watershed is Australia's largest and the home of the country's agricultural potential. The basin has suffered a once-in-one-thousand-year drought from 2003 to 2007, meaning a drought so severe that before man-made climate change intervened, such a drought was likely to occur no more than once in a thousand years! The ongoing drought is causing a sharp loss of crops and urgent and expensive measures of water conservation. The IPCC highlights the likelihood that global warming will lead to further drying in the basin and in other parts of Australia.

WATER STRESS AND CONFLICT

In all of these cases, the rising water stress, combined with other pressures, will worsen food security. Crop failures due to drought are likely to become much more frequent. Farm households will not only lose their food supplies but their livelihoods as well. At least in the poorer regions, water stress can end up in war. Indeed, as shown in Figure 5.1 (see insert), there is a powerful and disturbing overlap between dryland regions and many of the sites of ongoing violent conflicts in 2007. That is not just an environmentalist's worst nightmare but the grim record of recent years. A notable scientific contribution in establishing this link was made by Edward Miguel and his colleagues, who found that "drops in rainfall [in Africa] are associated with significantly more conflict. . . . There is strong evidence that better rainfall makes conflict much less likely in Africa." The key link seems to be that a decline in rainfall causes the economy to shrink, presumably through the adverse effects on harvests and food supply, and this in turn triggers conflict. What is important is that when the authors compared the explanatory power of rainfall with political variables (such as democracy, ethnic cleavages, religious divisions, colonial heritage) in accounting for the location, and timing of conflicts in Africa, the rainfall variable was more important than the political variables. The research team concluded as follows: "The most obvious reading of these findings is that economic factors trump all others in causing African civil conflicts, and that institutional and political characteristics have much less of an impact."

The role of extreme water stress is evident in Darfur, Sudan, which has experienced a sizable drop in rainfall during the past thirty years combined with a massive rise in population. This combination has added to a lethal brew of extreme poverty, ethnic clashes, and other contributing factors. We will return to the Darfur crisis in Chapter 10.

Water scarcity is, so far, mainly responsible for conflicts within countries rather than between them, yet cross-border confrontations will also become more likely to arise as water stress becomes more extreme. As Fred Pearce reminds us:

> All told, more than twenty nations get more than half of their water from their neighbors. Many should by rights get more than they do. Mexico receives virtually none of the flow of the Colorado River out of the United States. Most of the water of the Jordan River disappears within Israel and never reaches the country named after it. The Illi has shrunk by two thirds by the time it leaves China for Kazakhstan. The Karkeh, flowing west out of Iran, rarely makes it to Iraq anymore. Iran, meanwhile, has rarely seen the Helmand flow west over the border from Afghanistan since the 1990s. Given the extent of the damage caused by such disruption to the natural river flows, it is perhaps a wonder that there have not been more out-and-out wars.

It is extremely important that diplomats working to bring peace to conflict zones, such as Darfur and Somalia, and to prevent tensions in other dryland regions from erupting into full-scale conflict, should understand and address the ecological underpinnings contributing to the stress in the regions. One of the most important interventions—ensuring predictable and adequate access to water for human use and agriculture—is frequently overlooked in conflict avoidance and peacemaking.

A FRAMEWORK FOR ACTION

There is no single remedy for the rising water stress and rainfall instability. Countries need to develop holistic plans of action and will need international support to implement them. Plans should address the following five areas:

- Safe drinking water and sanitation for all

- Increased water efficiency in agriculture, including the development of drought-resistant seed varieties and new irrigation strategies

- Increased attention to droughts through improved water storage

- Reduced economic risks through rainfall insurance

- Economic diversification and international trade to reduce the dependency of livelihoods on rainfall

Let's consider each of these and then turn to the kinds of global cooperation that can make a difference. We should also underscore that every one of these challenges will be easier to meet if the country is also making overall progress in the fight against extreme poverty and is taking action to reduce high population growth rates through voluntary reductions of fertility.

Drinking Water and Sanitation

The Millennium Development Goals call for cutting in half the number of people without access to safe drinking water and sanitation. This is actually the easiest of all of the goals. While the appropriate water solution—wells, springs, piped water, community water stands—must be determined in every village and city, the basic problem is engineering and finance rather than the natural availability of water. That is because household water use for drinking and hygiene is only a small part of total water needs, while the bulk of water is needed for agriculture. In 2006, the UNDP estimated that the worldwide cost of meeting the water and sanitation targets would be about $10 billion per year, which represents a mere 0.03 percent of the rich-world national income of $35 trillion per year.

One popular solution for drinking-water needs much favored in Washington has been the privatization of urban water supply systems, with the belief that private operators will be more efficient, better capitalized, and perhaps more scrupulous than public water agencies. History has shown otherwise, however. Privatization, if done in a sloppy manner, can result in the changeover from a public monopoly to a private monopoly, with the private monopolist not even constrained by the need to win the next election. Private monopolies may have no interest whatsoever in ensuring access for the poor, specifically those households which are unable to pay the monopolist's profit-maximizing price of water.

One effective compromise between public ownership and privatization can be the insistence that private providers offer a lifeline tariff, which guarantees to each household a free fixed amount of water each day for uses that the household needs to stay alive (drinking, cooking, and hygiene). Water use above the minimum is charged by the meter, at the market rate, but in this way everybody, even the most indigent, is guaranteed a lifeline. This kind of smart subsidy has a general merit beyond water, and can be used for power, fertilizer, high-yield seeds, bed nets, and other basic needs. Larger buyers, and especially the rich, must pay at the market price. The poorest of the poor, however, need not meet that market test. Depending on the exact structure of the public-private partnership and pricing rules, the public-sector budget might reimburse the water provider for the free provision of the lifeline water supply.

More Crop per Drop

Increasing the productivity of agriculture vis-à-vis water, that is, getting more crop per drop, is a much greater challenge. Indeed, the Food and Agriculture Organization of the United Nations (FAO) has estimated that by 2030, the world cereal demand will have increased by almost 1 billion tons due to population growth and rising consumption per person. This must be accomplished in the face of more difficult climate conditions in large parts of the world.

Many technologies can play a role in improving agricultural productivity. A key technological option will be to engineer crop varieties that need less water and can thrive in drought-prone areas. Such varieties can be developed either through traditional breeding techniques or through transgenetic modification, meaning the transfer of genes from one species to another in order to increase drought resistance. Various scientific teams are working on transgenic crops that transfer genes from drought-resistant natural varieties to food crops, and they have achieved spectacular results in early trials.

A second option is to introduce mechanical or agronomic systems to maximize the crop per drop of rainwater. Drip irrigation is a prime example. Instead of flooding a field or bringing water to it via canals in which water can pool and evaporate, drip irrigation brings a constant, low-pressure stream of very small amounts of water directly to the crop roots. Water can simply be delivered through a perforated rubber hose placed on the ground near the plant's roots. This simple, affordable, and proven technology can prevent up to 90 percent of soil evaporation. Local innovations, such as the Indian Pepsee system of small plastic vials to deliver the water, have cut the operational costs of drip irrigation to very low levels.

Another crucial technique is rainwater harvesting. Farmers dig a small pond, or place small receptacles underground, to collect and store rainwater, and then use the stored water in the event of a temporary dry spell. While the rainwater is not enough for continuous irrigation, it is enough to supplement the rains in the event of a few days' dry spell. The method is also called supplemental irrigation. Rainwater harvesting in Gansu Province, China, for example, has been reported to increase crop per drop by 20 percent and wheat yields by 50 percent. Improving the productivity of rainwater is another fruitful approach. This can be done by limiting evaporation early in the growing season through techniques such as planting, mulching, and intercropping (growing other plants alongside the crop) in order to develop a canopy that can provide valuable shade cover.

A third innovation is a change in tillage systems, including low-till or no-till systems. Tillage refers to the farmer's preparation of the soils for planting. Standard practices involve plowing the fields, that is, digging up the soil to uproot weeds and to prepare the physical site for seeding and application of fertilizer. Low-till, or conservation tillage systems, are ways to plant the seeds with zero or minimal plowing and thereby accomplish several things: soil moisture evaporation is reduced; soil structure is better maintained; and erosion is reduced. Animals in the soil that improve soil productivity, such as earthworms and arthropods, are left undisturbed to do their productivity-enhancing work. Low-till agriculture introduces problems as well, which must be addressed. Because the weeds are not destroyed by plowing, the crops may face increased competition with weeds. Farmers may also need special equipment to enable them to plant in untilled soil. The feasibility of conservation tillage must be examined in each context, and impoverished farmers may require special help to get started.

In all of these cases, a price for use of water (together with a lifeline tariff) is needed to help induce farmers to shift from overuse of water supplies to sustainable use based on high crop per drop technologies. Just as with low-carbon technologies, it will be one thing to develop water-efficient seed varieties and more efficient irrigation methods, and quite another to have the technology widely accepted. To get these methods adopted in the place of unsustainable groundwater harvesting, farmers will need to face a market incentive. For the poorest of the poor, this might be a subsidy or grant for the improved technology. For richer farmers, it should be the contrary: a price of water tariff that reflects the true social costs of drawing unsustainably on groundwater or river-based irrigation.

Physical Infrastructure

There will be no shortage of freshwater on the planet as long as we are ready to produce it from seawater, and pay for it. Seawater can be turned into freshwater through desalination. Advances in desalination technology, such as the reverse-osmosis method, have dramatically lowered the costs of desalination compared with traditional distillation. Of course, desalination requires energy, and lots of it. That's why the hope for a radical cut in overall global energy use is unrealistic, since we will need more energy, not less, to solve crucial challenges, such as water security. Still, by harnessing wind, solar, or hydropower for desalination, it might be possible to bolster water supplies on a large scale cleanly and inexpensively. Unfortunately, desalination is likely to be economical only near coasts and near major energy sources (such as Middle East oil). Desalination is unlikely to provide much relief for inland and especially highland regions, because of the high costs of pumping water.

Physical infrastructure can also play a pivotal role in water storage, from farm ponds for small farms to giant water reservoirs along major rivers. With increasing rainfall variability likely in the years ahead, and the end of reliable glacier melt, there will be an extra economic benefit to water storage and availability of irrigation potential during droughts and dry spells.

Rainfall Insurance

Another potentially beneficial tool will be financial rather than physical. Rainfall insurance (or, technically, a weather-linked derivative) is a financial instrument to help insure against drought. The insurance company sells a bond that pays nothing in the event of a normal rain and pays a high amount in the event of a drought. The price of the bond reflects the probability of the drought and the size of the payout in the event that it occurs. For example, the bond may cost $100,000 and pay $1 million in the event of a severe once-in-ten-year drought, but it pays nothing if the drought does not occur. A farm cooperative might buy such a bond to insure its members against a crop failure due to drought. While markets will provide these insurance services in high-income settings, public finance may be necessary to provide rainfall insurance in the poorest countries.

Economic Diversification and International Trade

Farmers routinely adjust to rainfall risk by diversifying their crops. Drought-resistant varieties are intercropped with more vulnerable varieties in order to ensure against disaster. Nonagricultural activities (for example, commerce and small-scale industry) that are not directly dependent on the rains can be added to the mix of activities in rural communities. Long-distance trade, both regional and global, also allows communities to specialize in farm activities that are drought resistant (for instance, planting tree crops with deep root structures that resist short-term dry spells) and to use the cash income to import foodstuffs.

As climate change causes further stress in dryland regions, increased trade will surely have to play a critical role. Some parched regions will simply be incapable of continuing to produce food. Other regions will become their suppliers through international trade. A few regions, especially the high latitudes of the United States, Canada, and Russia, may experience a rise in farm productivity due to global warming, which might bring longer growing seasons and more rainfall. Some of these far northern regions might become important new breadbaskets for the world. We should not, however, believe that international trade will by itself simply save the day. If a region of subsistence farmers is no longer able to produce food, there is no guarantee that it will be able to shift to an alternative source of income in order to buy food. Many times the very poor are simply reshuffled out of one activity and are then left without the means to start up productive work in another. They can go hungry as a result, and many deaths can ensue. While it is true that trade can play a critical role in reallocating agriculture around the world, international markets cannot by themselves be relied upon to ensure that all people will survive the shocks.

TOWARD GLOBAL WATER COOPERATION

There is no coordinated water management authority or technical agency for water in the United Nations system. At least a dozen international or treaty organizations play some role—the UN Children's Fund (UNICEF), the World Bank, the Food and Agriculture Organization (FAO), the UN Educational,

Scientific, and Cultural Organization (UNESCO), the UN Industrial Development Organization (UNIDO), the United Nations Development Program (UNDP), the United Nations Environment Program (UNEP), the UN Convention to Combat Desertification (UNCCD), the UN Framework Convention on Climate Change (UNFCCC), the UN Convention on Biological Diversity (CBD), the International Water Management Institute (IWMI), the International Crops Research Institute for the Semi-Arid Tropics (ICRISAT)—and countless additional regional bodies are also involved. The problem is that this great mass of activities produces far less than the sum of the parts. There is no overall responsibility, accountability, or vision as to how to address the intermixture of climate change, agricultural stress, and water technologies, how to implement plans with global funding, or how to combine water programs with other development initiatives such as poverty reduction. Moreover, sound water solutions require local specificity and considerable cooperation among neighboring countries that share watersheds. This is a tall order. There are 273 international water basins in the world, which involve 145 countries covering more than 90 percent of the global population.

The necessity for an apical international body on water is urgent, given the scale of the challenge and the interconnected problems of technology, economics, and diplomacy. A first step, at least, would be to focus on the hardest-hit lands, specifically the world's drylands. Fortunately, these are covered by the UN Convention to Combat Desertification, which has 191 member governments as signatories. Unfortunately, the treaty as it now stands is little known and has little clout and financial backing. Rather than reinvent the treaty, however, it would be better to reinvigorate it.

A starting point would be for the Science and Technology Committee of the UNCCD to carry out a major international scientific assessment of the world's water situation focusing on the drylands, with a special charge to investigate each of the following:

- Priorities for improved water technologies

- Priorities for water efficiency in agriculture

- Hydrological risks from climate change

- Access of the poorest of the poor to water security (for household use and agricultural use)

- Financial requirements to achieve the Millennium Development Goal (MDG) for drinking water and sanitation

None of this will convey much interest or enthusiasm, however, if the result just sits as another empty document. What the drylands will need is help to *finance* the implementation of real solutions, including funding for research and development on drought-resistant farming systems (seeds, water management, tillage practices, crop choices, land management) and financing for efficient irrigation and safe drinking water, increased water storage capacities, and the like.

In 2003, the Global Environmental Facility (GEF), an international fund to support environmental programs, was charged with being the financial backer of the UNCCD. The GEF is a reputable choice, as it is the world's major environmental finance facility, operated jointly by the UNDP, the World Bank, and the UNEP. The problem, however, is that the scale of financing is no more than one tenth, if not one hundredth, of the magnitude needed to be taken seriously. The GEF allocation for dryland management was established at $250 million for the recent four-year period 2002–6, or roughly $60 million per year. Instead, to confront the dryland crises in places such as Darfur, Somalia, and Ethiopia, we will require funding of several billion dollars per year.

Chapter 6

A Home for All Species

THE GREAT EXPANSION IN HUMAN POPULATION and economic activity over the past two centuries has come at the expense of the other species with which we share the planet. Our own species' hunger for resources has led us to become the single most destructive force on Earth for the rest of life. The Millennium Ecosystem Assessment (MEA), a comprehensive study of the state of the world's ecosystems carried out over several years with the input of more than two thousand scientists, found that during the past fifty years humans have degraded most of the world's ecosystems and driven down the abundance of other species, some to extinction. Although humans have benefited greatly from our ability to exploit nature for food, water, energy, materials, and other uses, our appropriation of nature's services has become far too much of a good thing. We are devouring our very life-support systems, and finding excuses along the way not to care.

We are facing a biodiversity crisis, and we have already done irreparable harm to countless species, most of which we haven't begun to know, much less document. Our assaults are coming from so many directions that natural systems can't adjust. There is a pervasive drop in biodiversity and species abundance; the decline is summarized in the World Wildlife Fund's Living Planet Index, which illustrates the extensive decrease of species abundance since 1970 (Figure 6.1). The great evolutionary biologist E. O. Wilson has coined the acronym HIPPO to describe these multiple assaults: habitat destruction, invasive species, pollution, population increase, and overharvesting.

All of these changes will be enormously exacerbated by climate change. As the climate changes, the current habitat of countless plant and animal species will no longer be suitable because of changes of temperature, precipitation, chemistry (for example, ocean acidification from higher CO_2 levels), storm frequency, or the changing ranges of other species that are their predators,

Figure 6.1: The Living Planet Index from 1970 to 2000

The index currently incorporates data on the abundance of vertebrate species around the world, of which 555 are terrestrial, 323 are freshwater, and 267 are marine. While the overall index fell by some 40 percent between 1970 and 2000, the terrestrial index fell by about 30 percent, the freshwater index by about 50 percent, and the marine index by around 30 percent over the same period.

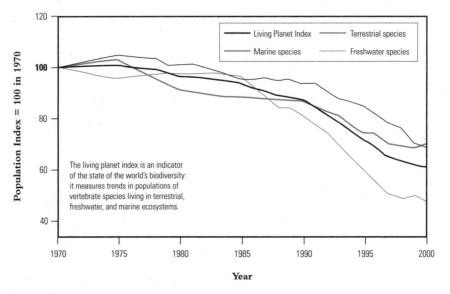

Source: WWF, UNEP-WCMC in Millennium Ecosystem Assessment (2005)

prey, or pathogens. As the planet warms, some species will be able to migrate poleward in order to keep within their temperature range, but others will not, because migration routes will be blocked or fragmented, or because the ability to migrate is too slow to survive the climate changes, or because they simply have no place to go. The last situation—no escape route—applies to alpine species that will try to go higher up the mountainsides to escape the heat until they've reached the upper limit, and to polar species, such as polar bears, whose habitat may disappear entirely from the planet. Recent studies have shown that an enormous proportion of species, even one third to one half, could be driven to extinction as a result of these changes.

THE PERVASIVE DAMAGE

The results of this multiple assault are everywhere. Virtually every ecosystem on the planet is degraded, and some are in a state of near collapse. Species abundance is declining across large categories of animals and plants. Some of the most notable are the following.

Fisheries

A recent study found that the rate of fisheries collapse has been accelerating over time, with 29 percent of currently fished species deemed collapsed in 2003. One major concern with fisheries loss is that it is often nonlinear. Fisheries populations are prone to sudden drops once the level of exploitation reaches a certain tipping point. Figure 6.2 and Figures 6.3(a) and (b) (see insert) very clearly show how such a dramatic and sudden collapse in the fish population occurred in the well-known case of the North Atlantic cod fishery in the early 1990s.

Corals

Coral reefs are under multiple assaults and pervasive threats. These include rising sea surface temperatures, which lead corals to expel the symbiotic algae that live within them; physical destruction of reefs from tourism, fishing,

Figure 6.2: History of Newfoundland Cod Fishery

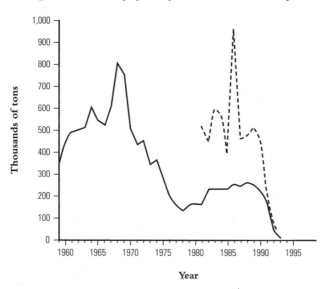

Annual harvest in thousands of tons is plotted as a solid line; stock size is plotted as a dashed line.

Source: Adapted from Roughgarden and Smith (Copyright 1995 National Academy of Sciences, U.S.A.)

boating, and other hazards; acidification of the oceans, with consequent destruction of carbonate structures; ocean pollution; and widespread harvesting of corals for ornamental purposes.

Amphibians

The world is currently suffering a crash of amphibian populations, including many species of frogs and toads. There are many simultaneous causes. Some of the culprits include habitat destruction and fragmentation of wetlands and forests; invasive species, for example, nonnative fish that eat the tadpoles; pervasive use of pesticides and herbicides; introduced pathogens, parasitic flukes, and destructive fungi; and perhaps the partial destruction of stratospheric ozone and a consequent rise of exposure to ultraviolet radiation.

Pollinators

Many fruits, vegetables, and flowering trees depend on pollinators, such as honeybees, for their reproduction. Indeed, the fruit industry spends vast sums of money on bee pollinators, including the roughly one million beehives brought into California each spring to pollinate the almond orchards. There is now a mass decline in the wild populations of many pollinators, including honeybees, and also a replacement of native pollinators by unsuitable invasive species. The results will be declining crop productivity and rising food costs. There is, as with the other areas of catastrophic biodiversity decline, a multitude of interacting factors, probably all of which are contributing to the decline. These include loss of habitat of the pollinators (for example, forests), invasive species of parasites (for example, mites and fire ants that attack honeybee populations), viral infections transmitted from abroad, and large-scale use of pesticides, which kill the pollinators.

Great Apes

There is a pervasive and acute threat to the great ape populations, including gorillas, bonobos, and chimpanzees. Many of the dangers revolve around the growing encroachments of human populations on the forest habitats of the great apes. Causes of the sharp decline of great ape populations and the extreme danger of their extinction include the small initial population of the great ape populations; the destruction and fragmentation of their forest habitats, especially caused by logging and violent conflict; the hunting of the apes for bush meat; and the mass epidemics of Ebola virus among the apes for reasons that are uncertain (and that may include environmental, climate, or habitat changes).

THESE HIGH-PROFILE THREATS are considered by ecologists to be the visible part of a mass human-led extinction era now under way. Human activity has long contributed to the extinction of megafauna, the large mammals that are easily hunted, such as American horses, camels, mammoths, saber-toothed cats, and other species driven to extinction by hunters (and perhaps climate change) in North America roughly ten thousand years ago. In the past half millennium, more than 750 species extinctions have been recorded by the International Union for Conservation of Nature and Natural Resources (IUCN), the keeper of the extinction accounts, including of the dodo, the Chinese river dolphin (declared extinct in 2006), and many other birds and marine life. A vast number of additional species have also been driven to extinction, perhaps by the millions, but these are typically smaller organisms that were not even documented before their disappearance. In its most recent survey of globally threatened species, in 2006, the IUCN evaluated 24,284 vertebrate species and determined that 5,624 of them were threatened; 3,978 invertebrates, of which 2,101 were threatened; and 11,901 plants, of which 8,390 were deemed to be threatened. (The category "threatened" includes species that are critically endangered, endangered, or vulnerable.)

The estimates of the mass extinctions rely not only on direct observation but on the crucial tool of the species-area relationship, which estimates how many species are likely to exist within a given area. As habitat is destroyed, it is possible to use the known species-area relationship to estimate the number of species that are lost along with the habitat. E. O. Wilson in *The Future of Life* (2002) has estimated that up to half of all species, an almost unimaginable proportion, faces a threat of extinction during the twenty-first century as a result of HIPPO and climate change.

THE WORLD'S MOST IMPORTANT UNKNOWN TARGET

The human assault on biodiversity has been recognized, though not its scale, extent, and imminent threat. In 1992 the world coalesced around a framework for action to protect biodiversity in the United Nations Convention on Biological Diversity (CBD). The objectives of the treaty are described as "the conservation of biological diversity, the sustainable use of its components and the fair and equitable sharing of the benefits arising out of the utilization of genetic resources." The treaty, at its core, calls on countries to take appropriate actions to conserve biological diversity. The rich countries promised additional financial resources for this effort. The following wide range of conservation actions was envisaged:

- Reduce the rate of biodiversity loss, including: (1) biomes, habitats, and ecosystems; (2) species and populations; and (3) genetic diversity.

- Promote sustainable use of biodiversity.

- Address the major threats to biodiversity, including those arising from invasive alien species, climate change, pollution, and habitat change.

- Maintain ecosystem integrity, and the provision of goods and services provided by biodiversity in ecosystems, in support of human well-being.

- Protect traditional knowledge, innovations, and practices.

- Ensure the fair and equitable sharing of benefits arising out of the use of genetic resources.

- Mobilize financial and technical resources for implementing the convention and the strategic plan, especially for developing countries, in particular the least developed countries and small island developing states among them, and countries with economies in transition.

The most specific of the treaty's goals was actually adopted by the treaty's signatories a decade later, in 2002, when the parties committed themselves to "achieve by 2010 a significant reduction of the current rate of biodiversity loss at the global, regional and national level as a contribution to poverty alleviation and to the benefit of all life on Earth." This target was also adopted at the 2002 World Summit on Sustainable Development and was incorporated by the UN General Assembly as a target under the Millennium Development Goals.

Alas, the commitment to slow the loss of biodiversity by 2010 must be re-

garded as the best-kept secret on the planet. The goal was set to at least modest fanfare but has now disappeared from the world's radar screen entirely.
There are many reasons, all relating to a lack of political leadership in all parts
of the world. The goal has been eclipsed by war, short-term crises, and pervasive neglect, and also by a blindingly misguided debate over the CBD itself.
The world's nations ended up focusing much of their debate, and ire, on the
question of how to share genetic riches for commercial use and on who would
own those resources. They also spent an inordinate amount of time on the
debate over genetic modification. But most important by far, the United States
signed but never ratified the treaty—ratification was defeated in the Senate
in 1994 by a coalition of farm and ranch groups who defended their grazing
rights over the conservation of the planet's biodiversity. The Clinton administration was unable to prevail over the farm lobby, despite the obvious fact
that sound rangeland and farmland management is in the long-term interest
of these lobbying groups as well.

THE VAST STAKES IN BIODIVERSITY CONSERVATION

E. O. Wilson has recently described biodiversity conservation as nothing less
than the protection of the Creation itself. Indeed, he has reached across scientific lines to American religious communities in order to find common
cause in the protection of the Creation, both from a scientific and a religious
point of view. This is not merely rhetoric. Protecting biodiversity is nothing
less than protecting the underpinnings of life itself. Ecology emphasizes the
interconnections of all living systems and that the destruction of biodiversity
at the current rate poses not only a spiritual loss but also a practical threat to
human food production, protection from pathogens, and sustenance of
countless other aspects of our lives and livelihoods.

This, too, was the theme of the Millennium Ecosystem Assessment, the
largest global effort ever undertaken to catalog the state of the world's ecosystems and the human effects on them. The assessment brings modern ecology
to the service of human well-being by outlining the various ways that our
well-being depends on ecosystem functions and how human activities are
undermining those critical functions. The study categorizes the functions of
ecosystems into four areas: supporting services, provisioning services, regu-

lating services, and cultural services. These in turn support well-being in several ways. *Supporting* services are the key basic processes of ecosystems that contribute to their ability to meet human needs. Supporting services include nutrient cycling (such as cycling of nitrogen and carbon, which is vital for life), soil formation, and primary production through photosynthesis. These basic functions then contribute to higher-order services. Ecosystems *provision* society in the forms of food, freshwater, wood and fiber, and fuels. Ecosystems *regulate* the natural environment to prevent floods, keep epidemics in check by limiting disease-transmitting species, purify water in wetlands, and stabilize the climate. And ecosystems sustain *cultural* and ethical values in beauty, relations with other species, scientific inquiry, and artistic endeavors.

Clearly, our well-being depends fundamentally on these ecosystem services. The MEA discusses four end points of well-being supported by these varied services: *Security* includes protection from natural hazards (floods, droughts, predators). *Material needs* include foodstuffs, building materials, fibers for clothing, and energy supplies. *Health* includes clean water and air, and relative safety from pathogens. *Social cohesion* includes community trust and well-being that is supported by a shared and trusting community commitment to a healthy environment. All of these are a form of empowerment of individuals and communities to meet desired objectives, material and spiritual.

The main lesson of ecology is the interconnectedness of the various parts of an ecosystem and the dangers of abrupt, nonlinear, and even catastrophic changes caused by modest forcings. We have already seen these threats in the case of climate change. The same is true regarding the loss of biodiversity. It is a basic finding that biological diversity increases the productivity and resilience of ecosystems. With more species filling more niches in a given location, a biodiverse ecosystem is better buffered against external shocks and is more adept at cycling nutrients, capturing solar radiation, utilizing water resources, and preventing the takeover of the system by single predators, weeds, or pathogens. In other words, preserving biodiversity helps to preserve all aspects of ecosystem functions. Removing one or more species from an ecosystem, for example, by selective harvesting of trees or fish or hunted animals, can lead to a cascade of ecological changes with large, adverse, and nonlinear effects on the functioning of the ecosystem.

Unfortunately, human activities are very often designed precisely to "simplify" ecosystems, often to their grave peril. In modern farming, monocultures of crops often replace multiple intercropped species and varieties, leading to a decline of biodiversity, genetic variation within species, and resilience to climate change or plant diseases. Fishing fleets often aim to harvest particular high-valued species, often the largest and slowest-growing carnivorous fish at the top of the food chain, yet the removal of a part of the food chain has ripple effects throughout the ecosystem. Fishing stocks have become smaller (because of the culling of the largest fish) and more concentrated at lower trophic levels (meaning the herbivorous prey rather than carnivorous predators). In some fisheries, the removal of the top trophic species has led to a cascade of species changes, such as when the overhunting of the sea otter along the Pacific coast of the United States led to a proliferation of sea urchins, the prey of the otter, which in turn led to a decline in the great kelp forests, the feed stocks of the sea urchins.

The MEA documents several "accelerating, abrupt, and potentially irreversible changes." These include:

- Disease emergence, as animal and human populations come into contact, which has occurred with HIV/AIDS (transmitted to humans through the mutation of a chimpanzee virus), SARS (transmitted to humans most likely by an infected civet), avian flu, West Nile virus, and Rift Valley fever

- Algal blooms, caused by the increase of nitrogen loading, which have led to massive fish kills and dead zones (for instance in the Gulf of Mexico)

- Fishery collapses, exemplified by the collapse of the great Newfoundland cod fishery off the coast of Canada

- The replacement of corals by algae in many locations caused by eutrophication and the decline in populations of fish that feed on algae and with a consequent long-term decline in the reefs' fish population and overall biological productivity

- Desertification, as land degradation exacerbated by climate change and other influences leads to a collapse of grasslands, moisture retention, and soil structure

- Massive vulnerability to natural hazards such as increased flooding, landslides, and storm surges

- Crop failures, caused by pests, pathogens, destruction of biodiversity (for example, the loss of pollinators), soil erosion, water pollution, and increased low-level (tropospheric) ozone

STRATEGIES FOR BIODIVERSITY CONSERVATION

At the core of long-term strategies, society must get the HIPPO and climate change elephant out of the room. Large-scale actions will be needed to reduce the human impact on natural habitats: to limit the introduction of invasive species through much better regulation of pathways by which those species are transported internationally (for example, in the bilges of transoceanic ships and in the illegal trade in exotic species); to reduce the growth of the human population; to reduce pollution; to control overharvesting of the commons (ocean fisheries, lakes, bush meat, tropical forests, and more); and, of course, to mitigate climate change. The agenda of biodiversity conservation in the long term is the agenda of environmental sustainability itself. Yet within these very broad and vital categories there are specific actions we can take to limit damage today and stop irreversible losses while global efforts on the big challenges are given time to scale up. I will focus on six specific interventions that can make a tremendous difference in a short period of time, indeed in time to point the world in another direction by the biodiversity target date of 2010.

Protected Habitats
One standard and successful approach to high-priority conservation is the establishment of protected habitats by regulation. These include national parks and refuges, protected marine areas, conversion of open-access sites to community management, and even private ecotourism sites, which under certain circumstances can harness the profit motive and biodiversity conservation. There is a long experience with terrestrial parks and refuges. The recent move to marine-protected areas is new and exciting. The idea is to define an area of ocean within which the rights to fishing and commercial exploitation are

severely curtailed. President Bush recently adopted such a protected area in Hawaii.

Avoided Deforestation

A powerful new approach will be international funding to give rain forest countries the incentive to avoid further deforestation. Rather than paying these countries to cut their forests (when we buy their lumber), the world would pay them to conserve their biodiversity and sequester the carbon in the forests. The Coalition for Rainforest Nations has proposed that countries be given carbon credits for avoiding deforestation. Under the Kyoto Protocol, rain forest countries can get carbon credits for reforestation and for afforestation (creating forests where they did not previously exist) but not for avoiding deforestation! The proposed change would pay countries if they agree to stop the current trend of deforestation and commit the country to a given assured level of forest cover.

Improved Agricultural Productivity

High-productivity farming is often seen as the foe of biodiversity conservation and, indeed, with bad farming practices, farming can be ecologically destructive. At a more basic level, however, high-productivity farming is vital for biodiversity conservation, since the higher the yield per hectare of arable land, the fewer hectares of arable land are needed to provision the population with foodstuffs. The Green Revolution in Asia saved vast areas of land by tripling the crop yields per hectare. Still, the Green Revolution also introduced several practices that were damaging to the environment, including overuse of fertilizers (often supported by generous subsidies), overuse of groundwater (often backed by free or heavily subsidized water), underutilization of improved irrigation technologies (such as drip irrigation), and massive use of persistent pesticides and herbicides. The core concept of a Green Revolution remains vital and, indeed, will be at the core of Africa's escape from extreme poverty. Yet the twenty-first-century Green Revolution needs to be environmentally friendly and ecologically savvy from the start. This would mean adopting the lessons of the new agroecology, which combines high-productivity agriculture with sustainable land management. Some of the techniques of agroecology include drip irrigation to conserve water use, integrated pest management to reduce or eliminate the need for chemical pesticides, low-tillage agriculture to reduce the churning of the soils and the resultant soil erosion, and water-efficient crop and seed varieties. The benefits of such practices in higher yields and lower environmental losses can be enormous. Also, smart subsidies for fertilizer that encourage fertilizer use by the poor without subsidizing overuse by the rich should be combined with the improved fertilizer practices described next.

Nitrogen Cycle Management

It is typical for half or more of the nitrogen applied to farm fields to be lost in water or in the air. Fortunately, there are techniques to limit those losses, such as dissolving the fertilizer in irrigation water and distributing it below the ground surface. Such fertilizer management techniques can make a tremendous difference when applied on a large scale. There are also agronomic techniques, such as low-tillage farming, that drastically reduce the runoff of nitrogen fertilizer into lakes, groundwater, and the sea. Wetlands and riparian zones (vegetated areas that form the border between land and a river or stream) are natural nitrogen sinks, yet they are also often drained of their water to make way for cultivable land. Preserving those areas or constructing artificial wetlands can be an effective way of trapping nitrogen before it reaches bodies of water in which it will act as a pollutant. Agroforestry techniques (planting certain species of trees and shrubs along with crops) can also help to fix nitrogen in the soil and prevent it from entering groundwater and rivers.

Sustainable Food Systems

As societies become more prosperous and more urban, they tend to consume more meat. This dietary transformation has been explored in detail by Vaclav Smil, among others. The basic issue is that meat is a roundabout and energy-inefficient way to get nutrients to the human population. To fatten a cow by one kilogram, around eight kilograms of feed grains must be fed to the cow, but if we take into account the fact that much of the cow is bone and fat, each kilo of edible meat product has used around thirteen kilograms of feed grains. The huge burden of meat consumption on land use should be apparent. To raise that many kilos of feed, we require massive pasturelands if the animals graze or vast croplands if the feed grain is obtained by the production of cereals, soybeans, and other farm products.

Currently, meat consumers do not face pricing that reflects the environmental consequences of their actions, in terms of the loss of biodiversity implicit in land use, in the costs of providing the freshwater, and in the environmental losses associated with the industrial production of feed grains and livestock (for example, the eutrophication of the waterways, with the consequent destruction of marine life). Meat is dramatically underpriced relative to plant products if we take into account the environmental costs of producing it. With more accurate environmentally based pricing (for example, charging appropriate prices for water use and grazing on pasturelands) and more accurate consumer information, it is likely that today's meat consumption would decline markedly, and would not rise as rapidly as it is in China, India, and other fast-growing markets. Given the adverse health consequences of a diet rich in red meats, the public health would also benefit markedly from such a policy. As one easy and practical step, Smil proposes incorporating vegetable proteins into ground meats and processed meat products such as sausage, in order to limit meat consumption without curtailing protein consumption.

Another major dietary change is to curtail the predilection for eating endangered species. China is a particularly remarkable example of such exotic tastes, ranging from rare frogs, turtles, and snakes to endangered fish and sea animals to bears and tigers, which are believed to have medicinal or aphrodisiacal qualities. China's colossal domestic demand and rising incomes mean that the market for endangered species is ever growing, and the global policing systems have not been ramped up to keep pace with China's growing consumer demand. Political measures, legislation, and public awareness campaigns must attempt to counteract such destructive appetites.

Protecting the Global Fisheries

Many of the world's major fisheries are in dire need of relief before they are fished to extinction. Fisheries management is divided between national regulation (generally within a two-hundred-mile nautical exclusive economic zone, or EEZ, of a country's coast) and the high seas, which are treated essentially as an open-access resource for the world. Within the EEZs, countries are responsible for sustainable fisheries management, but many have no capacity or interest. Beyond the EEZs, the situation remains lawless. There are, we have noted, several economic and regulatory means available to restore collapsed fisheries, improve those that are in decline, and preserve the few that are still healthy, for example, a system of tradable fishing quotas or permits, by which each fishery is limited to a catch of a certain size. In addition, governments should protect certain highly vulnerable marine areas entirely by closing all commercial activities in those waters. Governments may also finance the decommissioning of existing national fishing fleets to bring them into line with more sustainable catch levels, thus reversing the heavy subsidization of fishing by such fleets in the past.

On the high seas today, the most consequential single step available is the outlawing of bottom trawling on sea mounts. This is a remarkably destructive practice, in which the trawler drags a massive net on the sea bottom, destroying the marine ecology along the way in the interest of catching a modest number of fish of modest commercial value. The practice is carried out for one, and only one, reason: nobody is watching and nobody is charging for the extraordinary damage to vital and unique ecosystems. (Figure 6.4 in the insert illustrates the severity of the damage.) Fishing fleet nations such as Spain and Portugal have used every diplomatic maneuver to protect their right to pillage the ocean bottom, one of the richest and least understood of all of the world's ecosystems. There are few more egregious ecological practices on the planet with a higher ratio of damage to social benefit and, therefore, there are few if any that would be easier to eliminate without imposing a serious cost to consumers or producers.

Cultivating fish and other aquatic organisms rather than harvesting them from open waters is another crucial way to protect endangered fisheries and other marine species. Just as humans made the transition from hunting and gathering to agriculture around ten thousand years ago, they now need to make the same transition regarding the aquatic harvest. This blue revolution can match the Green Revolution and can relieve the pressure on the oceans, but only if the aquaculture is managed in an environmentally sound manner. Aquaculture includes a number of practices: fish farming, typically in ponds, for freshwater fish (carp, tilapia, catfish) or ocean species (salmon); mariculture, which is the farming in seawater of shrimp, mollusks, and ocean fish; and algaculture, which is the farming of algae and kelp. Fish farming reduces the demand for ocean catch to the extent that the farmed fish are herbivorous. When the fish are carnivorous, as are salmon, it takes between one and three kilograms of fishmeal, caught from the sea, to raise one kilogram of salmon, thus typically representing a net ocean burden.

Aquaculture is booming, led by China, partly as a result of favorable economics and partly as a reflection of brilliant breakthroughs that have raised the productivity and reliability of fish farms. Most of China's farmed fish are herbivorous (especially carp species), and China's total fish farm output has risen from roughly two metric tons in 1980 to around thirty-five million metric tons today. Worldwide, fish farming is now running at about fifty million tons per year, around half of the worldwide ocean catch, which has peaked at around one hundred million metric tons. Fish farming has accounted for all of the increase in the world's fish consumption during the past decade.

REVIVING GLOBAL COOPERATION BEFORE 2010

There is still time to rescue something of the shockingly neglected 2010 goal of biodiversity conservation. Given the stakes involved, it would be devastating to arrive at 2010 without progress, yet that is the course we are now following. By combining actions on the following ten fronts, it is still possible for the world to regain its footing.

1. The United States should ratify the Convention on Biological Diversity. The absence of the United States is a scandal and tragedy. The next president should prepare to put the CBD before the U.S. Senate in early 2009.

2. The world should arrive at 2010 with renewed global cooperation on population control, the Millennium Development Goals, and climate change (including the post-Kyoto settlement to be negotiated under the UNFCCC), all of which are crucial inputs for biodiversity conservation.

3. We should agree by 2010 to establish significant new protected areas, both terrestrial and marine, focusing on biodiversity hot spots under special threat.

4. We should increase international funding for biodiversity-protected areas by several billion dollars per year and direct the increase to the poorest countries through the Global Environmental Facility (GEF).

5. We should guarantee dedicated funding for avoided deforestation in the new post-Kyoto global climate strategy.

6. We should ban all bottom trawling in the open seas.

7. The Antarctic Ocean, which is under increasing threat, should be established as a marine-protected area in the same way that the Antarctic terrestrial habitats are now protected by the Antarctic Treaty.

8. We can eliminate one of the major sources of invasive species by requiring ocean vessels to heat-treat their ballast water (thereby killing potential invasive species) or to exchange the ballast water in the open sea rather than at port.

9. We should establish regulations under the CBD to ensure that aquaculture facilities use sustainable practices, including the farming of native species in coastal or oceanic waters to prevent the release of invasive species, and shift to herbivorous species and feeding practices that do not multiply the pressures on the open sea.

10. We should establish a worldwide, sustained scientific effort on global biodiversity conservation, with several components:

   • A commission on biodiversity and macroeconomics that would recommend guidelines for appropriate global pricing and regulation of ecosystem services of global consequence, such as conservation of endangered species, liability for the introduction of invasive species, enforcement of trade restrictions on endangered species, and global environmental levies or limits on various pollutants.

   • A millennium ecosystem fund, perhaps housed at the Global Environmental Facility that would help developing countries to incorporate environmental sustainability into their overall development strategy. The fund would enable local scientists to carry out comprehensive national ecosystem service assessments and continuous monitoring. The costs for global environmental sustainability need not break the bank, either. Conservation International concluded that substantial protection for 70 percent of land-dwelling flora and fauna could be achieved with a onetime payment of $30 billion to protect the twenty-five most important spots on the planet in terms of biodiversity, including the remaining tropical forest wilderness (in the Amazon, Congolian basin, and New

Guinea). Another study found that a global reserve network covering 20 to 30 percent of the oceans would cost between $5 billion and $19 billion annually, which could be met by cutting subsidies to the fishing industry.

- The Millennium Ecosystem Assessment should be institutionalized as an ongoing program, charged with providing up-to-date reports on the state of global biodiversity at least every five years, much as the Intergovernmental Panel on Climate Change does successfully with climate.

- A Web-based Encyclopedia of Life is a brainchild of E. O. Wilson's. Wilson has wisely argued that we will not succeed in conserving biodiversity unless we also create the tools for success, including an encyclopedia of the world's species in order to understand the targets and dimensions of the needed conservation effort.

PART THREE

The Demographic Challenge

Chapter 7

Global Population Dynamics

THOUGH THE WORLD'S POPULATION GROWTH RATE has declined, any complacency about global population growth would be misplaced. The global population continues to increase by large numbers and in the regions least able to ensure the health, stability, and prosperity of the population. Nonetheless, most mainstream economics now gives a pretty big yawn about the issue. Here is how *The Economist* magazine, the world's authoritative economics weekly, recently dismissed concerns about population growth:

> There doesn't seem to be much danger of a Malthusian catastrophe. Mankind appropriates about a quarter of what is known as the net primary production of the Earth (this is the plant tissue created by photosynthesis)—a lot, but hardly near the point of exhaustion. . . . Raw materials have become more abundant, not scarcer. Certainly, the impact that people have on the climate is a problem; but the solution lies in consuming less fossil fuel, not in manipulating population levels.

Yet we need to worry about population growth and take global public actions to address it. Here's what I shall argue:

- The world's population growth remains far too rapid.

- Resource scarcity is very real, especially regarding the impact of rising populations on the Earth's ecosystems and biodiversity.

- The rapid growth of populations in the poorest countries hinders economic development, condemns children in poor countries to continued poverty, and threatens global political stability.

Public policies can play an important and salutary role in assisting poor households in achieving a voluntary reduction of fertility rates. Fortunately, if today's high-fertility countries, especially in Africa, can follow the successful lessons of countries that have reduced population growth in the recent past, and if they are helped with increased assistance in that effort by international agencies, these countries can achieve a rapid and voluntary reduction in fertility, much to the benefit of economic development, the next generation, and global security. The world should embrace a set of policies to help stabilize the global population, through voluntary choices, at a population of roughly eight billion people, rather than the current trajectory, which is likely to take us to nine billion or more by 2050. This may seem like a modest difference, but the consequences would be large, especially since the population control would come mainly in the world's poorest places.

THE DEBATE OVER POPULATION

Economists tend to be divided into three camps: population optimists, who say that today's population growth is good for development or is at least neutral; population pessimists, who say that population growth has already gone too far to avoid disaster; and those (including myself) who believe in the importance of spurring the demographic transition to lower fertility rates in the poorest countries.

Population optimists maintain that there are no real bounds to the Earth's population because technology can and will keep ahead of the curve. One variant of this optimism is associated with the ideas of economists Simon Kuznets and Michael Kremer, who have each argued that a larger global population will tend to bring about the very technological advances that are needed to sustain that larger population. From their viewpoint, an important part of economic advance comes from the scientific and technological discoveries of geniuses in society. These extraordinary individuals represent a small but relatively constant proportion of the population. Therefore, a world of one billion people will tend to be populated by ten times the number of geniuses of a world of one hundred million people. Kuznets, Kremer, and other economists argue that the overall rate of economic progress depends not on the number of geniuses per million population, which is fixed, but on the total number of geniuses at any time, since each good idea that a genius brings forward can be adopted by the entire population. As we've noted earlier, ideas are nonrival in that the use of the idea by one person does not diminish the ability of others to use the idea as well. Therefore, a population of one billion people will generate a lot more brilliant ideas, and technological advance, than a population of one hundred million. If this is true, a larger population will experience faster growth than a smaller population. The very takeoff of modern economic growth, for example, might have been triggered by the fact that the world's population had gradually crept up to the one-billion mark by 1830, finally enough to trigger a worldwide technological revolution.

Population pessimists believe that humanity has lived not only on ideas but also on the rampant and ongoing depletion of natural resources, especially ecosystem services such as freshwater, habitat, and harvesting of plants and animals. They assert that we have still not proved that we can use technology to overcome natural resource limits, only that we can mine depleting resources fast enough to stave off collapse temporarily. To these pessimists, the current optimism is like the man falling from the thirtieth floor of a building who reports "so far so good" when he passes the tenth floor. In this interpretation, the test is not the first two hundred years of economic growth but the possibility of smooth landing this century.

The advocates of demographic transition, such as myself, remain cautiously optimistic. This group in the middle of the debate acknowledges that good ideas and man-made capital can substitute, though imperfectly, for ecological resources in fixed supply. High-yield seeds and improved irrigation, for example, can raise food production per hectare and thereby support a larger population on a fixed amount of arable land. Nonetheless, rising populations still weigh heavily on a fixed or depleting natural resource base, especially ecosystem services. Economic development, therefore, hovers between ecological constraints on the negative side and the benefits of technology and man-made capital on the positive side. The net outcome depends on the rate of technological advancement versus population growth and on the ability of man-made capital (for example, irrigation) to substitute for natural processes.

Advocates of speeding the demographic transition emphasize the need for public efforts to speed the voluntary reduction of fertility rates as rapidly as possible to achieve the stabilization of the world's population as well as the population of each major region of the world. Rather than depend only on technological advances to save the day, the world, they believe, should relieve the direct pressures of population growth through direct population policies.

THE TOTAL FERTILITY RATE (TFR) AND POPULATION GROWTH

For two and a half centuries, the world has been living through an explosion of the human population supported by remarkable technological advances in food production and disease control. During the first phase of the post-1750 population surge, the greatest increases occurred in today's high-income economies. These were, after all, the societies that first mastered the technological advances in food production and industrialization that could reduce mortality rates and support a booming population with increased food supplies. Those technological advances gradually spread to the rest of the world. As a result, the burst of population growth also transferred from the high-income world to the developing world. In recent decades, the growth of the developing-world population has dramatically outpaced that of the high-income countries, both in proportionate terms and even more widely in absolute terms (Figure 7.1). The rich world added roughly 400 million people between 1950 and 2005, a gain of some 50 percent. The developing world

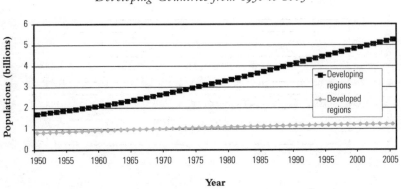

Figure 7.1: Human Population in the Developed and Developing Countries from 1950 to 2005

Source: Data from UN Population Division (2007)

added 3.5 billion people, a gain of 200 percent. In 1950, the developed world (United States, Canada, Europe, Japan, Australia, and New Zealand) was roughly one third of the world's population, and by 2005, it had fallen to roughly one sixth of the world's population.

Our societies and cultures are still adjusting to the happy surprise of falling child mortality and rising life expectancy. The decline of fertility lagged behind the decline of mortality, and a massive bulge of population ensued. Those population increases for a time were compatible in most countries with ecological limits, but as the world's population has continued to increase, the threats to human well-being from rising populations have also multiplied. In many developing countries, the rate of population increase has been so rapid and unprecedented that rising populations have destabilized the countries' politics and economics.

In recent decades, the population growth rate (the population increase as a percentage of the world's population) has slowed in most countries. While the world's population grew at around 2 percent in the 1960s, it is growing at around 1.2 percent today. Despite the slowdown, the absolute growth of the world's population—and hence the pressures on the Earth's carrying capacity—remains very high. With growth around 2 percent per year of the world's population of 3.3 billion in 1965, the annual population increase was around 70 million, which is actually slightly less than 1.2 percent of today's population of 6.6 billion, or roughly 78 million per year! Figure 7.2 illlustrates how the proportionate growth rate of population (measured on the right-hand

Figure 7.2: Population Growth from 1950 to 2050

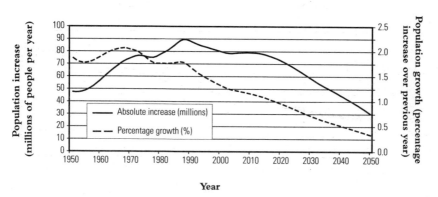

Year

Source: Data from UN Population Division (2007)

axis) has slowed significantly while the *absolute increase* of population per year remains high. The slowdown in the growth rate will likely continue, but the absolute increases in population will likely remain 70 to 75 million per year through 2020.

The slowdown in the growth rate of the world population reflects a decline in the total fertility rate, which measures the average number of children per woman during her reproductive years. Women in most parts of the world are choosing to have fewer children than in the recent past, contributing to the decline in the population growth rate. The most important reason for the fall in the TFR has been the decline in children's mortality. As newborns survive to adulthood with much greater frequency, it makes sense for households to reduce the number of births. Other forces have helped: female empowerment, female participation in the labor force, modern improvements in contraceptive technology, and the introduction and diffusion of family planning programs designed to encourage and help households to have fewer children. Yet, just as with the poverty trap, certain parts of the world, notably the poorest, are stuck in a demographic trap of high fertility.

The future trends in global population are startlingly sensitive to the TFR. Slight changes, up or down, from a given trend can mean differences of billions in population. Here's an illustration why: suppose that each woman in a particular society has five children, and one of them dies in childhood while the rest grow to adulthood. In that case, each woman will have four surviving children, and two, on average, will be girls. Therefore, each mother will be raising two girls who will survive to adulthood. We can say that each mother is "replaced" by two daughters in the next generation. This means that the population will tend to double each generation, or roughly every twenty-five years. The number of surviving daughters per mother is known as the net reproduction rate (NRR). When the NRR equals 1, the size of the population will tend to stabilize from one generation to the next. When the NRR is greater than 1, the population will grow. In the example just given, the NRR equals 2.

When the TFR is around 2, and almost all children survive, each woman will raise, on average, one daughter to adulthood. The population will be steady if this fertility rate is maintained over time. Specifically, suppose that the TFR is 2.1 and that 50 out of every 1,000 daughters (5 percent) die in childbirth. Each mother averages 1.05 daughters (half of 2.1), of whom 0.05 die. The NRR is therefore 1. We then say that fertility is at the "replacement rate," since each mother is replacing herself with one daughter in the next generation. For this reason, a TFR of 2.1 is conventionally taken to be the replacement rate, though in truth the precise level depends on the child mortality rate. The fertility rate therefore turns out to be the most crucial variable for determining the overall rate of population growth. When the TFR exceeds 5, as in much of Africa today, the population roughly doubles each generation. When the fertility rate falls to 2 or below, the population tends to stabilize or even begins to decline.

Figure 7.3 shows the TFR profile today and what is projected to be most likely in the future for various regions of the world. The projections are made by the UN Population Division, the keeper of the "official" global population forecasts. The "more-developed regions," or rich countries, have a TFR of 1.6, below replacement, while the least developed countries (and especially African countries) have a TFR of around 4.6. With roughly 0.8 of children dying before adulthood, the net reproduction rate in those countries is roughly 1.88 (equal to 3.84 surviving children, divided equally between girls and boys), meaning a doubling of population approximately every thirty years. The projection is that all regions of the world will gradually converge at the replace-

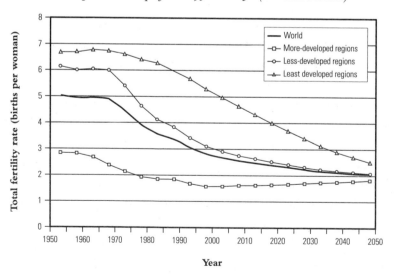

Figure 7.3: Total Fertility Trajectories of the World and Major Development Groups from 1950 to 2050 (medium variant)

Source: United Nations Population Division (2007)

ment rate. The TFR of the more developed regions is forecast to rise very gradually from its current low level, reaching 1.8 as of 2050. The TFR of the less developed regions is assumed to decline to 2.05 by 2050, just about the replacement rate. And the TFR of the least developed countries is forecast to decline to 2.5 by 2050, much lower than today but still above the replacement rate.

THE WORLD'S POPULATION IN 2050

The world's population prospects as of 2050 will be determined mainly by the evolution of TFR in the poor countries. If the fertility rates remain constant, not declining from today's high rates, the global population will soar to nearly unimaginable levels and will almost surely trigger Malthus's "positive checks" (war, disease, famine). If the fertility rates come down according to the medium forecasts or low variant, then the global population can actually stabilize within a half century or so. The UN Population Division puts forward four variants of future TFR and population. The medium forecast is deemed to be the most likely, and it is flanked by a low-fertility variant and a high-fertility variant as well as a fourth variant that assumes an unchanged TFR in the future. The low variant assumes a TFR roughly one-half child lower than in the medium forecast, and the high variant assumes a TFR roughly one-half child higher. In all of these variants except the fourth, the TFR of the poor countries is assumed to decline gradually over time from high levels today toward the replacement rate by midcentury.

The global population trends associated with these alternative TFR assumptions are shown in Figure 7.4. In the medium (most likely) forecast, the world's population is carried to 9.1 billion in 2050, which is pretty much the peak of the world's population. When this forecast is extended beyond 2050, the global population rises a tiny bit more and then declines gently to 9.1 billion, after which it stabilizes according to the long-term TFR assumptions used in the scenario. In the high-fertility variant, in which the TFR is just one-half child higher, the slight difference in fertility rates is enough to carry the world's population to 10.6 billion instead of 9.1 billion! In the low-fertility variant, in which the TFR of the developing world comes down more quickly to the replacement rate, the world's population reaches "only" 7.8 billion. If the TFR remains unchanged between now and 2050, the population will rise

*Figure 7.4: Population of the World from 1950 to 2050,
According to Different Projection Variants*

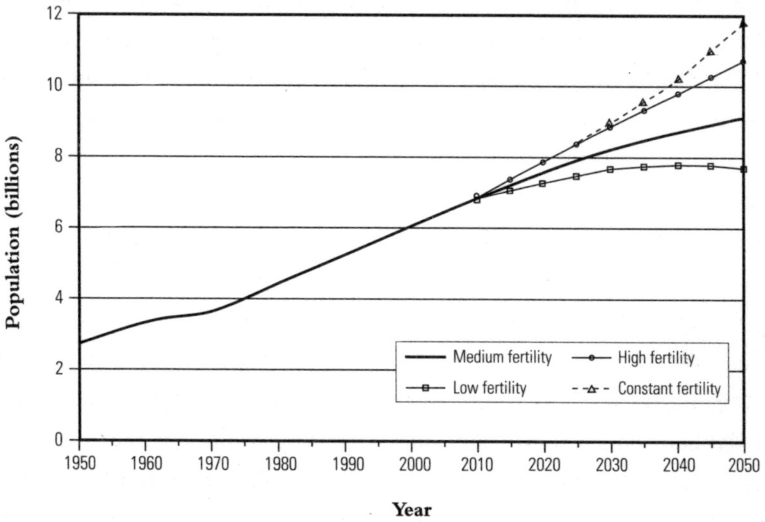

Source: United Nations Population Division (2007)

to a startling 11.7 billion. Crucially, in the medium variant the population stabilizes by around 2070 at 9.2 billion; in the low variant, the population stabilizes by around 2035 at roughly 7.8 billion.

The stunning fact is that all of the world's population increase will come in today's developing countries (though many of these countries will become developed countries based on successful economic development). Today's high-income countries will have little overall change in population, remaining at about 1.2 billion. The developing world will experience a rise from 5.2 billion to 7.8 billion in the medium forecast, equal to the world's projected rise in population. And of that 2.6 billion rise, a stunning 1 billion will be in Africa and 1.3 billion in Asia. Not only will the world's population increase, but the shift in composition will reshape the world as well. From today's share of the global population of around 12 percent, Africa's share will rise to a remarkable 20 percent by midcentury and to around 24 percent by 2070 in the medium forecast. India will overtake China as the world's most populous nation.

These projections need some digesting. Not only will the world's population continue to soar by another 2.6 billion or more in the medium and high forecasts of fertility, but it will soar in precisely those parts of the world that are struggling the most today with extreme poverty, disease, famine, and violence. Both cause and effect are at play. Poverty contributes to high fertility rates, while high fertility rates prolong poverty. The poorest countries in the world are stuck in a demographic trap as much as a poverty trap. Fortunately, there are solutions—good ones—for achieving a rapid and voluntary reduction of the fertility rate in these countries if we pay attention and coordinate our global efforts.

POPULATION MOMENTUM

In all cases, there will be a substantial increase in the global population before we are through with population increases. In fact, even if the TFR falls magically and instantly to the replacement rate in all countries, the world will still experience an overall population increase of more than one billion people! This is the consequence of population momentum. It works as follows: Suppose, to illustrate, that a country with a TFR of 5, a child mortality rate of two hundred per one thousand, and therefore a net reproductive rate of 2, has been doubling in population each generation. Currently there are two million older people, four million childbearing adults, and eight million children. The total population is fourteen million. Now suppose that the TFR immediately falls to the replacement rate, and the NRR immediately falls to 1. When today's children become parents, they will just replace themselves. In the coming generation, there will be four million elderly (the same as today's four million who are of childbearing age), eight million childbearing adults (the same as today's eight million children), and eight million children (born to the new adult population). The next generation's population will therefore be twenty million, up from fourteen million, despite a TFR that has been at the replacement rate during the entire generation! In the generation after that, the population will grow one more time. There will then be eight million elderly, eight million childbearing adults, and eight million children, or twenty-four million in all. From that point on, the population momentum is over, and the population will thereafter remain stable at twenty-four million. Population momentum by itself has therefore carried the original population from twelve million to twenty-four million, a doubling, even after the TFR fell to the replacement rate. The reason, simply, is that the original population had a massive youth bulge, which grew up to become childbearing adults and then the elderly.

This is our situation in the world today. We are at 6.6 billion people. If somehow, miraculously, the TFR were to fall today to the replacement rate, the world's population would still grow by approximately another one billion (depending on the precise assumptions made). We would end up with a planet of 7.5 billion. That's true even with the so-called baby bust in the more developed regions. In the coming decades, the momentum of population growth in the developing countries, with their very young population, will simply overwhelm any tendency to population decline in the high-income countries. This is why, in essence, we need to be working much harder to reduce the fertility rates in those regions, for their benefit and for the world's.

FERTILITY AND AGE STRUCTURE

The TFR largely determines not only the population growth rate but also the age structure of the population. When the TFR is high, say 5 or more, there will be a bulging number of youths relative to the number of adults. When the TFR is close to 2, the number of adults and childen will be similar (at least in the long term, after the population momentum has worked itself out). The population age structure is summarized by the so-called age-population pyramid, which shows the number of males and females in the population for each age cohort, usually designated in five-year intervals. The age-population pyramid for three types of countries is shown in Figure 7.5. On the horizontal axis is the number of males and females in each five-year age cohort as a percentage of the total population. On the vertical axis is the age category. In the Democratic Republic of the Congo (DRC), the TFR is around 6.7 and around one fifth of the children die in childhood. Each mother raises around four surviving children and, therefore, an average of slightly more than two daughters. The age-population pyramid has a broad base (children roughly twice as numerous as their parents) and a narrow peak (few people living to old age). In the United States, where the fertility rate is 2 and fewer than ten children per one thousand die before their fifth birthday, the age-population profile is more like a rectangle than a pyramid. The numbers of parents and children are similar. In Germany, where the TFR is only 1.4, below the replacement rate, there are fewer children than parents! The age-population

Figure 7.5: Three Patterns of Population Age Structure in 2000

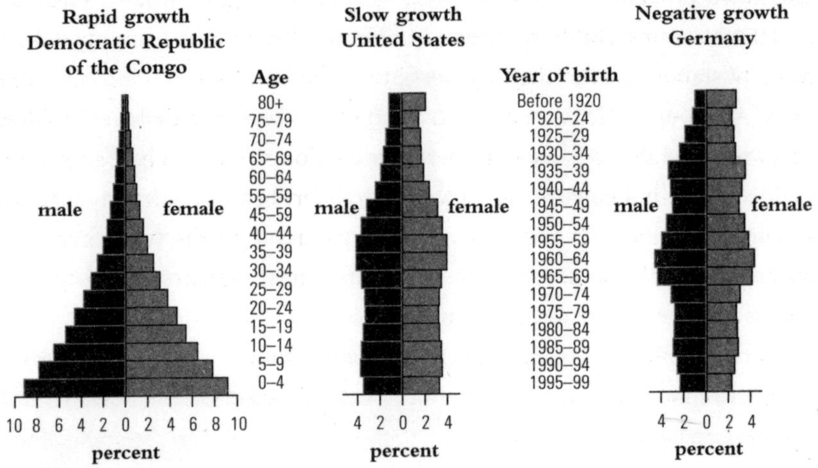

Source: United Nations Population Division (1999)

profile resembles an inverted pyramid for the population born after 1959. This is characteristic of a population whose numbers will gradually decline in the future.

An age-population pyramid like that of the DRC has huge implications for national stability and global security, as we will see in the next chapter. Regions with bulging youth populations are less stable than those with older populations. There are too many young people for every adult. In particular, there are too many potential young male fighters, aged fifteen to thirty, for every more mature social elder and potential peacemaker. Young men, especially impoverished young men without reliable employment, are fodder for the nightmarish dreams of political manipulators. This is not to blame the poorest countries for their plight, or to fear them. It is to suggest to them, and to us, that reducing the TFR from very high levels is part of their own security and ours.

SPEEDING THE DEMOGRAPHIC TRANSITION

The world is not locked in a demographic straitjacket but is instead in a transition, albeit one that is stretched out over many decades and with large differences across regions. The core idea is known as the demographic transition, illustrated in Figure 7.6. A society begins with very high mortality rates (especially of young children) and very high fertility rates. The population is roughly stable because the high fertility rates are offset by high mortality rates. As an example, suppose that the TFR is 5, but three of five children never reach adulthood. Then the net reproduction rate would be 1, despite the high fertility. In the figure, note that the high fertility and mortality rates are shown not by the TFR and deaths per one thousand births, but by what demographers call the crude birth and death rates, measured as births and deaths per one thousand of total population.

According to the theory of the demographic transition, the child mortality rate declines ahead of the total fertility rate. For example, the spread of immunizations, improved food production, safer water supply, and availability of antimalarial medicines and antibiotics cuts the mortality rate from three out of five children to one out of five children (still extraordinarily high from the perspective of modern public health). This is illustrated in the figure by the fall in the crude death rate from forty per one thousand down to ten per one thousand. Only later, with a lag, does the total fertility rate come down commensurately. In the interim, labeled as Stage 2, the crude birth rate exceeds

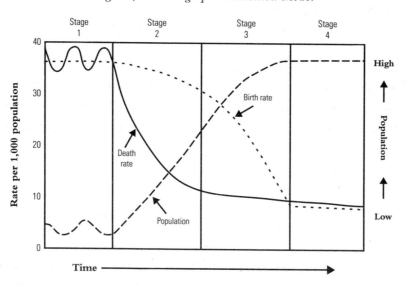

Figure 7.6: Demographic Transition Model

Source: Haggett (1975)

the crude death rate by as much as thirty per one thousand, at the maximum gap. At that point, the population will be growing rapidly, indeed at 3 percent per annum. A population growth rate of 3 percent per annum leads to a doubling of the population in twenty-three years. Roughly speaking, a 3 percent annual growth rate corresponds with a net reproductive rate of around 2.

Let's take the case of Kenya during 2005–10 as an illustration. The under-five mortality rate has declined to 1 in 10 children (104 per 1,000 for the period 2005–10 in the UN Population Division projections). This corresponds to a crude death rate of 12 per 1,000. The total fertility rate remains high at 5, which translates to a crude birth rate of 39 per 1,000. The difference between the two, 39 minus 12, results in a net annual population increase of 27 per 1,000, or an annual growth rate of 2.7 percent per year. The net reproduction rate with a TFR of 5 and an under-five mortality rate of 104 per 1,000 is just a sliver under 2 (1.96).

The upshot of demographic transition theory is that the total fertility rate declines with a lag, leading to a massive onetime bulge of population as the society transitions from high fertility and high mortality to low fertility and low mortality. At both the start and the end of the transition, the overall population growth is low, but during the transition, the population soars. The world has been in that transition, claims the theory, for the past two hundred years. In fifty years' time, or earlier with good policies, the world will complete the transition and enter an era of population stability. Note that in Stage 4 of the transition, the birth rate dips below the death rate. This would be the case if the TFR remains below the replacement level. That is possible. In that case, the world's population would begin to decline after nearly three centuries of bulge. There is nothing in the laws of demographics that would prevent a gradual and voluntary decline in overall world population. A long-term decline of the European population has, perhaps, commenced.

One key question, which drives the policy judgments of the next chapter, is why the decline in fertility lags behind the decline in mortality, and what can and should be done about it. There are three kinds of answers, all contributing to a realistic picture. First, fertility choices are built into the culture. The age of marriage, the social expectations of the number of children a family should have, the beginning of the childbearing age, the use of contraception, the birth spacing, and the like, are cultural as well as economic choices. Societal norms and expectations play a role in determining the choices. Even when the fundamental determinants of fertility choice change—for example, a steep drop in child mortality—the resulting change in actual fertility practices might take a generation or more.

Second, there can be a recognition lag, during which the parents are unsure that child mortality rates have really declined. The parents maintain high fertility rates just to be sure. Once the reduced mortality is firmly believed in, the fertility decline picks up speed. Third, and perhaps most important, there is nothing automatic about the transition of fertility following a decline of child mortality. Fertility choices represent the active decisions of households (including differing views and interests of fathers and mothers). The continuation of high fertility rates in the face of falling mortality rates might reflect a rational calculation by the parents, given the socioeconomic conditions of the household. When families live by subsistence farming and children provide labor and old-age security, and when the mother and daughters have few alternative means of livelihood, high fertility rates may be accepted as the preferred option for women, or at least the decision imposed on them by their husbands and the community. Moreover, contraception may be prohibitively costly for a family living at subsistence. Health care and family planning advice may be nowhere to be found.

Consider one more illustration. Suppose that children are the main old-age security for their parents, especially in the countryside. To ensure that old-age security, the household would like to ensure a surviving son with a very high probability, which we'll put at 97 percent for purposes of illustration. The household then chooses the number of children needed to ensure at least a 97 percent chance of a surviving son. If the probability of each child dying is one in five (20 percent), then having one son only won't be enough to ensure a 97 percent survival rate. The chance of a single son surviving is only 80 percent, not high enough for the parents' security. Having two sons is still not enough. The chance that both would die would be 20 percent multiplied by 20 percent, or 4 percent (if their survival probabilities are independent of each other). The chance of at least one surviving son would therefore be only 96 percent (equal to 100 percent minus 4 percent).

Having 3 sons would do it. The chance that all 3 would die before adulthood would be 20 percent times 20 percent times 20 percent, or 0.8 percent. There would be a 99.2 percent chance that at least *1* of the sons would survive. For families to have 3 sons, they would need, on average, to have 6 births, half girls and half boys. A child mortality rate of 20 percent (200 deaths per 1,000 births) would therefore induce a TFR of 6 in this illustration. The population would soar. Of the 6 children, 4.8 would survive on average (since 20 percent of the 6 children, or 1.2 children, would die). Each mother would be raising 2.4 girls (on average). The population would more than double each generation!

Now consider the implication of a drop of the child mortality rate, from 20 percent to 3 percent (thirty deaths per one thousand births). In this case, the chance of a son surviving is 97 percent. The parents will be satisfied to raise one son or just two children on average. The TFR will be two, and the population will be stable. (Actually, in this example it would decline slightly, since only 97 percent of the daughters would survive, and the NRR would be 0.97).

Now here is the implication: a drop in the child mortality rate must be large enough to induce the risk-averse parents to cut back on the number of children. If the mortality rate is three hundred per one thousand births, they will choose to have six children (for the reasons just argued). If the mortality rate drops from three hundred to two hundred per one thousand, they will *still* choose to have six children. The population growth rate will speed up, without a decline in the fertility rate! If the mortality rate drops further, to thirty per one thousand, the parents will choose to have only two children.

THE COMPELLING CASE FOR FERTILITY DECLINE

There are four compelling reasons why the poorest countries need to speed the demographic transition, and why we need to help them do it. The first, and most important, is that poor families cannot surmount extreme poverty without a decline in the fertility rate. Parents may think that they are providing security for themselves, but it is coming at the cost of continued extreme poverty for their children. An impoverished subsistence family in a rural village in Africa cannot raise six healthy, educated, well-nourished children. The parents face what economists call a quality-quantity tradeoff. With six children, a poor household must severely ration the investments per child. Perhaps only one of the children (typically the eldest son and none of the daughters) is able to go to secondary school. Often, all of the children will be chronically undernourished. Several may succumb to malaria or other killers because the family cannot afford basic health care and emergency transport to a local hospital. Studies find that large households are impoverished households. While the causation runs in both directions, with poverty conducive to large households, and large households exacerbating poverty, the pernicious effects of large families on the well-being of the children should not be doubted.

Second, what is true for the family is true for the society as a whole. A poor country cannot afford to equip its communities with schools, clinics, new roads, and other public facilities to accommodate a population that doubles each generation. A country with rapid population growth faces intense fiscal challenges just to keep up with the population, not to mention achieve economic progress.

Third, the ecological and closely related income consequences of such rapid population growth are devastating. The poorest countries are rural and usually in fragile ecologies, especially drylands. Desperately poor subsistence farmers with rapidly growing populations face constantly shrinking farm sizes that are already too small (0.25 hectares or less in parts of Africa) to provide a farm livelihood even with the best of technologies. African farms are already the smallest in the world on average (Figure 7.7). Falling farm sizes mean falling incomes per farm family, unless the shrinking land-family ratio

Figure 7.7: Average Farm Size by Continent from 1930 to 1990

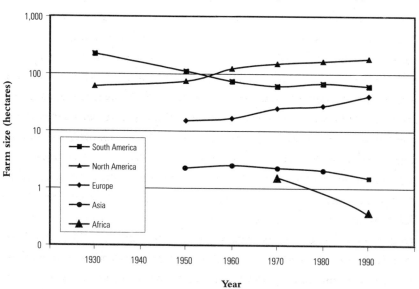

Source: *Estimates from Eastwood et al. (2004)*
Note: *Vertical axis on logarithmic scale*

is somehow compensated for by a sharp rise in the value of output per hectare. When farms become as small as they are in many parts of Africa today, it will be extraordinarily difficult to overcome poverty through farm incomes. These communities are also deforesting the local environment in search of fuel wood (Ethiopia, for example, is now 80 percent deforested), overpumping underground aquifers, depleting soil nutrients, overgrazing the pasturelands, and generally mining the environment in a desperate struggle for survival. Land is so scarce that the farmers can no longer afford to leave the land fallow for several years to replenish nutrients. These problems can still be overcome by helping impoverished farmers to adopt improved technologies and diversified income strategies, but such gains will not be sufficient to keep ahead of a doubling of population every generation!

Fourth, and finally, there are the threats to the rest of the world. Rapid population growth raises the pressures for mass migration and local conflict. Today's conflicts in Africa mainly reflect a breakdown of order among hungry and impoverished communities. Violence is not just a matter of poverty but also of the age-population structure. Higher fertility rates, we've seen, lead to age-population pyramids with a wide base and a narrow apex: too few elders per adolescent. The evidence points to added risks of violence and even war, a link that we will explore further in the next chapter.

HIGH FERTILITY RATES AND LOW ECONOMIC GROWTH

We have seen that high fertility rates should impede per capita economic growth for both microeconomic and macroeconomic reasons. At the household level, higher fertility means less investment in each child's human capital (including nutrition, health care, and education). At the national level, higher population growth means that more capital investment must be devoted simply to expanding the number of schools, clinics, paved roads, and other infrastructure just to keep up with population growth, and less can therefore be devoted to improving average services (per person). In economic jargon, we say that saving must be devoted to "capital widening," to keep up with population growth, rather than "capital deepening," to raise the capital stock per person.

One test of this is the cross-country evidence on economic growth. We can examine whether countries with high fertility rates indeed have lower growth rates of income per person. The standard tests have been carried out by the leaders of empirical growth modeling, Robert Barro and Xavier Sala-i-Martin. Their statistical model accounts for each country's average annual growth rate of income per person according to various characteristics of the country, including the level of income per person, the average educational attainment, the life expectancy, an indicator of the "rule of law," and other variables, including the total fertility rate. The TFR is shown to have a strong, statistically significant negative effect on economic growth. Consider two countries that are identical in all respects except that one has a fertility rate of 6 and the other a fertility rate of 2. According to the statistical result of the Barro and Sala-i-Martin study, the high-fertility country will have per capita income growth that is 1.3 percentage points per year lower than the growth of the low-fertility country. That's a whopping negative effect of high fertility.

POPULATION POLICIES AND THE REDUCTION IN FERTILITY

It might be supposed that fertility choices are among the most private of all decisions and the least amenable to government action (except, perhaps, by coercion). Yes, societies will pass through a demographic transition, but it would seem to be one that can, should, and will be determined by individual choices, not by government policies. Indeed, for today's rich countries of Western Europe and the United States, the demographic transition that took place during the twentieth century occurred largely through such decision making of individual households.

Yet the same has not been the case in the poorer countries. Their demographic transitions, where they have occurred, have typically been accelerated, and even triggered, by proactive government policies. Since governments have played a key role in the rapid decline in mortality rates of young children, for example, through provision of immunizations and safe drinking water, they have also had to step in to promote a rapid decline in fertility to accompany the decline in mortality. Experience has shown that households must be made aware of their legal rights (for example, to contraception) and technological options. Recent decades have brought enormous advances in contraceptive choice, including the pill, intrauterine devices, injectables, implants, and more.

Government programs have been critical in making households aware of the safety, convenience, and efficacy of these options, often providing contraceptive services to the many households in the developing countries that are too poor to afford contraceptive services on their own. Without government support, fertility rates will remain far above desired levels. This is also the case because fertility choices are strongly conditioned by social norms. Government-led advocacy can play an important role in changing ancient customs, which generally favor large families. After all, these customs emerged over centuries or even millennia of high rates of child mortality from infectious diseases.

The case for public leadership in fertility reduction was increasingly accepted throughout the world after 1960, as former colonies gained their independence and the family planning successes of one country spread to the next. The first family planning program was initiated by Prime Minister Jawaharlal Nehru of India in 1951. Pakistan's came soon after. Private foundations and nongovernmental organizations joined the effort, including the formation of the Population Council in 1952 and the start of Ford Foundation financing of India's population programs in 1959. By the 1960s, continued rapid population growth in the poor countries was being viewed as a global threat. The U.S. government came to understand rightly that very high fertility rates threatened political stability by creating a huge bulge of youth, often carrying the burdens of household poverty, hunger, and rural underemployment. Moreover, there were increasing fears that the global population boom would outstrip the world's food supply, making Malthus's original prediction come true one and three-quarter centuries after the prediction was first made.

The adoption of birth control as a U.S. government priority required the fortitude of U.S. political leaders to wade into highly charged and culturally contested waters. As late as 1959, President Dwight Eisenhower rejected the advice of a blue-ribbon committee on U.S. aid that called for U.S. government support for birth control in developing countries. "This government will not . . . as long as I am here, have a positive political doctrine in its program that has to do with birth control. That's not our business." Three years later, however, President John Kennedy agreed with his advisers that U.S. aid efforts should be extended to support family planning services, and as America's first Catholic president, he also made efforts to forestall direct criticisms from leading church officials of such U.S. government actions. U.S. support helped lead to the establishment of the UN Fund for Population Activities (UNFPA) in 1967, later renamed the UN Population Fund (with the original acronym unchanged). The UN made major efforts to train family planning specialists and demographers, and established regional demography centers to support this global work.

Fertility rates began to drop sharply in much of Asia in the 1960s and then, a decade or so later, in North Africa as well. Countries with higher levels of literacy, women's rights, and per capita incomes achieved the demographic transition earlier, but family planning programs also provoked rapid changes in countries with pervasive rural poverty, rigid gender roles, and widespread illiteracy. The transitions to low fertility were often very rapid. Thailand, for example, reduced its TFR from 6.4 in 1960–65 to 2.9 in 1980–85. Egypt, India, Indonesia, and Nepal achieved a sharp and voluntary drop in fertility rates even at relatively low levels of socioeconomic development through a highly proactive national family planning effort.

Family planning thereby emerged from an effort by a few specialists in a handful of countries into a worldwide effort. From two countries (India and Pakistan) with national family planning programs in the 1950s, more than a dozen countries had established family planning programs as of the 1960s, and several dozen had them by the 1970s. A series of major global conferences on population both spurred and underpinned this phenomenal worldwide shift in public policy. The first two global population conferences, in Rome in 1954 and Belgrade in 1965, were mainly scientific gatherings without direct political input. In 1974, the UN organized the world's first major intergovernmental conference on population in Bucharest. The official delegates, representing thirty-five countries, adopted a twenty-year World Population Plan of Action, which emphasized that countries should launch national population plans of action and that they could expect international support in so doing. The Plan of Action underscored that fertility choices should be left to voluntary decisions of households; that population policies should be seen holistically to include policies related to fertility, mortality, education, and research; and that in the end, such policies are a matter of national sovereignty, not international compulsion. The United States played a major role in Bucharest, urging the widespread adoption of bold population programs backed by U.S. support.

A decade later, the world's governments met again, in Mexico City, to review progress and make midcourse corrections to the Bucharest Plan of Action. Much had been accomplished. The fertility rates in much of the developing world were falling sharply. Yet the political circumstances had changed a bit. With Ronald Reagan as president, the U.S. delegates argued that fertility reductions were natural results of development and that family planning was much less important. They also suggested that population growth had only "neutral" effects on overall economic development prospects, a change of viewpoint from the earlier (and more accurate) position that high fertility rates are deleterious to long-term development. Most of the other governments, however, continued to maintain that reductions in fertility rates were needed to ensure long-term sustainable development. Nonetheless, despite such contention and a bruising battle over the specific issue of abortion rights, the conference concluded with a continuing global commitment to family planning services, and to the Bucharest Plan of Action in particular.

In 1994, the world assembled in Cairo for the next population conference, with political conditions altered yet again. This time, the major theme, promoted by a global activist community, was that population policies needed to be broadened beyond the narrow gambit of fertility to a much wider integrated approach on sexual and reproductive health, based strongly on the empowerment of women. The International Conference on Population and Development (or ICPD, as it came to be known) certainly did not reject family planning per se, but it sought to put family planning in the context of access to a much wider array of sexual and reproductive health (SRH) services, including safe pregnancy and delivery and sexual health more generally (including the control of sexually transmitted disease). In truth, these issues had long been on the table, but the ICPD changed the rhetoric and emphasis. The most important specific commitment regarding family planning to emerge from the ICPD was the commitment to universal access to sexual and reproductive health services, including family planning services, by the year 2015. This commitment was backed up by a call for increased development aid for the poorest countries and for the levels of aid needed specifically to ensure universal SRH coverage by 2015.

In summing up the results of a half century of family planning advocacy, funding, and organization, leading demographers emphasized the crucial role played by all of these global efforts. As John C. Caldwell and coauthors put it:

National family planning programs have been an important instrument in accelerating global fertility decline and in restricting ultimate world population to a level probably below ten billion. . . .

Those of us who have worked with contemporary family planning programs have been convinced of these programs' impact by the certainty of their clients that they could not control their fertility without the support of the program and that their parents' uncontrolled fertility was the inevitable consequence of the absence of such programs in their time.

The spread of changed ideas about family size and the legitimization not only of the use of contraceptives but also of their provision by governments was not a haphazard affair. International organizations played an increasingly important role. . . .

FULFILLING THE MILLENNIUM PROMISE OF REPRODUCTIVE HEALTH

The ICPD Plan of Action (or Cairo Plan of Action) forms one of the most important Millennium Promises. It underscores that population policy is integral to the overall challenge of sustainable development. A UN summary of the ICPD Plan of Action notes that "efforts to slow population growth, reduce poverty, achieve economic progress, improve environmental protection and reduce unsustainable consumption and production patterns are mutually reinforcing." The plan makes clear that one objective is "to facilitate the demographic transition as soon as possible in countries where there is an imbalance between demographic rates and social, economic and environmental goals," thereby contributing "to the stabilization of the world population." To underscore the multidimensional nature of reproductive health, the ICPD Plan of Action puts the goal of universal access in this way:

All countries are called upon to strive to make reproductive health accessible through the primary health-care system to all individuals of appropriate age as soon as possible and no later than 2015. Such care should include, *inter alia*: family planning counseling, information, education, communication and services; education and services for prenatal care, safe delivery and post-natal care, especially breast-feeding and infant and women's health care; prevention and treatment of infertility; abortion as specified in paragraph 8.25; treatment of reproductive tract infections, sexually transmitted diseases (STDs) and other reproductive health conditions; and information, education and counseling on human sexuality, reproductive health and responsible parenthood.

What is also important, the conference underscored the need for global cooperation, including financial assistance from rich to poor, in order to meet this goal of universal access, and put quite specific financial targets in place:

> The international community should strive for the fulfillment of the agreed target of 0.7 per cent of GNP for overall official development assistance (ODA) and endeavour to increase the share of funding for population and development programmes commensurate with the scope and scale of activities required to achieve the objectives and goals of the Programme of Action. . . . Given the magnitude of the financial resource needs for national population and development programmes, and assuming that recipient countries will be able to generate sufficient increases in domestically generated resources, the need for complementary resource flows from donor countries would be (in 1993 US dollars): in the order of $5.7 billion in 2000; $6.1 billion in 2005; $6.8 billion in 2010; and $7.2 billion in 2015.

The UN Millennium Project's special report on sexual and reproductive health (2006) came up with estimates of the scale of donor effort that would be needed to achieve the goal of comprehensive access to basic sexual and reproductive health in the poor countries, including safe childbirth, emergency obstetrical care, and family planning services. The estimate came to around $25 billion per year as of 2015, which would be roughly 0.06 percent of the income of the donor countries. This estimate would ensure broad coverage not only of contraception and family planning but also of safe childbirth, the key step in meeting the Millennium Development Goal of cutting maternal mortality by three fourths by 2015. Alas, to date, those financial goals have not yet been met. We now turn to reviving the global cooperation on family planning and fertility reduction.

Chapter 8

Completing the
Demographic Transition

SINCE THE BEGINNING OF THIS DECADE, population policy has been hijacked by shortsighted ideology. Leaders of the U.S. religious right have called for ending U.S. support for family planning. While that has not happened entirely, the Bush administration has slashed aid to the UN Population Fund and recommended large cuts in direct U.S. funding of family planning services. It's hard to think of a single more misguided policy; it runs directly against American interests in the reduction of conflict and terror, as well as against the support of economic development and environmental sustainability more generally.

The future trend of the global population will be a matter of choice, not fate. If the rich countries, including the United States in the next administration, honor their commitments at Cairo to help the poor countries invest in family planning and reproductive health more generally, the world's population can be stabilized at around 8 billion. Table 8.1 sketches how this would be achieved. In the current medium-fertility UN forecast, the world's population rises to 9.2 billion by 2050 and is roughly stable thereafter. A plausible policy alternative is to assume a faster demographic transition in the developing countries, as presented in the UN's low-fertility forecast. This low-fertility scenario puts the TFR at 0.5 lower than in the medium forecast. This alternative results in the stablization of global population at roughly 8 billion, with almost half of the reduction from 9.2 billion to 8 billion resulting from lower populations in India and sub-Saharan Africa. Per capita economic growth in Africa and in other regions of current high fertility would be powerfully promoted. The Earth's environment, first and foremost in the poorest regions, and also globally, would be much better protected. If the United States persists in its war against family planning, or simply continues the cur-

Table 8.1: Global Population with Faster Demographic Transition (billions)

REGION	2005	2050 (MEDIUM FERTILITY)	2050 (LOW FERTILITY)
Developed	1.22	1.25	1.25
Less-developed	5.3	7.95	6.73
World	6.52	9.2	7.98
of which: India	1.13	1.66	1.39
Sub-Saharan Africa	0.77	1.76	1.52

Source: Data from the UN Population Division (2007). The low-fertility forecast is for the less-developed countries only. The developed-country population forecast uses the medium-fertility assumption in both columns.

rent neglect and underfunding of global efforts, we are much more likely to find ourselves in more real wars instead.

Continued rapid population growth has given an air of Malthusian inevitability to Africa's travails. Many people suppose that any help for Africa in the form of disease control or increased food production will simply be offset by increased mouths to feed. On countless occasions in recent years, somebody has approached me after a lecture and in a whisper asked a question they found deeply unsettling and even embarrassing: "If we save all those children, won't they simply starve as adults? Won't we be creating a population explosion?" These questions are reflecting deeply ingrained thinking but also flawed reasoning. There is nothing static or inevitable about high fertility rates in Africa or anyplace else. These questioners are usually relieved—indeed, very relieved—when I explain three points. First, fertility rates in Africa can be brought down, quickly and voluntarily, just as in other parts of the world. Second, saving children through increased access to public health services and nutrition is actually a major stimulus to reduced fertility. Parents will choose to have fewer children in the first place if they are assured that the children will survive. Third, any sensible development policy for Africa or any other high-fertility region should integrate aid for economic development (including health, agriculture, education, and infrastructure) with aid for family planning. We should view the fertility transition and the economic development takeoff as a package deal.

COMPLETING THE DEMOGRAPHIC TRANSITION

Family planning, a worldwide policy-led effort since the 1950s to empower households to reduce their fertility rates through access to contraception and health services generally, is one of the great success stories of modern times. Without that effort, our global population pressures would be vastly more stark than they are today. Through ample global experience and scholarship, we know a great deal about the strategies that can succeed in shifting the world from the medium or high trajectories to the low trajectory in the interest of ending poverty and strengthening global political stability. The targets of opportunity are those regions with continuing high TFRs, as shown in the map in Figure 8.1 (see insert). Fertility rates remain high (above 4) in sub-Saharan Africa, the landlocked countries of South America (Bolivia and Paraguay), several countries of the Persian Gulf other than Iran (more on that below), and some parts of South and Southeast Asia. Even within countries such as India, where the national average TFR is now around 3, the population growth rate remains rapid, and rural fertility rates are above 4.

A rapid, voluntary reduction of fertility rates can be achieved through a package of efforts, some strictly within the family planning tool kit, such as free availability of contraception in the low-income countries, and some that are far more general, such as the promotion of child survival, the empowerment of women in the labor market, and the national leadership of politicians, celebrities, and the business community—all emphasizing that smaller families are a better economic investment for the parents (especially in the context of greatly improved child survival) and vastly better for the children.

Nine factors have proved time and again to be important in leading to a rapid or slow decline in fertility rates. Not all are needed, but each can contribute to a rapid voluntary reduction in the fertility rate.

Improving Child Survival

The decline in mortality rates of infants and young children is probably the single most important step in encouraging poor families to reduce fertility rates. When families have confidence that their children will survive, they are much more likely to choose quality over quantity in their family strategy. The

Figure 8.2(a): Child Mortality and Total Fertility Rates in 2005

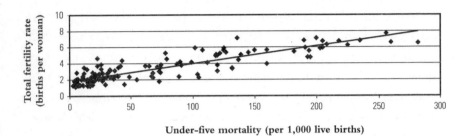

Under-five mortality (per 1,000 live births)

Source: Data from World Bank (2007)

scatter plot of 150 countries in Figure 8.2(a) shows that lower rates of under-five mortality are associated with lower rates of total fertility. The scatter plot in Figure 8.2(b) shows that lower under-five mortality is associated with a lower overall rate of population growth, suggesting that the decline in mortality is more than offset by an accompanying decline in fertility. Correlation does not prove causation, but ample experience, and more sophisticated statistical testing, does. By saving children's lives, and reaping the benefits in lower fertility rates, societies not only save their children but also help to stabilize their populations at the same time.

Figure 8.2(b): Population Growth and
Child Mortality Rates in 2005

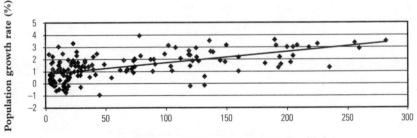

Under-five mortality rate (per 1,000 live births)

Source: Data from World Bank (2007)

Education of Girls

Girls' education has time and again been shown to be one of the decisive entry points into the demographic transition. Girls' education has multiple effects, all leading in the same direction: lower fertility (see Figure 8.3, which shows lower TFR in countries with higher girls' enrollment rates). There is the most direct effect: girls in school, notably in secondary school, are likely to remain unmarried until a later age and, therefore, are likely to begin child rearing much later than girls without schooling. Of course, the content of education matters as well. Girls can and should be educated about sexual and reproductive health, and about the options for contraception. They can learn to analyze the quality/quantity tradeoff in the size of families and thereby overcome preexisting cultural biases more easily. This is critical, since the cultural assumptions may have developed under a set of demographic conditions (for example, very high child mortality rates) that are no longer applicable. Girls' education will empower them as young women to negotiate more effectively with their spouses, including on the issue of family size. Last, and perhaps most important for the long term, education empowers women in the labor market, raising the value of their time by imparting labor-market skills. The more skilled the mother, the higher her value will be in the labor market

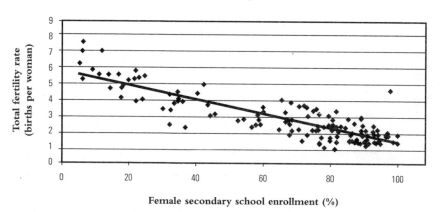

*Figure 8.3: Female Secondary School Enrollment
and Total Fertility Rates in 2005*

Source: Data from World Bank (2007)
Note: Where 2005 data not available, most recent available year is used

and the higher the opportunity cost will be (or foregone market earnings) of the time devoted to child rearing. Women with a high market value, and thus a high opportunity cost of time spent in child rearing, on average choose to have fewer children.

There is very likely to be another more subtle effect. Female education will also raise the future market earnings of daughters. This, in turn, will reduce the preference for sons, which often prevails in low-income settings. When a household is aiming for three sons, it will need to have six children on average, half girls and half boys. If the household decides instead that it wants three children of *any* gender mix, it can reduce fertility by half and still achieve its objective. As son preference diminishes, therefore, the overall fertility rate will fall as well.

Empowerment of Women

Empowerment of women through legal protection (for example, against violence), property rights (land and inheritance), microfinance (lending for small businesses) and in the labor market (nondiscrimination) serves double duty. When women are empowered, they have greater opportunities in the labor market. This leads them to shift from quantity to quality in child rearing because of the much higher opportunity cost of the mother's time. Husbands are also much more likely to agree to fewer children when their wives are money earners in the labor market. This kind of empowerment is also likely to strengthen the mother's bargaining power vis-à-vis the husband in case of a difference of opinion between the spouses.

Access to Reproductive Health Services

Even when households would prefer to reduce fertility, they need reproductive health services, including family planning and contraception, in order to turn aspirations into reality. Yet in large parts of Africa and other very poor regions, health services do not reach the households. Families cannot afford contraception at the prices that are charged, and they lack access to clinics where the contraceptive services would be obtained. Social marketing schemes, in which poor households are granted access to contraception at subsidized prices, may work in some poor settings, but they often exclude the poorest of the poor, who have no money, even when the subsidized prices are quite low. Experience has shown, moreover, that while a clinic in a village can make a huge difference, additional door-to-door outreach to households by trained community health workers can be decisive. Many women in poor societies are not empowered enough within their communities to travel to public clinics to seek health care. When outreach health workers come to them, however, they may be able to make critical choices within the privacy of their own households.

Green Revolution

A boost in farm productivity has two effects, one self-evident and the second a bit more subtle. The direct effect is to raise the value of the farmer's time (in most cases in Africa the farmer is the mother). The higher value of the mother's time in turn induces the household to shift to fewer children and higher investment per child, along the quality/quantity tradeoff. The second effect is to raise the economic benefits of keeping children in school for additional years. When farmer communities are working with improved technologies, they are more likely to benefit from extra schooling. Thus, when a community is introduced to Green Revolution technology, it benefits the community to keep the children in school for more education. Yet this extra schooling is costly for the parents, so they in turn will choose to have fewer children and to provide more education for each child. Once again, the household moves toward quality and away from quantity. India's Green Revolution was a spur to reduced fertility rates in the districts covered by the high-yield technologies. The same can and should happen in Africa.

Urbanization

One common observation is that urban households tend to have fewer children than rural households, holding constant other socioeconomic characteristics of the households. Children are economic assets in rural areas because they help with the farm chores from an early age. In the cities, however, children are generally a much greater net cost, with little compensating contribution to home production. While urbanization is not a policy target per se, the trend to urbanization is likely to be a factor in speeding the demographic transition.

Legal Abortion

Even with widespread contraception available, many pregnancies will be accidental and unwanted. Abortions will take place, legally or illegally, as has been found in all parts of the world. The mortal risks to the mother in the case of illegal abortions are vast, and both these risks and costs will lead to many unwanted children being born as well as many women dying in botched abortions. In countries with legal abortion services, households have a lower-risk and lower-cost option, and there is strong evidence that the legalization of abortions reduces a country's TFR significantly, by as much as half a child on average, and also reduces maternal mortality.

Old-Age Security

Government provision of social security for the elderly directly substitutes for one motivation for large families. Even poor countries can gradually provide pensions for the old and can give confidence to today's young generation that such pension coverage will rise over time with economic development.

Public Leadership

Fertility choices reflect not only individual tradeoffs in the marketplace but also community norms as to the "appropriate" behavior of young men and women. The age of marriage, the spacing of children, the appropriateness of choosing sterilization (for example, vasectomy or tubal ligation) as a long-term fertility-control method after the family size is complete, and public attitudes toward women in the workforce are all culturally conditioned. Public leadership by authority figures in favor of voluntary fertility reduction has played an important role in shifting cultural norms (for example, in accepting modern contraceptive use) and has emboldened women in tradition-bound rural areas to seek family planning services. On the other hand, where authority figures such as religious leaders oppose contraception and family planning, the fertility transition can be delayed.

THESE NINE FACTORS AFFECT FERTILITY DECISIONS, and when all of them point in the same direction of reducing the fertility rate, a country can achieve dramatic results of slowing the population growth through voluntary means in just a few years. Moreover, there are successes in all parts of the world and in all cultures and religions. The common claim, for example, that fertility declines will not occur in the Islamic world is belied by the experience in Iran after the 1979 Iranian revolution (Figure 8.4). In the 1970s, Iran began introducing family planning ideas and services, though with very low usage. Immediately after the Iranian revolution, the new ruling religious authorities

Figure 8.4: Iran's Demographic Transition

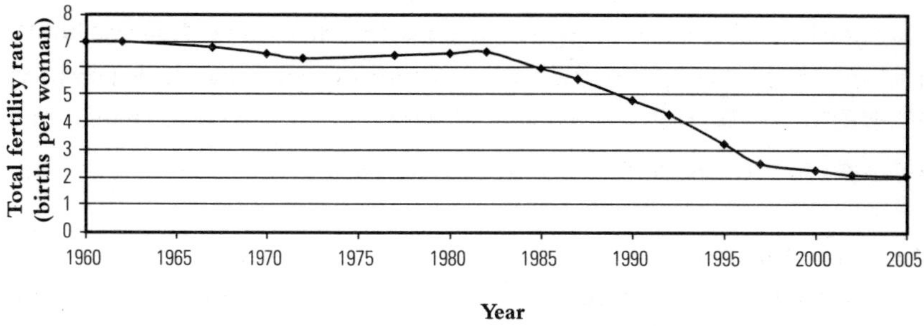

Total fertility rate (births per woman)

8
7
6
5
4
3
2
1
0

1960   1965   1970   1975   1980   1985   1990   1995   2000   2005

Year

Source: Data from World Bank (2007)

embarked on a short-lived pronatalist position. This was exacerbated by the disastrous and bloody Iran-Iraq War, which further disrupted family planning and decreased the motivation to reduce fertility. The result was a slight increase in fertility rates until the mid-1980s. The TFR averaged 6.6 during 1980–85. Yet soon afterward, the attitude of the political and religious leadership reverted to family planning, and this time with far more energy and cultural legitimacy than before. The TFR actually plummeted from 6.6 in 1980–85 to an astounding 2.1 by 2000–05. Many factors played a role, including increased access to family planning services, a change in public attitudes, and urbanization. One of the major factors, interestingly, was the rising rate of girls' school enrollment. It seems that religiously conservative fathers were more likely to send their daughters to school after the revolution than before. With higher female enrollment and literacy came later marriages and a steep reduction in desired family size. It is ironic that the Bush administration's attitudes toward family planning are in many ways more fundamentalist than Iran's.

AFRICA'S PROSPECTS

Africa's fertility decline lags behind the rest of the world. The progress is real, but far too slow. Africa's TFR during 2000–05 averaged around 5, the highest of any region in the world. In the poorest countries of Africa, the fertility rates are even higher, often well above 6.0, with cases such as Chad, 6.5; Mali, 6.7;

Burkina Faso, 6.4; Sierra Leone, 6.5; and Niger, 7.5. These countries have every risk factor imaginable: very high child mortality rates, a high proportion of the population in rural areas, largely illiterate populations, lagging women's rights, very low agricultural productivity and hence low market value of a mother's time, low girls' attendance at school (and even when recorded enrollments are rising, actual attendance can remain extremely low), little or no access to formal health systems and contraception, and no social safety net.

In addition to these standard factors, there are other more subtle barriers that have contributed to the lag in Africa's demographic transition. First, since Africa has by far the highest disease burden in the world and the highest rates of mortality of infants and young children, the cultural norms for large families—to offset these extraordinary mortality rates—have been very powerful. African culture, traditionally, has been strongly pronatal, with nearly all girls getting married, onset of marriage and childbearing at a very young age, strong preference for sons leading to even larger demand for children, and religious rites of various sorts emphasizing the importance of large families and surviving sons (for example, to perform funerary rites). Second, during much of the twentieth century—though no longer—there was ample extra land to expand the number of farms in order to absorb burgeoning rural populations. Only in the past generation have farm sizes been dangerously squeezed by the rising rural population. Cultural practices of extended families, with the common fostering of children outside of their parental households, and communal land ownership, broke the direct link between the number of children and the family's cost of child rearing. The community (or extended family), rather than the nuclear household, bore the brunt of the added population, including in the allocation of land. And the common practice of polygamy in some regions further breaks the responsibility of the biological father for the financial costs of child rearing, which are assumed to be borne by the biological mother. The diminished responsibility for the father means he has less incentive to limit fertility, and the fact that these are often male-dominated societies means that the father may have the last word. Polygamy may also raise the bride price for girls (the amount the groom's family pays the bride's family), thereby leading to an indirect incentive for parents to increase their "supply" of marriageable girls.

Africa's special conditions also include the strong role of religious leaders from many religious affiliations that discourage public discussion of contraception and family planning, and in some cases oppose their use outright.

Public discussions about sexuality have traditionally been taboo. Abortion is illegal throughout most of sub-Saharan Africa. Then, to top off the problems, the structural adjustment era of the IMF and World Bank, during the period from 1980 to around 2000, led to a cutback on public health initiatives, including family planning. The Washington-imposed policies of that era led to the dismantling of public health services and the imposition of user fees at public health facilities, at a time when the poorest countries needed greatly improved access to public health services.

Yet now all of this can and should change quickly. African leaders are recognizing that population policies are needed. Structural adjustment cutbacks in the health sector are being reversed, and public health is being scaled up. Many young African women are seeking contraception if they can obtain it inexpensively and discreetly. On just about every cultural, political, and economic level, the pendulum is now swinging toward a chance for rapid voluntary fertility reduction, if Africa grabs the opportunity and the world helps it to do so. Nonetheless, African countries will need an integrated strategy backed by global support to bring down the fertility rates in impoverished rural areas, since there are so many risk factors conducive to a prolongation of high rates.

There are three key changes now under way. First, the topics of sexuality and fertility are no longer taboo in the age of AIDS. Issues of family formation, sexual activity, polygamy, and access to contraception have become the fare of daily discussion. With rising population pressures, a squeeze on farm sizes, and increasing rates of urbanization, African leaders are poised to take up the population challenge in ways they've ducked in the past. Because Africa's continuing higher fertility rates are now sorely the exception on a global basis, Africa's leaders have a much clearer sense of the continent's unfortunate "exceptional" situation, and they are also aware of the possibility for rapid and voluntary reductions in fertility in view of the successes achieved elsewhere in the developing world. They are also painfully aware that several generations of rapid population growth have filled the countryside and now pose dangerous threats to farm sizes and environmental sustainability.

Second, for the first time in a generation, there is the movement and confidence to launch comprehensive development strategies that embrace the crosscutting and synergistic challenges of disease control, family planning and reproductive health services, girls' education, and farm productivity. The Millennium Development Goals foster precisely the kind of comprehensive approach that is so vital for success in voluntary fertility reduction. Model approaches such as the Millennium Villages, described in Chapter 10, will demonstrate the feasibility of implementing such packages of interventions, and the fertility trends within the Millennium Villages will likely provide a demonstration of the possibility of the rapid and voluntary reduction of fertility rates in rural Africa. Even in the first year of operation, many of the Millennium Villages experienced a dramatic increase in the use of modern contraception, once the contraceptives became widely available within the village.

Third, we have learned many important specific lessons for program implementation, which should help speed the effort in Africa. One of the most important is the need for outreach to women by community health workers in circumstances where cultural norms make it difficult for women to attend family planning clinics. John C. Caldwell and Pat Caldwell stress the importance of privacy to women's use of contraception in Africa. Community health worker visits to households would seem to be crucial under those circumstances. Yet ironically, donor cutbacks in funding have forced the curtailment of such programs just as their efficacy was being established. Caldwell and Caldwell also emphasize the need for family planning programs to cater to the needs of adolescents as well as to married households. Indeed, these great demographers provide a list of seven requirements to enable family planning programs to accelerate the decline in fertility:

- Heads of state should support the programs.

- International aid should be maintained or increased.

- Family planning service-delivery points should be densely located.

- A range of alternatives should be provided.

- Contraceptives should be available without prescription (to protect privacy).

- Additional mechanisms should meet the needs of adolescents, men, and unmarried people of either sex.

- Abortion should be legalized.

Several African countries, some with a TFR of around 6 today, are likely to adopt bold fertility objectives, such as a reduction of the TFR to 3 or below

Figure 4.3: Schematic Diagram of Possible Carbon Capture and Storage (CSS) Systems

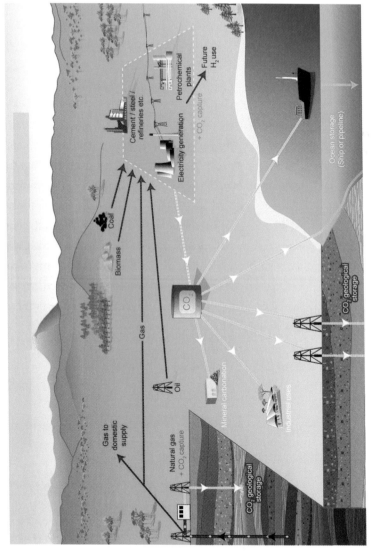

Source: IPCC (2005)

Figure 5.1: Drylands and Conflict

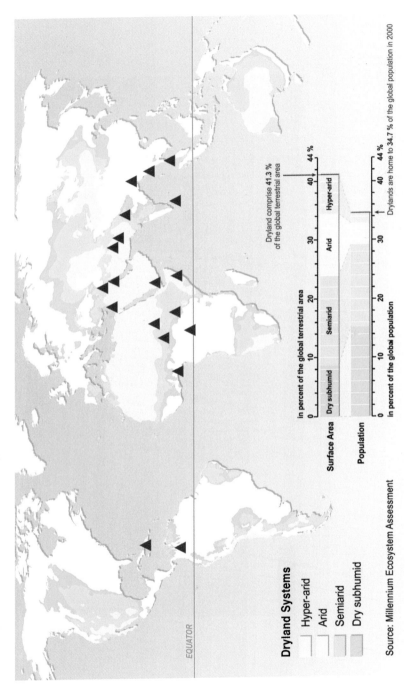

Dryland comprise 41.3 % of the global terrestrial area

in percent of the global terrestrial area

0	10	20	30	40	44 %

Surface Area | Dry subhumid | Semiarid | Arid | Hyper-arid

Drylands are home to 34.7 % of the global population in 2000

in percent of the global population

0	10	20	30	40	44 %

Population

Dryland Systems

Hyper-arid
Arid
Semiarid
Dry subhumid

EQUATOR

Source: Millennium Ecosystem Assessment

Drylands include all terrestrial regions where the production of crops, forage, wood, and other ecosystem services are limited by water. Formally, the definition encompasses all lands where the climate is classified as dry sub-humid, semiarid, arid, or hyper-arid. This classification is based on aridity index values[†].

Notes: The map is based on data from UNEP Geo Data Portal (http://geodata.grid.unep.ch/). Global area based on Digital Chart of the World data (147,573,196.6 square km); data presented in the graph are from the MA core database for the year 2000.

▲ Major episodes of political violence ongoing in 2007 involving the systematic use of lethal violence and terror by organized groups and/or states that substantially affect the society or societies that directly experience the armed conflict (resulting in at least five hundred directly related fatalities, substantial destruction of infrastructure, and population displacements). Episodes may involve states, a state and non-state group, or non-state groups only, including interstate and independence war, ethnic and revolutionary (civil) war, inter-communal warfare, genocide, and communal massacres. Each episode is rated on a ten-point scale according to its total impact on the society or societies that are directly affected by the violence. (Marshall, 2007)

[†]The long-term of the ratio of an area's mean annual precipitation to its mean annual potential evapotranspiration is the aridity index (AI).

Figure 6.3(a): Biomass Distribution for High-Trophic Level Fishes in the North Atlantic in 1900

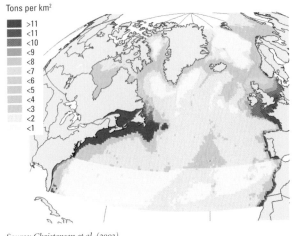

Source: Christensen et al. (2003)

Figure 6.3(b): Biomass Distribution for High-Trophic Level Fishes in the North Atlantic in 1999

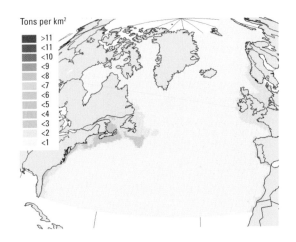

Source: Christensen et al. (2003)

Figure 6.4: Ecosystem Devastation in the Atlantic Ocean

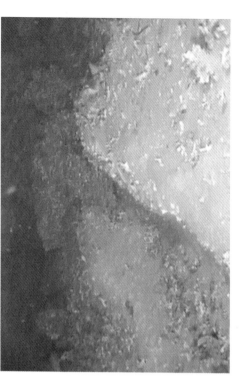

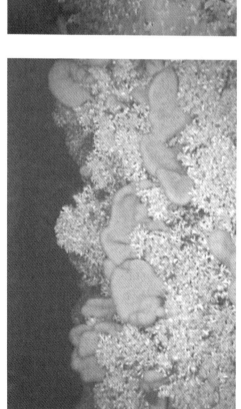

Sea Change: the photograph on the right shows the devastation wrought by trawlers on ancient corals (left, before fishing) in the northeast Atlantic Ocean.

Source: Nature *(2002)*

Figure 8.1: Total Fertility Rates in 2005

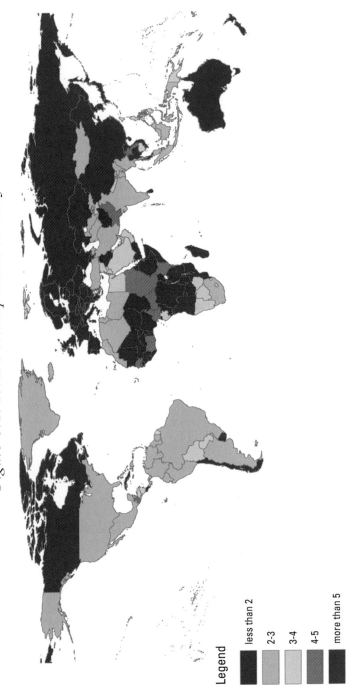

Legend

less than 2

2-3

3-4

4-5

more than 5

Note: Where 2005 data is not available, most recent available data is used.

Source: Data from World Bank (2007)

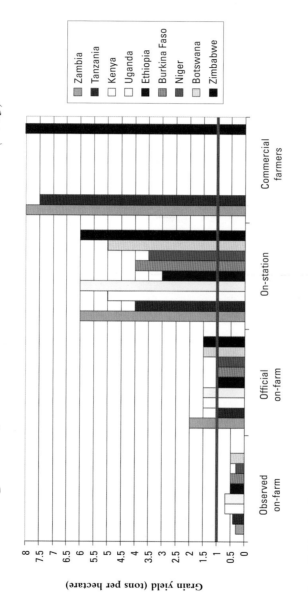

Figure 10.4: Grain Yields in Selected Countries (2003)

Source: Rockstrom (2003)

Figure 10.6: Millennium Villages

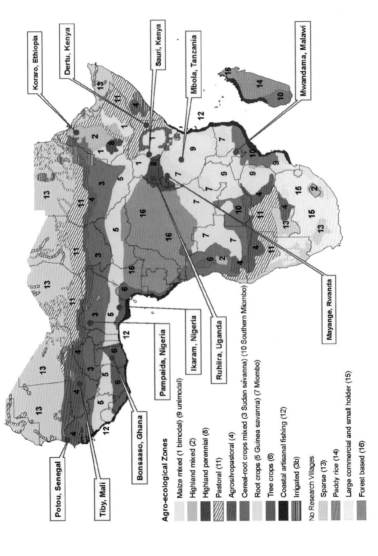

Koraro, Ethiopia

Dertu, Kenya

Sauri, Kenya

Mbola, Tanzania

Mwandama, Malawi

Pampaida, Nigeria

Ikaram, Nigeria

Ruhiira, Uganda

Mayange, Rwanda

Bonsaaso, Ghana

Potou, Senegal

Tiby, Mali

Agro-ecological Zones

Maize mixed (1 bimodal) (9 unimodal)

Highland mixed (2)

Highland perennial (8)

Pastoral (11)

Agrosilvopastoral (4)

Cereal-root crops mixed (3 Sudan savanna) (10 Southern Miombo)

Root crops (5 Guinea savanna) (7 Miombo)

Tree crops (6)

Coastal artisanal fishing (12)

Irrigated (3b)

No Research Villages:

Sparse (13)

Paddy rice (14)

Large commercial and small holder (15)

Forest based (16)

Source: Pedro Sanchez & Rafael Flor
Adapted from Dixon et al. 2001. Farming Systems and Poverty. FAO

during 2015–20. Let's look at what such a bold policy would accomplish when combined with an equally bold MDG-based effort to reduce infant and child mortality rates.

How will Africa's population, on balance, evolve if both mortality and fertility rates are sharply reduced within the context of a bold development program? To be specific, let us suppose that the African countries succeed in reducing the child mortality rate by two thirds as of 2015 compared with the 1990 baseline, as called for by the MDGs. Specifically, instead of a business-as-usual (BAU) gradual decline of under-five mortality from 167 per 1,000 in 2005 to 141 per 1,000 in 2015, let us assume an accelerated decline to 63 per 1,000 in 2015, as shown in Figure 8.5. We then assume (for purposes of illustration rather than realism), that the under-five rate remains level till 2050, when the business-as-usual gradual decline of mortality rate would finally catch up with the mortality rate of the accelerated track. We also assume that the TFR will decline sharply as well, from the current average of 5.5 in 2005 to 2.9 in 2015. Again, for purposes of specificity rather than forecast, we then assume that the TFR remains constant at the lower level till around 2040, when the BAU path would actually reduce the TFR still further. After 2040, we then follow the BAU path. The alternative paths for the TFR are shown in Figure 8.6.

Let us assume, as I believe to be the case, that the rapid declines in both mortality and fertility can be achieved with bold policies. The question for us

Figure 8.5: Projected Child Mortality Rates in
Sub-Saharan Africa from 2005 to 2050

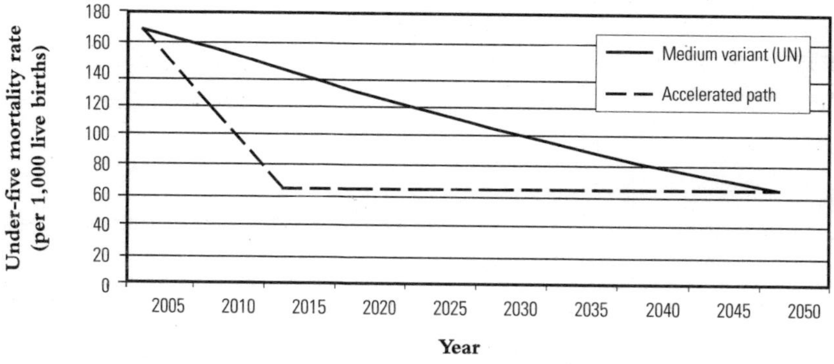

Source: Data from UN Population Division (2007) and author's calculations

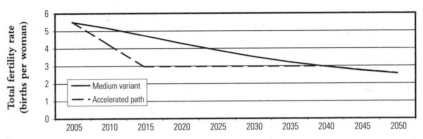

Figure 8.6: Projected Total Fertility Rates in
Sub-Saharan Africa from 2005 to 2050

Source: Data from UN Population Division (2007) and author's calculations

here is the net balance of results: will population growth rise or fall when a steep reduction in child mortality is combined with a rapid decline in the fertility rate? The effect of the fertility decline is greater in the sense that Africa's population at midcentury will be lower if Africa puts in place a joint program of mortality and fertility reduction, in comparison with a continuation on the BAU path (Figure 8.7). The bold intervention program would reduce Africa's population by roughly 300 million people as of 2050 compared with the BAU trajectory. Africa's population still increases significantly, even with the rapid TFR decline, because population momentum in Africa is enormous, but by much less than it would if the BAU trajectory remained in place. Our finding is broadly similar to the comparison between the UN Population Division's low-fertility versus medium-fertility scenario, where the low-fertility projection implies a 2050 population that is 280 million lower than in the medium forecast.

Note that if Africa were to introduce a child-survival program alone, without the accelerating decline in the TFR, the population increase would be faster than the BAU path. To achieve a reduction of population, it is necessary to combine fertility decline and mortality decline. Fortunately, the evidence is overwhelming that mortality decline is a major success factor for achieving the needed fertility decline.

The bottom line is clear: it is possible to save children's lives and to reduce Africa's overall population at the same time. *Indeed, saving children's lives is a precondition for success in voluntary fertility reduction!* We can therefore go boldly forward in disease control and improved food production without fear of being overtaken by Malthusian disaster if the African governments and

Figure 8.7: Projected African Population from 2005 to 2050

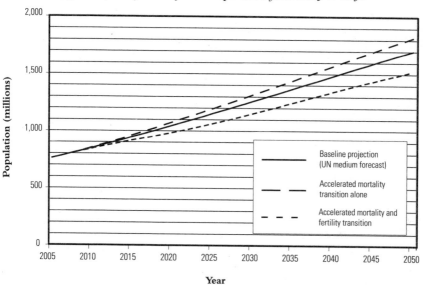

Source: Data from UN Population Division (2007) and author's calculations

their development partners follow through on their commitments to family planning.

THE BUSH ADMINISTRATION'S WAR ON FAMILY PLANNING

Such commitments, alas, are bigger ifs today than they should be. U.S. financial support for family planning services in low-income countries has been hamstrung in the past twenty-five years by the U.S. religious right, which has stymied overall funding for planning services, slashed support for the UN Population Fund, and instituted a so-called gag rule against support for any organizations that receive funding from any other source for legal abortion or for counseling on the option of abortion (even where legal). In Figure 8.8 we see that in constant dollars, correcting for inflation, the level of population assistance spending has, despite ups and downs, remained the same since 1970. Given the 2.5-fold increase in the population of the least developed countries, and the persistence of very high fertility rates in those countries,

Figure 8.8: U.S. Official Development Assistance
for Population Programs

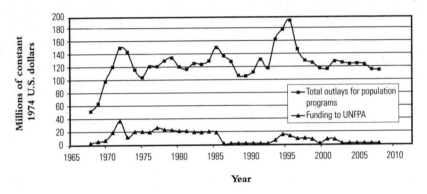

Source: Data from Population Action International (2007)

the freeze on overall aid represents a sharp cut on a per capita basis for the populations most in need. Total population assistance is currently about $450 million ($120 million in 1974 dollars), which represents around 60 cents per person in the least developed countries. Of course, only part of the 60 cents is available for local services and commodities in any event, since much is absorbed in overhead. In its 2008 budget request, the Bush administration called for a 25 percent cut in this budget line.

The U.S. government's assault on the UN Population Fund (UNFPA) has been particularly vindictive, as is also evident in Figure 8.8. It began with assaults during the Reagan and Bush Sr. presidencies and has continued with the Bush Jr. presidency, after a slight recovery during the Clinton years. The current Bush administration wrongly accused UNFPA of aiding China in coercive measures and cut off all U.S. funding for UNFPA. The U.S. State Department investigated and in 2002 recommended that funding be restored, but it did not succeed in overturning a White House political move. Narrow politics prevailed over America's foreign policy interests.

U.S. policy neglect is especially surprising in view of the our concerns over the threats of failed states. The youth bulge of high-fertility countries—measured as the share of youth (aged fifteen to twenty-four) in the entire adult population (aged fifteen and above)—should be a matter of national concern. The evidence, summarized in powerful reports by Population Action International (PAI) and by the demographer Henrik Urdal, is that a *youth bulge significantly raises the likelihood of civil conflict*, presumably by raising the ratio of those who would engage in violence relative to those who would mediate disputes. Most directly, unemployed young men become prime fodder for militias, raiding parties, terrorist groups, and armies. In PAI's analysis, three kinds of demographic stressors are related to the likelihood of civil conflict: the youth bulge, the shortage of arable land per capita, and the rapid growth of urban areas. All, of course, are related to the persistence of high total fertility rates.

Urdal summarizes the results of his own research on civil unrest as follows:

> The results of my internal armed models suggest that the presence of youth bulges increases the risk of conflict outbreak significantly. The statistical relationship holds even when controlling for a number of other factors—such as the level of development, democracy, and conflict history—and is also robust to a variety of technical specifications. For each percentage point increase of youth in the adult population, the risk of conflict increases by more than 4 percent. When youth make up more than 35 percent of the adult population, which they do in many developing countries, the risk of armed conflict is 150 percent higher than in countries with an age structure similar to most developed countries.

He also notes that microdata, based on interviews of young soldiers, validates the macro results: "A recent study based on interviews with young soldiers presents strong micro-level support for the expectation that poverty, a lack of schooling, and low alternative income opportunities are important reasons for joining a rebel group."

It is illustrative to compare the youth share in a number of countries. In Afghanistan, youth make up 37 percent of the population. In Iraq and Somalia, 34 percent, and in Pakistan, 35 percent. In the UN's grouping of more developed (high-income) countries, including mainly the United States, Western Europe, and Japan, the youth cohort is a mere 16 percent of the adult population.

Recent undermining of family planning efforts in the developing world by the United States is all the more ironic given U.S. leadership in mobilizing aid for family planning early on, beginning in the early 1960s. Led by USAID, the Ford Foundation and the Population Council, family planning at the national level led to tremendous successes in countries such as Brazil and

Bangladesh, which had drastic fertility reductions within one generation. Brazil, for example, saw its TFR go from 6 births per woman in 1960–65 to 2.5 in 1990–95. Despite desperate rural poverty, Bangladesh achieved similar results, with its TFR declining from roughly 7 in 1970 to 3.4 in 1993. Throughout Asia and Latin America, comprehensive family planning programs have led to decisive reductions in TFR and slowing of population growth rates, and have done so in Christian, Muslim, Buddhist, and other religious and cultural settings. Crucially, these changes in fertility were *voluntary*—they were achieved without compromising freedom of choice.

IS A BABY BUST A RISK FOR THE RICH WORLD?

With all of the urgency of reducing the fertility rates in the poorest countries before we add another 2.5 billion more people to the planet by midcentury, it is perhaps paradoxical to hear calls for pronatalist policies in the rich world. With fertility rates below replacement levels, there is some prospect for a modest decline of populations in the rich countries, especially in Europe and Japan. In the United States, the TFR remains at the replacement level rather than below, and in-migration remains very high, so the U.S. population is primed to continue to grow even as many European countries and Japan decline in population. On the UN's medium forecast, Europe's population (including both Western and Eastern Europe as well as Russia, Ukraine, and Moldova, of the former Soviet Union) is set to decline from around 731 million to 664 million in 2050. It's true that if extrapolated for the long term, below-replacement fertility rates can be startling. If Italy holds its current TFR of 1.3 till 2300, the UN calculates that the population would decline from 58 million to 600,000! It might not be all bad: an estate and vineyard for all. But it's also very unlikely to happen in that way.

The most widespread concern is that the social security systems of the rich world will go bust as more retirees live longer and have fewer and fewer workers to support them. There is some truth to the message. The ratio of those older than sixty-five to those aged fifteen to sixty-five, called the old-age dependency ratio, will indeed take a big surge in the high-income world, as shown in Figure 8.9. The ratio basically doubles from around 23 percent to

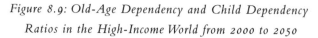

Figure 8.9: Old-Age Dependency and Child Dependency
Ratios in the High-Income World from 2000 to 2050

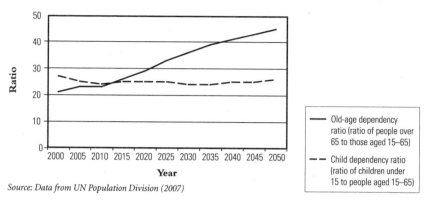

Source: Data from UN Population Division (2007)

around 46 percent, while the child dependency ratio (children under fifteen relative to the fifteen-to-sixty-five cohort) declines slightly.

It is true that these changes will impose stresses on pension systems, but it is simply not true that the costs are likely to be large. First, with slower population growth or even outright decline, society will not need to invest in major infrastructure (roads, power, and the like) merely to keep up with population growth. This marks an enormous social saving. Second, it is likely that

Figure 8.10: Median Age of High-Income Countries and
Least Developed Countries from 2000 to 2050

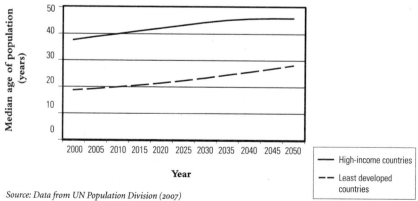

Source: Data from UN Population Division (2007)

retirement ages will rise, probably with more flexible work times. We are, mercifully, not only living longer but living better, with more healthy life years. If sixty is the new forty-five, in terms of stamina and productivity, then who knows what seventy-five will bring in a few decades? Retirement ages will likely rise gradually by a few years. Of course, continued improvements in overall economic productivity may mean that we can work less in total and capture some of the advances in productivity through greater leisure time. There is one point on which we can be confident: we will be older in the future (Figure 8.10). The median age of the rich world is projected to rise from thirty-eight in 2005 to forty-six in 2050, and in the least developed countries from nineteen to twenty-eight in the medium-fertility forecast. In the low-fertility variant, the median age rises from nineteen to thirty-one. Older and wiser has a nice ring to it. Let us hope.

PART FOUR

Prosperity for All

Chapter 9

The Strategy of Economic Development

THE TWENTY-FIRST CENTURY CAN BE a century of shared prosperity, a great convergence, as we termed it earlier. The global economy can be marked by a narrowing of the income gap between rich and poor countries, not because of a decline in incomes in the richer societies but because of a rapid catch-up by the poor. Shared prosperity would not only mean the end of massive and unnecessary suffering among those who are now trapped in extreme poverty but would also mean a safer and more democratic world as well, with rising incomes underpinning political stability and increasingly open societies. Moreover, resentment along class and ethnic lines would diminish if all income groups and cultures had the chance to share in a growing global economy. It is when one region or group is excluded that hatred and unrest are likely to follow.

The fundamental reason for believing that prosperity can spread to all corners of the world is that the very science and technology that underpin prosperity in the rich world are potentially available to the rest of the world as well. If the rich countries are rich because they have adopted these improved technologies—power generation, medicine, transport, construction, and much more—the same improved technologies can also be adopted in today's impoverished countries. As we noted earlier, technology has the wonderful property of being nonrival; each person, business, or country can adopt the technology without limiting the ability of others to adopt the technology as well. Unlike a given number of barrels of oil, which are available either for you or for me, but not both, the fruits of scientific advancement such as the human genome or the Internet are available for any and all, without the need to ration the knowledge. Moreover, for many advanced technologies—the Internet, computer operating systems, vaccinations, insecticide-treated bed nets, mobile phones—the benefits are greater the more that others are using the technology. Such technologies are often called network technologies, and the benefits of mass use are called network externalities. Fittingly, we live in a networked age, where the advent of such technologies has soared.

Note that the focus on technological improvements is starkly different from the failed Marxist notion that the rich are rich because they successfully exploit the poor. If the rich get rich only because the poor get exploited, then world income would be roughly constant, and all of the economic action would be about the distribution of a given level of economic output. That, indeed, is what Marx had in mind. But world output is not constant, precisely because technological improvements allow the world to get a lot more economic value out of a given level of inputs. We've already seen how the world average income per person rose from around $650 in 1820 to around $6,000 in 1998, an increase of nine times.

TAPPING INTO ADVANCED TECHNOLOGY

Even though the knowledge that underpins prosperity is potentially available to all, not all parts of the world are rich—indeed, far from it. While the world's average per capita income has increased by roughly ten times since 1820, some parts of the world have had much larger increases than ten times, and others much smaller. The actual increase in per capita income between 1820 and 1998, stated as a multiple of the 1820 level, is shown for the major regions of the world in Table 9.1.

One of the core challenges of the science of economic development is to understand these regional differences. Another is to understand how to unlock faster economic growth in the laggard regions. Why did Africa's income per person rise by a mere 3.5 times between 1820 and 1998 while the United States enjoyed a twenty-two-fold increase? Can Africa now narrow the vast gap in per capita income with the high-income countries through faster economic development? What about other laggard regions?

There are four hurdles that an economy must surmount in order to mobilize a new technology. By understanding these hurdles, we can understand many of the mysteries of economic development, including the highly varying performance of different regions. Indeed, by recognizing and respond-

Table 9.1: Increase in per Capita Incomes by Region from 1820 to 1998

REGION	INCREASE IN INCOME (MULTIPLICATION FACTOR)
World	9*
Africa	3.5
Asia	3
China	6
India	4
Eastern Europe	9
Former USSR	7
Latin America and Caribbean	8.5
Middle East	9
Western Europe	16
United States	22

Source: Calculated using data from Maddison (2001) and World Bank (2007)
*Increase was eleven times between 1820 and 2006.

ing to the four hurdles, governments can adopt strategies to accelerate their nations' economic growth and the ability to tap into global advances in technology.

Saving and Investment

Most new technologies are embodied in specific kinds of machinery (such as a new computer or mobile phone) or in specific skills (such as medical training). In other words, even when the ideas behind a technology are available for the whole world, the use of the technology requires investment in physical capital (machines) and human capital (skills). Investment, in turn, requires savings. In order to invest in a machine or in training for new skills, some part of current income must be set aside to pay for the capital good rather than spent on current consumption. Every dollar of investment must be financed by a dollar of savings. If the economy is too poor to save, for example, it may be impossible to finance the uptake of the technology.

Exports and Imports

Most of the time, the new technology is imported from abroad, where it was first developed. Suppose that the Brazilian government or a private Brazilian company wants to order a capital good made in the United States. It must have the dollars to pay for the import. Those dollars are earned by Brazilian exports. Thus, for a country to be able to import technologies from abroad, it must be a successful exporter of products as well. If a country can't develop export markets, it will find itself cut off from the advance of technologies as well.

Public and Private Capital

Even when technologies are invented by the private sector, the use of new technologies usually depends on public-sector investments as well. For example, cars require roads, electrical machinery requires a reliable power grid, and imported medicines in the poorest countries require public-sector hospitals and clinics. If the government is not holding up its end of the deal by making the needed public investments, then the private sector will not be able to make profitable private investments in new technologies. Thus, a failed state, or a bankrupt government that can't pay for public investments, or a wildly corrupt government, will result in a technologically stagnant private sector as well.

Adaptation to Local Ecology

Many technologies work right out of the box, irrespective of the local physical environment. Many, however, require significant adaptation to local biophysical conditions. Agronomic practices, public health methodologies, construction methods and materials, and infrastructure design all must adapt international practices to local conditions. That translation often requires significant local investments, most notably when the new technologies have arisen in one ecological zone (for example, the temperate zone of the United States, Europe, or Japan) and must be adapted for another (for example, the tropics). A poor country, alas, may not be able to muster the local investments to adapt international technologies to local needs.

ECONOMIC DEVELOPMENT, therefore, requires that each economy overcome four hurdles: there must be adequate domestic savings, a competitive export sector that can earn the foreign exchange needed to pay for imported technology, a financially strong government that can finance needed infrastructure (roads, power, and clinics) to complement private-sector investment, and the ability to adapt international technologies to local ecological conditions and needs. Countries can be trapped at a low level of economic development because they lack adequate domestic saving, are not competitive in exports, cannot finance public-sector investments, or lack the ability to adapt international technologies to local needs.

CLIMBING THE DEVELOPMENT LADDER

To see how economic growth can actually be achieved, it is useful to trace the progression of economic development through four basic stages, each stage representing a higher level of income and development than the preceding one. The progression is from a subsistence economy, to a commercial economy, to an emerging-market economy, to a technology-based economy. Each stage represents a higher level of well-being and a higher level of capital per person.

Consider first a *subsistence economy,* characterized by low agricultural productivity, poor coverage of public services and infrastructure, and a small amount of exports, all concentrated in a narrow range of primary agricultural commodities (for example, horticulture, raw cotton and yarns, and so forth). In such an economy, living standards are near subsistence, even below. There is little margin for saving, since income must be used for basic needs. Without private saving there is little or no private investment. There is also very little opportunity for government to collect taxes, since the population is so poor. As a result, there is little public investment. Infrastructure is lacking. There are few roads, an inadequate power grid (especially in rural areas), and limited access to safe drinking water and sanitation. As explained in previous chapters, one of the few things that grows is the human population, so each succeeding generation actually has less farmland per person than the preceding generation. Average income per person is on the order of $300 per year.

Many economies remain stuck in the poverty trap of subsistence farming, while others experience economic development. In the places that break out of poverty, it may be that local agronomic conditions are sufficiently favorable that even poor farm families are able to save for the future, and governments are able to mobilize tax revenues for public investments. Perhaps a technological breakthrough—a Green Revolution in agriculture—raises farm yields to the point where smallholders can save and accumulate capital. It may be that the economy has access to other resources—oil earnings, foreign aid, tourism—that enable it to save and invest beyond the stage of subsistence farming. It may be that the economy is proximate enough to a richer neighbor that the neighbor's infrastructure and market demand can provide the jobs and income needed for growth.

With sufficient saving and investment, the government builds roads, a power grid, an effective port, and a basic education and health system. The private sector achieves increased productivity and can invest in export-oriented activities. Agricultural exports include cash crops (spices, beverages, meat products, fibers). Manufacturing exports might include processed agricultural commodities (cotton-based fabrics, confectionaries, ethanol) as well as labor-intensive assembly operations (apparel, shoes and other leather goods, electronics assembly). Typically, the export sectors benefit from various kinds of imported technologies (machinery, technical know-how, process improvements).

As a result of economic growth, the economy becomes a *commercial economy* in which both rural and urban households are part of the monetary economy. Both rural and urban areas save and invest. Export earnings rise, and the range of exports also increases beyond a few primary commodities. Population growth rates begin to decline as families adopt birth-control methods. Educational standards rise as government services in education are expanded and as families seek higher educational attainment. Literacy among the young becomes nearly universal. Average annual income levels are on the order of $1,000 per person.

With sufficient growth in exports and domestic saving, the commercial economy becomes an *emerging-market economy,* characterized by the nearly complete coverage of basic infrastructure (roads, power, telecoms, ports), basic education (universal literacy and primary education), basic health services, safe drinking water, and sanitation. The economy by now is an exporter of both manufactures and services. Manufacturing exports include industrial products (automobile components, semiconductor products, consumer appliances), information-based services (business process operations, software, business consulting), and perhaps construction services as well. Foreign investment plays a growing role in economic development. Foreign investors bring not only capital but also know-how, technology, and linkages to global production and distribution systems. Major government responsibilities include the extension of secondary education and vocational training, improvements in port services (for example, paperless customs clearance, efficient containerization), the promotion of the financial sector (for example, through a sound regulatory system), and various environmental investments to stop or reverse environmental losses that accompanied the early stages of economic development. Average annual incomes have reached $4,000 per person.

By the time an economy has become a middle-income emerging market, there is an important measure of domestic technological innovation under way. The economy is no longer simply importing technologies from abroad but is also improving them and beginning to export technology-based manufactures and services. Tertiary education reaches perhaps 10 to 20 percent of the university-aged population. National laboratories have started up. Scientists in the country are beginning to be part of global research teams. Foreign enterprises are setting up research and development operations within the country, though initially at a very small scale and often mainly to train locals.

The final major step to becoming a high-income country is the transition to full-fledged science-based innovative activities. A *technology-based economy* is characterized by widespread tertiary education (perhaps 30 percent or more of the university-aged population), extensive public financing of scientific studies (1 percent or more of GNP), extensive private-sector-led research and development (another 1 percent or more of GNP), a sophisticated information-based society (high Internet use, large circulation of daily newspapers, nearly universal use of mobile telephony and universal access to computers in schools). The economy continues to import technologies from abroad, but now foreign exchange is also earned by exporting knowledge and technological advances. Annual income per capita has reached $15,000; it will reliably grow at a slightly faster rate than in the richest countries, so the proportionate gap between the "leaders" and the domestic economy will continue to shrink.

At every step along the growth path—from subsistence to commerce to emerging markets to high-tech—both the public and private sectors have responsibilities. The idea that growth is market based is true, but that is only half of the story. Government action provides the foundations for long-term economic growth by ensuring that key parts of the social and physical infrastructure are in place and working effectively. At a low level of economic development, government responsibilities involve investing in basic infrastructure, especially roads, power, primary schools, clinics, and water and sanitation. At the next stage, the government must concern itself with highways, Internet connectivity, containerization, and intermodal transport (the interface of sea-, air-, and land-based freight). At a still later stage, the government must invest heavily in scientific capacity and higher education.

At all stages of development, the government must also ensure that the basic conditions of a functioning market-based economy are in place. These include a relatively stable monetary unit, a banking system adequately buffered against banking crises, reasonable physical security for persons and property, a rudimentary legal system to enforce contracts and property rights, and a modest level of official corruption that is kept from getting out of hand. Nothing is ever perfect, even in the high-income countries, in these various dimensions of social order and rule of law. Still, outright lawlessness and violence must be eliminated for there to be hope of climbing the development ladder.

HOW GEOGRAPHY CAN AFFECT THE CLIMB UP THE DEVELOPMENT LADDER

Geography helps shape economic development for clear and understandable reasons. Consider a subsistence economy. If the soils are poor, the rains erratic, and the crop varieties very different from those in rich countries (for which advanced technologies are available), then the economy may well remain stuck in extreme poverty. Farmers will not grow enough food to make ends meet, and there will be little surplus available for private saving or for taxation to support public investments. If the country is in the tropics, the advanced technologies that are available from rich temperate-zone countries of Europe, the United States, and Japan are likely to require extensive and costly adaptation to local conditions, with few scientific institutions, if any, to bring that adaptation about.

The problems will be compounded if the country is landlocked or far from seaports. Overland transport might be long and hazardous, with traders having to brave congested, poorly maintained, and unpoliced roads. The port itself may be far from the main global sea routes, so sea-based cargoes must be transshipped, at high expense, from regional trading centers (like Hong Kong, Singapore, and Dubai). Such geographic obstacles are not insurmountable. Roads can be built, treaties can be negotiated between inland and coastal countries, agricultural conditions can improve with research and development. Geography is not destiny. But geography shapes economic costs and the investment needed to move from one rung of the economic ladder to the next.

Five key aspects of geography help to shape a region's economic success or failure.

Agricultural Productivity

Crop productivity depends on many ecological factors: soils, water availability, topography, pests and pathogens, and local crop varieties. Some parts of the world are favored with deep and nutrient-rich soils, ample water availability (both rainfall and river-based irrigation), plains rather than steep slopes, and long growing seasons. Other farm regions are burdened by poor soils, droughts, limited access to irrigation, steep mountain slopes, and short growing seasons. One of the basic differences between Asia and sub-Saharan Africa, for example, is that most African smallholder farms are located in drought-prone regions without access to river-based irrigation, whereas Asia's river-based irrigation is extensive. Roughly 39 percent of South Asia's farmland is irrigated and 48 percent of China's, compared with just 4 percent in sub-Saharan Africa.

Energy and Minerals

Any process that creates order out of disorder, including economic development, requires energy. For most of human history, this energy came in the form of food to sustain human physical activity and animal power. To a modest extent, wind and water power were also harnessed. The single greatest trick of the modern era has been to tap new stores of energy, starting with coal and expanding to other fossil fuels (oil and gas), nuclear power, and increasingly efficient ways to convert wind, water, and solar radiation into electricity. It stands to reason that places well endowed with primary energy resources have an economic advantage over energy-scarce economies, and this has been generally the case. In the nineteenth century, local availability of coal was virtually a sine qua non of industrialization. In the twentieth century, availability of hydrocarbons was generally a great advantage.

There are a host of qualifiers to this rule, however. First, the usefulness of a particular energy resource depends on the technology that is available. Coal made only a modest difference before the invention of the steam engine. Most water power could not be usefully tapped before the invention of the electrodynamo, by which falling water can be converted into electricity. Oil became valuable with the invention of the internal combustion engine. Perhaps in the twenty-first century, sunshine will become the resource of choice as solar power is more effectively harnessed. Second, most energy resources are tradable, so even countries lacking in key energy resources can import their energy needs as long as they earn foreign exchange through exports. For this reason, availability of energy is a help but not a necessity. Third, energy resources, like any kind of wealth, can be squandered. Plentiful reserves of oil have fueled wars, coups, and mega-greed, a pattern commonly known as the resource curse. While it's fair to say that countries with energy resources have outperformed those without, it's also fair to say that many, if not most, energy-rich countries have underperformed their potential as a result of mismanagement of the energy resources.

A few other valuable minerals have an economic effect similar to energy resources. Countries rich in copper, diamonds, gold, platinum, and valued mineral stocks have a ready source of export earnings they can convert into energy imports or other needs. But like oil, valuable mineral deposits are easily squandered and are often the source of crippling political intrigue and violence. Diamonds have helped to finance successful economic development in Botswana and Namibia in southern Africa, but they have also helped to incite and finance wars in West African countries, such as Sierra Leone.

Transport

Trade is absolutely vital for economic development, both to import advanced technology and to export goods and services to pay for the imports. The costs of shipping goods play an enormous role in facilitating or hindering trade, and therefore, development. Transport costs are lower by sea than by land (and much lower than by air). Sea-based transport costs are lower in main trading lanes than in remote reaches of the world. Transport costs are obviously lower to reach a neighboring market than a distant market. These differences give Singapore a profound economic advantage over, say, Fiji. Singapore is on the world's main trade route between Europe and Asia. A ship going from Osaka, Japan, to Rotterdam, Netherlands, will pass by Singapore as it traverses the Strait of Malacca. Fiji, by contrast, is far away in the South Pacific. That may contribute to its exotic reputation, but it certainly does not contribute to its economic development.

Table 9.2 shows the world's twenty biggest container ports in 2005. Of those, thirteen are in Asia, three are in Europe, three are in the United States, and one, Dubai, is in the Middle East. Not one is in Africa or in Latin America. Of course, as Africa develops, major ports will develop as well. Yet to build a major port with major industries around it poses a chicken-and-egg problem. Port services and ocean shipping both have strong economies of scale. Small-scale ports and small-scale ships have high operating costs compared with larger ports. Thus, if a port starts small, its costs will be very high, and this tends to discourage further development of the port area. If the port succeeds in reaching a critical mass, however, its operating costs per user will decline sharply, and much more business will be developed. The key then is to make the breakthrough to an adequate scale of operation.

Since three fourths of the world's population lies in the northern hemisphere on the Eurasian landmass, coastal populations in Europe, the Middle East, and Asia find themselves on great sea-lanes, while Africa's population finds itself comparatively out of the action. Similarly, North America has an intrinsic transport advantage over South America. Australia and New Zealand may seem like exceptions—prosperous yet distant—but both countries benefit by having small populations compared with enormous land areas. The favorable land-to-person ratio helps keep incomes high.

Disease Ecology

A heavy disease burden frustrates economic development in countless ways. Individual productivity is impeded by illness, if not ended by premature mortality. Childhood diseases can lead to a lifetime of adverse health conditions. Regions prone to disease are less likely to attract tourists, skilled migrants, and foreign investment. As we've noted earlier, where children die in large proportions, the transition from high fertility rates to low fertility rates is far slower. Parents are less likely to reduce family size if they lack the confidence that each one of their children will survive beyond the first few years of life. Somewhat surprisingly, perhaps, the regions of the world differ not only in the

Table 9.2: The World's Busiest Container Ports in 2005

RANK	PORT	COUNTRY	TEUs (THOUSANDS)
1	Singapore	Singapore	23,192
2	Hong Kong	People's Republic of China	22,427
3	Shanghai	People's Republic of China	18,084
4	Shenzhen	People's Republic of China	16,197
5	Busan	South Korea	11,843
6	Kaohsiung	Taiwan (Republic of China)	9,471
7	Rotterdam	Netherlands	9,287
8	Hamburg	Germany	8,088
9	Dubai	United Arab Emirates	7,619
10	Los Angeles	United States of America	7,485
11	Long Beach	United States of America	6,710
12	Antwerp	Belgium	6,482
13	Qingdao	People's Republic of China	6,307
14	Klang	Malaysia	5,544
15	Ningbo	People's Republic of China	5,208
16	Tianjin	People's Republic of China	4,801
17	New York/New Jersey	United States of America	4,785
18	Guangzhou	People's Republic of China	4,685
19	Tanjung Pelepas	Malaysia	4,177
20	Laem Chabang	Thailand	3,834

Note: "TEU" stands for "Twenty-foot Equivalency Unit," that is, a twenty-foot shipping container. Thus a forty-foot container is two TEUs.
Source: American Association of Port Authorities, (2005)

kind of health care they can provide to their people but also in their intrinsic susceptibility to key diseases. Since malaria and a host of other insect-borne diseases are transmitted overwhelmingly in tropical climates, while many other diseases are worldwide in impact, the overall impact of infectious disease on the tropics is much higher than in the temperate regions. For various ecological reasons, tropical Africa has the heavest tropical disease burden of all regions. Most important, Africa's malaria-transmitting mosquitoes are especially deadly, since they have evolved to bite only humans while the malaria-transmitting mosquitoes in other continents bite animals, as well as humans. The consequence is a much higher rate of malaria transmission in Africa than elsewhere, and the malaria disease burden is correspondingly devastating.

Natural Hazards

When Hurricane Katrina hit New Orleans, that city's economic prospects were set back for years, perhaps for decades. And for the same reason, countries that are repeatedly hit by natural disasters face the risk of long-term setbacks to development. Repeated blows to the economy can add up to a long-term poverty trap. Natural hazards, of course, come in many forms. So-called hydrometeorological hazards (meaning water-related hazards) take the greatest overall toll. Droughts cause massive loss of human livelihoods and livestock; floods cause even greater dislocations. Many countries face both kinds of hazards, sometimes simultaneously in different parts of the country or within the same area over the course of a year. Other weather shocks include hurricanes (called typhoons in Asia), tornadoes, heat waves, and more. Another major category of hazard is seismological, including volcanoes, earthquakes, and tsunamis.

Tropical and subtropical economies near continental shelves in Asia and the Americas face the worst combination of seismological and hydrological risks. The Philippines, for example, faces heavy threats of typhoons, droughts, floods, volcanoes and earthquakes. The same is true of the Central American nations. Africa is especially vulnerable to drought, which has repeatedly devastated vast parts of the continent and has become considerably more frequent in the past quarter century, partly as a result of long-term global climate change.

GEOGRAPHY IS NOT DESTINY

The geography argument has been seriously misconstrued in two ways. First, it has been interpreted to mean geographic determinism, the false argument that a country's fate is settled by its geography, not merely shaped by it. The purpose of understanding geographical challenges is not to submit to fate but to identify practical steps to overcome barriers posed by specific natural endowments. If disease epidemiology identifies a special burden of malaria, the argument is not to give up but to increase investments in fighting malaria. If highly variable rainfall threatens crop yields, the response should probably be a focus on supplemental irrigation to protect against dry spells. If landlockedness hinders trade, then special efforts need to be made to build roads to seaports and to build diplomatic ties with coastal neighbors. In short, geographical impediments suggest priorities for public investment efforts, rather than reasons for surrender.

Second, the geography argument has been misunderstood to imply that certain places in the world are for all time more advantaged than others. The counterargument is that since leader and follower countries have traded places throughout history, geography must not be so important. This line of reasoning misses the point. Without being deterministic, the role of geography changes in line with changes in technology. Before the steam engine, coal deposits were not as valuable. Before the internal combustion engine, the same was true of oil deposits. And before Columbus's voyage to the Americas, the Americas suffered from the lack of access to the Old World's technological advances (and benefited from the lack of access to the Old World's epidemic diseases). Before the advent of the Internet, landlocked regions were much more disadvantaged than they are now. In today's Internet-empowered world, a major noncoastal city such as Bangalore, India, can export knowledge-based services to the world's markets via the Internet without having to worry about access to shipping routes. In other words, changes in technology shift the particular advantages of geography (from coal to oil, for example) and also eliminate certain geographical barriers altogether (think of air freight or the Internet).

When correctly understood, a geographical analysis helps to frame a country's development strategy by identifying areas of priority public investment and by suggesting how a country's underlying production costs are likely to shape the industrial structure. Geography will shape the balance between light and heavy industry, between industry and services, between types of agricultural crops, and between alternative locations for urbanization and trade. A region's natural resource deposits, disease patterns, climate, and soils are all critical inputs into designing a proper development strategy.

DESIGNING A DEVELOPMENT STRATEGY

According to the free-market textbooks, countries should simply open their markets, enforce property rights, and ensure macroeconomic stability. Economic development will follow. No place in the world, including the free-market United States, actually pursues development policy in this manner, and for very good reason. At every stage of development, and for every sector of development, the public sector and private sector have mutually supportive roles. Public-sector capital—roads, clinics, schools, ports, nature reserves, utilities, and much more—are essential if private capital in the form of factories, machinery, and skilled labor are to be productive. Economic development is a complex interplay of market forces and public-sector plans and investments.

There is no single trajectory from destitution to development. Iceland, India, and Indonesia are in alphabetical sequence, but their development trajectories could not be more distinct. As a small North Atlantic island economy, Iceland has leveraged its plentiful fish stocks and geothermal energy into spectacular development, mainly by reinvesting its natural resource earnings into very high levels of education and skills for its small population. Iceland has used its mid-Atlantic proximity to the United States and Western Europe to foster an open society in which its leading students, businessmen, artists, and entrepreneurs move effortlessly between two vast markets, equally at home in both.

India, of course, is at the opposite extreme, with a population that is five thousand times larger than Iceland's. India's challenge, completely different from Iceland's, is to transform a densely populated subcontinent of subsistence farmers into a modern and largely urban society. Hundreds of millions of people live in poverty. Population growth has been high, with India's population tripling between 1950 and 2000 from 350 million to 1 billion. In the past two decades, India has finally achieved a long-awaited development breakthrough. A big boost of agricultural productivity in the 1960s and 1970s, supported by international science and donor assistance, began to transform large parts of subsistence-farming India into commercial agricultural regions. Gradually in the 1980s and then rapidly in the 1990s, several urban centers became internationally competitive in exports of manufactures and information-based services. Fertility rates came down and literacy rates rose, and both trends helped to strengthen India's economic transformation. Yet with 70 percent or so of India's population still living in villages, and with profound ecological stresses, India continues to face an enormous challenge of development and transformation.

Indonesia is yet a third case, a tropical archipelago densely populated like India but more open to international trade as a result of its insular geography. Approximately 95 percent of Indonesia's population lives within sixty miles of the coast, compared with only 38 percent of India's. The coastal proximity of Indonesia's population is conducive to international trade, so it is not surprising that the ratio of exports to GNP in Indonesia stood at 31 percent in 2003, compared with India's 14 percent. The same proximity has no doubt supported Indonesia's relatively quicker urbanization, which in the same year stood at around 46 percent compared with just 28 percent in India.

These brief examples underscore the fact that each country faces a distinctive challenge based on its own unique geography, demography, and history. Nonetheless, we can offer at least a few valid generalizations. First, a sound development strategy for any country requires attention to three geographic dimensions: the rural (largely agricultural sector), the urban (largely manufacturing and service sector), and the national infrastructure grid (roads, power, telecoms) that links together all parts of the economy, and connects the economy with neighbors and with world markets.

Second, at each stage of transformation from a subsistence economy to a knowledge-based economy, both the public sector and private sector have important and complementary roles to play. Without adequate public-sector investments and leadership, the private sector will be unable to operate effectively. Development is inherently an interplay between market forces and public policies. Even though we expect the private sector to be the engine of growth, the public sector must provide critical public goods such as infrastructure, which cannot be adequately provided by the private market and without which the private sector cannot thrive.

There are six kinds of public interventions of great importance. The first is help for the destitute (who constitute a very significant proportion of the population in the poorest countries) so that the poor can stay alive, meet basic needs, and step onto the ladder of development. That requires public financing to ensure that the poor have access to basic health care, adequate nutrition, primary education, safe drinking water, and other essential needs.

The second is the public provision of key infrastructure (roads, ports and air-ports, power, telecommunications, and broadband connectivity, all of which are required by the private sector in order to flourish) as well as other public goods such as infectious disease control and environmental management. If core infrastructure is left to the private market, there will tend to be under-provision, monopoly prices, and exclusion of the poor. Other public goods such as disease control are also dramatically underprovided by the market. The third is the provision of a sound business environment, including mon-etary stability, protection of property rights, contract enforcement, and open-ness to international trade. The fourth is the provision of social insurance, to ensure that all parts of the population can maintain their economic security and well-being in the face of inevitable economic dislocations. The fifth is the promotion and dissemination of modern science and technology. Like infra-structure, scientific inquiry can be left to the market, but the benefits of new knowledge do not reach all of society, since they are protected by copyrights and patents for commercial reasons. The sixth is proper stewardship of the natural environment.

The relative importance of these six challenges varies systematically dur-ing the climb up the technology ladder, as emphasized in Table 9.3. Public pro-vision of basic needs must come first, at the very bottom of the ladder. The public sector's support of science and technology, while important at every stage of development, surely must expand as an economy develops. Similarly, basic infrastructure and primary education are vital at the lowest economic rungs, while high-quality university education for much of the population is vital for a highly developed economy.

Implementing a development strategy presents several deep challenges of governance. The first and most basic challenge is to ensure that politics and policy choices actually support development. Before World War II, imperial rule by Europe over much of Africa and Asia was a major obstacle to devel-opment, since the imperial powers were interested in exploiting natural re-sources in the colonies rather than in their long-term economic development. Once independence was achieved, the newly independent states had to take on the challenge of good governance. Governance could fail for many reasons: civil strife; massive corruption; ethnic divisions; the concentration of power in the hands of a narrow, unaccountable elite; and more. Bad policy choices were also an obvious threat. Many well-intentioned leaders of poor countries simply made poor policy decisions, for example, by adopting state ownership

Table 9.3: Climbing the Ladder of Development

RUNGS OF THE DEVELOPMENT LADDER	PUBLIC-SECTOR CHALLENGES	PRIVATE-SECTOR CHALLENGES	NOTABLE GEOGRAPHICAL CHALLENGES
Innovation economy	Excellence of universities, public funding for science	Management of knowledge workers, quality of life for employees	Establishment of high quality of life in "creative" urban zones, with top-flight universities, entertainment, access to global travel and markets
Emerging-market economy	Deepening of financial markets, commercial law, public-sector pensions, judicial systems, universities and technical schools	Creation of research capacities, logistics systems, quality control, worker training	Need for competitive transport and communications services, linking national economies with international suppliers and customers
Commercial economy	Establishment of well-functioning industrial parks and zones; promotion of ports, airports, telecoms, Internet, and power; universal secondary education; completion of the demographic transition; labor codes	Export financing, operation in industrial zones, contractual relations including joint ventures with international buyers and suppliers, adoption of labor standards	Transport and communications conditions, reliability of electricity, promotion of urban infrastructure and policy support to accommodate rapid urbanization
Subsistence economy	Creation of basic network of roads, power, health, primary schools, teachers' colleges; universal primary education; training of skilled workers for education, health, agriculture, and infrastructure	Promotion of cash-earning agriculture, small-scale rural enterprises, microfinance	Vulnerability to drought, epidemics, agricultural pests, and other hazards

Climbing the ladder

of farms and factories and imposing trade barriers that blocked the inflow of technologies.

Even when governance is good, however, another major challenge remains:

public finance. Successful development requires public investments, but governments in impoverished countries are often too cash strapped, and too indebted, to finance the requisite investments. When the government is unable to build roads, a power grid, and other basic infrastructure, the private sector languishes. The result is a fiscal-poverty trap in which poverty leads to low public investments, and low public investments reinforce poverty. This kind of fiscal collapse is one of the most important causes of economic development failures in the poorest countries. The fiscal trap is all the more debilitating because the poorest countries face geographical obstacles that cry out for remedial investments, but those investments are simply unaffordable. A fiscal collapse is also often a cause of subsequent poor governance. When the government lacks the revenues to ensure basic needs, it loses legitimacy in the population and is unable to prevent extreme factional infighting or even to defend against internal insurrection and coups.

DIAGNOSING DEVELOPMENT FAILURES

Only the developing countries in East and Southeast Asia have systematically achieved economic development at rapid and sustained rates in the past fifty years. Other regions, notably South Asia, have more recently picked up the pace. Africa has fallen backward in extreme poverty, and Latin America, though richer than both Asia and Africa, has also languished for decades without a decisive breakthrough. Identifying the bottlenecks to faster progress and mobilizing policies to overcome those bottlenecks constitute the greatest challenges of development economics. In *The End of Poverty*, I describe this identification process as a differential diagnosis akin to clinical medicine and suggest a systematic template that could be useful to carry it out. What follows is a snapshot tour of some of the overarching challenges faced by major world regions.

In Latin America, the main obstacles are probably social divisions and economic strategy rather than basic geography or disastrous governance (though there certainly has been some of that as well). Latin American societies tend to be divided by race, ethnicity, and class. For centuries, the populations of European descent ran the show and displayed scant interest in the education, health, and economic well-being of indigenous Amerindians or Afro-Latin descendants of former slaves. The result was sharp social conflict and chronic underinvestment in education, skills, and public health. Politics oscillated between a populist left appealing to the masses and an authoritarian right defending the privileges of the rich. At the same time, the elites underestimated the importance of investing in technology and higher education, since they were used to living off the income from natural resources and vast farms. The result has been a long period of economic stagnation in Latin America, from the 1970s until recently.

Things are finally beginning to change. Old class and ethnic cleavages are diminishing under the force of democracy. Politicians are responding not only to traditional elites but also to society more broadly. The case for education and investments in knowledge is much better appreciated throughout the region. While populism and instability remain a threat, there is also a real prospect of Latin America finally taking up the challenge of mass education and the transformation to a high-tech society.

Most of Asia, by contrast, has been achieving rapid economic growth for the past fifteen years, and in some cases longer. Back in the 1960s and 1970s, East Asia and much of South Asia had already succeeded in making the transition from subsistence to commercial economies. In the past quarter century, they have taken another step up the development ladder as they transformed themselves from largely agricultural economies to industrial and service-sector economies. Massive inflows of foreign investment and technology are fueling spectacular growth. Basic infrastructure is in place through most of the region, and wherever it is in place, economic growth tends to be very rapid. Policy leaders have relentlessly focused on technological advance and thus have fast-forwarded the region into the information age.

Geography will play a key role in future threats to Asia's economic convergence. On the one hand, Asia's landlocked and mountainous countries— such as Afghanistan and the former Soviet republics in Central Asia— continue to severely lag behind their coastal neighbors. Similarly, water-stressed regions tend to severely lag behind irrigation-based regions. In addition, virtually all of Asia is highly vulnerable to climate change. Rising temperatures will threaten crop yields in the tropics and subtropics, and climate change threatens to destabilize reliable access to water for agriculture and household use.

The Middle East possesses conditions not seen in any other part of the world. On the positive side, by virtue of its situation between Europe and Asia, the region can surely be a center of global trade and cultural exchange. That, after all, was its vocation a millennium ago, and it is the role that the United Arab Emirates have been successfully re-creating as the Middle East's trading and tourist center. Being in the "middle" has also exposed the region to centuries of interference and meddling by neighboring countries and distant powers. It is a region that is particularly difficult to defend militarily because it is vulnerable to attack from so many directions.

Outside interference reached extraordinary and dangerous levels in the twentieth century, and it continues today, as a result of the region's vast oil holdings. The imperial powers of Europe before World War II, and the United States after the war, relentlessly manipulated the region, always with both eyes firmly on the prize (appropriately enough, *The Prize* is the title of an epic history of oil in the region by Daniel Yergin). Such manipulations have often achieved short-run benefits for the intervening power—control over oil—and long-term instability within the region and inflamed opposition toward the meddling power. Now the United States has created a region inflamed with anti-American sentiment, which the United States continues to feed with short-term sales of advanced weaponry to one side or another: one year Saudi Arabia, the next Iraq, and then Iran, and so on.

Yet it is the underlying ecology that truly defines the region. The Middle East is arid and likely to become even more so as climate change proceeds. Oil-rich states can convert their oil wealth into the world's most expensive freshwater through desalination. The rest of the region, such as Yemen, Syria, Jordan, and Palestine, faces fearsome and growing water challenges. Until recently, ecological stress had been compounded by an extraordinary population increase, which raised the population of the Middle East from 50 million in 1950 to 212 million in 2005. Fortunately, most of the region has experienced a significant fertility decline in recent decades, from an average TFR of 6.5 during 1950–55 to 3.2 during 2000–05. And some of the countries, notably the United Arab Emirates, are quickly becoming global trading hubs.

It is in Africa, though, that the difficulties of geography, fiscal distress, and governance come together to create the epicenter of the world's development challenge. For a generation the region has suffered rising poverty, hunger, disease, and environmental stress. Geography affects African development in every direction. The tropical environment, combined with poverty, results in the highest disease burden in the world. Much of the population is far from coasts and navigable rivers, perhaps partly the result of moving to the interior to flee the depredations of slavery in earlier centuries and partly because farming conditions are better in the interior highlands. Hazards of drought are severe in the drylands and savanna ecozones, where roughly two thirds of the population lives. Yet even in Africa solutions abound to break the poverty trap. Public investments in agriculture, health, education, and infrastructure can unlock the private investments in agroprocessing, manufacturing, and services. Africa could begin to boom. We take up that possibility in the next chapter.

Chapter 10

Ending Poverty Traps

AFRICA IS FACING A TRIPLE WHAMMY in economic development. Its agricultural performance is the worst in the world, measured as cereal yields (food production per hectare Figure 10.1). Yields have barely budged for half a century, remaining stuck at roughly one ton per hectare. Cropland cannot expand commensurately with the rapidly growing population, so farm sizes are shrinking. The combination of stagnant yields and fewer hectares per person has caused a decline in food output per person in contrast with all other parts of the world (Figure 10.2). The result is a continent in the chronic throes of hunger.

Africa's disease burden is similarly unique in the world. Life expectancy is forty-six years on average, roughly thirty-three years less than the average in high-income countries. The under-five mortality rate is a staggering 179 per 1,000, signifying that 179 of each 1,000 newborns die before their fifth birthdays. That compares with 6 deaths per 1,000 in the high-income countries. With the risk of children's death so high, so too is fertility, as we've discussed at length. The TFR averaged 5.5 in sub-Saharan Africa during 2000–05, compared with 1.6 in the high-income countries.

Africa's connectivity to world markets is similarly burdened by geography, history, and now by extreme poverty itself. Unlike the Eurasian landmass, sub-Saharan Africa is inherently isolated by the Sahara and by the lack of rivers navigable from the oceans to the interior. Moreover, the colonial powers did not build much infrastructure in the interior of Africa. In India, the British raj constructed a thorough rail network, often connected to rural roads, in part to bring India's rural cotton production to British factories. In Africa, by contrast, rails were not built to reach villages but rather a few diamond and gold mines. The result was not a rail network but some disconnected rail capillaries that reached only a tiny proportion of Africa's rural

Figure 10.1: Cereal Yields from 1960 to 2005

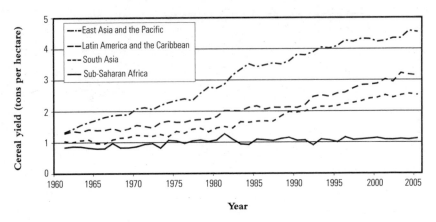

Source: Data from World Bank (2007)

population. Figures 10.3(a) and 10.3(b) show the remarkable difference of this contrasting colonial legacy. When India needed to bring fertilizers into the Punjab and food surpluses out of that region to trade with the rest of India to achieve the Green Revolution, the rail network proved to be critical. Africa had no such good fortune.

Figure 10.2: Cereal Production per Capita,
by Region from 1961 to 2004

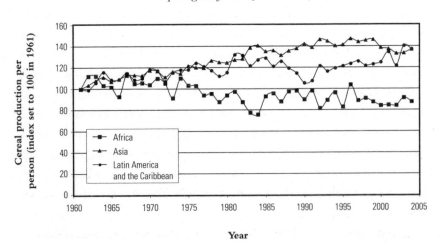

Source: Data from FAO (2007), World Bank (2007)

Figure 10.3(a): Africa's Railroads

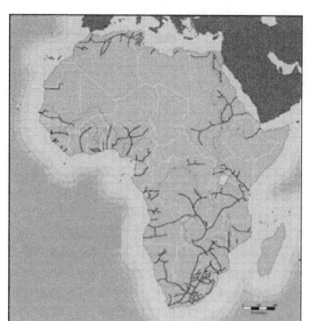

Source: *Africa Studies Center, Michigan State University*

ESCAPE FROM POVERTY

These burdens are surmountable, and at a remarkably low cost. Food production can be increased; diseases can be controlled; education and literacy
can be expanded to ensure universal coverage of the young; and infrastructure—especially roads, power, water, and sanitation—can be put in place.
Indeed, these things can happen rapidly if the projects can be implemented.
While in a handful of cases the limiting factor is poor governance, in most
cases it is finance. The poor know what to do but are too poor to do it.
Since they can't meet their immediate needs (food, safe water, health care)
they also can't afford to save and invest for the future. That is where foreign
assistance comes in. A temporary boost of aid over the course of several
years, if properly invested, can lead to a permanent rise in productivity. That
boost, in turn, leads to self-sustaining growth. The logical chain is the following:

| Temporary aid | → | Boost of productivity | → | Rise of saving and investment | → | Sustained growth |

Figure 10.3(b): Railway Network of India

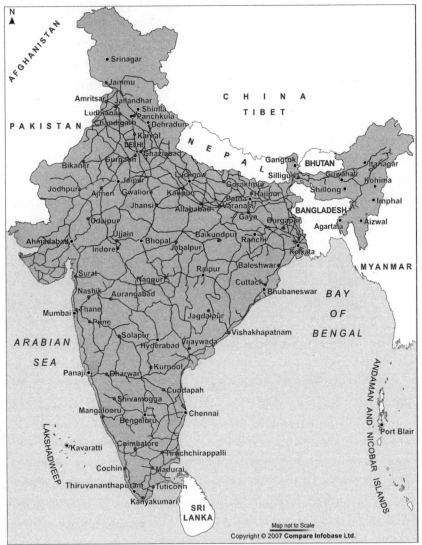

The escape from extreme poverty requires four basic types of investment. The first is a boost to productivity of the core livelihood, agriculture. This is the hallowed Green Revolution that initially lifts smallholder farmers out of subsistence. The second is health, including control of the main killers— infection, nutritional deficiencies, and unsafe childbirth—through the pro- vision of preventative and curative health services. The third is education, which ensures that households develop the requisite skills to navigate the local global economy. The fourth is infrastructure, essential for productivity in every sphere, including power, roads, safe water for drinking and sanitation, phone and Internet connectivity, and port services. The boost of farm production has very often been the deus ex machina that triggers the long-term growth process. It is also a process that often starts with outside help, as when the United States funded the initial research and many of the inputs (improved seeds and fertilizer) that went into India's Green Revolution, which began in the second half of the 1960s. In the urban areas, the initial investment will not support agriculture but rather manufacturing or services. Perhaps the trigger to growth will be improved roads that facilitate trade or an improved port that permits the start of an apparel sector or a power plant that provides vital power for factory production. Whatever the particular investment, the concept is the same: raise productivity above subsistence in order to trigger a self-sustaining process of economic growth.

If the outside world funds these start-up investments in agriculture, health, education, and infrastructure, the situation can change rapidly and decisively. Consider first the benefits of investing in agriculture. Figure 10.4 (see insert) shows striking evidence of the potential for yield increases in African agriculture. Johan Rockstrom collected four types of yield data for nine countries from smallholder farms, official data, research stations, and commercial (large-scale) farms. The data show that the average yield of smallholder farmers is close to 0.5 tons per hectare. The official reports put the yields closer to 1 ton per hectare, roughly twice the observed yields. The crucial point is in the third block of data, the on-station yields, where demonstration plots are planted with best-option technologies, notably with fertilizer and proper agronomic methods (for example, row planting), and small-scale water management. Indeed, on-station yields are often ten times the observed yields on smallholder farms, with 5 tons or more per hectare. The commercial farmers do even better than that (though the data are limited).

The package of inputs required for a one-hectare farm might be roughly $200, while the added food yield is one to two tons, or even more, with a market value beyond $450. Fertilizer and high-yield seeds, therefore, have a spectacular rate of return. However, these results are not yet realized because smallholders lack their own cash to finance the inputs and are unable to obtain credit.

The returns to investing in health are similarly dramatic. The huge burden of disease among the poorest of the poor results from a relatively small number of conditions: infectious diseases, nutritional deficiencies, and unsafe childbirth (resulting in both maternal and infant deaths). The infectious diseases include: AIDS, TB, malaria, diarrheal disease, respiratory infection, vaccine-preventable diseases (measles, polio, tetanus, diphtheria), and helminths (worms). As with agriculture, a proven set of investments can slash the deaths and dramatically raise the well-being, energy levels, and productivity of the community. As just one illustration, consider the challenge of malaria. Malaria is the greatest killer of African children among the infectious diseases causing up to three million deaths per year (most of them children) and up to one billion clinical cases of illness! Yet the disease is largely preventable and entirely treatable if the treatment is timely. Prevention depends on stopping the mosquito from biting, either through indoor spraying of insecticide or by using an insecticide-treated bed net. Treatment requires prompt attention after the onset of symptoms. Highly effective medicines (notably those based on the Chinese herbal extract artemisinin) can cure the disease but only if the child is treated before life-threatening complications set in. That generally requires attention within the first few hours of fever.

Communities know what to do to protect themselves from malaria—spraying, nets, medicines—but as with agriculture, they cannot afford the interventions. When increased help arrives, as it did from the Global Fund to Fight AIDS, TB, and malaria (starting in 2003) and from the United States (starting in 2006) for the two islands of Zanzibar, Tanzania, the results can be spectacular. Beginning in 2003, Zanzibar started to introduce and make widely available a new generation of highly effective medicines. Starting in 2005, bed nets were distributed for free and in large numbers on the two islands. Then in mid-2006, the bed net distribution was followed by a campaign to spray all households with an indoor insecticide called ICON, which lasts for four to six months before the need for respraying. Up until the campaign malaria was a major killer and source of illness, accounting for around half of the deaths of children under five and around 40 percent of outpatient consultations in Zanzibar. The results of the control campaign have been spectacular, as shown by the data of the Abdalla Mzee Hospital, the main receiving hospital on the northern island of Pemba (Figure 10.5.) During the first half of

Figure 10.5: Malaria Cases at Abdalla Mzee Hospital, Pemba Island

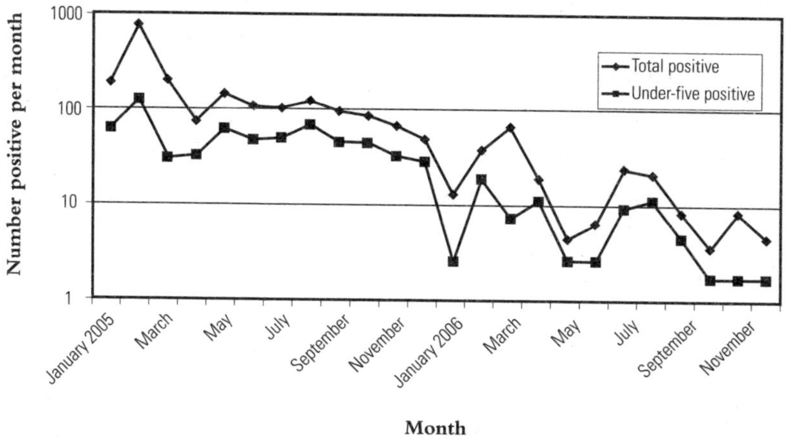

Month

Source: Ministry of Health, Government of Zanzibar
Note: Vertical axis on logarithmic scale

2005, there were regularly more than one hundred cases per month, including dozens of cases of children under age five (the group most vulnerable to death). Mass bed net distribution commenced in the northern district on the island in October 2005 and was completed throughout the island during January 2006. The number of cases plummeted thereafter to around twenty during the first half of 2006, and roughly one half of the total was among young children. After spraying, the number of malaria cases fell again, to single digits. The results are startling and heartening, but not unusual by the standards of malaria control. Tremendous results can be expected once the implementation of bold control programs are under way.

Similarly dramatic gains can be achieved through a boost in education and literacy, which can quickly open up opportunities for employment and exports in many new branches of industry, such as textiles and apparel, agricultural processing, and assembly operations. Large productivity returns to schooling have been verified over decades of studies. Infrastructure certainly plays the same transformative role. Industrial zones newly equipped with power, water, connectivity and transport to ports enable the inflow of foreign investment. Infrastructure also makes possible new economic connections between currently isolated rural areas and urban markets.

STRATEGIES FOR
REGIONAL DEVELOPMENT

Geographically distressed impoverished regions need a temporary helping hand to reach the bottom rung of the economic development ladder. Because these regions lack the benefits of easy transport, productive agriculture, or a low-disease environment, they easily get trapped without saving and invest-ment, and thereby fall ever further behind the rest of the world. An investment push is needed to establish a productive base in such places. The approach has been blocked for a generation, roughly since 1981, ever since the United States decided to cut back sharply on development aid as an active instrument of na-tional policy. Since then, aid has been small scale and has been under attack by ideological foes.

The idea of helping laggard regions is routinely applied within countries. National governments channel funds to assist the regions falling behind and to ensure that all parts of the country have adequate infrastructure. Laggard regions within a country also benefit from internal migration. Young men often leave the less favored places in search of jobs in the more favored places, and send home remittances to those left behind. Foreign aid should be seen as standard regional development policy for lagging re-gions, albeit for regions outside of the national boundaries of the aid giver. Still, the economic principles and policy motivations are roughly the same. Rich regions have an incentive to help poor regions within national borders, and rich countries have an incentive to help poor countries across national borders.

Two successful regional development programs help us to understand how international development assistance can succeed. In the United States one of the most famous projects to emerge from the New Deal was the Tennessee Valley Authority (TVA), which oversaw construction of a vast net-work of hydroelectric dams, flood control projects, and waterways for navi-gation in the Tennessee River Valley, covering seven states in the southeastern United States. In addition to creating thousands of jobs in a time of profound economic crisis, the TVA provided the Southeast with critical infrastructure, including plentiful cheap electricity, improved channels for commercial navigation, and a large network of dams to protect the valley's inhabitants from floods. The TVA also successfully eradicated malaria, which had hitherto been endemic in the region, and significantly improved environmental conservation practices in the area.

The TVA was, in fact, part of a more general New Deal approach to fight poverty in the rural United States through public investments. The Rural Electrification Administration (REA), established in 1935, provided government credits and financial guarantees to rural cooperatives in order to extend electrification to American farms, ranches, and other rural locations. The effect was galvanizing, even in the midst of the Great Depression. In 1935, only 11.6 percent of U.S. farms had electricity. By 1940, that number had reached 30.4 percent, and by 1950, 77.2 percent of farms had access to electricity. In 1949, the REA was similarly empowered to finance the extension of telephone service to the rural United States. In just one decade, service coverage doubled, from 36 percent in 1949 to 64 percent in 1959. This role of the federal government in financing the uptake of infrastructure in rural America is rarely acknowledged by free-market ideologues, and it certainly is not mentioned by U.S. and World Bank officials who have championed the full privatization of utilities in rural Africa and other impoverished regions.

More recently, the world's largest regional development project is the Western China Development Project, by which the Chinese government is spreading economic development beyond the booming coastal regions to the lagging regions in the interior. Since 2000, the Chinese government has invested more than 1 trillion yuan ($125 billion) in western China development. The government has invested heavily in infrastructure (it has built 250,000 kilometers of highway and 4,000 kilometers of railroad), foreign investment promotion, education, and environmental conservation (reforestation mainly) to help the western regions catch up. The results have been impressive: between 2000 and 2006, western China's production nearly doubled, equivalent to annual growth rates of more than 10 percent over that period. At the same time, massive migration from the interior to the coastal provinces, and from the rural areas to the cities, has also helped the development process in two ways. It has provided jobs and improved incomes for more than one hundred million migrants. Many of these migrants were unemployed or working at very low productivity in their home villages. Second, part of that increased income has been sent back to the villages to support local consumption, business formation, and investments in homes and farms. The costs, however, are high, since the mass migration has very often meant separated families, and even mothers and children left behind in the villages, with the husbands not seen again.

THE BENEFITS AND LIMITS OF INTERNATIONAL MIGRATION

One solution for desperate regions is out-migration. The solution for China's poor interior is clearly a combination of out-migration and investment and remittances in. When a country has both geographically stressed regions and geographically favored regions, out-migration from the difficult regions is both inevitable and salutary. The Chinese migrate from west to east. Brazilians have long migrated from the arid northeast to the temperate southeast. Italians moved from the subtropical south to the temperate north. But things become much trickier when an entire country is geographically stressed. Out-migration, in that case, must cross national boundaries.

In some regions, such as within Southeast Asia, the Middle East, and parts of Africa, large-scale migration among poor countries is already pervasive, sometimes with little monitoring or control. The landlocked countries typically export a significant part of their labor force to their coastal and richer neighbors. This can be a peaceful affair, but it can also erupt into ethnic violence and even war, as was the case in Côte d'Ivoire, where tensions were deeply exacerbated in the 1990s by the massive influx of workers from Burkina Faso at a time of economic crisis in the receiving country. Eventually, the rising tensions contributed to civil war in 2002.

A more deeply contentious route is migration from the poor countries to the rich countries, such as from Latin America into the United States, or from Africa into Europe. Immigration is certainly a hot-button issue. Developed countries are happy to accept highly skilled migrants—doctors, nurses, computer engineers—from anywhere at any time, and, indeed, they compete aggressively for them, attracting the few doctors and nurses from the poorest countries. The developed countries, meanwhile, are deeply conflicted internally about absorbing large numbers of low-skilled workers. The economics of such in-migration are more favorable than the politics.

In economic terms, such in-migration of low-skilled workers tends to be a win for the source country, the host country, and the migrant. A low-skilled immigrant arriving in a rich country experiences an immediate jump in income that can be a factor of ten or more. The migrant's employment tends to be in areas that are largely complementary with the host-country labor force, for example, in low-cost labor-intensive services (personal services, delivery boys, busboys, child care) that offer significant benefits for the host population. And part of the income earned is sent home as remittances, leading to a significant rise of consumption expenditures among family members left behind in the villages. While the low-skilled migrant might compete with low-skilled host-country workers, and lower their wages as a result, that effect tends to be small. Migrants are, in the economics jargon, mainly complements rather than substitutes for the host-country workforce.

At the political and sociological level, however, the issues are decidedly more complicated. Low-skilled migrants very often do not assimilate with the local population—or are not allowed to do so—as they are relentlessly separated by economic class, legal status, residential neighborhoods, language, religion, and culture. Legal and illegal migrants arrive without families, leaving behind wives and children who suffer the pangs of separation. The migrants are inevitably in legal flux, without property rights and highly fearful of judicial processes, especially forced deportation. They may lack access to basic health services. Children, when they are present, may have only a tenuous connection with the schools and public health systems. Separation, discrimination, and mutual fear can be flashpoints of violence, as has been the case repeatedly in the United States and Europe for years.

Nor can migration and remittances alone solve the development problems back home. The developing world will add another one to three billion people by 2050, compared with a total population in today's developed world of around one billion. Only a small fraction of the unskilled workers in the poor countries will be allowed to migrate legally to the developed world, and only another modest fraction will make their way illegally. While the benefits of increased remittance incomes for source-country economic development can be real, the remittance income will not finance the public investment needs nor more than a small part of the private investments of the developing countries. We should understand, therefore, that the imperatives for homegrown economic development in the poorer regions must continue to have center stage, with or without migration.

THE MILLENNIUM VILLAGE STRATEGY

The concept of quick-impact investments that help to lift disadvantaged regions from extreme poverty were at the core of the recommendations of the UN Millennium Project, which I was fortunate to direct for former UN secretary-general Kofi Annan. In each sector of the economy, including agriculture, health, education, and infrastructure, the project identified practical investments that can be readily applied, successfully monitored, and easily adapted to local conditions. It is the kind of aid that can work fast, providing a reliable investment that is easy to monitor and protect against corruption. Indeed, as I noted earlier, it is the kind of aid that even the fierce aid critic William Easterly has recommended (when he calls for aid for "obvious goods," such as "the vaccines, the antibiotics, the food supplements, the improved seeds, the fertilizer, the roads, the boreholes, the water pipes, the textbooks, and the nurses"). This focus on quick-impact investments was also endorsed by the world's governments at the 2005 UN World Summit, which formally adopted the core recommendations of the UN Millennium Project.

The UN Millennium Project has also moved quickly to support the implementation of its recommendations to show what can be accomplished. Hence the Millennium Village Project (MVP) was born, a program developed and led by a three-way alliance including The Earth Institute at Columbia University, Millennium Promise (an NGO devoted to promoting the MDGs), and the United Nations Development Program, and implemented by the local communities in Africa. The MVP draws on the financial analysis of the UN Millennium Project. A set of quick-impact investments is made in impoverished villages according to a budget that shares the burden among outside donors, the local community, NGOs, and government. The five-year effort aims to spend approximately $120 per villager per year in each community of roughly five thousand people, with the goal of empowering the community to achieve sustained long-term growth. The $120 is allocated among several key sectors: agriculture, health, education, and infrastructure, and it is shared roughly as follows: $60 per villager from external donors, $30 from the host government, $10 from the community (in kind), and $20 from other partners, including NGOs. The Millennium Village Project received financial support from private philanthropies and the government of Japan, which together cover the $60 portion from the external donors.

In total, about four hundred thousand people in seventy-eight villages were part of the project as of the end of 2006. As seen in the map in Figure 10.6 (see insert), the villages as of the end of 2006 are distributed across Africa in ten countries and twelve sites. The sites were chosen because of their extreme poverty and because the host governments were interested in partnering in the project. The sites were also distributed across the various agroecological zones of Africa so that lessons could be learned from a variety of underlying conditions. Some sites are in well-watered rain forest environments, while others are in extreme drylands. There are highlands in Ethiopia, Uganda, and Rwanda, and lowlands in West Africa. In 2007, three more countries joined Millennium Villages Project: Liberia, Mozambique, and Madagascar.

Five goals are set for each village in the first year: a good harvest using improved inputs (high-yield seed and fertilizer); malaria control based on bed nets and medicines; clinical health services including construction of new facilities if necessary; improved water sources for household use; and improved attendance of children at school supported by a midday feeding program (using locally produced food if possible). The goals are quantified, budgeted, and evaluated. The initial results have been very positive. Table 10.1 shows some early results for food production in the longest-running village programs, in Kenya, Ethiopia, and Malawi. In all cases, yields in the pre-intervention year were far below the potential, and yields have since soared with the introduction of high-yield seeds and fertilizer inputs. The combination of improved yields and expanded planted land area has meant that overall food production has risen substantially, for example, around eight times in the Ethiopian village compared with the base year, and fifteen times in the village in Malawi. (The actual multiple can be a bit high when the baseline was a drought year, as in these two cases.) Similar results are evident in many other areas, including quick progress against malaria, and implementation of school feeding programs. Malaria incidence and parasitemia (infection in the bloodstream by the malaria pathogen) drop sharply once long-lasting insecticide-treated bed nets and effective antimalarial medicines are available to all villagers. School attendance and national exam scores soar when school feeding programs are introduced.

Table 10.1: Food Production in the Millennium Villages

MILLEN-NIUM RESEARCH VILLAGE	YEAR	GRAIN YIELDS (TONS PER HECT-ARE)	AREA PLANTED (HECT-ARES)	PRODUC-TION (TONS)	PRODUC-TION INCREASE (TIMES FROM*)
Sauri, Kenya	2004*	1.9	220	418	
	2005	5.0	325	1,625	3.9
	2006	6.2	364	2,257	5.4
Koraro, Ethiopia	2004*	0.13	1,067	139	
	2005	0.58	1,970	1,148	8.3
Mwandama, Malawi	2004–5*	0.8	690	552	
	2005–6	6.5	1,272	8,268	15

*Refers to a year before the Millennium Village Project began in that village
Source: Adapted from Sanchez et al. (2007)

The early lessons of the Millennium Village Project are already being taken to heart by several of the host governments, which are looking to scale up this kind of holistic, practical, community-based development program. The scale-up will come in four ways. First, some of the key interventions, such as mass distribution of antimalarial bed nets, will simply be introduced on a national scale, as has now happened in Ethiopia, Kenya, Niger, Togo, and a growing list of other countries. Second, the existing village areas will expand their coverage, from around fifty thousand people per cluster to a full district of perhaps ten times that size. Third, clusters of Millennium Villages will be introduced in districts throughout each country, donor support permitting. And finally, countries not yet part of the project are asking to join. There are thirteen countries with Millennium Villages as of 2007 and several more countries planning to join by 2008. I hope that by 2010, nearly all countries in sub-Saharan Africa will have similar programs.

As usual, the limiting factor is donor resources. The project itself requires $60 per villager per year for five years. This amount falls squarely within the aid levels promised, but not yet delivered, by the G8. At the 2005 summit in Gleneagles, Scotland, the G8 countries promised to reach $50 billion per year in aid for Africa by 2010, doubling the aid level of 2004. With roughly five hundred million Africans living in rural villages, and with each villager targeted to receive assistance of $50 per year, the total cost of expanding the Millennium Village strategy across rural Africa is about $25 billion per year (or roughly half of the promised G8 aid). The limiting factor, therefore, is not the lack of potential financing; it has already been promised. If the powerful countries follow through on their commitments, we could make decisive progress against extreme poverty in a very short period of time. The Millennium Villages concept, brought to scale and combined with other worthy initiatives on agriculture, health, education, infrastructure and private-sector development, can yet make the difference in achieving the Millennium Development Goals.

TODAY'S WINNERS AND PAST HELP

"How soon they forget" might as well be the rallying cry of foreign assistance. Most successful countries, including most of today's donor countries, required outside donor help at critical moments in their histories. An irate e-mailer once attacked me for promoting help for Africa when his model country, Israel, had clearly made it on its own. Little did this gentleman realize that U.S. aid to Israel, with a population roughly one hundredth of Africa's, has been roughly equal to American aid to all of Africa! I am often told, in a similar vein, that India, Korea, and Taiwan each "made it on their own" without an understanding that U.S. foreign assistance in the 1950s and 1960s, as well as investments by Japan, set the stage for their later economic development. And, of course, today's European donors were themselves Marshall Plan recipients, with an average annual grant in the Marshall Plan countries of around $85 per European per year (in 2004 dollars) during the late 1940s and early 1950s. Interestingly, the Marshall Plan's $85 per recipient is close to what the G8 has promised (but not yet delivered) to sub-Saharan Africa (since the promised $50 billion would be divided among roughly six hundred million recipients).

The cases of Korea, India, and Taiwan are especially pertinent because simplistic and invidious comparisons are often made between these successful economies and the impoverished economies of Africa. For example, Korea and Taiwan are often compared pointedly with Ghana, with the assertion that all three economies had roughly the same starting point in 1960, so the subsequent divergence in performance was homegrown and due to better economic governance and management in Asia. In fact, the economic take-off of Korea and Taiwan in the 1960s was built on foundations laid by Japanese investments during the colonial era and by infrastructure financed by U.S. aid in the late 1950s and early 1960s. Most important, and without downplaying the darker sides of colonial rule, Japanese policies and investments laid the foundation for high-productivity agriculture in both Korea and Taiwan, and thereby laid the foundations for food security and industrialization.

A leading economic analyst of Asia's successful industrialization, Robert Wade, has usefully summarized some of the key investments that Japan made in rural Taiwan:

> A good communications infrastructure was laid down, designed not with the narrow purpose of extracting some primary raw material but with the aim of increasing production of smallholder rice and sugar, both wanted in Japan. Under these policies, "expansion in irrigation and drainage, dissemination of improved or better seeds, and spread in the use of fertilizers and manures were all energetically attempted, sometimes even with the aid of the police force; the statistics indicate continuously rising trends" [quoting Ishikawa, 1967:102]. Farmers were grouped into farmer cooperatives, irrigation associations, and landlord-tenant associations so as both to accelerate the spread of technical knowledge and to keep them under control.

After the end of Japanese colonial rule in 1945, Taiwan invested heavily in rural infrastructure and irrigation, backed by U.S. aid. Again, as Wade summarizes:

> Agricultural production grew at 4.4 percent a year between 1954 and 1967, faster than just about anywhere else in Asia. The surge of agricultural growth checked discontent with the Nationalist regime in the countryside, helping to stabilize the industrial investment climate. By 1960, rice yields per crop reached three tons per hectare, the highest in Asia outside of Japan. Agriculture could thus provide a generous investable surplus for the rest of the economy, and in the 1950s, for export.

No such investments were made in Ghana's agriculture, or for that matter in most of Africa's. While Korea received U.S. aid amounting to about $65 per capita per year (in 2005 dollars) during 1953–61, U.S. aid to Ghana amounted to $2 per capita per year during the same period. Initial conditions of these countries as of 1960 could not have been more different. Korea and Taiwan had high literacy, high food yields, and high life expectancy. Ghana had the opposite. As early as 1960, Korea and Taiwan had cereal yields of 3 tons per hectare, while Ghana's yields were a meager 0.8 tons per hectare. As early as 1960, South Korean farmers were applying 155 kg of fertilizer per hectare, while Ghana's were averaging less than 1 kg per hectare (Table 10.2).

India is yet another example that is frequently cited as self-made development, whereas, in fact, external assistance also played a critical role. As in Korea and Taiwan, the colonial era bequeathed to India some vital infrastructure, especially the rail system, which served India in crucial ways during its recent economic takeoff. Even more important, India's Green Revolution of the 1960s and 1970s was strongly supported by external assistance. Though India has wonderful indigenous scientific capacity, the Rockefeller Foundation's support for improved wheat varieties also was crucial. Two great scientists, Norman Borlaug, of the Rockefeller Foundation, and M. S. Swaminathan, India's director of wheat research in the 1960s, teamed up to disseminate the improved seed varieties first developed by Borlaug in Mexico and selected for applicability to Indian conditions by Swaminathan's

Table 10.2: Development Indicators in Ghana and South Korea in 1960

	GHANA	SOUTH KOREA
Life expectancy at birth (years)	46	54
Under-five mortality rate (deaths per 1,000)	215	127
Cereal yields (ton/hectare)	0.8	3.2
Fertilizer consumption (kilogram/hectare)	0.4	155
Aid from United States, 1953–61 (constant 2005 dollars per recipient per year)	2.2	65.2

Source: Calculated from World Bank (2007), USAID (2007)

team. Their work took on special urgency after back-to-back droughts in 1964–65, which required India to rely on massive shipments of emergency U.S. food aid.

Borlaug's message to India was that there was need for a mass scale-up of high-yield agriculture, supported by strong and consistent government guarantees to farmers of fertilizers, high-yield seeds, credits, and guaranteed sale prices for output. In a 1968 speech, Borlaug declared, "I wish I were now a member of India's Congress; I would stand up out-of-order every few minutes and shout in a loud voice: *What India needs now is fertilizer, fertilizer, fertilizer, credit, credit, credit, and fair prices, fair prices, fair prices!*" (emphasis in the original).

The U.S. government strongly heeded the call by financing the vital inputs. As explained in 1968 by USAID administrator William Gaud:

> [T]he developing nations—their governments, their institutions, and their farmers—cannot sustain the Green Revolution without outside support. They lack the skills to do the necessary adaptive research. They lack the capital to build fertilizer plants. They lack the facilities and the technicians needed to train their people in the new ways.
>
> If this agricultural revolution is to succeed, it can only do so as the result of a working partnership between the advanced and the developing nations. . . .
>
> This is why fertilizer is rapidly becoming the largest single element in the A.I.D. program. This is why A.I.D. is backing a growing number of American companies in their efforts to put up fertilizer plants in countries which are seeking to expand their production of food.

Fertilizer for India was the largest single item in the USAID budget at the end of the 1960s. All told, India has received around $160 billion in aid since 1960, a sum that has been vital in helping India to achieve the Green Revolution, build infrastructure, control disease, and strengthen science and higher education.

SCALE AND SUSTAINABILITY

In addition to the mythology of self-help, the other two myths about aid involve the challenges of scale and sustainability. It is often claimed that foreign aid can succeed on a small scale but not on a large scale, and that demonstration programs don't reflect sustainable success. Such generalizations are false. There are countless aid-based programs of mass scale-up, like the Green Revolution, which indeed went quickly from small trials to implementation at country or even continental scale. These include smallpox eradication (carried out worldwide), malaria elimination (successful throughout the subtropics and other regions of low or moderate transmission), vaccine coverage (led by UNICEF from the 1980s until the present), family planning and contraception (a worldwide, aid-based scale-up in the 1970s and 1980s), and countless programs of specific disease control (polio, African river blindness, leprosy, and Guinea worm, all of which have been brought substantially under control through mass scale-up efforts during the past two decades).

Nor are the costs of scaling up prohibitive. The UN Millennium Project demonstrated that comprehensive investments in the critical areas—agriculture, health, education, and infrastructure—if taken to scale for the poorest countries, can be covered within the international commitment of 0.7 percent of donor income as development aid. With a rich-world annual income of roughly $35 trillion, 0.7 percent of GNP is around $245 billion per year, compared with actual aid flows of roughly $100 billion per year. The additional $145 billion per year would be sufficient to close the financing gap for the Millennium Villages, disease control, national-scale infrastructure, and much more.

The other even more hoary myth is that aid might work, but it is not sustainable. The notion is that any advance in development resulting from aid will simply collapse when the aid is ended. That can be true if the aid is not sufficient or is not designed to enable the recipient countries to escape from the poverty trap. Yet if aid helps to break the poverty trap, as it should, then aid has served its purpose and can be phased out. Self-sustaining economic development will continue. Increased household and budgetary incomes will provide the wherewithal to cover the costs of clinics, schools, agricultural inputs, and infrastructure that were previously supported by the aid flows and will create a tax base for continued public investments. There is even a term for such a process: *graduation from aid.* India is in the process of graduating from aid. China, the recipient of about $60 billion in aid from all donors since 1980, has already graduated from grants and subsidized loans from the World Bank because it has become too rich to need them. Any new credits come at market terms.

Here is a rule of thumb: an economy can generally graduate from the need for aid when the national income has reached around $4,000 per person, measured at purchasing power parity (PPP) or roughly $1,000 at market prices. China's income in 2003, for example, had reached $5,000 per person (PPP). This graduation point compares with current incomes in sub-Saharan Africa of roughly $1,400 per person (PPP). Africa needs, roughly, to triple its per capita income per person to graduate from aid. At a 7 percent per annum per capita growth rate, Africa would triple its per capita income in sixteen years. Economic growth per person in sub-Saharan Africa could be sustained at 7 percent per annum in the foreseeable future if external aid helps the continent to achieve the needed preconditions of infrastructure, public health, high agricultural productivity, and universal primary and secondary education. Therefore, with a determined effort, and with ample aid between now and then, *Africa could graduate from aid by the year 2025*. And that, indeed, should be our goal, remembering that to achieve it we will have to provide adequate financing between now and then.

Fortunately we've already promised to do just that. In addition to the specific G8 commitment to double aid to Africa by 2010, each major donor country has promised in the Monterrey Consensus (signed March 2002) to "make concrete efforts to reach 0.7 percent of the Gross National Income as official development aid." In 2005, the European Union declared that it would reach that goal by 2015. Others, including Australia, Japan, and the United States, should do the same. The combined national income of donor countries is now around $35 trillion per year and can be expected to reach roughly $44 trillion by 2015. Meeting the 0.7 percent pledge, therefore, would mean approximately $300 billion in total annual aid as of 2015, with perhaps $120 billion of that (or 40 percent) destined for Africa. With roughly eight hundred million African recipients as of 2015, the per capita aid to Africa would be on the order of $150 per African per year. If the donors scale up to that level of aid by 2015 and then sustain it to 2025, there would be ample opportunity to invest in Africa's villages and urban areas and to create the infrastructure, health, and education that Africa will need for self-sustaining growth after 2025.

IF WE FAIL TO ACT

The important new collection of essays *Too Poor for Peace?*, which I cited earlier regarding the youth bulge, describes more generally how extreme poverty leads to violence, terror, and mass displacement of populations. As the editors of the volume describe:

> In a world where boundaries and borders have blurred, and where seemingly distant threats can metastasize into immediate problems, the fight against global poverty has become a fight of necessity—not simply because personal morality demands it, but because global security does as well.
>
> Extreme poverty exhausts governing institutions, depletes resources, weakens leaders, and crushes hopes—fueling a volatile mix of desperation and instability. Poor, fragile states can explode into violence or implode into collapse, imperiling their citizens, regional neighbors, and the wider world as livelihoods are crushed, investors flee, and ungoverned territories become a spawning ground for global threats like terrorism, trafficking, environmental devastation, and disease.

I had also made this point in the summer before 9/11, in an essay entitled "The Strategic Significance of Global Inequality," though at the time I certainly did not expect it to become so painfully relevant so quickly. Afghanistan had become the quintessential mix of desperation and instability, and the home base of global terror. The great powers, of course, had not only failed to help solve Afghanistan's poverty, they had preyed on it. The Soviet Union invaded Afghanistan in 1979, and the United States promoted a religious-based insurrection in response, one that would come back to haunt the United States as a terrorist movement in subsequent years. Even today, because of Afghanistan's extreme poverty, the invasion of Afghanistan by the United States and NATO has failed to bring stability.

Afghanistan's crisis had simmered for decades before exploding. Its hardships were and remain extreme. Afghanistan faces severe ecological difficulties from aridity, desertification, overgrazing, soil erosion and degradation, and deforestation. The country is landlocked and located in mountainous Central Asia, resulting in isolation. The population has tripled from eight million to twenty-five million since 1950. A remarkable two thirds of the population is under the age of twenty-five, and the total fertility rate is 7.

Afghanistan exemplifies the end of the line for desperately poor countries when poverty, overpopulation, and environmental degradation are allowed to continue unchecked for decades. Solutions that were once at hand can be lost for decades because the land simply can no longer sustain the population, except perhaps by reliance on poppy production and other desperate stratagems. The greatest swath of instability today comprises the group of dryland countries from Africa through the Middle East and Central Asia that relies on pastoralism as a principal livelihood. The group includes the Sahel (Senegal, Burkina Faso, Mali, Niger, Chad), the Horn of Africa (Ethiopia, Eritrea, Somalia, and Sudan), East Africa (northern Uganda, northeast Kenya), the Middle East (Yemen), and Asia (Afghanistan, Pakistan, Uzbekistan, and Tajikistan, among others). All of these countries are besieged by problems that no military can solve: remarkably rapid population growth, a youth bulge, deeply degraded environments, and a lack of economic alternatives. The poverty trap, and instability, deepen as the world delays a sensible response.

DARFUR AS A DEVELOPMENT CHALLENGE

Only Darfur rivals Afghanistan today as a case of extreme desperation leading to mass violence. The rebellion in Darfur against the Khartoum government and the brutal violence among the various groups within Darfur reflect the desperation of a population that cannot meet its most basic needs. The world's politicians have focused on Sudan's politics as they've flailed about for an international response to the brutality of the conflict, but they have largely missed the central point: the only true solution for Darfur is economic development assisted by the rest of the world.

Consider briefly the particulars. Darfur has long been the development backwater of an impoverished country. As a landlocked region in the west of Sudan, Darfur is far from the irrigation, power grids, and transport networks of the more developed part of the country. It has always been among the poorest regions in Sudan, both during the British dominion and Sudan's independence. Northern and southern Darfur have poverty rates between 41 and 60 percent, while western Darfur, on the Chad border, has a poverty rate between 61 and 72 percent.

Throughout modern history, Darfur has lacked basic infrastructure (roads, power, safe water, and sanitation) as well as political representation. During the British Empire, Darfur was neglected in favor of the irrigated cotton plantations along the Nile. The only reliable growth in Darfur was its population, from less than one million at the start of the twentieth century to an estimated six to seven million today. But as the population has soared, the carrying capacity of the land has declined because of long-term diminished rainfall, shown in Figure 10.7 for the El Fasher weather station of north Darfur. The figure reports the July–September rainfall each year. The striking pattern is the decline of rainfall starting at the end of the 1960s, a pattern that is evident throughout the African Sahel. While there has been a bit of recovery in recent years, the rains have remained deficient, especially in view of the sevenfold increase in population over the last century. The results have been predictably disastrous. Competition over land and water has become lethal. Nomadic communities, who move between Chad and Darfur to find water for their livestock, have increasingly had to encroach upon sedentary farmers. Since there are ethnic and linguistic divisions between the nomads, mainly from northern Darfur, and the farmers in South Darfur, the clashes increasingly have taken on an ethnic and political character. The national Sudanese government acted ruthlessly in the face of rebellion by the mainly sedentary groups, and has used the horrible tools of ethnic cleansing to try to put down the rebellion.

The most authoritative recent study of the links of environment and con-

Figure 10.7: Precipitation in the Sahel (El Fasher Station)
from 1917 to 2006

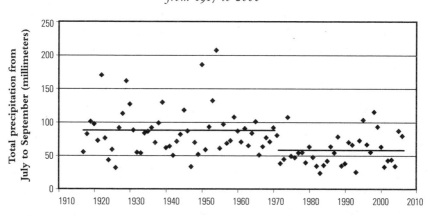

Source: Vose et al. (1992)
Note: Lines represent average values for 1917–1970 and 1971–2006

flict in Sudan gives strong support to the linkages of ecological stress and conflict. The United Nations Environment Program's excellent report *Sudan: Post-Conflict Environmental Assessment* notes that "there is a very strong link between land degradation, desertification, and conflict in Darfur," that northern Darfur "can be considered a tragic example of the social breakdown that can result from ecological collapse," and that "long-term peace in the region will not be possible unless these underlying and closely linked environmental and livelihood issues are resolved." While emphasizing desertification, land degradation, and climate change as "major factors in these conflicts," the report also wisely notes that "they are generally *contributing* factors only, not the sole cause for tension."

Darfur, therefore, presents a critical case, as does Afghanistan, where a different kind of security thinking is needed. Sanctions, peacekeepers, and the like will not solve the problem. Any lasting end to the violent conflict in Darfur will need to address the causes of the conflict, which lie in the extreme poverty of the region. Five key development challenges will need to be addressed to overcome Darfur's extreme poverty and economic insecurity: the lack of essential social services and infrastructure; adverse hydrology and rapid desertification; extremely low productivity in agriculture and animal husbandry; poor governance and breakdown of dispute-resolution mechanisms; and rapid increase in population that exacerbates ecological and economic conditions.

Peace in Darfur will require solutions to the development crisis alongside strategies that address immediate security and humanitarian needs. While the need for such a three-pronged strategy—security, humanitarian relief, and development—is widely accepted by experts on the ground, the political discussions often focus exclusively on short-term security and humanitarian interventions, with little or no attention paid to the longer-term development needs.

The development response to the crisis could start with the same kinds of quick-impact interventions for development as in the Millennium Villages. Following a successful stabilization within some two to three years, a longer-term strategy can be built around the Millennium Development Goals, which provide a comprehensive and pragmatic basis for setting quantitative objectives. It is notable, and promising, that the parties to the Darfur Peace Agreement, including the government and rebel groups, have themselves put an enormous emphasis on economic development as key to long-term peace. They have identified the Millennium Development Goals as the cornerstone for Darfur's development: "The Parties agree to make every effort to bring Darfur states up to the national average level of human development in the shortest possible time with a view to attaining the Millennium Development Goals (MDGs)."

At the core of the quick-impact strategy is the goal of a rapid and sustainable increase in agricultural and livestock productivity, including a shift of practices to slow, and eventually to reverse, severe environmental degradation in Darfur. Additionally, nonrural livelihoods need to be promoted, including meat processing and trade. Key social services (health, education), improved governance, and core infrastructure (particularly transport) underpin this quick-impact strategy. Quick-impact measures should include:

- Improving water access through the construction of small-scale water storage, shallow tube wells, and repair of water management infrastructure that has been damaged or fallen into disuse

- Controlling disease through distribution of antimalarial bed nets, essential medication (immunization, oral rehydration therapy, antibiotics, antimalarials, antihelminthics, and so forth). In a second phase village health workers can be trained in three-to-six-month courses to deliver 50 percent of medical interventions needed to achieve the MDGs.

- Opening or reopening schools (including, as appropriate, opportunities for boarding children for the migrant population) to permit the return to some degree of normalcy for children and families and ensure that no children are left without access to primary education

- Establishing comprehensive school feeding programs using locally produced food (if available) to improve nutrition and educational outcomes, and to generate demand for local food production

- Increasing agricultural productivity through the mass distribution of improved seeds (sorghum and millet), fertilizers, improved tools and animal-drawn plows, and simple rainwater harvesting techniques

(these simple interventions can be delivered within one growing season and will lead to a doubling of food crops)

- Improving livestock health through the free mass provision of veterinary services, and improved breed varieties

- Creating safe corridors for livestock movement from the north to the south during the dry season to minimize the damage to croplands and reduce sources of conflict

- Introducing an early warning system for drought in western Sudan that comprises low-cost meteorological stations, access to satellite data on regional oceanic and atmospheric conditions, and climate forecasting software

- Creating food-for-work or labor-intensive construction programs for roads, bridges, repair and construction of buildings, and other public works (to the extent possible, food for the food-for-work programs should be sourced from the Darfur region to increase demand for locally produced food)

- Installing mobile-phone-based services. (In a large, sparsely populated arid region like Darfur, in which populations are seminomadic and often large distances from cities, the advent of the cell phone offers remarkable new opportunities: phones can provide connectivity between parents and children left at boarding schools, support for emergency health services and transport to health facilities, market information, information on weather and natural hazards, and more.)

- Curtailing gender-based violence and women's vulnerabilities through safe houses, safety kits for women and girls at risk, and distribution of firewood and drinking water to reduce the need for foraging

- Removing mines and the explosive remains of war and promoting the rule of law and safe areas that include provision of safe houses for people where supplies and important documents can be stored

Ending the Darfur crisis, and others like it, will require a new approach that should become central to security thinking in the years ahead. When regions like Darfur are in crisis, we must think first of the underlying causes of such crises from the outset, which in many cases are extreme poverty and deprivation, and then think of practical investments that can save lives and give hope for the future. Soldiers, peacekeepers, and sanctions should be diplomatic tools of last resort, not of first resort. If we focus initially on the underlying causes of these crises, we will discover that our ability to achieve lasting solutions to them is far greater than we now imagine.

Chapter 11

Economic Security in a Changing World

WHEN COUNTRIES ARE STRUGGLING TO break free of extreme poverty, the role of the state is clear: to help the population meet basic needs (food, safe water, shelter, health services, nutrition) and to invest in agriculture and in the core infrastructure (roads, rail, power, telecoms, Internet, ports) to provide the foundations for private-sector-led economic growth. As countries break out of extreme poverty and begin to acquire wealth, another public-sector role emerges: social insurance. Social insurance expands the concept of social protections beyond the most basic needs to include universal access to an expanded range of health services, universal access to education services in addition to the primary level (including preschool, secondary, vocational, tertiary, adult, and job retraining), unemployment insurance, old-age pensions, insurance against various natural hazards, and income transfers to households in the event of job loss, disability, or extreme poverty for other reasons.

Peter Lindert has beautifully told the story of the expanding social outlays of the high-income economies in his comprehensive history *Growing Public: Social Spending and Economic Growth Since the Eighteenth Century.* Social expenditures on health, education, pensions, and social insurance for unemployment, work injuries, and job loss began in the late nineteenth century and developed in earnest in the twentieth century. Germany's chancellor Otto von Bismarck is often credited with having established, in 1889, the first old-age security system based on a payroll-financed public pension, partly as a tactic to deflect the growing mass support for socialism. Britain followed suit in 1911 with its own contributory pension system. Social expenditures in the high-income world went from nearly nothing in the mid-nineteenth century to more than a quarter of GNP in most cases today.

CLAIMS AND COUNTERCLAIMS
ON THE WELFARE STATE

There is a long-standing debate about the extent of the social safety net. How generous should it be? Is there a point at which it gives too much and provides disincentives to hard work and personal initiative? That debate is very much alive today in the United States and Europe. The political right calls for tax cuts and reforms of the public outlays to reduce their cost and to target them more specifically at the poor. The left calls for higher taxation to finance a greater degree of social outlays and to expand protection beyond the indigent to all of society in universal programs. For the most part, however, this debate takes place without much evidence being invoked. It is dominated by ideology rather than fact. I hope to remedy that deficiency here.

Interestingly, the debate has flared in the wake of globalization. As globalization has proceeded, the working class in the high-income world has suffered a relative decline in income compared with more highly educated knowledge workers, and two sharply contrasting lines of thought have emerged. Free-market ideologues warn that competition in the international system has become even more intense. The perceived threat to a country's prosperity from overseas competitors means that all attention must be refocused on economic competitiveness and growth. Obstacles to business development and to saving and investment must be eliminated. Taxes must be cut and profits encouraged. A country's standing in the world economy will collapse if it is burdened by expensive social outlays. At the other end of the spectrum, proponents of social investment opine that social spending must be raised dramatically, precisely because globalization is tearing at the fabric of economic equality. The rising income gap between skilled and unskilled workers, for example, requires higher taxes on the richer skilled workers, if only to help finance social outlays for those who are left behind.

Many economists have argued that the social safety net should remain limited, lest the incentives for innovation and risk taking be diminished. Economist and political theorist Joseph Schumpeter developed the very influential theory of creative destruction in the 1940s, according to which economic success inherently requires the failure of some sectors in order to make room for the rise of new leading sectors. New ideas are constantly entering the market, jostling with old ones, and often defeating them; the weakest workers, businesses, and industries lose in this process. Economic growth and development are thus inherently painful for the victims of creative destruction. In some interpretations, a social safety net would slow the turnover from lagging to leading sectors, and frustrate the returns on entrepreneurship and innovation. A contrasting view, very popular in Sweden and some other social welfare states, holds that precisely because capitalism is so turbulent, a social safety net is vitally needed to win the public's support for an economy in constant flux. The argument goes that without social insurance, the public would be likely to demand protectionism and nonmarket guarantees of employment.

Another major criticism of the social welfare state from the right is that it represents a direct threat to personal freedoms. Economist Friedrich Hayek argued in his influential work *The Road to Serfdom* that large-scale involvement of the state in the economy would lead to the collapse of individual freedoms. Although he first aimed those criticisms at the centrally planned communist economies and their controls on industry, he later extended them to the so-called social democracies with their expensive welfare policies.

The U.S. and European political right wing regularly depicts social spending as a threat to economic efficiency and personal liberties. Social programs are viewed as imposing an excessive burden of taxation on citizens and corporations. Expansive (and expensive) social programs are thought to undermine market mechanisms and to distort the incentives vital to healthy economic growth and performance. The idea is that the world will have winners only if it also tolerates losers. Markets should be left to provide the bulk of the services otherwise provided by the welfare state. The opposing view is that a large social safety net actually ensures confidence in the future, enables people to take risks, and also allows for a redistribution of wealth that prevents the most extreme economic inequality. Redistribution of wealth ensures that the most acute inequalities are avoided. While there will still be inequality, there will be no deprived underclass at the low end of the income spectrum nor a wealthy plutocracy at the other.

Proponents of an expansive welfare state also argue that relying on markets to ensure help for the poorest of the poor within a society is futile. Even in the rich countries, markets do not reach the very poor, who have too little income to afford health insurance, to rebuild their homes after a flood, or to pay the rent if they lose their jobs. Absent a safety net provided by the government, the poorest are left to fend for themselves and languish in miserable conditions. Second, markets do not actually provide the adequate protection attributed to them by their supporters. Only governments will provide unemployment insurance or recovery funds when major natural disasters strike. It is naive to assume that markets will offer the appropriate protection to those who need it under such unique and dire circumstances.

The debate over economic security is like the debate about poverty, environment, and sustainable development. Because it is seldom tethered to the facts, the debate generates fierce heat, great rhetoric, and little resolution. In the case of social spending, much more is known and proved (and also disproved) than the protagonists of the debate either recognize or want to acknowledge. By turning directly to the evidence, we find that the choices faced by the rich countries are considerably less stark than America's free-market ideologues pretend. Capitalism is not a fragile reed that will collapse with the slightest investments in social insurance. Capitalism is robust. It is possible to combine a high level of income, growth, and innovation with a high degree of social protection. The Nordic societies of northern Europe have done it, and their experience sheds considerable light on the choices for others.

THE SOCIAL-WELFARE AND FREE-MARKET STRATEGIES

Let us examine three kinds of capitalist societies. The first group is the social-welfare states of Denmark, Finland, Norway, and Sweden. All of these countries maintain very extensive systems of social insurance and very high levels of social expenditure as a share of gross national product. The second group of countries includes the core European continental countries of the European Union: Austria, Belgium, France, Germany, Italy, and the Netherlands (although the Netherlands straddles both the mixed economies and the social-welfare models). I will call these the mixed economies because they fall between the social-welfare system and the free-market system. The third group of countries includes the (relatively) free-market countries: Australia, Canada, Ireland, New Zealand, the United Kingdom, and the United States. These countries tend to believe more in free markets and lower social insurance. They have much lower social spending as a share of GNP than do the mixed economies and the social-welfare states. Figure 11.1 shows the different

Figure 11.1: *Average Government Spending as a*
Percent of National Income in 2004

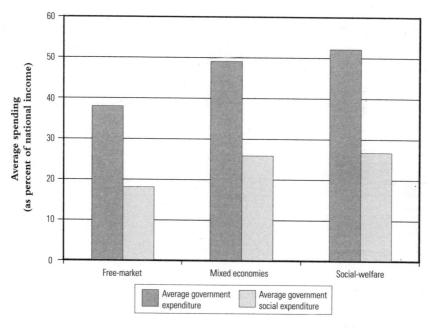

Source: Data from OECD Economic Outlook (2006)

levels of government spending as a share of GNP among the three groups. As
we can see, the free-market countries have the smallest share of government
spending, at roughly 38 percent. The mixed economies have about 49 percent
government spending as a share of GNP, while the social-welfare countries
spend the most, at 52 percent. The key difference in overall levels of government spending is the difference in levels of social spending as a share of GNP,
also shown in the figure.

SPENDING ON SOCIAL INSURANCE

Public-sector social outlays may be divided between cash transfers, direct
government provision of services, and active labor-market policies (for example, job training and government hires under public-sector employment
programs). Cash transfers include transfers to retirees (pensions and survivor
benefits) and cash transfers to working-age households. Government social

*Table 11.1: Breakdown of Public-Sector Social Outlays as
a Share of National Income in 2001*

COUNTRIES	CASH TRANS- FERS	DIRECT GOVERN- MENT PRO- VISION OF SERVICES	ACTIVE LABOR- MARKET POLICIES	TOTAL PUBLIC- SECTOR SOCIAL OUTLAYS
Free-market	9.8	7.2	0.4	17.4
United States	7.9	6.7	0.2	14.8
Mixed economies	16.8	8	1	25.8
Social-welfare	14.2	11.4	1.2	26.8

Source: Data from OECD (2004)

services are divided between health and nonhealth services (such as child care and disability care). The breakdown of these main categories of social outlays is shown in Table 11.1. I will refer to the sum of the first two categories (cash transfers plus direct government provision of services) as direct public social outlays. These plus spending on active labor-market policies equal total public-sector outlays.

We see that the social-welfare states are distinctive not only in their overall high level of social expenditures but also in their high direct provision of services. These directly provided services, such as child care and care for the elderly, are important not only for the services themselves but also for the public employment positions they represent. The social-welfare states have hired many otherwise hard-to-employ individuals (for example, with disabilities or low school performance) into the government social sectors in the past twenty years as part of their labor market strategy.

SOCIAL SPENDING AND ECONOMIC OUTCOMES

The evidence suggests that the high social spending in the social-welfare states is indeed very effective in reducing poverty and inequality and in promoting

Table 11.2: Inequality and Poverty Indicators in 2004

COUNTRIES	POVERTY RATE (%)	SHARE OF DISPOSABLE INCOME TO LOWEST QUINTILE (%)	GINI COEFFICIENT
Free-market	12.6	7.3	32
United States	17.1	6.2	35.7
Mixed economies	9	8.4	28
Social-welfare	5.6	9.7	24.7

Source: Forster and Mira d'Ercole (2005)

health and prosperity. Table 11.2 shows three different measures of poverty in the three country groups: the poverty rate (the percentage of people living at less than half the average national household income); the share of disposable income (after taxes) received by the poorest 20 percent of the population; and the Gini coefficient on income, which measures how equally wealth is distributed across the country (o is perfectly equal, 100 is entirely unequal). As the table shows, the social-welfare states outperform the other two groups across all three measures. The mixed economies of Europe are the next best. The average poverty rate in the social-welfare states in 2004 was just 5.6 percent of households, compared with 9 percent in Europe and 12.6 percent in the free-market countries. The United States, among the richest of all of the countries in per capita GNP, also has the highest poverty rate by far, at 17.1 percent of households living on 50 percent or less than the average household income.

Free-market critics of the welfare state have long believed that high social spending, paid for by high rates of taxation, would be harmful to economic prosperity by reducing the incentives to hire workers and the incentives to save and invest. Yet these arguments are not supported by the evidence. The surprising fact is that the social-welfare states have an even higher employment rate (number of workers as a share of the working-age population) than the free-market countries. The free-market countries in turn have a higher employment rate than the mixed economies. The key here is that the social-welfare states have very high rates of female labor-force participation. The social-welfare system ensures day care and schooling for the children, so mothers have the time and means to enter the labor market.

The social-welfare states have been successful in maintaining very high employment rates for two other reasons. First, social support for the working-age population has been tied to specific policies that require those receiving benefits to seek employment with the assistance of government programs. Second, the government itself has acted as an important employer of last resort. Many older, lower-skilled, and partially disabled workers are employed in the public sector, and especially by local governments, in the provision of public-sector social services, including day care, health care, and support for the disabled population. Those policies have allowed the social-welfare states to use government programs to ensure outstanding employment levels.

In terms of wealth and per capita income, the social-welfare states again defy the stereotype that high taxation leads to lower living standards. On average, the social-welfare states have a higher per capita GNP than the free-market countries, with the mixed economies coming in third. The high tax burden in the social-welfare states has obviously not crushed the economy. And when we look not only at average income but also at its distribution among the citizenry, the social-welfare states achieve their high incomes with greater equality. The poorest 20 percent of households in the social-welfare states take in around 9.6 percent of the national income, as opposed to only 7.3 percent of the national income in the free-market countries. Thus, if we look at the poorest 20 percent of households in each group, the average annual income comes to $24,465 for the poor in the social-welfare states, compared with just $17,533 in the free-market countries.

Thus, the social-welfare states have achieved high levels of income, low rates of poverty, and a more equal distribution of income than the free-market societies. This is powerful evidence of the advantages of an extensive social-welfare state. These countries have also achieved many other notable successes in their governance and economic management. They are rated very highly for having low corruption and high public trust in government institutions. They are rated very highly in their international competitiveness and in rankings by the World Economic Forum and others. They achieve high rates of national saving, despite the high tax burden. They achieve balanced budgets, despite the large social outlays, because the high public spending is matched by adequate taxation. In short, they have achieved vibrant, well-functioning democracies that assure a very high level of social well-being for all of the citizens.

Another striking fact about the social-welfare states is their very high rate of technological excellence. Sweden and Finland prosper on their high-tech sectors in information and communications technologies, notably led by Ericsson and Nokia, respectively. Table 11.3 shows the ranking of countries in the World Economic Forum Technology Index, which is built upon evidence of innovation, R & D, and mobilization of information and communications technology. The social-welfare countries score exceptionally well on the technology index. They are heavy investors both in R & D and in higher education, and they have very high rates of patents per capita as well.

As a final point, social-welfare spending not only reduces inequities and uncertainties within a rich society but also bolsters the confidence and trust within the society to be more generous on the international stage. Countries treat the world's poor and vulnerable as they treat their own. U.S. policies, by pursuing a constricted notion of social insurance, foster a society of fear and vulnerability that lacks the readiness to contribute more to global cooperation. Mainstream Americans feel increasingly unnerved by widening income inequality at home, and are therefore less likely to support assistance for the poor abroad.

Figure 11.2 illustrates the relationship between domestic social policies and international aid policies. The horizontal axis measures each country's social spending as a percent of national income, and the vertical axis measures the country's development aid as a percent of national income. There is a

Table 11.3: Technology Index and R & D as Share of Income in 2006

COUNTRIES	WORLD ECONOMIC FORUM TECHNOLOGY AVERAGE RANK*	R&D IN 2003 (AS PERCENT OF GDP)
Free-market	16	1.8
Mixed economies	24	2.0
Social-welfare	6	3.0

Source: World Economic Forum (2006) and OECD (2006)
* 1 is top rank

Figure 11.2: Domestic Social Expenditure and
Foreign Assistance in the High-Income Countries in 2005

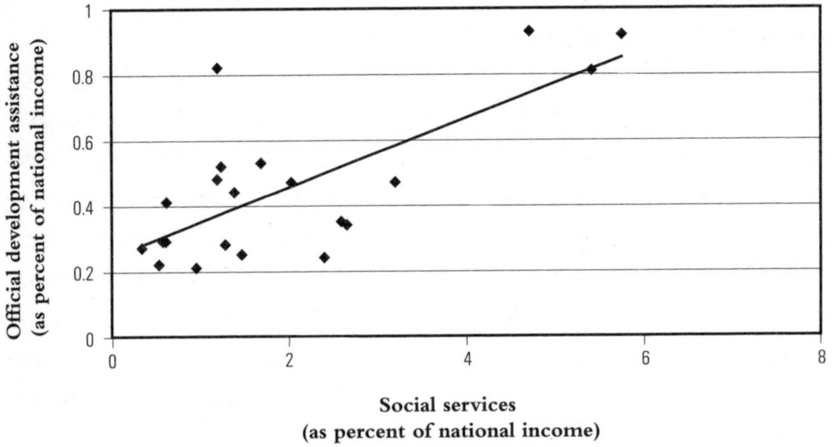

Source: Data from OECD/DAC (2007), using social expenditure other than health.

striking positive correlation. Countries like the United States with very low social spending at home are also the countries with low levels of international development aid. Countries like Sweden with very high levels of social spending are also countries with high levels of international aid. In essence, countries treat their own poor and the world's poor with a similar approach: either extending ample help through social spending (as in Sweden) or leaving the poor to fend for themselves (as in the United States). The social-welfare state, in this sense, can be a powerful instrument for enlightenened globalization, both within the rich countries and in fostering sound relations between the rich and the poor countries.

IS THE SOCIAL-WELFARE MODEL TRANSFERABLE AND SUSTAINABLE?

The Nordic commitment to the social-welfare state is long-standing and dates back at least to the post–World War II political scene. Social Democrats have governed in northern Europe for most years since 1950. Social spending as a percent of GNP has been relatively high in the social-welfare states for at least forty years. In this sense, there is a long-standing social-welfare model of social democracy. We have shown that the social-welfare model of high social spending has not led to long-term political or economic deterioration. The social-welfare states tend to outperform the other countries on most economic and governance indicators.

There are still important questions regarding the transferability of the social-welfare model. There is probably little room for doubt that Nordic ethnic homogeneity has been an important enabling social factor in the success of the social-welfare state. In a wonderful series of articles, Alberto Alesina and colleagues have shown that social spending tends to be highest where social and racial cleavages are the smallest. This is true across U.S. states and apparently across countries as well. White Americans living in states with higher proportions of African Americans, for example, seem to be much less likely to support high levels of social spending. The authors summarize matters as follows:

> Racial discord plays a critical role in determining beliefs about the poor. Since minorities are highly over-represented amongst the poorest Americans, any income-based redistribution measures will redistribute particularly to minorities. The opponents of redistribution have regularly used race based rhetoric to fight left-wing policies. Across countries, racial fragmentation is a powerful predictor of redistribution. Within the US, race is the single most important predictor of support for welfare. America's troubled race relations are clearly a major reason for the absence of an American welfare state.

In the end, the social-welfare model relies on a form of trust. It seems people are more willing to withstand high rates of taxation if they know that their taxes are paying for programs that help people like them. Because poor people in the social-welfare states are of the same cultural and ethnic background as the rest of the population, it is politically easier to promote programs that support the poor. The social-welfare model underlines how important it is for the success of the welfare state that citizens identify with the beneficiaries of government programs. They are less likely to do so if socioeconomic divisions coincide with racial or ethnic divisions. This is a central point. The costs of racism are great. Racial and ethnic diversity in the United States, and in many countries in Latin America, has led to divided and unequal societies. It has also contributed to the failure of the welfare state. In order to combat poverty and inequality in those racially divided societies, it is also essential to combat racism and intolerance.

FURTHER REFLECTIONS ON THE UNITED STATES

The oddest fact about U.S. politics in the past quarter century is that income inequalities have widened considerably, the number of families living in poverty has stopped declining, the size of the prison population is sky-high, the underclass has become even less socially mobile than before, and yet American politics has increasingly favored the rich: in hefty tax cuts, reduced outlays for the poor, the lack of progress on expanded health care coverage, and much more. Democracy has not brought home the benefits for the bulk of the population, but instead has favored the super-rich. Yet perhaps none of this is surprising, since the heightened inequality of income has been accompanied by an even more ruthless penetration of big money into national politics. The cross-country evidence that we've just reviewed puts to rest the false proposition that the growing income inequality in the United States is the inevitable price to pay for a highly productive economy. The social-welfare states enjoy high productivity and much greater economic fairness, and with much less poverty. While there is no doubt that the U.S. super-rich are benefiting in terms of personal wealth and megaconsumption, there is no evidence that the rest of the population has been a beneficiary of the strategy of stingy social outlays.

One of the best books on U.S. politics in recent years is *The 2% Solution*, by Matthew Miller, who shows how little it would take to make a big difference in addressing the needs of the U.S. poor. Even without going all the way to a social-welfare strategy, the United States could smooth the hard edges of American inequality, just as increased rich-country help could make a huge difference among the world's poor. Miller's title refers to the idea that 2 percent of U.S. national income, if devoted to increased social outlays, could address some of the profound inequities of U.S. society, especially the lack of universal health coverage (which would require less than 1 percent of national income in added spending to ensure) and the poor quality of public schools for the children of U.S. poor and working-class families. It is important to note that President George W. Bush's tax cuts, which went overwhelmingly to the rich, amount to around 2 percent of national income each year. The Iraq War costs roughly 1 percent of national income each year in direct outlays. Thus, by reversing the tax cuts and ending the Iraq War, it would be possible to pay more for the U.S. poor—to ensure, for example, universal health care coverage within the United States and to improve public schools—while also increasing U.S. outlays for the world's poor to the 0.7 percent of U.S. GNP that we promised.

Another recent and powerful book is Jacob Hacker's *The Great Risk Shift*, which describes how the United States not only lacks an adequate social insurance system today but has also substantially dismantled the limited system that was in place during the past forty years (with the peak years of social insurance identified as the mid-1960s, during Lyndon Johnson's War on Poverty). Hacker demonstrates the great rise in risk facing the American middle class as well as the poor and shows the remarkably high proportion of the middle class in the United States who are vulnerable to spells of poverty. He describes vividly and persuasively how a great right-wing attack on social insurance has systematically reduced the scope of the social-welfare system in health care, job protection, child support, housing support, and retirement security. He recounts all that is misguided about the constricted philosophy of self-help and market-based solutions that has dominated U.S. politics in recent years:

> Our framework of social protection is overwhelmingly focused on the aged, even though young adults and families with children face the greatest economic strains. It emphasizes short-term exits from the workforce, even though long-term job losses and the displacement and obsolescence of skills have become more severe. It embodies, in places, the antiquated notion that family strains can be dealt with by a second earner—usually a woman—who can easily leave the workforce when there is a need for a parent at home. Above all, it is based on the idea that job-based private insurance can easily fill the gaps left by public programs—when it is ever more clear that it cannot.

There are five main conclusions to our investigation of social insurance in the United States and abroad:

- The United States does not have to accept continued high rates of poverty as the price to pay for a vibrant market economy, since social insurance can be combined with a high-productivity market economy.

- The United States does not have to choose between its own poor and the world's poor. It can help both, at modest cost, and with budgetary funding sources that are easy to identify.

- The United States can learn from the success stories of social-welfare states how to foster a greater degree of social harmony and confidence in public institutions.

- The U.S. social insurance system is even more tattered than it looks, because of the increased variability of incomes and risks facing American households.

- The costs of major corrections are small relative to U.S. national income.

Those lessons, of course, can be applied beyond the United States to other high-income countries as well, and can be guideposts for middle-income countries on their way to high-income status. Our focus on the United States is due, in no small part, to the fact that the United States, uniquely among the world's high-income countries, has carried on a decades-long assault on social insurance in a manner contrary to the evidence, and with increasingly adverse results.

PART FIVE

Global
Problem Solving

Chapter 12

Rethinking Foreign Policy

EVERY COUNTRY WILL NEED TO RETHINK its foreign policy strategy in the twenty-first century. None is yet equipped to put proper focus on global challenges around the environment, population, and global poverty. No government is properly organized to absorb the complex scientific information needed to make sound decisions. This chapter puts special emphasis on U.S. foreign policy because of the phenomenal gap that exists today between America's current role in the world and its potential role in helping to solve critical global problems vital to its own security and the broad global interest. The United States is on the wrong track in foreign policy and is thereby endangering itself and the world. The lessons extend beyond one country. Every nation will need to reassess its own international strategies along the lines discussed below.

The foreign policy of President George W. Bush's administration has been particularly misguided, but the flaws go beyond this administration. American political leaders have lost perspective on the post–Cold War world and on the real challenges facing our crowded planet. Since the end of the Cold War, the United States has failed to play a leadership role in global poverty, environmental and climate policy, energy policy, and global population change. The Clinton administration stood by while the AIDS pandemic soared in Africa, and the Bush administration's actions have been too little, too late, and too ideological. American foreign policy in the Middle East has failed time and again, putting the United States and the world at risk. The Iraq War is a foreign policy disaster that rivals the Vietnam War in cost, human tragedy, and misdirection of human energies.

Democrats and Republicans have agreed on the characterization of the United States as the world's colossus, the indispensable power, the new Rome, the twenty-first-century empire, the sole superpower. These ideas seem so normal that they've hardly been debated. Americans have bitterly debated the future course of action in the Iraq War, but they have not analyzed deeply how we got into this mess. Every analyst who explains our debacle in Iraq as the result of tactical failings—not enough troops, not enough prewar planning, too much corruption from American contractors—fails to understand the true risk facing the United States. Our problem is that our government has been flying blind, unable to comprehend the new realities taking shape in the world. When we examine the nature of American policy making, it's no surprise. Our government is simply not properly organized to absorb and process meaningful data from abroad.

I will discuss five points that threaten American security. First, we greatly overinvest in military approaches, though the great foreign policy challenges are political, economic, and environmental and are unsolvable by military means. Second, we neglect the power of foreign assistance as a tool to promote global stability. Worse yet, we mock it. Third, we believe in our own press releases about our dominance, failing to understand the limits of American power in today's world. Fourth, we caricature our adversaries, and reject dialogue and negotiation with them. We act as if negotiation is appeasement, despite the overwhelming evidence to the contrary. Fifth, our government is poorly organized to do better. Without antennae, we grope helplessly from one crisis to the next.

We need to fundamentally revamp our foreign policy strategy and organization. We cannot achieve national security strictly through military outlays. Instead, we need international partnerships and goodwill, and greater stability in today's fragile and failing states. We need to use development assistance to promote global stability. Finally, we need to reorganize government so that the deeper challenges to our stability—extreme poverty, failed states, environmental threats—can be addressed with knowledge and capacity.

THE LIMITS OF MILITARY POWER

Figure 12.1 shows an astounding fact. U.S. military spending in 2006 was nearly equal to the military spending of the *rest of the world combined*. By now, after large increases in the U.S. budget in fiscal years 2007–8, it's very likely that U.S. military spending now exceeds the rest of the world's. Since the United States constitutes just 5 percent of the world's population, the impli-

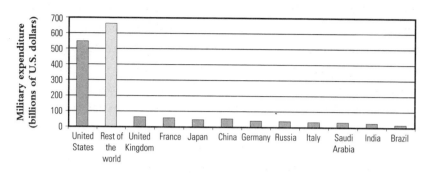

Figure 12.1: Military Expenditure in
Selected Countries in 2006

Source: Data from Stockholm International Peace Research Institute (2007)

cation is that U.S. military spending per person is nearly twenty times the world average.

It is a hallmark of U.S. national security doctrine that U.S. security rests on the pillars of defense, diplomacy, and development, but to understand the true nature of policy, it's good to follow the money. As shown in Figure 12.2, in fiscal year 2007 the United States spent an estimated $572 billion on the military, $11 billion on international security (security assistance to countries such

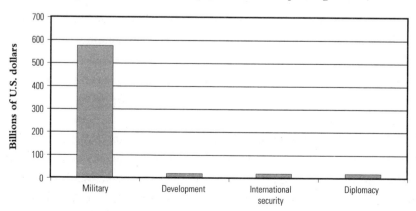

Figure 12.2: U.S. Military and Overseas Spending in 2007

Source: White House Office of Management and Budget (2007)

as Iraq and Afghanistan), $14 billion on development and humanitarian aid, and $11 billion for diplomatic functions (State Department, embassies, and so on). The figure is a startling and vivid display of the lopsided nature of our national security investment.

We should understand these allocations as *investment choices* in our national security, with a startling and threatening imbalance. Let's just consider one example. Part of the great development challenge in Africa is disease control, with malaria control ranking at or near the top of priorities. Malaria causes up to one billion clinical episodes per year, and between one and three million deaths. It impedes African economic development. It is a stated priority of the Bush administration. Now we will follow the money.

There are three hundred million sleeping sites in Africa in regions of malaria transmission. These sites should be protected by long-lasting insecticide-treated bed nets (LLINs). With recent technological improvements, these nets last for five years, cost $5 per net, and on average three nets are required to protect five people in the household. (There are an average of three sleeping sites for the five people in the household, and each of these sleeping sites should be covered). This comes to 60 cents per person per year. Even the small price of $5 per net puts them out of reach for hundreds of millions of impoverished people. Note that the total cost of bed nets for every sleeping site in Africa for a five-year period would be $1.5 billion (= $5 per net for three hundred million sleeping sites). Yet that is less than what the Bush administration spends on the Pentagon every day (the Pentagon has a $572 billion budget in fiscal year 2007, which translates into $1.6 billion per day). It's a striking truth worth pondering: *One day's Pentagon spending would provide enough funds to ensure antimalarial bed net protection for every sleeping site in Africa for five years.*

A fully comprehensive malaria control program for all of sub-Saharan Africa, including bed nets, medicines, community health workers, diagnostics, training, and indoor residual spraying, would require around $3 billion per year, or less than two days' Pentagon spending. The president chose to allocate a little under 10 percent of the total need, roughly $240 million per year. The choices are all illustrated in Figure 12.3.

This fiscal choice is certainly not guided by management or the administrative difficulties of doing more. The International Red Cross and partners (including UNICEF, the U.S. Centers for Disease Control, national govern-

Figure 12.3: Pentagon Spending and Malaria Needs

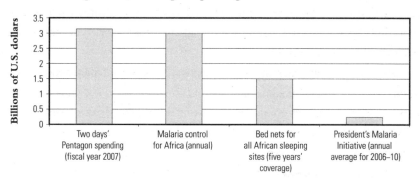

Source: *White House Office of Management and Budget (2007) and Teklehaimanot, McCord, and Sachs (2007)*

ments, and other NGOs) have demonstrated the ability to distribute bed nets on a remarkably widespread basis in a very short time, even in the poorest and most difficult rural settings. Yet these proven national campaigns led by the International Red Cross must struggle for cash to buy nets and other commodities. Money is the obstacle to scaling up, not logistics, politics, absorptive capacity, or other excuses that are often made.

Of course, it could still be argued that the military preponderance of U.S. security spending is sensible. We are in a war against terror, claims President Bush, and wars are costly. The problem, however, is a failure to understand how to achieve true security in the twenty-first century. The issue is not winning against a conventional army but removing the fundamental sources of instability. By that standard, the Pentagon spending is misguided. We are spending in ways sure to lead to sorrow and frustration, rather than true national and international security.

WARS OF IDENTITY

One of Britain's leading soldier-statesmen, General Sir Rupert Smith, has made the point in his recent book *The Utility of Force* that conventional military advantage may prove useless in facing the real security threats of the twenty-first century and, indeed, has regularly done so in the wars of the past half century. Our military thinking, says Smith, is still bound up in the vision of "industrial conflict" of mass armies, as in the Napoleonic wars, World War I, and World War II. Yet in recent decades, and for the foreseeable future, countries are faced with a very different kind of security challenge, which Smith labels as "wars amongst the peoples." War is "no longer a single massive event of military decision that delivers a conclusive political result." Conflicts are waged for political advantage and public opinion as much as for battlefield victory. The conflicts are open-ended. The sides are often non-state actors. In these circumstances, the vast industrial might of the U.S. military can easily prove useless.

Table 12.1 reminds us that all of America's battles in recent decades have taken place in the developing world, and often to disastrous political effect. The United States failed in Vietnam, Lebanon, Somalia, and now Iraq and mostly likely Afghanistan as well. In none of these cases has the military superiority of the United States proved at all useful in achieving political ends. But the

Table 12.1: Selected U.S. Military Operations since 1959

COUNTRY	YEAR OF INTERVENTION	MILITARY AND POLITICAL OUTCOME
Vietnam	1959–75	U.S. military defeat and withdrawal
Cambodia	1970	Temporary incursion, followed by mass genocide by Khmer Rouge
Iraq-Kuwait	1991	Military victory in forcing Iraq from Kuwait with Saddam Hussein remaining in power
Lebanon	1992	U.S. military withdrawal after suicide bomber
Somalia	1992	U.S. military withdrawal after downing of Blackhawk helicopter
Afghanistan	2001	Ongoing civil war and insurgency; growing political instability and heroin trade
Iraq	2003	Ongoing civil war and insurgency; no political resolution

Sources: Various

United States is not alone in experiencing a series of such debacles. The European imperial powers withdrew from their colonies after World War II not because their armies were militarily defeated but because their armies could not secure the political objectives of maintaining imperial rule and legitimacy.

At play is a fundamental issue of politics. In the post–World War II era, after generations or centuries of colonial rule, the forces of nationalism and self-determination became irresistible in the developing countries. The idea that human dignity requires freedom from foreign occupation has become the most powerful political idea of our time. All of this was immeasurably strengthened by the spread of literacy, mass communications, and a modicum of economic development. Yet even as the United States has proclaimed its fundamental commitment to human freedom, it has disregarded its own anticolonial history and the basic facts of modern history. Thus, the United States substituted for France in Vietnam's struggle for independence, and could not understand that the Vietnamese were fighting a war of national liberation. The United States replaced Britain as the chief outside meddler in the Middle East oil states—Iran, Iraq, Saudi Arabia—but could not understand that every U.S. manipulation of local Middle East politics ignited powerful anticolonial antibodies.

President Bush imagines that the United States has liberated Iraq, but to the Iraqis the United States is yet one more occupying power, indeed one that has partnered with Britain, Iraq's original imperial power. Moreover, the United States has not tried to understand the roots of Arab views of Israel as a colonial imposition. While compromise is the only productive approach for both parties to the conflict, the Arab view reflects Arab nationalism and anticolonialism. For these reasons, military adventures such as the Iraq War are bound to fail, and I wrote as much in 2003 during the lead-up to the war:

> Under much worse circumstances [than even Afghanistan, Lebanon, and Somalia], the United States is about to insert itself for years into the vicious internecine struggles of Iraq, where tens of thousands of angry young men will be keen to pick off the occupying force. Our smart bombs won't prove as helpful on ground level as they do at 35,000 feet.

The military should not have been sent to Iraq in the first place. We needed diplomacy, not war.

FUNDAMENTAL DRIVERS OF VIOLENCE

The United States does need a powerful military that can defend against conventional forces. However, most American military engagements since 1960 have been in developing countries that had recently experienced a state failure. Figure 12.4 shows, in fact, that the second half of the twentieth century brought a sharp increase in civil conflicts within countries, while the number of interstate conflicts remained far fewer.

The links between the lack of development and state failure are clear. When a country is too poor to provide its people with basic necessities such as health care, and when the underlying ecology makes agriculture difficult without fertilizer and irrigation, any change can push a society off the edge and into outright desperation. As described in Chapter 5, something as sim-

Figure 12.4: The Annual Number of Civil
and Interstate Conflicts from 1946 to 2001

Civil conflicts greatly outnumber interstate conflicts. Since the 1950s, the number of interstate conflicts (warfare between the governments of two or more countries) has shown no upward or downward trend, while civil conflicts more than doubled, peaking in the early 1990s.

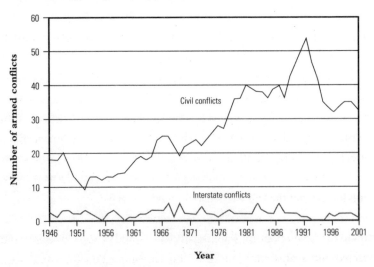

Source: Population Action International (2003)

ple as bad rains can trigger internal conflict when a society is living at the edge of survival. In Chapter 8, we also discussed how a youth bulge, which results in a high ratio of easily inflamed youths relative to those who might mediate disputes, tends to raise the likelihood of civil conflict. Young men are even more likely to join armed groups and engage in violence when economic activity is weak and other income-earning opportunities do not exist. In a similar vein, the work of Colin Kahl shows how demographic and environmental stress—in the form of rapid population growth, environmental degradation, and unequal distribution of renewable resources—leads to violent state failure or violence instigated by elites to further their interests. In particular, Kahl argues that demographic or environmental stresses are most likely to lead to state failure in societies that are deeply divided along ethnic, religious, or class lines and in societies where large parts of the population have little influence over the government.

At the core of the failed state problem are problems of poverty, the youth bulge, and rapid urbanization, all of which have sustainable development as their only real solution. None of these problems can be adequately addressed by the militaries of rich countries, powerful as these militaries may be. Our other tools, such as well-targeted foreign aid to promote development and sustain the environment, are likely to be much more effective at relieving desperation, fostering economic activity, and reducing the likelihood of conflict and subsequent U.S. military involvement.

FOREIGN ASSISTANCE AND U.S. SECURITY

Most of today's politicians in the United States have a primitive view of foreign assistance, when they think of it at all. There was once a glorious tradition—at the start of the postwar era—when General George C. Marshall recognized that aid to Europe would be vital for achieving American postwar political goals. As Marshall famously put it:

> It is logical that the United States should do whatever it is able to do to assist in the return of normal economic health in the world, without which there can be no political stability and no assured peace. Our policy is directed not against any country or doctrine but against hunger, poverty, desperation, and chaos. Its purpose should be the revival of a working

economy in the world so as to permit the emergence of political and social conditions in which free institutions can exist. Such assistance, I am
convinced, must not be on a piecemeal basis as various crises develop.

Truman's aid to Greece and Turkey, Eisenhower's aid to Taiwan and Korea,
Kennedy's launch of the Peace Corps, and Johnson's support for India's Green
Revolution evinced the same guiding purpose: to use aid to further economic
recovery and development, and by doing so, further the long-term stability
and goodwill of the countries in question. Unlike aid today to Iraq, or the ongoing funding of Israel and Egypt, aid in its heyday was seen not merely as a
payoff to allies but as a true instrument of development. It was understood
that poverty could foment violence and instability, so the ultimate goal of aid
as development assistance needed to be taken seriously.

Even today the U.S. security doctrine officially recognizes the linkage of
aid to overseas stability and thereby to U.S. national security. The 2006
National Security Strategy states:

> Effective economic development advances our national security by help-
> ing promote responsible sovereignty, not permanent dependency. Weak
> and impoverished states and ungoverned areas are not only a threat to
> their people and a burden on regional economies, but are also susceptible
> to exploitation by terrorists, tyrants, and international criminals. We will
> work to bolster threatened states, provide relief in times of crisis, and build
> capacity in developing states to increase their progress.

Yet the United States fails to act on that linkage: it has promised time and again
to support impoverished countries in order to help them escape from poverty,
but then it has failed to deliver, except in a few exceptional projects. In 2002,
the United States committed to "make concrete efforts towards the international target of 0.7 percent of gross national product (GNP) as [official development assistance (ODA)] to developing countries . . ." in the Monterrey
Consensus at a global conference attended by President Bush. Yet senior U.S.
officials then rejected that goal and disowned any such effort. The United
States said that it would not be pinned down to a numerical aid target, even
one to which it had agreed, and even one to which the European Union had
set a timetable for delivery.

The extreme of U.S. disdain for foreign assistance came in 2005, in the lead-up to the United Nations World Summit. The U.S. ambassador to the UN, John Bolton, tried to expunge the very concept of Millennium Development Goals from the outcomes of the summit, even though the MDGs were the centerpiece of the fight against poverty. At high cost to U.S. prestige, the U.S. government put itself squarely, if briefly, on the record as disowning the shared international objectives. A firestorm ensued in which virtually every country of the United Nations objected to the U.S. proposal. The United States backed down under the furious protest, but great damage had been done. The U.S. government had shown an ugly side, one ready to launch a war in Iraq but not ready to honor even the most basic commitments to the world's poorest and dying people. Ironically, on the opening day of the World Summit, September 13, 2005, President Bush not only declared America's commitment to the MDGs ("We are committed to the Millennium Development Goals"), but he also thanked more than 115 countries and nearly a dozen international organizations for offers of help to the United States in the wake of the devastation of Hurricane Katrina.

President Bush is sometimes praised for reinvigorating aid to the poorest countries, but this is mostly the result of starting from a meager base, not a true reflection of the adequacy of the U.S. aid effort. The president launched one respectably funded development program—the President's Emergency Plan for AIDS Relief (PEPFAR)—but even that effort has been hamstrung by right-wing ideology preaching a scientifically unjustified and ineffective strategy of abstinence rather than condom use to prevent HIV transmission. He also launched two other programs, the Millennium Challenge Account and the President's Malaria Initiative, but both were poorly funded relative to needs. As for the rest of the assistance effort, the president has actually cut other aid programs in Africa to make room for spending in Iraq. And, as discussed previously, the administration gutted the U.S. support for family planning, again an assault from the right-wing constituency.

AMERICA'S REAL SECURITY NEEDS

The United States is not threatened by an armed invasion of a foreign standing army. The age of industrial war has passed, at least for now. Our threats are more complex and less amenable to military solutions. First, we face a continuing dire threat of nuclear proliferation, both by governments and by rogue groups seeking such weapons from wayward states. Second, we face dire threats to the global environment that put the United States and the rest of the world at risk. Third, we face the risks of failed states—Somalia, Afghanistan, and many more—which can foment cross-border war and the spread of disease and refugees, and which can provide a harbor for terror.

None of these issues can be solved unilaterally. All require a highly sophisticated network of cooperation on a daily basis over years and decades. Security is a daily challenge to be achieved through cooperative efforts, not a prize to be won by a decisive military battle or change of regime. Yet cooperation requires trust, and trust requires that parties to an effort understand one another's needs and support them. The United States rejected this approach in recent years, abandoning UN treaties (such as the Kyoto Protocol), launching the Iraq War over the objections of the UN Security Council, forsaking basic principles such as the Geneva Conventions against torture, and rejecting the jurisdiction of the International Criminal Court.

The results are plain to see, and startling. Rather than achieve cooperation on crucial issues of common concern, America has squandered its reputation. In many parts of the world, the United States is seen as the greatest threat to the planet, not its hope. Few parts of the world see the United States as a reliable partner. A recent BBC-PIPA GlobeScan survey tells the grim story, summarized in Figure 12.5.

More than half of the eighteen thousand respondents in eighteen countries

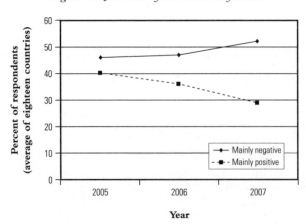

Figure 12.5: Views of American Influence

Source: BBC-PIPA GlobeScan Poll (2007)

held a "mainly negative" view of the United States, up from 46 percent in 2005. Even more dramatically, the proportion with a "mainly positive" view plummeted from 40 percent in 2005 to just 29 percent in 2007. An overwhelming but not surprising 73 percent opposed the U.S. war in Iraq. The collapse of support is found among traditional allies of the United States. In Germany, for example, only 16 percent said that they held a mostly positive view of the United States, down from 21 percent the year before! In Britain, 57 percent see the U.S. role as mostly negative. In Poland, a traditional mainstay of support for the United States, approval plummeted from 62 percent in 2006 to 38 percent in 2007. In Egypt, positive views declined from 21 percent to 11 percent. Under these circumstances, there is little chance for creating long-term strategies of mutual cooperation. Governments abroad come under tremendous domestic political pressure when they overtly support U.S. foreign policy initiatives, such as an expansion of a U.S. military base or flyover rights, or, especially, when they participate in a military effort led by the United States.

The most basic norm of cooperation is reciprocity: I will assist you if you will assist me. But the U.S. attitude has been different: "You are either with us or against us," as President Bush declared, with no recognition of the interests of the other country. The United States has demanded allegiance in the war on terror, without reciprocal support for the war on poverty, disease, or climate change. The UN has been attacked relentlessly by the American right wing as a threat to American sovereignty, as if American objectives could be accomplished unilaterally. This whole approach has by now imploded.

PICKING UP THE PIECES

The United States must take six steps to transform its security policy into a workable framework for the twenty-first century:

- Embrace multilateralism and international law

- Create a Department of International Sustainable development

- Shift financing from the military to an international sustainable development budget

- Address demography and the environment

- Reinvigorate the framework for nuclear nonproliferation

- Understand the Middle East and respond appropriately

Embrace Multilateralism

The neoconservative mistake, at the core, is the misreading of U.S. power. Why cooperate when we can have it all? Yet the bravado is misplaced. Four years and $500 billion later, Iraq cannot be secured and tens or hundreds of thousands are dead. The unilateral doctrine is even more preposterous when it comes to global threats such as nuclear proliferation, terrorism, climate change, or avian flu and other epidemics. Inherently, each of these requires thorough and meticulous cooperation from other countries. Much of that cooperation is already cemented in international treaty law and global regulation. In public health, for example, international cooperation to limit the global transmission of disease is codified in a series of international health regulations that enable the World Health Organization (WHO) to call upon member governments for various kinds of urgent actions. Such cooperation must start with the governments involved, but those governments ultimately depend on the support of their populations. U.S. objectives, therefore, depend deeply, not superficially, on global public opinion. The much-quoted Roman aphorism *Oderint dum metuants,* "Let them hate us long as they fear us," is a failure—if it was ever truly believed.

Department of International Sustainable Development

The United States is unable to pursue a sensible foreign policy today in part because our government is a blind giant stumbling from one crisis to the next. We have no governmental capacity to understand the interconnected problems of poverty, environment, and political instability in the developing world. We have "explained" those problems as being the result of tyrants and thugs rather than the result of politics, economics, and ecology. We have pretended that terrorism has no political dimension at all, only the theological dimension of "evil." Our aid agency, USAID, was long ago gutted of much of its talent, and now often operates as an employment agency for consulting firms. Virtually no single serious analysis has come out of USAID for a decade, despite a tradition of excellence and a long-suffering group of skilled development workers who somehow have survived the mix of faith-based politics and naïveté that has characterized our recent aid disbursements.

The next administration should take its cue from the United Kingdom's Department for International Development (DFID) and Sweden's International Development Agency (SIDA). Both are cabinet-level ministries with highly professional teams tasked with analysis as well as implementation. They have both been charged with ensuring policy coherence across a number of objectives, including development aid, governance, international objectives (especially the MDGs), trade policy, global public health, and environmental policy. They study, and know, the developing world in detail.

Financing for Development

Development aid should not be used to buy friends (such as when notorious Cold War–era payments were made to the dictator Mobutu Sese Seko in Zaire) but rather to promote long-term development. The strength of the linkages from economic progress to democracy and reduced warfare are powerful. Economic development promotes stability, while poverty and disease promote state failure. We have seen in earlier chapters that crises such as Darfur and Somalia must be understood as failures of development first and foremost, and only secondly as failures of politics. Trying to solve such crises through peacekeepers and sanctions alone, without the prospects of long-term development, is like putting a Band-Aid on an infected wound. The bleeding might stop temporarily, but the risk of continuing infection, even death, remains.

Impoverished governments cannot keep order, maintain the rule of law, or police their borders. Threats and sanctions are likely to add to destabilization rather than solve long-term problems. Indeed, economic development is so important for stability, yet so difficult to achieve, that we should put sanctions back into the drawer in almost all cases; they merely cripple an economy without reliable political effect. Carrots, in the form of assistance for development, are vastly more effective than sticks, in the form of sanctions and disinvestment, for creating long-term solutions for chronic instability.

The United States will spend in fiscal year 2008 more than $600 billion on the military and around $20 billion on all of development aid, of which half or so is for the war on terror (Iraq, Pakistan, Afghanistan, and Palestine), and only around $4 billion is for all of Africa. It's time to get serious by cutting the military budget by at least $150 billion per year (by withdrawing from Iraq and reducing outlays on nuclear weapons technology) and devoting roughly half of the saving to development aid, thereby meeting the promise by the United States to make concrete efforts to reach 0.7 percent of GNP in official development assistance (which amounts to approximately $90 billion in today's $13 trillion economy). This sum, when combined with Europe's aid scale-up, would provide the financial wherewithal to enable all impoverished countries with adequate governance to escape from extreme poverty. Crises in Sudan, Somalia, Afghanistan, and elsewhere could be solved at the core for a tiny fraction of the resources now wasted in open-ended military commitments.

Demography and Environment

As I've noted, the Bush administration has sharply reduced funding for population programs. The results run directly counter to U.S. security interests. The demographic bulge of young men in high-fertility countries feeds directly into the heightened threats of violence in those societies. We ignore uncontrolled fertility at our long-term peril, especially as these countries approach ecological crises and the shrinkage of farms to minuscule plots that can no longer support livelihoods. The neglect or disdain for environmental threats has been even more dangerous. The climate is already changing in all parts of the planet, and is leading to an increased frequency of droughts and floods throughout the world. Yet to date, the United States is hardly engaged in support either of mitigation or adaptation. A coherent development and security strategy will integrate ecology, climate, agronomy, demography, and public health into an integrated policy framework.

Nuclear Nonproliferation

The gravest terrorist threat is weapons of mass destruction, especially errant nukes. Nuclear technology today is such that the construction of a bomb requires massive state support, at least for the fissile materials. Our attention needs to remain, therefore, on government commitments to a global regime of nonproliferation, and on the protection against transfers of nuclear weapons from state to private or rogue hands. That is partly a matter of intensive policing to prevent fissile materials from leaving military compounds, and it is partly a matter of diplomatic efforts to keep countries within a nonproliferation regime. American militarism has proved to be a reckless foundation for such efforts. Rather than persuade rogue nations to desist from weapons creation, the threats against these countries and unwillingness to engage in negotiations accelerated such efforts. It was only when negotiations with North Korea were resumed in 2006 that real progress was made. When countries have come in from the cold, as South Africa and Brazil did in the 1990s, and Libya more recently, it has inevitably been through diplomacy and positive incentives, mainly the ability of countries to win broad diplomatic approbation and trade, investment, and development assistance from the United States.

The nonproliferation regime is splintering under multiple factions. The United States tolerates Israeli nuclear weapons while demanding that other countries in the Middle East reject such weapons. Similarly, the United States undermines the Nuclear Non-Proliferation Treaty, which calls on the nuclear powers to dismantle their own weapons stocks. Instead, it continues to construct new weapons systems in violation of the commitments to nuclear disarmament.

Middle East

The Middle East has experienced a century of Western imperial meddling. Britain and the United States toppled governments (Iran in 1953, Iraq in 1968), supported wars (Iran-Iraq in 1980–87), tolerated tyrants when convenient (Saddam Hussein in the 1970s and 1980s), and toppled them when inconvenient (Saddam Hussein in 2003). The United States supported Osama bin Laden and his mujahideen in the Afghan civil war (against the Soviet Union) only to help create Al-Qaeda. The United States and Europe have routinely peddled massive weapons systems, sometimes with bribery, which have frequently ended up in the hands of adversaries after the fall of a regime (Iran after 1979). The United States has stood by as Israel undertook an enormous and costly error, the post-1967 expansion of settlements into the West Bank and Gaza despite UN resolutions and the evidence that the settlements constitute a clear obstacle to peace. Through all of this, the West has talked about freedom, good governance, and democracy.

A viable Middle East strategy would start again from basic principles. It would include a settlement of the Israel-Palestine conflict along the 1967 boundaries, with both states having a capital in Jerusalem. It would aim at a nuclear-free Middle East, with Israel and the Arab states credibly abjuring nuclear weapons. It would focus attention on urgent development needs throughout the region, especially the challenges of job creation for the bulging youth population and massive environmental threats, particulary the shortages of water for households, industry, and agriculture.

AVOIDING GLOBAL WAR

Early in the twenty-first century we can envision three grave threats to global peace. In all three cases, the risks of a self-fulfilling descent into violence are far greater than the objective threats of war. The first, of course, is the prospect of a spreading conflict in the Middle East, one which could easily engulf the world. After 9/11, the American political leadership displayed the same kind of self-fulfilling paranoia that gripped Germany at the beginning of the last century. Vice President Richard Cheney enunciated the One Percent Doctrine, according to which a 1 percent threat against the United States would be regarded as a certainty rather than a low-probability event. Yet in a world in which cooperation can so easily collapse, Vice President Cheney's (alleged) morbid fixation on low-probability threats was much more likely to lead to self-fulfilling conflict than to true security for the United States. Sure enough, Cheney's fears led to a disastrous and unnecessary war in Iraq, one which continues into 2008 without surcease and continues to threaten a bonfire of violence engulfing hundreds of millions more people. Similar worst-case planning seems now to trap U.S. policies vis-à-vis Iran. Rather than negotiate with Iranian leaders, American leaders focus at every turn on Iran's perfidious intentions. This is viewed by many as tough-minded realism. In truth, it can create a self-fulfilling path to war.

The second threat, closely related to the first, is the unbridled spread of nuclear weapons. The Nuclear Non-Proliferation Treaty seems to be breaking down, or at least to be at the breaking point. Iran's move toward nuclear status follows the recent spread of nuclear weapons to India, Pakistan, and North Korea. Each country has its reasons for seeking these weapons, the most important being that one or more of its feared enemies already possesses nuclear weapons.

The third threat involves a replay of the disastrous military competition of the twentieth century between leading and rising powers, but with China now playing the role of the rising power and the United States the role of the defensive leader. The twenty-first-century rise of China will challenge global geopolitics at least as much as did the rise of industrial Germany and Japan in the twentieth century. As a crowded and resource-poor industrial power-house, China will look to international markets and foreign alliances to secure its vital primary resources, just as Germany and Japan did in the twentieth century.

There is nothing inherently frightening about the rise in China's influence. A stronger China can be an ally that bears more of the global responsibilities. Yet many in America will no doubt feel threatened by the surge of Chinese power. Grievances will mount as Chinese diplomacy trumps the United States on repeated occasions, whether in securing oil fields in Asia and Africa, selling military equipment to other countries, or challenging U.S. positions in global negotiations. Already, some right-wing voices in the United States are calling for the containment of China, as if 1.3 billion people, with the world's fastest-growing economy, could conceivably be contained. These calls for containment are heard clearly by Chinese leaders, who in turn call for a strengthening of China's military power to defend against U.S. threats. A Chinese military buildup, of course, would then be a self-fulfilling prophecy of the fearmongers. It should be no surprise that 2006 brought such titles to American bookstores as *The Coming China Wars: Where They Will Be Fought and How They Can Be Won; Showdown: Why China Wants War with the United States;* and *America's Coming War with China: A Collision Course over Taiwan.*

Our very survival in the long run will be achieved by recognizing that the vast majority of people in the Middle East, China, India, and the rest of the world, just as in the United States, long for their own prosperity and security, not for domination over others. Our fears can easily get the best of us. We must therefore train ourselves and orient our foreign policy to understand the world not only as we would see it but how others see it as well. That is the key to appreciating our common fate, and common wealth, on the planet.

Chapter 13

Achieving Global Goals

THE MILLENNIUM PROMISES ARE THE WORLD'S goals for sustainable development and they should guide our common actions. Accomplishing those goals requires a complex global process, one that is beyond the capacity of governments alone or any other single sector of society. In an age of global networks, these cross-cutting goals will require that we harness the energies and talents of all parts of society.

This chapter lays out a general blueprint for meeting the Millennium Promises. The process will necessarily involve many actors: scientists, entrepreneurs, activists, politicians, and private citizens. The first essential process is the mobilization of science around the issue. The second step is entrepreneurship: various incentives push businesses, innovators, and social entrepreneurs to come up with practical solutions. The third step is scaling up: taking proven solutions and applying them globally. Fortunately, history is replete with examples of successful scientific mobilization, practical innovation, and scale-up. We can build on these past successes.

GLOBAL PROBLEM SOLVING

Throughout the book, I have described progress in the areas of environmental sustainability, population stabilization, and poverty reduction. There have been marked global successes in each area, yet each is also an unfinished project. Nonetheless, we can discern the basic patterns that have proven successful at a global scale.

First, the public sector, private sector, and not-for-profit sector (including foundations and academia) have always played interlocking roles in global problem solving, especially the promotion of sustainable technologies. The *public sector* has four core responsibilities:

- Funding basic science
- Promoting the development and demonstration of early stage technologies
- Creating a global policy framework for solutions
- Financing the scale-up of successful innovations and technologies

The *private sector* has two core responsibilities (besides making profit, of course):

- Investing in R & D, often with public funding
- Implementing large-scale technological solutions in partnership with the public sector

The *not-for-profit sector* has five key roles:

- Public advocacy
- Social entrepreneurship and problem solving
- Seed funding of solutions
- Accountability of government and the private sector
- Scientific research, notably in academic institutions

These distinctive roles are played out in a complex ballet of interwoven actions. There is rarely a single conductor to keep the actions on time and harmonious. Only clearly stated shared goals can orient the multitude of individual actions that add up to global success.

Consider the ways that these actions may be mobilized for success. The process starts with the problem itself, such as desertification, anthropogenic climate change, excessive fertility rates, or extreme poverty. The problem is perceived first by experts, typically trained scientists. Often the scientific analysis runs a decade or more ahead of public opinion. The scientists usually form hypotheses, such as the growing risks of climate change, or the disappearance of the ozone layer, or the spread of HIV/AIDS. As those hypotheses are borne out, the scientific analysis becomes more broadly known in the public and in policy making circles. A specific event (a famine, a heat wave, a catastrophic storm, photographic evidence of ozone depletion) may provide an added crucial stimulus to public awareness.

The global policy community is often able to muster an early reaction, perhaps a loose framework for global cooperation, but one that does not produce a high level of action. In every case we've considered, the environment, disease, population, and poverty, there were early and mostly toothless international agreements that harnessed increasing scientific attention and increasing public awareness but not solutions commensurate with the scale of the challenge. United Nations framework conventions—for example, on ozone and climate change—are critical steps, but they do not mark the breakthrough to real action.

It is often in the foundation sector, the business sector, or academia where real solutions are first pioneered. The Rockefeller Foundation, for example, was the early champion of high-yield seed varieties that became the Green Revolution of the 1960s and onward. Individual drug companies often spearheaded projects to use their proven medicines in the fight against diseases of the poor, as with Merck and African river blindness. Academic scientists championed the control of chemical pollutants (CFCs) that contributed to ozone depletion. Often communities of experts (termed epistemic communities by political scientists) become the champions for a new approach to address the underlying ills.

Public policy plays a role at this stage as well by providing seed funding for the early solutions. Most of these are carried out on a small pilot scale. These pilot projects are proving grounds for what must come later at a national and global scale. Nongovernmental organizations and policy activists may also play a critical role. Philanthropists may support these early start-ups. Public service organizations, such as Rotary International, Doctors Without Borders, or Care International, can begin implementation.

As time progresses, three things come into sharper view. First, the problem itself becomes much clearer. Perhaps a public disaster (for example, Hurricane Katrina) becomes a moment of public epiphany. Second, the failure of the early steps or market forces alone becomes widely evident. This leads to growing calls for stronger public actions. Third, field trials and pilot projects give much stronger guidance on what can work at a large scale.

The next step is a global agreement for real action rather than a mere framework for recognizing the problem. This tipping point has arrived, at various historical moments, with ozone depletion, HIV/AIDS control, malaria control, and the fight against extreme poverty. At this point, a global treaty or protocol is agreed on, and a funding mechanism is put in place to take solutions to scale. Innovative economic frameworks—a new global fund, an international permit system, or a new global standard—are adopted to guide the actions of governments and the private sector.

Then comes the scale-up, the time when solutions proven at the pilot scale are brought to the global scale. Ozone depletion is controlled by a large-scale substitution of safe chemicals for the ozone-depleting CFCs. HIV/AIDS treatment is taken to millions in the developing world. Antimalarial efforts are financed on a large scale by the Global Fund to Fight AIDS, Tuberculosis and Malaria. National population control policies are backed by large-scale international funding.

Ideally, the global scaling up, which will last years or decades, is guided by a high-profile and transparent process in which clear goals are established, and all stakeholders are judged according to their contribution to the solutions. Success is achieved by constant feedback as actions and results are compared with targets and time lines. Without clear goals and accountability, the global stamina and cooperation needed to achieve the goals will surely fall short.

While humanity currently seems a bit adrift and is gripped much more by what divides us than what unites us, we should remember that the five Millennium Promises provide a unique and vital compass for steering global cooperation. The three Rio treaties, the Plan of Action on Population and Development, and the Millennium Development Goals all contain targets, time lines, and even formal treaty processes required to make headway. The Millennium Development Goals are vital, just to take one example, precisely because they set time lines and quantitative targets such as reducing maternal mortality by three fourths by 2015 compared with 1990. If the statement was merely that we should reduce maternal mortality, there would be little practical benefit in such an affirmation. It is the specificity and quantification of the goals that give them traction. Experts can monitor progress. Activists can gain leverage in fighting inaction and high-handedness of policy makers, and communities can set benchmarks and plan actions accordingly.

REINVENTING GLOBAL COOPERATION

Global processes have taken us halfway toward the goal of sustainable development. The world has achieved marked success, backed by remarkable global cooperation, in the fight against environmental degradation, population increases, and extreme poverty. Yet our combined efforts, great as they have been, have fallen far short of what is needed. The world is far off course from achieving the Millennium Promises, and far off track in securing sustainable development for the planet.

At the core of our problems today is the collapse of faith in global problem solving, and a widespread cynical disbelief in global cooperation itself. Opinion leaders dismiss global objectives such as the Millennium Development Goals or the mitigation of greenhouse gas emissions as unrealistic or even utopian. This pessimism is in part the result of the changes in global politics from a time after World War II when the United States took the lead in providing many global public goods to today, when a surly and fearful United States during the Bush administration has championed the ideology of unilateralism and narrow self-interest.

The achievement of global goals can no longer depend on U.S. leadership alone but requires robust global cooperation. That cooperation depends on an active network of governments, international organizations, the private sector, and academic and nongovernmental organizations.

We need, therefore, to reinvent global cooperation in a manner that recognizes certain key requirements:

- Clear goals and time tables, as contained in the Millenium Promises

- The need for public financing to be shared among the developed countries and a broadening network of middle-income countries

- The need for global participation in global problem solving by developed and developing countries alike, rather than by an exclusive group of countries, such as the G8

- The need to mobilize the private and not-for-profit sectors as partners in the global effort

- The need to harness expert scientific and technical knowledge at every juncture

- The need to support innovation at each stage, from start-up to scale-up

THE SOURCES OF PAST SUCCESS

The greatest successes in global cooperation in the past have combined a clear objective, an effective and scalable technology, a clear implementation strategy, and a source of financing. Smallpox eradication, for example, started with a clear objective (the eradication of the disease) and an effective and scalable technology (the immunization against smallpox). It built on a clear implementation strategy in which mass free immunization was combined with active case identification and localization of outbreaks. It built on a sustained funding effort by several donor governments. There are many other cases. The Green Revolution built on a clear objective (raising food yields), an effective technology (high-yield seeds, fertilizer, and water management in irrigated zones), a clear implementation strategy (mass distribution of the input package at below-market cost and a government commitment to buy the resulting increased harvest from the farmers), and large-scale funding (from private foundations, the U.S. government, and national financing). One can find this four-part package in the case of polio eradication (still under way), family planning and expansion of modern contraceptive use, children's schooling, rural electrification (where it has occurred), the expanded programs of immunization (championed by UNICEF), and more.

Failures of development aid have come when one or more of these four elements is lacking. Either there is a deep division between means and ends when goals are not set, or there is no proven way to achieve them if there is no obvious scalable technology, or the technology sits on the shelf when there is no clear implementation strategy, or the process ends in recrimination and finger-pointing if there is no financing to accompany the high-minded rhetoric that brought the major stakeholders to the table. The focus on practical deliverables can unite aid supporters and critics.

In many of the great challenges that we now face, such as climate change, biodiversity conservation, and the struggle to improve livelihoods in the dry-lands, no single technology will be the magic bullet. There are many candidate technologies for large-scale adoption, but many of these are as yet unproven. In such circumstances the four-part strategy of goals, technology, implementation, and finance for scale-up must be augmented by three other critical processes: an ongoing scientific assessment (such as the IPCC), public financing for basic science and early-stage technologies, and public-private strategies to bring newly proven technologies to mass scale. Science and public policy must work more closely than ever when we are in a situation where the preferred technological strategies are not yet clear.

Our recent failures to make faster progress to achieve the Millennium Development Goals and to mitigate anthropogenic climate change are largely attributable to the inability of international leaders to put key pieces into place. Seven years after the launch of the MDGs, and after countless promises of increased financing from the donor countries, including a promise to double aid to Africa between 2005 and 2010, the commitments remain un-fulfilled. Quite incredibly, debate reverts to first principles (Is aid effective?) even after financial promises have been repeatedly made and endlessly re-confirmed. In the 1950s and 1960s, U.S. leadership often was the deus ex machina that ended such paralysis. In this decade, the United States has become the biggest free rider, the one country seemingly least interested in stepping up to finance the globally agreed-on public goods.

LEARNING FROM THE GLOBAL FUND TO FIGHT AIDS, TUBERCULOSIS AND MALARIA

We need a new global architecture that relies less on U.S. leadership and more on global cooperation, and that puts added focus on science, technology, and the combined efforts of public, private, and not-for-profit stakeholders. A great success story, filled with larger lessons, is the Global Fund to Fight AIDS, Tuberculosis and Malaria (the Global Fund), in existence since 2001 and demonstrating what can be accomplished when the right pieces are put in place. Its performance vastly outpaces that of the rest of the development community in recent years.

The Global Fund was born at the height of the AIDS pandemic, when the donor-country governments, international financial institutions such as the World Bank, and the business sector were unable to organize an effective response to the epidemic within the existing institutions. As late as 2001, there was not a single HIV-infected African who was supported for antiretroviral treatment by a Western government aid program or by the World Bank. The developed countries were standing by as millions died each year despite the availability of medicines that could save them at a cost of roughly $1 per day at the time (the cost is now considerably less). Despite all of the hand-wringing about AIDS, and the existence of a highly effective treatment, three components of global cooperation—targets, implementation strategy, and financing—had not been put in place. The same could also be said about TB and, especially, malaria. Though proven strategies existed to fight both diseases, there was a general paralysis. Millions died each year as the world looked on, or more accurately, averted its gaze.

In 2000–2001, I was given a chance to help push the agenda forward as chair of the Commission on Macroeconomics and Health of the World Health Organization where my colleagues and I spelled out the links of finance, technology, and disease control. It became dramatically clear that the package of goals, technology, implementation, and finance could indeed be harnessed. In a July 2000 speech at the World AIDS Conference in Durbin, South Africa, I called for the establishment of a Global Fund to fight AIDS. In the fall of 2000 and early 2001, a faculty group at Harvard documented how AIDS treatment could be expanded to the poorest of the poor, drawing inspiration and insight from the path-breaking work of Dr. Paul Farmer and Dr. Jim Kim in Haiti, where they were successfully treating impoverished AIDS patients using antiretroviral therapy. The Harvard group demonstrated how AIDS treatment could be expanded on a large scale to the poor. Most important, Secretary-General Kofi Annan led the worldwide effort for action, first by leading the adoption of the MDGs in September 2000 and then by launching the proposal for a Global Fund to fight AIDS, TB and malaria in the spring of 2001.

The subsequent success of the Global Fund is especially notable because it has come in the aftermath of much backbiting, skepticism, and outright opposition over the years. Many people claimed that it would be impossible to treat AIDS in Africa because Africans would not adhere to drug regimens (the incoming USAID administrator at the time, Andrew Natsios, said that Africans could not tell Western time and would therefore not know when to take their medicines) and because drug resistance would soar. Similarly, there was widespread belief that it would be impossible to achieve large-scale malaria control because there would be no way to get the vital technologies— insecticide-treated bed nets and antimalarial medicines—into African villages because the nets would be diverted by corrupt officials or left unused by the households. And then once in the villages, the nets would be misused. There were similar excuses for inaction against TB control, which requires many months of directly observed therapy to cure the disease, and was also regarded as impossible to achieve in the impoverished and corrupt African context.

Six years later, all of these doubts and worries have proven to be vacuous. Africans did adhere to regimens, drug resistance did not grow, bed nets were used and few were stolen or mislaid. The accomplishments of the Global Fund as of mid-2007 are remarkable, and include:

- Program funding for 132 countries

- More than thirty million bed nets distributed

- More than 1 million people put on antiretroviral treatment

- 2.8 million people treated for TB

There have been serious glitches, to be sure. The United States opposed a strong link between the Global Fund and the World Health Organization out of a general antipathy to the United Nations, and this has weakened both organizations in recent years. The Global Fund would have helped to make the WHO more operational, and the WHO staff in the field could have done much more to support the Global Fund programming. The United States also went off on its own in disease-control efforts to control AIDS and malaria, unnecessarily complicating, and sometimes politicizing, the global support. This was another symptom of the Bush administration's unilateralism. On a technical level, there can be many improvements in the interface of the Global Fund with national programs, in clarity of funding, in design of projects, and in procurement of commodities. Yet the practical results of the Global Fund far outweigh all of these limitations.

The Global Fund also demonstrated a core lesson in political economy. Before 2001, poor countries were unable to access funding to fight AIDS, TB, and malaria. International donor agencies, such as the World Bank, engaged in lots of rhetoric but little action. Yet the lack of action was not easily discernible from the outside. It appeared, because of all of the hand-wringing, meetings, and speeches, that vastly more was being done than actually was. Moreover, if governments appealed for support, they could be brushed aside without any public awareness. The aid community was not taking any action, and there was no real recourse for suffering countries.

The Global Fund changed the dynamics dramatically by suddenly creating a highly visible place where governments could seek help. If the governments were turned down, that, too, was transparent. Indeed, scientific review panels were established for each disease in order to give an objective evaluation of country proposals. The existence of a clear source of funding, with a clear mission and backed by science, was galvanizing. Dozens of countries began to formulate plans and programs with the growing confidence that actual funding would be available to put those programs into action. The world moved quickly from speeches, theory, and debate to action.

A NEW FINANCIAL ARCHITECTURE FOR SUSTAINABLE DEVELOPMENT

The Global Fund points the way for success on a much broader array of challenges. When it comes to the MDGs, climate change, and population policy, we are wallowing in speeches and rhetoric, as we were in 2001 with regard to AIDS, TB, and malaria. Countries have no place to turn to get expanded programs under way. The poor have been told time and again to plan to achieve the Millennium Development Goals, only to find that the promised international support is not available. Taking a cue from the Global Fund, we should plan to simplify the global aid architecture and make it more transparent, science based, and responsive to the level of actual needs. This can be accomplished by establishing a few high-level funds targeted at critical dimensions of the Millennium Promises, and concentrating our aid efforts through those funds rather than a plethora of bilateral programs. Some funds already exist and need to be expanded. Others need to be started.

Seven global funds would cover the vast range of sustainable development needs:

- *Global Fund to Fight AIDS, Tuberculosis, Malaria and Other Diseases.* The Global Fund could usefully be expanded to cover additional infectious diseases (for example, worm parasites) as well as provide expanded support for operating the core health infrastructure in the poorest countries.

- *Global Fund for an African Green Revolution.* This fund would put its focus on expanding sustainable agriculture in low-income countries, with a special focus on Africa. It would put emphasis not only on high-yield seeds but on high efficiency of water use and sustainable land management practices.

- *Global Environment Facility.* This existing fund, jointly managed by the UN Development Program, the UN Environment Program, and the World Bank, would be expanded dramatically in scale and would have mandates in four priority areas: (1) sustainable energy for low-income countries; (2) adaptation to climate change; (3) biodiversity conservation; and (4) drylands management.

- *UN Population Fund.* The UN Population Fund (UNFPA) would be reinvigorated with greatly expanded funding in order to comply with the commitments to ensure universal access to sexual and reproductive health services by 2015. The UNFPA would be the focal point for the effort to stabilize the global population at eight billion or fewer by 2050.

- *Global Infrastructure Fund.* The World Bank, the regional development banks, the European Investment Bank, and perhaps other donors would pool financing efforts to expand public monies for infrastructure in the poorest countries, especially in sub-Saharan Africa.

- *Global Education Fund.* Of all of the MDGs, universal access to basic education is surely the easiest to achieve. The technology is the best understood and most straightforward. Yet funding has consistently run far behind promises. The United Kingdom has promised $15 billion over ten years for basic education, and this could form the corpus of a multilateral rather than bilateral effort.

- *Global Community Development Fund.* In addition to all of the targeted sector programs (health, education, infrastructure, population, and so forth), there is also the need to support community-based development efforts that cut across individual sectors. As countries seek to expand their Millennium Villages into Millennium Districts and Millennium Provinces, they need a place to turn to for reliable and predictable funding for the vital village-based investments in agriculture, health, education, and local infrastructure in order to jump-start development.

The point of this list is to ensure that there is a place for each country to turn to to meet crucial needs. These funds should take country applications for program funding in a public and transparent way, and should be replenished by the donor countries in line with needs and performance on preceding grants, and with proof of credible, scientifically valid plans. The mere existence of these funds would energize each country to establish serious and responsible plans of action across the gamut of the sustainable development challenges. With the prospect of timely financing for real investment needs, the world could move decisively from words to deeds.

SOCIAL VENTURE CAPITAL

These global funds would have as their main task the scaling up of proven solutions. When a technology and an implementation strategy have been verified, the relevant fund would be the guarantor of follow-up action commensurate with the challenge. Yet we also need seed funding to find solutions in the first place, a kind of social venture capital financing for early-stage problem solving. This is the ideal role for fast-moving and creative private foundations, which can take risks with their own money in ways that public funding agencies find much harder to do. It was the role played by the Rockefeller Foundation in championing the Green Revolution in the twentieth century. It can be the role played by the Gates Foundation and other partners in the twenty-first century.

Even with Bill Gates's vast wealth, the foundation by itself can't finance the scaling up of solutions at a global level. The Gates Foundation has been spending a bit more than $1 billion per year in recent years, and this will rise by $2 billion to $3 billion per year with the recent infusion of funds from Warren Buffett. Still, even with these vast sums, the global needs across poverty, disease, climate, energy systems, and population will be in the hundreds of billions of dollars per year, vastly beyond the means of even the largest private foundations.

The real work of great foundations lies elsewhere, in spearheading the search for solutions. This can come in the form of basic science, such as the Gates Foundation funding for vaccine and drug research and development. It can also come in the form of innovative delivery approaches, such as a Gates Foundation project to provide comprehensive malaria control in Zambia in order to learn about practical implementation strategies. Once the solutions are identified, however, then the larger-scale capacity of government-backed global funds would have to finance the scale-up of these solutions. If the Gates Foundation, with its financial weight, can promote new discoveries in science, technology, and implementation strategies for the poor, and can continue to inspire other philanthropic donors as it has done with Warren Buffett, the chances for the Gates Foundation to make world-changing contributions and then mobilize government funding to take its discoveries to scale are indeed very high. Many other foundations and philanthropists, by operating with insight, creativity, and boldness, can also make their mark on the history of sustainable development.

FUNDING FOR R & D

One of the greatest unmet challenges is a mechanism to support basic scientific research for sustainable development at a level and allocation across sectors that is commensurate with global needs. Raising money for global public goods is hard enough; raising funds for scientific research and technology development is harder still when the targets of the research are for global needs, not national economic advantage or private profits. The world can mobilize, with some difficulty, billions of dollars to support actual service delivery, but it has had an extremely daunting time in mobilizing support for the research and development of needed technologies.

The issue here is not one of principle, for example, a free-market opposition to public financing of science. Even staunch free-market economies invest heavily in national science and technology. The issue is much more practical: how to mobilize global funds for global purposes when the target of the funding is the world's poor or the global commons (such as improved conservation of biodiversity, management of the high seas, or sustainable energy technologies that will be difficult to patent).

The problems are threefold. First, the multilateral financing agencies, such as the World Bank, are not well staffed with research scientists. Second, the national research agencies, such as the National Institutes of Health in the United States, are charged with addressing national rather than international concerns. There is a National Cancer Institute, for example, but not an institute for tropical infectious diseases. And third, there is the problem of cost-sharing among the potential funding agencies. Global public goods require pooled financing, and free riding is pervasive.

There is no easy fix. In each area of concern, an international science committee should evaluate promising areas for R & D, and make recommendations on the allocation of research funds. Such R & D committees are needed for disease control, agriculture, climate science, sustainable energy, water-management technologies, and biodiversity monitoring and conservation. The Gates Foundation and the World Health Organization could take the lead on convening the panel on health issues. The Gates Foundation, the Rockefeller Foundation, and the Food and Agriculture Organization could take the lead on agriculture. The UN Environment Program and the UN Development Program could take the lead on water and biodiversity conservation. There is no single champion in any area. The pressing need, however, is to get started.

INNOVATIONS BY NONGOVERNMENTAL ORGANIZATIONS

Ideas, which are the key to global solutions, start with individual entrepreneurs. Once the problem is known, and early public policy has started, a field of incentives is created to foster the multiplication of ideas. Innovators can be motivated by the promise of future profits derived from patents, prize money offered by foundations and governments (as with the Gates Foundation's Grand Challenges in Global Health Initiative), purely socially minded aims (as with social entrepreneurs), and the desire to solve technical problems (as with engineers). Nongovernmental organizations have repeatedly played a pivotal role in identifying local needs, proving new technologies, and perhaps most important, identifying novel implementation strategies.

Perhaps the leading example of NGO leadership in recent years has been in the area of microcredit, pioneered by Nobel laureate Muhammad Yunus of Bangladesh and described in his book *Banker to the Poor*. Microcredit has revolutionized banking by making it possible for the very poor to take out small loans without collateral. The idea is that by lending to small groups rather than to individuals, collateral can be replaced by trust and group enforcement, since the group monitors its own members and ensures repayment. If one member of the group defaults, the whole group is held responsible and must pay back the defaulter's loan. Dr. Yunus also decided to lend almost exclusively to women, whose role as primary caregivers in rural Bangladesh makes them on average more responsible and less likely to squander the loan.

Making credit available to previously noncreditworthy microscale entrepreneurs enabled those people to break the trap of low income, low saving, and low investment. Even a very small loan makes it possible to purchase crucial materials or equipment to start a small, income-generating business. The loans also have the advantage of breaking the reliance of the poor on moneylenders who charge such high interest rates that the poor who borrow from them can never repay their debts.

Microcredit was unrolled gradually, first at the level of one village, then across one district, followed by several districts and, eventually, the entire country. The model evolved into a full-fledged financial institution, the Grameen Bank, which has more than seven million borrowers today. Grameen's model has been replicated across the developing world, and microcredit is now a widely used tool in the fight against global poverty. The Grameen model exemplifies how innovative solutions are first tried on a small scale and are gradually scaled up once their success has been proven.

In this vein, Grameen Bank expanded into mobile telecommunications when it started Grameenphone in 1997 with partner Telenor, a Norwegian mobile telecommunications firm. Grameenphone, in addition to now being the largest mobile phone service provider in Bangladesh, with more than ten million subscribers, is also responsible for the Village Phone Program. Based on the idea that a mobile phone can provide a source of income for its owner, Grameen Bank lends money to a microentrepreneur (almost always a woman) to buy a Grameenphone mobile and to be trained in its use. The owner can then charge others to use her phone for a profit, repay the loan, and have a sustainable livelihood. The Village Phone provides a fundamental public good to rural Bangladeshis: affordable connectivity. More than 260,000 Village Phones have been deployed in Bangladesh, covering roughly fifty thousand villages around the country. Village Phones have dramatically affected village life, notably by offering real-time access to market information for agricultural producers. The success of the model in Bangladesh has led to the development of similar programs in other countries and has also illustrated the far-reaching impact of mobile telecommunications technology on the rural poor.

Large humanitarian organizations also can be the source of important, life-changing innovations that can be scaled up and affect the lives of millions. The International Red Cross has long had expertise in mass immunization campaigns for children against such diseases as measles and polio. These campaigns mobilize hundreds of health workers and volunteers to reach thousands of children in a very short amount of time and immunize them. Mass immunization is the only way to ensure that the disease is properly controlled and, it is hoped, eradicated.

In 2002, the Red Cross decided to integrate its efforts to combat malaria with its mass immunization campaigns. The idea was to take advantage of the mobilization of resources and personnel for the immunization campaigns to also distribute free, long-lasting insecticide-treated antimalarial bed nets. To prove the effectiveness of the concept, the Red Cross first distributed 15,000 nets in one district in Ghana during a measles immunization campaign. The campaign's effectiveness was scientifically measured and evaluated through a series of follow-up surveys to see how many people still had the nets and were using them, and what had happened to the burden of disease. The results there and in other trials (next in Zambia) were impressive, so much so that the approach was then taken to national scale in Togo in 2004, with the distribution of 875,000 nets during the nationwide measles campaign, and again in 2005–06 in Niger, where 2.3 million nets were distributed during the national polio immunization. This gradual, methodical scale-up has proven that rapid, free distribution of bed nets can achieve tremendous results at a national scale. The rest of Africa can now follow this model, so that a long-lasting insecticide-treated bed net protects every sleeping site in the malaria-transmission zones of Africa.

SUSTAINABLE DEVELOPMENT IN A NETWORKED AGE

Modern information and communications technology (ICT) also boosts our capacity for effective global cooperation and provision of public goods. The advent of modern ICT is revolutionizing every aspect of development practice, and will enable more and more countries and isolated regions within countries to join the convergence club. Mobile telephones are perhaps the greatest development tool of our age, breaking isolation at remarkably low cost and drawing even the most remote regions and poorest communities into the global economy.

I count eight distinct contributions of ICT to sustainable development. The first is connectivity. Regions once separated from local and regional markets and from the flow of information are now instantly connected to the world. In the world's most remote villages, the conversations often now turn on the most up-to-date political and cultural events, or to changes in commodities prices, all empowered by cell phones even more than radio and television. The second is the division of labor. Connectivity to information means the ability to participate in finely divided production chains, in which distant communities provide inputs to a global supply network. Remote villages in Africa increasingly deliver flowers, vegetables, or sewn fabrics to markets in Europe and the United States, linked by cell phones, bar-code monitoring, GPS tags (to monitor physical location), and other instantaneous tracking devices. The third is scale. ICT permits messages to go out over vast networks, to provide guidance and vital information to thousands or millions of individuals.

The fourth is replication. ICT permits standardized processes, for example, online training or production specifications, to reach distant outlets instantaneously. The fifth is accountability. ICT provides a technological platform for audits, monitoring, and evaluation. Banking transactions can be made online (including more and more payment settlements by cell phone). Arrivals of products or their successful distribution in villages can be monitored in real time. Cold chains for vaccines can be verified by remote teleme-try, as digital devices give real-time readings of the temperatures in refriger-ated shipping containers. The sixth is matching, meaning the ability of the Internet to bring together remote buyers and sellers. The seventh is building communities of interest. Web sites that build on the new social networking technologies (for example, wikis, Facebook, MySpace, and more) allow for group activities, social activism, coalition building, and peer monitoring that were unimaginable just a few years ago. Within weeks it is now possible to build coalitions of hundreds of thousands or even millions of like-minded in-dividuals for social causes, political rallies, or other group events.

The eighth is education and training. Distance learning is now ubiquitous in countless informal ways, and will become the standard for much formal ed-ucation and training as well. Classrooms will go global, with lectures and stu-dent participation taking place in several countries simultaneously. Poor rural communities can be trained to perform IT services online or by videoconfer-encing. Telemedicine is already enabling doctors in India's urban centers to at-tend to patients in rural areas, and will soon be expanded to enable Indian doctors to attend to patients in Africa as well. Village health workers around Africa will be able to receive training, feedback, and guidance over the Internet.

The necessary next step for all of this is the ICT platform itself, the phys-ical hardware on which these vast applications can flourish. The platform is now, finally, being built. Mobile telephony is nearly ubiquitous today, even in impoverished regions where almost nobody has a phone, because those with phones demand universal access to their networks. Broadband Internet will not be far behind, especially if public financing is devoted, as it should be, to ensuring universal coverage of Internet services.

PUTTING A PRICE TAG ON SUCCESS

In the last dozen chapters, we have explored the challenges that will likely de-fine this century in humanity's history. We must strive to increase well-being around the world through economic growth, yet do it without wrecking the planet's climate or damaging ecosystems to the point where they fail to pro-vide the services we need and sustain the biodiversity of our planet. To syn-thesize each of the major challenges discussed in this book—climate, water, biodiversity, population, extreme poverty, and global politics—Table 13.1 shows

Table 13.1: Meeting Our Millennium Challenges

OUR GEN-ERATION'S CHAL-LENGES	BUSI-NESS AS USUAL	MILLEN-NIUM PROMISES	ACHIEVING OUR GOALS	THE COSTS OF FAILURE
Environmental degradation	Climate change in excess of dangerous thresholds, massive species extinction, growing water stress	To avoid dangerous anthropogenic interference in the climate (UNFCCC), significantly cut the loss of biodiversity (CBD), meet the challenges of dry lands (UNCCD)	Regulation of greenhouse gases to keep temperature change below 2 degrees centigrade; species conserved and ecosystems managed sustainably; water security for farming and drinking	Massive dislocations and deaths due to crop failures, famine, and failures of critical ecosystems
Population change	Population rising to more than 9 billion, and possibly more than 10 billion	Universal access to family planning by 2015 (ICPD)	Global population stabilized at 8 billion by 2050 through voluntary fertility reduction	Massive youth bulge, environmental pressures, and unchecked global migration
Extreme poverty	1 billion people stuck in a poverty trap	To cut extreme poverty and hunger in half by 2015 and reduce disease by more than half (MDGs)	MDGs achieved by 2015 and extreme poverty ended by 2025.	A world of instability, failed states, and uncontrolled pandemic diseases
Global problem solving	Growing tensions combined with the failure of global goals	Global cooperation to achieve the Millennium Promises	Success in meeting the great challenges of sustainable development by 2050	The risk of global conflict, provoked by growing sources of instability—economic, demographic, environmental, and social

the challenges of the twenty-first century, with the corresponding treaties and goals (our Millennium Promises) and the consequences of failure.

In Table 13.2, we've made rough estimates of the amount of global financing that may be needed to achieve the Millennium Promises in each area. The transition to sustainable energy will likely require no more than 1 percent of rich-world income and less than that in low-income countries. The enhanced conservation of biodiversity will require perhaps $35 billion

Table 13.2: Financial Needs for Meeting Our Millennium Promises

GLOBAL GOAL	FINANCIAL NEED	ILLUSTRATIVE ANNUAL OUTLAYS FOR GLOBAL COOPERATION
Climate change mitigation	Adoption of sustainable energy systems, with support for the poorest countries	1.0 percent of GNP (donor countries) 0.5 percent of GNP (low-income countries)
Climate change adaptation	Assistance to support the poorest countries with adaptation	0.2 percent of GNP (donor countries)
Biodiversity conservation	Financing of protected areas	0.1 percent of GNP (donor countries)
Combating desertification	Financial assistance for water management in low-income dry lands	0.1 percent of GNP (donor countries)
Stabilizing global population	Assistance for universal access to reproductive health services	0.1 percent of GNP (donor countries)
Science for sustainable development	Global public financing of research and development of new technologies for sustainable development	0.2 percent of GNP (donor countries)
Millennium Development Goals	Assistance to help the poorest countries to escape from the poverty trap	0.7 percent of GNP (donor countries)
Total	Budgetary outlays for global sustainable development	2.4 percent of GNP (donor countries)

per year, or 0.1 percent of rich-world income. Science for sustainable development—in energy, health, agriculture, climate, water, and other areas—might be targeted at $70 billion per year, roughly 0.2 percent of rich-world GNP. Extreme poverty, we've suggested, can be ended within the envelope of 0.7 percent of rich-world GNP, an amount long promised but not delivered. The illustrative sums, added up in Table 13.2, are very modest compared with our incomes, and very modest compared with the great gains in well-being that we can achieve. The difference between the dangerous and unsustainable global trajectory we are on now and a sustainable trajectory that addresses the challenges of environment, population, and poverty, is a modest 2 to 3 percent of annual income. Yes, that is politically large, but it is not large in terms of human well-being, or investments needed to save the world from dire and growing risks. In the United States it is around half of our military spending.

These estimates are necessarily uncertain, a rough guess at what lies ahead. We will gain financial precision only as we move forward and learn by doing. But as in so many cases in the past, the ultimate costs of action are likely to prove far smaller than we fear today, since we are more clever than we know once we've mobilized our efforts.

Chapter 14

The Power of One

After the final no there comes a yes
And on that yes the future world depends.

SO WROTE THE POET WALLACE STEVENS, and so goes our generation's challenge to turn the world from its unsustainable course. Our problems are solvable, but as we try to solve them, we will hear a million noes. No, we need not change; no, we cannot change; no, we must prepare for war; no, we cannot risk making peace. Yet after that final no will come a yes.

It has been said that the most important trait in a successful politician is persistence. As our task—achieving cooperation at a global scale—is political at the core, persistence will be our greatest asset as well. We will have to believe in our own Millennium Promises despite a global chorus of pessimists who pronounce those promises to be unattainable. Yet persistence will pay off in the end. The goals are achievable, as we have seen, and at vastly lower cost and vastly greater benefit than is currently imagined.

We have to gird ourselves against the unholy trinity of reactionary rhetoric identified by the great development economist Albert Hirschman. He noted that every new idea for constructive change is met with three attacks. The first is *futility*: the course of reform cannot work because the problem is unsolvable. The second is *perversity*: any attempt at solution will actually make matters worse. The third is *jeopardy*: attempting to solve the problem will take attention and resources away from something even more important. This negativism is a state of mind, not a view based on facts. Vigorous debate over the methods of change is, of course, healthy and vital, but relentless acceptance of the status quo is not acceptable in the face of the challenges we confront.

I have sketched a model of global change based on the idea that shared global goals, with timetables and targets, can create a slipstream of change. If the world hews to the Millennium Promises, they will induce each of us—in our personal lives, our work, and our communities—to move toward the shared global objectives. As the world converges toward those objectives, the force of convergence will strengthen. What seems impossible at the start, requiring billions of fragmentary and uncoordinated actions, will ultimately take shape as a global movement to achieve peace, prosperity, and environmental sustainability.

However, we are not only the subjects of history, carried along by blind forces, but also the agents of history. Our intentions help determine whether the world converges to shared goals or breaks apart into war and distrust. The chances for success will depend on the extent to which each of us, in our many roles in society, becomes a positive force for change. In the end, as John Kennedy said, peace will be a process, not the result of a grand or magic formula but "the sum of many acts." Or in his brother Robert's famous formulation:

> It is from numberless diverse acts of courage and belief that human history is shaped. Each time a man stands up for an ideal, or acts to improve the lot of others, or strikes out against injustice, he sends forth a tiny ripple of hope, and crossing each other from a million different centers of energy and daring those ripples to build a current which can sweep down the mightiest walls of oppression and resistance.

The energy and daring is to resist the noes, until the final yes has been achieved.

THE STAKEHOLDERS OF CHANGE

Human activity is organized through institutions that facilitate long-term cooperation. That begins with the family and extends into larger groups, including the clan, the community, business enterprise, government, all the way to global apex organizations such as the United Nations, with its membership of 192 governments. Each of these institutions arose because it facilitated some kind of specialized cooperation not available in the other institutions. Institutions die when they no longer serve a useful role in coordinating such activities.

We have seen in the case of economic development, cooperation is needed at all levels, from the most micro, within the household, to the most global, for example, in treaties at the World Trade Organization to manage international trade. The households manage certain kinds of cooperation on the smallest scale, between parents and children, husbands and wives. The community is vital for other kinds of cooperation, for example, to build and manage schools and clinics, to tend to the local environment, to settle local disputes. Higher levels of government are needed to pave the roads that connect communities and to create the power grid that brings electricity to them; and national governments are needed to look after national borders, seaports, and international airports, and to support the basic and applied sciences needed to address complex economic and social problems. Of course, business organizations, from a one-person shop to a global multinational corporation, manage technologies and the international coordination of the workforce needed to supply goods and services to customers.

The challenges of sustainable development, whether in heading off climate change, fighting extreme poverty, stabilizing populations, or ensuring adequate water supplies for human use and crops, all must harness actions from a wide array of institutions. No major problem can be solved by government, or the business sector, or one community alone. Complex social problems have multiple stakeholders who are all party to the problem and who generally must all be part of the solution. Gaining that cooperation among the disparate stakeholders is the toughest challenge of all.

If market forces alone could solve these problems, the challenge of cooperation would be fairly straightforward. Markets are wonderful because they coordinate the actions of a vast number of suppliers and customers who can remain largely anonymous to one another. No great ethics or acts of courage, or virtues of coordination are needed, only the decentralized self-interest of each business and each consumer. Adam Smith memorably noted, "It is not from the benevolence of the butcher, the brewer, or the baker, that we expect our dinner, but from their regard to their own interest."

This has led some economists into the erroneous and simplistic viewpoint that markets can be relied on to solve all problems. William Easterly, for example, attacked the notion that large-scale plans and coordination are needed to get medicines to the poor by noting that millions of copies of Harry Potter books have gotten into the hands of readers without any such grand plans. The difference, of course, is that Harry Potter's readers have money to buy the books, while the poorest of the poor lack the means to buy, for example, life-saving medicines. If a child doesn't have the money to buy the book, the child nonetheless survives (with a touch of disappointment), whereas a child without the money for medicine could die before morning. Ten million of them do each year. If our goal is merely to get large numbers of vaccines to the public, markets would suffice. If our goal is to get vaccines to *all* children who need them, markets cannot do the job by themselves. If our particular focus is on the very poorest people, who lack any financial resources and who live far from paved roads, transport, clinics, and health information, then markets may be very far down on the list of institutions we need to muster.

Markets fail, we have stressed, when the poorest of the poor cannot afford to take part in them or when private incentives don't operate properly to provide public goods, such as environmental protection or disease surveillance or scientific breakthroughs, which are predictably underprovided by market forces alone. In those cases, more complex forms of cooperation are required, with a wider range of institutions that include not only businesses and consumers but also the public and not-for-profit sectors.

To say that such cooperation is hard is not to say it shouldn't be attempted. John Kennedy said the following about the challenge of going to the moon:

> We choose to go to the moon in this decade and do the other things, not because they are easy, but because they are hard, because that goal will serve to organize and measure the best of our energies and skills, because that challenge is one that we are willing to accept, one we are unwilling to postpone, and one which we intend to win, and the others, too.

We can say the same about global cooperation to end poverty and save our planet.

THE CASE OF ANTIRETROVIRAL MEDICINES

Consider further the problem of medicines for the poorest of the poor and specifically the life-and-death challenge of HIV/AIDS medicines, or antiretroviral medicines. This will help us to see the vast range of stakeholders whose actions are critical to address a complex need and the complex forms of cooperation required when markets alone will not solve the problem.

From the mid-1990s, scientists and clinical practitioners, backed by large-scale public funding, identified a class of drugs that successfully controlled the replication of the HIV virus in infected individuals, thereby stopping the progression of AIDS in treated individuals. The underlying scientific work was itself a complex partnership of government (for example, the National Institutes of Health), private pharmaceutical companies, and academic scientists. Given the complex incentive systems that have been devised to promote such discovery, several pharmaceutical companies ended up with patented medicines of high efficacy. Scientists determined that these medicines should be taken in a three-drug "cocktail" to forestall a patient's development of drug resistance to any single one of the medicines.

Patent-protected drug cocktails have sold for around $10,000 per patient per year since the first years of the twenty-first century. In most high-income countries, the vast majority of these costs are borne by health insurance, whether public or private, or by government-financed programs (such as the Ryan White program in the United States). In some cases, but only a few, individuals are forced to pay out of pocket, and the more fortunate among those can afford to do so. By the time the drug cocktails came into widespread use in the rich countries, Africa harbored between ten and twenty million HIV-infected individuals. Neither their governments nor the individuals themselves could come anywhere close to paying the $10,000-per-person costs of the medicines (or even the low costs for preventative methods and testing, for that matter). Indeed, nearly all Africans with HIV simply progressed to death from AIDS without the benefit of the antiretroviral therapy that could keep them alive. No miracle of the market was in sight. Indeed, official institutions, such as the World Bank, simply operated on the assumption that antiretroviral medicines were for rich people, not for Africans. The World Bank even avoided mention of antiretroviral medicines in its articles about AIDS.

Here is a complex problem par excellence. A pandemic disease is ravaging Africa, a technical solution exists to transform the disease from a killer to a manageable condition, yet that solution is utterly beyond reach of those who need it. The injustice was immediately stark, but the solutions less so. The first breakthrough came when some generic drug producers, notably in India, reverse-engineered the medicines and announced that they could produce the drug cocktails at a tiny fraction of the market price. Of course, so too could the patent-holding pharmaceutical companies, who were reaping high prices for the medicines only by virtue of their patent protection (and the temporary monopoly that the patents provided). In 2000 and 2001, several generics companies announced that they would provide the medicines to low-income countries at around $1 per day per patient for the drug cocktail, that is, roughly $350 per year. The major patent-holding companies confirmed that they, too, could produce at such a low cost, but they argued that the lower cost would not recoup the preceding R & D, and even worse, would adversely affect their incentives for future R & D.

Through heated discussions and vociferous debate, the multiple stakeholders in this crisis—including the World Health Organization, the patent-holding pharmaceutical companies, various groups representing HIV-infected individuals, academic groups, and African governments—came to several realizations. First, they realized (with varying time lags) that the patent-holding pharmaceutical companies could "afford" to sell their antiretroviral medicines at production cost in Africa (that is, at $350 or so per year), while maintaining their patent-protected margins in the rich countries (that is, at $10,000 per year). This would not lose money, even potential revenues, since the patent-holding companies in any event had no real market in Africa at a price of $10,000. Moreover, it would be possible, through normal policing, to "segment" the African markets from the high-income markets. The drugs destined for Africa could not legally be sent back across the borders of the rich countries, and effective policing could realistically be put in place (as has proven to be the case).

Second, even when the drugs were offered at marginal production cost, the African countries (governments and households) could not afford them. Health budgets in these countries are roughly $10 per person per year or less, and cannot cover drugs that cost hundreds of dollars per year. Therefore, donors would be required to buy the drugs at reduced prices on behalf of African patients and then provide them in Africa for free, or at prices that are a tiny fraction of the $350 per patient per year. This was one of the reasons for establishing the new Global Fund to Fight AIDS, Tuberculosis and Malaria.

Yet the parties to the emerging strategy then faced a third set of obstacles. Even when the drugs got to the warehouses in Africa, they were hard to move to the patients. The "last mile" of the supply chain, from the drug inventories to the dying patients in huts in rural villages, could not be bridged through automatic market forces. The challenges of scaling up basic health services—including public education, counseling and testing, medical care, patient oversight, and drug logistics to transport medicines from regional health centers and hospitals to local villages—are all part of the daunting challenges. At the end of the supply chain is an impoverished household that cannot afford to cover even a pittance of the costs.

Actually, even this description is too simple. Some drug companies, for example, Bristol-Myers Squibb (BMS), launched wonderful philanthropic programs of HIV-drug delivery, supporting their own teams or independent NGOs in the medical supply chain and delivery. But they then discovered yet another obstacle facing the poorest of the poor. Many lacked the means even for a minimum of daily caloric intake, and the HIV medicines don't function well with a chronically undernourished patient. A group of project leaders from BMS at one point came to my office for advice on how they might grow food in their HIV project site!

Actually, by 2007, many of these problems have been recognized and are being addressed on a large scale. Roughly one million Africans are now on HIV treatment supported by donor funding, compared with almost none in the year 2001. Each of the multiple stakeholders is performing a piece of the magic. Markets are not the drivers of this success, though of course market returns helped to make available the medicines in the first place and helped to generate the income in the high-income world needed to finance access to antiretrovirals for the poorest of the poor. The actual institutions delivering AIDS medicines include a bewildering array of market-based, public-sector, and not-for-profit nongovernmental actors, including the drug companies, NGOs such as Partners in Health and Doctors Without Borders, the Global Fund, national African governments, local communities, and volunteer village health workers. The common thread is not market returns but rather commitment to a common goal: AIDS treatment for all who need it, even the poorest of the poor.

CORPORATE SOCIAL RESPONSIBILITY

The overriding job of business is to make money for the owners, but that in no way precludes an active role for business in solving nonmarket problems such as access to HIV medicines. Indeed, CEOs understand that if they neglect the nonmarket side of their activities, they can risk the very success of the company. The reputational costs to business of blocking solutions to vital challenges can be devastating to shared values, customer loyalties, worker morale, the ability to recruit new employees, and even the social acceptability of their continued operations. As one businessman has put it, "Either we're at the table on these issues, or we're on the menu!"

During the AIDS episode in 1998–2001, before the start of the Global Fund, the major pharmaceutical companies were threatened by just such a debacle. The companies were getting heatedly attacked by highly visible activists because of the cruel neglect of Africa's dying AIDS victims and the seeming unwillingness of the companies to reduce prices. The companies aimed to maintain the high patent-protected prices for the high-income markets, but they didn't yet recognize that they could and should segment the markets vis-à-vis the poorest countries. They also understood, if only intuitively, that it would never be enough to simply ship low-cost drugs to Africa. There would need to be a system-wide scale-up of health care capacity in the receiving countries.

At the time, I met with several CEOs to encourage them to cut their prices to production cost and to encourage the industry as a whole to rally to this standard. I told them that such market segmentation would be crucial for them to keep their good names. I also suggested, in every way that I could as chairman of the WHO Commission on Macroeconomics and Health and as director of the UN Millennium Project, that the ancillary supply chain needs (logistics, health workers, local clinics, and the rest) should be met by other donors. The pieces of the puzzle began to fall into place and former president Bill Clinton and the Clinton Foundation moved things forward significantly by helping developing-country governments negotiate low-cost agreements on antiretrovirals. The CEO of Merck Pharmaceuticals at the time, Ray Gilmartin, later told me about a moving lesson for the company. After Merck agreed to cut its prices to a no-profit basis for the poor countries, the employees in the company responded with enormous pride and enthusiasm. Gilmartin said it was the greatest boost to company morale that he had seen as CEO. All of us want to work in institutions that are part of the solution, not part of the problem.

The difficulties are not over, to be sure. Some pharmaceutical companies still resist the intrusion of generics producers, or they try to negotiate for higher prices or royalties on new drugs even in the lowest-income countries. Some patent-holding companies continue to delay the introduction of new life-saving drugs in low-income countries produced by generics companies even when the new drugs may be more effective than older versions or may be better suited for the poorest of the poor (because they do not require re-frigeration or are easier to ingest). Most problematic, there is no agreement internationally on where to draw the line between the poorest countries, other low-income countries, and middle-income countries (like Brazil and Thailand) that are rich enough to pay some amount above the zero-cost level for international medicines but are too poor to pay the same market prices as the rich countries. Standards of fairness, justice, and above all, public health, have not yet been agreed upon, and acrimony still flares. Nonetheless, I would emphasize that it is possible, indeed in the interests of all parties, to find workable solutions that constructively engage the world's major companies, respect their fundamental position as profit-making rather than charitable en-tities, and call for goodwill and adequate public funding to enable public-private partnerships to work effectively on behalf of the poor.

This is the general message that I give to all CEOs regarding the Millennium Promises. Each company needs to be part of the solution and needs to stretch its activities beyond normal market activities. This does not mean to turn the company upside down or into a charitable institution, but rather to identify the unique contribution the company may make as part of a broader effort to solve a major social challenge. This is the real meaning of corporate social responsibility: to operate in a manner that promotes broad social objectives, including nonmarket goals, in a way consistent with core business principles, values, and practices. It means much more than simple corporate philanthropy. It demands creativity.

In most cases, a company's main assets are its proprietary technologies, its supplier and customer networks, its good name, and its workforce. These are the assets that it can bring to bear in the fight against poverty, disease, hunger, and environmental degradation. In the case of extreme poverty, for example, companies should examine their technologies to identify those that can be of significant value to the world's poorest people. This might be medical equip-ment, high-yield seed varieties, chemical fertilizers, computer hardware and software, telecommunications equipment, trucks, financial service expertise, or more. In many cases, as with the antiretroviral medicines, the market prices for such goods and services are well above the marginal production costs, so the technologies could be extended to impoverished regions without jeopardizing the bottom line. Doing so will not only have minor immediate costs but will also have enormous long-term market benefits by bringing the firm into new markets that may grow significantly in the coming decade or two.

There is almost always a major problem, however, and once again, it is one that is familiar from the HIV experience. The technologies in question are often of enormous benefit only in conjunction with other goods and services. Computers might be great for rural schools but only if there is electricity. Trucks might be vital for farm communities but only if there are roads. Hospital equipment, of course, requires a hospital. Corporate philanthropy cannot be too complicated, or it can punish a company attempting to do the right thing. No private company can realistically be required to ensure a community's access to roads, power, schools, clinics, and the rest of the community's basic needs. A company is not a charity, nor is it a development agency. The companies should be pressed to contribute, most critically though not exclusively, by supplying their own technologies on favorable terms and provide the training and guidance in adapting those technologies and skills to local needs.

My own somewhat serendipitous discovery is that business philanthropy works best as part of a holistic development effort, where many partners—including philanthropists, donor agencies, and private business—come together to make their mark. The HIV episode, ultimately backed by billions of dollars from the new Global Fund, was one such approach. In the Millennium Villages throughout Africa, a large number of companies have lent a hand, largely by focusing on their core competency in a network of like-minded and farsighted businesses. Each of the following companies has helped to solve one part of the puzzle of extreme poverty in these villages: Yara for fertilizer; Monsanto for high-yield seeds; Sumitomo Chemical for antimalarial bed nets; KPMG for financial expertise; General Electric for surgical equipment; Ericsson for mobile phone and Internet connectivity; Novartis for malaria medicines; Becton, Dickinson for medical supplies and diagnostics. The list continues to grow.

A special kind of cooperation, pioneered by the Gates Foundation, has been public-private partnerships (PPPs) around research and development in which the philanthropies support research costs carried out by laboratories and research scientists of major academic and private-sector institutions. These PPPs have been established for the discovery and development of new medicines, diagnostics, vaccines, and other crucial medical inputs for major killer diseases including AIDS, TB, malaria, and several parasitic diseases. In each case, market forces alone would not justify the outlays of R & D. There is no market to solve the problems of the poorest of the poor. The Gates Foundation, in partnership with cutting-edge scientific enterprises, is stepping in where markets do not reach.

Companies should stretch in three ways. First, they should agree to focus on the Millennium Promises as part of their commitment. Second, they should work creatively to see how their particular technologies, networks, and expertise can become part of the solution. This process is one of discovery, in which the company works iteratively with on-the-ground problem solvers in different parts of the world. Third, they should agree to operate in places they've not yet reached. Perhaps they will not make much of a profit when they first open operations in Mali, Malawi, Tajikistan, or Bolivia, but they won't lose much either, especially if companies enter these new places in partnership with other like-minded firms. The Millennium Villages Project and others like it offer a basic platform upon which each company can leverage its special role and can help this entry process enormously.

Companies can play a huge role not only as providers of technology but also as customers of local output from impoverished regions. When companies like Starbucks, Nike, or the Gap source from low-income communities, they are not creating poverty (as is sometimes alleged) but reducing it. Of course, this is only true if these companies abide by internationally recognized labor standards and human rights principles related to community rights, workers' health, and so on. Thanks to relentless and dedicated pressure by NGOs, the major companies, intent on burnishing their names, are working toward or fulfilling those standards in many important cases. Many NGOs—such as Global Witness, Oxfam, the Interfaith Center on Corporate Responsibility, Amnesty International, and CERES—are performing a vital and heroic service in exposing companies that continue to abuse the privilege of their position and power. Yet there needs to be a situation of long-term trust and mutual accountability. When companies do the right thing, the watchdog NGOs should be prepared to praise them, thereby adding weight and support to the arguments being waged *inside* those companies. If bad performance is punished, good performance requires reputational rewards. This is a valuable point emphasized by the director of the Novartis Foundation, and one of the great leaders in corporate social responsibility, Klaus Leisinger.

The worst abuses have come—and continue to come—from the extractive industries, especially hydrocarbons (oil and gas), precious gems, gold, and other sectors where it is easy for companies to make a fortune by extracting high-value resources at a rapid rate without care for local communities or the physical environment. Oil companies may complain about lawlessness in the Niger Delta, but we must be clear that many among them were themselves agents of lawlessness when they paid massive bribes to national authorities over the heads of impoverished and local communities, and relentlessly cheated on contracts, records of shipments, reports on costs, and other aspects of business operations that affected their taxes and production-sharing arrangements. These efforts are hidden from view except when pried out by aggressive NGO monitors. Part of the hiding has been achieved by excluding Africans from senior ranks in some of the companies.

The most important global initiative to address the often egregious practices in this sector is the Extractive Industries Transparency Initiative (EITI). The basis of the initiative is "to support improved governance in resource-rich countries through the verification and full publication of company payments and government revenues from oil, gas, and mining." The EITI prepares a technical sourcebook to support companies and countries seeking to join the transparency initiative. As of mid-2007, fourteen resource-rich African countries, mainly in West Africa, had joined the initiative.

THE NONGOVERNMENTAL SECTOR

No part of the modern world has played as constructive a role in the challenges of poverty, disease, hunger, and the environment as the NGO sector. The scope of NGO activity, if defined broadly, is absolutely immense. There are millions of NGOs around the world and hundreds of billions of dollars of NGO activity each year. A precise accounting is not possible, but the sector is undeniably vast and growing much faster than the host economies themselves. The sector includes a huge array of institutions: large parts of academia, philanthropic foundations and individuals, activist groups, professional associations, scientific organizations, the social service divisions of religious groups, and many more. The common attributes are that the activities are nongovernmental and not for profit.

NGOs are crucial, of course, precisely because market forces by themselves do not optimally allocate society's resources, especially when it comes to poverty and the global environmental commons. In theory, governments could step in where markets fail to perform, but governments are only effective at covering a part of market failures. Governments are rarely entrepreneurial. They operate best when approaches have been tried and proven successful, and the challenge is to bring them to scale. Then the heft of the government's tax-raising and borrowing abilities can be crucial in providing the needed financing for scale-up. But the ideas about *what to do* require exploration and entrepreneurship, and that is where the NGOs have played such a vital and unique role.

The storied successes of NGOs are far too vast to canvass. Several NGOs have received the Nobel Peace Prize in the past half century, a vivid indicator of the path-breaking leadership that has emerged from the nongovernmental sector. We have already discussed the winner in 2006, Muhammad Yunus, whose name is synonymous with microfinance and whose institution, Grameen Bank, is a model of NGO activity throughout the developing world. Wangari Maathai, the 2004 winner, is the founder of Greenbelt, the tree-planting environmental movement in Africa. Jimmy Carter won the 2002 prize in significant part for guiding the path-breaking work of the Carter Center, an NGO devoted to the promotion of social and economic development. In 1999, Doctors Without Borders won for pioneering the delivery of life-saving health care to the most impoverished and troubled regions of the world. The International Campaign to Ban Landmines won in 1997, and Joseph Rotblat and the Pugwash Conferences on Science and World Affairs won in 1995 for NGO activity devoted to nuclear disarmament. Amnesty International received the prize in 1977 for NGO leadership in putting human rights at the forefront of global political and social awareness, and in 1970, Norman Borlaug won the prize for the Green Revolution technologies he helped to develop and bring to India, all with the backing of the Rockefeller Foundation.

One can say that the most important economic development institution in the world during the twentieth century was a path-breaking NGO, the Rockefeller Foundation. No other organization—not the World Bank, USAID, or any other international body—came close to playing the transformative role of the Rockefeller Foundation during its first seventy-five years. The Rockefeller Foundation is a special kind of institution, that of transformative philanthropy, in which a world-class philanthropist commits vast sums to improving the world. Until recently this has been largely a U.S. activity, though now billionaires from around the world are joining the effort. It is a storied list, starting with Andrew Carnegie and John D. Rockefeller and including Andrew Mellon, Edsel Ford, John D. and Catherine T. MacArthur, George Soros, David Packard, William Hewlett, and now Bill and Melinda Gates and Warren Buffett, among a growing list.

Rockefeller was deeply impressed with the example and leadership of the steel and railroad magnate Andrew Carnegie, who pioneered the role of philanthropy in social transformation. In 1889, Carnegie wrote that "the day is not far distant when the man who dies leaving behind him millions of available wealth, which was free for him to administer during life, will pass away unwept, unhonored, and unsung." Carnegie acted upon that by establishing the Carnegie Foundation. Rockefeller similarly rose to the challenge, telling the U.S. Congress in 1907 that he would endow a federal institution to fight disease, poverty, and ignorance. At the time, political hotheads attacked him rather than welcomed him, claiming that he was just trying to buy a good name. Congress demurred, and the offer was withdrawn. Instead, Rockefeller set up shop in New York State, establishing the Rockefeller Foundation in 1913 with two initial gifts totaling $100 million. No institution did more in the twentieth century to further the cause of international development. Almost everything that the Rockefeller Foundation undertook during its first sixty years turned to gold. Around 170 scientists supported by the foundation have gone on to win Nobel Prizes.

The foundation led the eradication of hookworm in the U.S. South, helping to pave the way for the South's economic development. It revolutionized the teaching of medicine. It founded schools of public health. It supported the Nobel Prize–winning work that established the yellow fever vaccine. It established the University of Chicago as a world-leading university. It helped Brazil to eliminate a dangerous malaria-transmitting strain of mosquito. And stunningly, it funded the science and transfer of knowledge that produced the Asian Green Revolution, the transformative agricultural success that enabled India and other countries to escape from the endless cycles of famine and poverty, earning another Nobel Prize along the way. The key to the foundation's success was its investment in knowledge and its capacity to identify crucial needs (public health, clinical medicine, vaccine development, Green Revolution seed varieties, and much more). Its modus operandi was a dream for the recipient scientists. The foundation would choose a subject of interest and a leader in the field, and then invest heavily and patiently, without micromanagement or strings attached. The foundation ended up supporting many of the most fertile minds of twentieth-century science and public policy.

Now Bill and Melinda Gates can do the same, backed by $25 billion of their own funds and another $30 billion or so contributed by Warren Buffett. The Gateses have rightly focused on extreme poverty and disease as their main targets. And like the Rockefeller Foundation, the Bill & Melinda Gates Foundation looks to technology for the breakthroughs that can end extreme poverty on a global basis. The original focus had been on health technologies, but now the foundation is expanding to agriculture, water, and other areas that are also critical in the fight against poverty. Of course, Bill and Melinda Gates are not alone in transformative billionaire philanthropy in recent years. George Soros's well-targeted support for brave truth tellers in Central Europe and the former Soviet Union helped to catalyze the peaceful end of communism. The Google team, Larry Page and Sergey Brin, are out to prove how information technologies can also be transformative. They've recently partnered with Amnesty International to post satellite imagery of Darfur in order to raise awareness, accountability, and technical support for solutions in that violence-ravaged region.

With the recent publication by *Forbes* magazine of the ranking of the world's richest people, a new prospect comes into focus. According to *Forbes,* there are now around 950 billionaires in the world, with an estimated combined wealth of $3.5 trillion. That's up an amazing $900 billion in just one year. Even after all the yachts, mansions, and luxury living that money can buy have been funded many times over, these billionaires will still have nearly $3.5 trillion to change the world. Suppose they pooled their wealth, as Buffett has done with Bill and Melinda Gates. By standard and conservative principles of foundation management, a $3.5 trillion endowment would have a 5 percent payout of around $175 billion, an amount sufficient to extend basic health care to all the poorest of the world; end massive pandemics of AIDS, TB, and malaria; jump-start an African Green Revolution; end the digital divide; and address the crying need for safe drinking water for one billion people.

The group of fewer than one thousand people would outstrip the entire $105 billion development aid of the twenty-two donor governments that represent a combined population of nearly one billion people. This speaks both to the incredible wealth of the super-rich and to the current shortsightedness of Washington, Tokyo, and much of Europe. In short, this billionaires' foundation would be enough to end extreme poverty according to the calculations we made earlier. All in all, it's not a bad job for men and women who have already transcended the daily economic struggle faced by the rest of humanity!

THE UNIQUE ROLE OF RESEARCH UNIVERSITIES

Among nongovernmental organizations, the institutions of higher learning and the research universities, especially, have a unique role in meeting the Millennium Promises. Only universities have within their walls the vast range of expert scientific knowledge that is vital for deep problem solving on the issues of sustainable development. Moreover, universities bring three other fundamental strengths to bear on global problems.

First, as much as any of our social institutions, universities take the long view. Harvard University predates the establishment of the U.S. government by 143 years, and my own academic home, Columbia University, was founded a quarter century before the U.S. government. Great centers of learning in the Middle East and Europe are, of course, even older: Al-Azhar University in Cairo (founded 988), Bologna (1088), the University of Paris (1150), Oxford (1167), and Cambridge (1209). These institutions are built to last, and for that reason they can take the long-term perspective.

Second, universities can approach global problems with less bias— political, social, and economic—than just about any other social institution. They are not for profit (alas, often decisively so!). They do not represent specific commercial interests. They are not, in most cases, beholden to the state and thereby not an agent of national policy. They are typically self-governing, often by a combination of faculty-based institutions and elected overseers. Senior scholars usually have lifetime tenure, resulting in an added measure of independence from political control. As a faculty member of a major research university, I have invariably felt welcomed in all parts of the world and have felt the confidence of my counterparts that I am there as an independent truth seeker, not as an agent of private or governmental interests.

Third, major universities were established, in most cases, with a mission to improve the world and to do so not only by shining light on problems through research and education but by making a difference in their community and others. There is, of course, a very long tradition of engagement by universities in *local* problem solving. The U.S. land-grant universities, first established by President Abraham Lincoln in 1862, have the responsibility to promote local agricultural development. For example, land-grant universities receive, under the 1887 Hatch Act, funding to operate an agricultural experiment station affiliated with the university. The U.S. tradition, therefore, of universities stepping outside of the ivory tower to support economic development is robust, but it is mainly local. The challenge today is to extend such local actions to global problems, with universities taking on the challenges in other parts of the world.

These characteristics of universities—scientific expertise, the long view, an unbiased position, and a mission of service to the community—are a unique combination among major societal institutions. Yet this uniqueness does not quite mean that universities will immediately and automatically assume leadership on the great global challenges. There are also three obstacles to that leadership. The first is the tradition of most universities of seeing themselves as national rather than international institutions. While this is changing rapidly, especially at the graduate level, most colleges and universities in the United States and Europe still draw the preponderance of their students from the home country, and most alumni are, of course, nationals as well. This leads to hesitancy in the universities to seize opportunities abroad. Even so, students are clearly pushing university administrations, faculty, and alumni to internationalize college life, including more options for study abroad.

Second, universities are often reluctant to take on practical challenges of sustainable development in developing countries, such as projects to promote public health or economic development in poor countries. Such projects are seen as risky and may be criticized as involving too little basic research. Yet the dichotomy between research and practice is miscast. Stay-at-home research on sustainable development is often impossible to do well. In most kinds of complex problem solving in sustainable development, there can be little chance of grasping truly fundamental issues—whether in business, law, public health, ecology, or governance—by theory alone. Engagement in actual problem solving is vital in order to construct a sound theoretical explanation of complex problems.

Third, universities, like governments, are actually not well organized to take on the intellectual challenges of sustainable development. Faculties and research activities are divided among traditional academic disciplines, such as economics, politics, or ecology, rather than along problem-solving lines. The problems themselves—such as poverty, environmental degradation, climate change, water stress, and biodiversity loss—don't come packaged along the traditional lines of inquiry. They require cross-disciplinary teams and research strategies. This creates tensions throughout a university in hiring, resource allocation, research funding, student enrollments, and project oversight.

Cross-disciplinary efforts, such as the one I direct at The Earth Institute at Columbia University, are promising ways to recast the conventional disciplinary lines so that the expertise of the university can be harnessed on complex interdisciplinary challenges. In 1993, the father of the Green Revolution, Nobel laureate Norman Borlaug, summarized beautifully the case for such a multidisciplinary science-based unit:

> It seems to me that as our science becomes more specialized, each of us is inclined to give more emphasis to our own specialty, our own discipline. This creates great difficulties when we are trying to transmit the global picture of the impact of science and technology, not just on one discipline but on all of them, including economics, for the benefit of the policy maker, so that he can gather the true essence of what we are talking about, in many different languages as it were. What it seems to imply—and I say this having worked in many different countries—is that we need to encourage a certain attitude among our young scientists: that while some of them stay with their own specialty or discipline, some others among them should work in an integrated way across disciplines. Their voice would be the one most likely to be heard, with the least confusion, by the policy makers in government. I do not know how we can encourage this, but I see a real need for it, and I think the unique opportunity of working in many countries of the world has brought that home to me.

In the case of The Earth Institute, the leadership of Columbia University has made a strong multiyear commitment of financial support that enables the complex cross-disciplinary activities to gain a foothold inside the university and around the world. Several universities, including Yale, Duke, Berkeley, Stanford, and Harvard, are experimenting now with similar cross-disciplinary efforts in sustainable development and global health.

THE SINEWS OF GLOBAL SOCIETY

Nongovernmental organizations, including academic institutions, fill multiple roles that markets and governments cannot. NGOs can be socially entrepreneurial, while governments are cautious and bureaucratic. Academic institutions harness cutting-edge science and technology in ways that government cannot. Just as important, nongovernmental organizations form the sinews, the connective tissue, of our new global society. Market forces are anonymous. Government interactions are formal and diplomatic, or even overtly hostile. Nongovernment groups put faces to names by deepening the person-to-person connections that must undergird global trust and cooperation.

A good example is the world of science. With few exceptions, scientific organizations and their membership work easily across cultures and across political divides. Physicists or biologists or ecologists speak the same language across ethnic, racial, and religious lines. Scientific academies can easily work together on scientific projects and, indeed, have come together now in a worldwide network of ninety-four national science academies as the new InterAcademy Council (IAC), headquartered in the Royal Academy of Arts and Sciences of the Netherlands in Amsterdam. The IAC is designed to provide sound scientific advice to international organizations and the United Nations. An early influential report by the IAC was on prospects for improved agricultural productivity in Africa. The report has contributed to the current efforts to achieve a new African Green Revolution.

At a time when our governments are far too prone to using threats, sanctions, and war in response to problems of instability, nongovernmental contacts across countries and cultures become ever more important as builders of trust, understanding, and a common global ethic. The global links that scientists make regularly should also be encouraged in countless other human endeavors. Artists, athletes, jurists, doctors, and engineers all speak their own distinct languages that bridge cultural divides. Sports events such as the World Cup and the Olympics play a vital role in forging global linkages, even though such events are from time to time hijacked for narrower political purposes. Global concerts, such as the Live 8 concerts, which were staged simultaneously in many parts of the world at the time of the 2005 G8 Summit, and the Live

Earth concerts in July 2007 to promote action on climate change, can have a similar effect.

Communications technology makes possible seamless linkages that were unimaginable just a few years ago. The concerts were not only simultaneously presented on television and the Internet, but they were mutually broadcast between the various concert sites. It was a worldwide gathering, not merely a simultaneous broadcast of distinct events. Creative educators are increasingly forging global classrooms in which lectures and scientific symposia link multiple sites around the world through live videoconferencing. Group meetings by Skype or other digital platforms can meld together teams in dozens of countries. Social networking tools such as MySpace and Facebook are becoming crucial tools for cross-cultural contacts and group mobilization as well.

These social networking tools, which connect tens of millions of individuals in online networks of friends, hobbyists, fans, and bloggers, are now turning to mobilization for social causes. Online social networking allows friends to know who is participating in what causes, to give social approbation for such participation, and to facilitate linkages of the network of friends with particular social service organizations. These tools will allow people with shared interests and commitments to organize at vastly lower transaction costs than in the past and to use gentle social cues to promote participation and avoid free riding.

NEW FORMS OF GOVERNANCE

Corporations, academic institutions, NGOs, and professional bodies are all being reshaped by the forces and opportunities of globalization. Governments need an even greater overhaul. The consistent driver of organizational change must be that government form must follow function. Governments and intergovernmental organizations such as the UN agencies need to be reshaped to give substance to the Millennium Promises. Nation-states were originally forged in the cauldron of war, or for the purpose of creating a national market for goods, services, capital, and labor out of a congeries of local markets. Yet these original drivers of political organization are increasingly passé. National governments are too small to address global economic, demographic, and environmental threats, and yet too big to preserve cultural diversity and traditions, which are found at the local level.

Nor are governments well organized to process the scientific knowledge regarding sustainable development that cuts across multiple disciplines. They therefore flail blindly when challenged by global forces they cannot comprehend. Challenges of extreme poverty and environmental stress get repackaged as traditional security threats. Military responses yield pitiful results. We've already argued for a new U.S. foreign policy backed by a major institutional reorganization, and the creation of a Department of International Sustainable Development. Governments will need such restructuring so that they can better understand and respond to the complex forms of environmental change, demography, and economy that are reshaping geopolitics.

Intergovernmental processes must also change in fundamental ways. The European Union is surely the harbinger of further regional integration. As our problems have become global, old nation-state boundaries have become too small to provide many of the public goods required at a transnational scale. The EU not only makes war unthinkable among its member states but also provides critical Europe-wide investments in environmental management, physical infrastructure, and governance "software" such as monetary policy, food safety, and financial market regulation. Other regions in the world, notably Africa, will follow Europe's lead in forging a much stronger transnational organization. Even the United States, relentless in its pursuit of its own destiny, has, of course, bound some of its national economic and environmental policies to the transnational North American Free Trade Agreement (NAFTA), including Canada and Mexico.

These transnational organizations have had a difficult time achieving direct democratic legitimacy. They are often remote and theoretical, run by an appointed civil service or appointed representatives of member countries, rather than by direct democratic engagement of the people. Part of the answer is to empower transnational democratic institutions such as the European Parliament. Information technology can help as well. A wonderful new project, e-Parliament, aims to knit together the world's parliaments and assemblies via videoconferencing and the Internet to forge a new kind of hybrid democratic institution at a transnational and even global scale. An e-Parliament that links national parliaments could help solve a host of problems. How can a challenge such as global climate change be addressed in a democratic manner when global institutions lack adequate democratic legitimacy? If the world's parliaments would hold simultaneous hearings, for example, with leading scientists and policy analysts presenting evidence to dozens of parliaments simultaneously, the world's democratic bodies could engage sensibly and jointly in a global undertaking. Even global legislation, or at least global resolutions on crucial topics like climate change, could be debated and adopted across the world. I believe that the sense of legitimacy and global connectedness that would result would be galvanizing. The imagination would expand as all of us better appreciated how common our challenges are.

Another fundamentally important trend is localization, in which public goods are provided by the lowest feasible level of governance. While nation-states are too small to address many environmental challenges that are regional or global, they are too big and too unaccountable to provide many public services that should be the purview of local communities and subnational regions. Many countries have regions with powerful and distinctive ethnic, linguistic, and historical identities. Cases include Quebec within Canada; Basque Country and Catalonia within Spain; Scotland and Wales within the United Kingdom; Flanders and Wallonia within Begium; Tamil Nadu and West Bengal within India. The list is endless. Devolution of power to these regions in areas of education, health, social security, and regional development policy is a global phenomenon, and a healthy one. Regional governments have been among the most dynamic in architectural and cultural pursuits in recent years. Power to the regions signifies power to maintain cultural diversity, and to share that diversity with the world.

THE UN DELIVERING AS ONE

The United Nations serves three vital roles: as a meeting ground for the world's governments, as a kind of secretariat for global goals and treaties, and as a provider of urgent public goods when national governments cannot or do not provide them (such as emergency relief operations and peacekeeping when national governments have collapsed or are overwhelmed by conflicts or natural disasters). In the United States, the face of the UN is mainly in its first role, as a debating shop in the UN Security Council. In fact, the UN's most powerful contributions probably fall into the second and third categories. The UN remains the world's repository of shared commitments on global objectives, whether in the environmental treaties, the Millennium Development Goals, or the protection against global pandemic diseases. Its agencies are the indispensable providers of public services in the poorest and most vulnerable places on the planet, a role that is almost invisible in the rich countries but nearly omnipresent in the poorest.

Beyond the specific acts of peacekeeping and the countless individual development initiatives of UN agencies, the deepest measure of UN success will be whether the Millennium Promises are sustained over time as shared active global goals and whether these goals are achieved in practice. Given the centrality of the United Nations to this overarching challenge, the UN itself needs to be reformed to fulfill these leading tasks. For example, the Millennium Promises require actions on the ground that cut across multiple UN agencies, connecting the work in agriculture of the World Food Program and the Food and Agricultural Organization with the public health work of the World Health Organization and the poverty reduction work of the United Nations Development Program, to name just a few of the relevant agencies.

The organizational challenge for the UN will be to press its diverse and often loosely managed institutions into a cohesive force, thereby giving strong and creative backing to global goals. On paper, this has recently been described as the UN "delivering as one." Such an outcome will sound unlikely to many, almost the opposite of what they expect from a global bureaucracy. Yet it is not impossible. If the secretary-general charges the UN agencies, above all else, with supporting member governments to implement the global goals, UN teams operating within each of the member countries will become much more actively engaged in real problem solving. Form will then follow function within the UN itself. UN agencies would find themselves working together despite the odds, and working against the calendar and against the skeptics.

THE POWER OF ONE

We are all shaped by our countless and cross-cutting individual identities— as citizens of a nation, residents of a local region, members of cultural groups, workers in an enterprise, members of civil-society organizations. Our multiple identities, as Amartya Sen has brilliantly emphasized in *Identity and*

Violence, allow us each to connect not just to one place or culture or region or religion but to multiple facets of our world. Each of us is, at least potentially, a node of a truly global network in which we help to weave together diverse traditions, areas of knowledge, and cultural pursuits on the global tapestry. We are each the potential shapers of a global society that can share values and address common global challenges.

I believe that it is as citizens of the world that we can flourish in the coming generation. As individuals we will find the maximum outlet for our creative energies and income-earning potential when we are part of global networks, at work and at play. Workers in enterprises that are active on the global stage, in finance, tourism, information technology, or manufactures, will have more opportunities in the growing global economy. An expanding world market will offer avenues of advancement for professionals engaged with China, India, and other emerging markets. Being part of such global networks will force each of us to be acutely aware of global trends. We will understand much better the forces of global politics, demography, economics, and ecology that are reshaping the world and that will provoke new forms of global cooperation. In short, being part of the global networks means being ahead of the curve.

As individuals, our most important responsibility is a commitment to know the truth as best we can, truth that is both technical and ethical. Our saving grace will be a broadened scientific awareness combined with an empathy that enables us to understand the plight of the poor, the dispossessed, the young people without hope, or the rural communities challenged by bewildering change. Gandhi called his life an experiment in "living in truth." That approach will have to become the experiment of our generation as well. Without the commitment to truth, we will be blinded by false and provocative divisions across religions, regions, and countries. Without the commitment to science, we will be prey to false and messianic claims without real substance. Without a determined effort to build understanding and empathy for other societies, cultures, religions, and the voiceless poor, we will risk a downward spiral of distrust and even hate across the divides of "us versus them."

Here are eight actions that each of us can take to fulfill the hopes of a generation in building a world of peace and sustainable development.

First, learn about this generation's challenges. Become acquainted with the underlying science of sustainable development. Those in school should take classes in environment, development economics, climate change, public health, and other relevant fields. For those out of school, find ways to stay abreast of scientific developments. The weekly and monthly leading scientific publications—*Nature, Science, New Scientist, Discover, Scientific American*—are must-reads for our age. Nobody can master each article, or even a modest fraction of the most technical of them, but each of these publications gives a general update of recent discoveries as well as coverage of the main challenges of science policy. Countless high-quality Web sites, such as realclimate.org (on climate change), also enable each of us to stay aware of serious scientific thinking and advances.

Second, to the extent that it is personally possible, travel. Seeing other places and cultures is the best way to understand the common interests and aspirations that unite us as well as the special challenges that are unique to different parts of the world. The travel can be a trip across town, across the country, or for the fortunate, abroad. Students have a special opportunity as they forge their careers and their life commitments. There are new opportunities to travel and work abroad. A travel year between high school and college gives today's students the opportunity to learn about other cultures and about the great gaps between rich and poor. Students can see firsthand the despoiled planet, the regions of water stress, and the risks of climate change. Most colleges promote years of foreign study, with the opportunity for immersion in a foreign culture and society. These are life-changing and life-shaping opportunities not to be missed whenever available. They are the window not just to other parts of the world but to the future as well, since globalization and the rising role of today's emerging markets bring us even closer to each other in the decades to come.

Third, start or join an organization committed to sustainable development. Many new and established organizations are doing wonderful work on some aspects of the challenge. On campuses across the United States, there has been a surge in recent years in activism regarding extreme poverty, public health, and environmental threats, opening new lifelong opportunities for students to become involved.

You and your organization may change the world and inspire others to do so as well. Muhammad Yunus began Grameen Bank and gave life to the worldwide microfinance revolution. Paul Farmer started Partners in Health, and has shown the world the true possibilities of health for all. Norman Borlaug helped to establish the wheat research institute CIMMYT, and thereby helped feed the world. Today's new leaders will promote the African Green Revolution, the control of malaria, new solutions for dryland crops, Internet connectivity in villages, and much more.

Fourth, encourage the engagement of your community and inspire others to join the cause of global sustainable development. In 2007, ballet star Jacques d'Amboise turned his National Dance Institute (NDI) to the cause of African development, inspiring thousands of New York City schoolchildren in the process. NDI teaches dance in the public schools, often in difficult, low-income neighborhoods, raising kids' sights about excellence, beauty, and personal accomplishment. When he dedicated NDI's 2007 program year to the dance, culture, and rhythms of African villages, the children themselves responded magnificently, with countless creative ways to get their schools, families, and neighborhoods involved in raising funds to support the Millennium Village in Potou, Senegal.

Fifth, promote sustainable development through social networking sites, which deploy the most popular and advanced tools of the Internet for the spread and support of social activism. Go out of the way to be the link across the nodes of your own social network—friends, school, workplace, blog sites—to bring different communities together in a common purpose.

Sixth, get politically engaged, demanding of our politicians that they honor our government's Millennium Promises. If the public insists on our government's follow-through, politicians will respond accordingly. Politicians should be pursued during election campaigns, through letter writing, visits to their offices, and at public rallies.

Seventh, engage your workplace. Every company can add to global sustainable development. First and foremost, each company should abide by standards of corporate social responsibility, for example, by adhering to the norms and standards of the United Nations Global Compact. But more than that, each company has special technologies, organizational systems, employee skills, and corporate reputations that can contribute to meeting the Millennium Promises. We've emphasized that corporate social responsibility is not philanthropy but good business practice. Customers, suppliers, and, most important, employees themselves rally to the cause of companies that take these responsibilities seriously.

Eighth, live personally according to the standards of the Millennium Promises. Seek out contacts across countries, cultures, and class divides to ensure that we can each appreciate the common interests of our generation.

Donate time, dollars, and the energy of your social networks. Lead among your friends and colleagues. Act honorably as a consumer, choosing the products and technologies that support sustainability. Act honorably as a citizen, making clear to our politicians that the Millennium Promises are the commitments of each of us, to be upheld by elected representatives.

Our generation's greatest challenges—in environment, demography, poverty, and global politics—are also our most exciting opportunities. John Kennedy bracingly told Americans in his inaugural address that while Americans faced the challenge of defending freedom in its hour of maximum danger (in the context of the Cold War), "I do not believe that any of us would exchange places with any other people or any other generation." I'm sure that the same is true today. Ours is the generation that can end extreme poverty, turn the tide against climate change, and head off a massive and thoughtless extinction of other species. Ours is the generation that can grapple with, and solve, the conundrum of combining economic well-being with environmental sustainability. Ours is the generation that can harness science and a new ethic of global cooperation to bequeath a healthy planet to future generations.

Acknowledgments

Sustainable development will be achieved through global cooperation across nations, institutions, and intellectual disciplines. In writing this book, I have been extraordinarily fortunate to be able to call upon the support and guidance of many leaders and experts from all parts of the world. I wish to thank them for their remarkable skills, commitment, and hard-won knowledge, and their graciousness in sharing their expertise while of course absolving them of any responsibility for errors of fact or interpretation that remain in the text.

I begin with special thanks to the global institutions of the United Nations with which I have been proud to be affiliated during this decade. I was thrilled to head the Commission on Macroeconomics and Health for the World Health Organization during 2000–2001, under the brilliant leadership of Dr. Gro Harlem Brundtland, and then to head the UN Millennium Project, under the unique global stewardship of former secretary-general Kofi Annan and Deputy Secretary-General Mark Malloch Brown. Currently, I am honored to advise UN Secretary-General Ban Ki-moon and Deputy Secretary-General Asha Rose-Migiro on the Millennium Development Goals, and to contribute to their unflagging efforts to bring this fifteen-year initiative to success. It is my pleasure to work closely with colleagues at the UN Development Program (UNDP), including Administrator Kemal Dervis, Associate Administrator Ad Melkert, Regional Bureau for Africa Director Gilbert Houngbo and Olav Kjorven, director of the Bureau of Development Policy. I also give special thanks to Robert Orr, Ambassador Won-soo Kim, and Ambassador Vijay Nambiar in the secretary-general's office. Many other UN leaders add their profound talents to the efforts for sustainable development. I would like to express special thanks to Ann Venneman (UNICEF), Achim Steiner (UNEP), Margaret Chan (WHO) and Josette Sheeran (World Food Program). I am also grateful to the many country-level UN leaders with whom I have been privileged to work closely, including Alberic Kacou, Michael Keating, Elizabeth Lwanga, Turhan Saleh, Oscar Fernandez Taranco, and many others.

International efforts succeed because of national leaders committed to them. In the course of working on the MDGs and sustainable development, it has been my profound privilege to collaborate with Prime Minister Manmohan Singh of India, Prime Minister Gordon Brown and colleagues in the UK, President Jakaya Kikwete of Tanzania, Prime Minister Abdullah Ahmad Badawi of Malaysia, President John Kufour of Ghana, President Amadou Touré of Mali, President Olafur Grimsson of Iceland, former president Jimmy Carter, former vice president Al Gore, and many others. To all I express my admiration and deepest appreciation. I am also grateful to world-leading artists and humanitarians including Bono, Angelina Jolie, Quincy Jones, John Legend, Madonna, and Roger Walters for their unstinting commitment, generosity, leadership, and outreach to millions of fans.

The UN Millennium Project and the UNDP Millennium Development Goal Support Program have brought together hundreds of scientists and development leaders in pursuit of practical approaches to achieve the MDGs. I especially want to thank my close colleagues John McArthur, Guido Schmidt-Traub, Chandrika Bahadur, and Erin Trowbridge, all of whom have been remarkably skilled and committed leaders of the MDG effort from the start, and who have made unique and world-class contributions in advancing the goals. I also thank colleagues Bashir Jama, Annette Karenzi, Johnson Nkuuhe, George Sempeho, Colleen Zamba, Gonzalo Pizarro, Margo Buchanan, Matthias Johansson, and others in the MDG support team for their unwavering dedication and skill.

In recent years, the private sector has stepped forward with wonderful contributions to the causes of sustainable development, many of which have helped to inspire the specific ideas in this book. I am especially grateful for the wonderful leadership of Ray Chambers, philanthropist and business leader extraordinaire, who is cofounder with me of Millennium Promise Alliance, an NGO that mobilizes businesses, philanthropists, other nongovernmental organizations, and the public, to achieve the Millennium Development Goals. Jeff Flug is the hugely talented and committed CEO of Millennium Promise, and I am grateful for his partnership in these efforts. The dedicated board of Millennium Promise brings its powerful business acumen to the cause in an unstinting and inspiring manner, with special thanks to Jean Case, Volkert Doeksen, Tracey Durning, Maria Eitel, John Fitzgibbons, Ben Goldhirsh, Rajat

Gupta, Leo Hindery, Donald Keough, Josephine Linden, Marjorie Magner, John Megrue, Jeff Walker, and Gary Wilson. Amanda Steck, Paula Zamora, Jennifer Cho, and the rest of the Millennium Promise staff have been instrumental in helping to mobilize a new movement for the MDGs. My deep gratitude as well goes to Millennium Promise Japan, with the leadership of Ambassador Shinichi Kitaoka and Rieko Suzuki, and to Millennium Promise Canada, with the bold efforts of Joey Adler and Belinda Stronach.

George Soros continues a quarter century of path-breaking and world-changing philanthropy, philosophy, and business leadership. Other business leaders who have personally assisted me in thinking through these issues and who have provided powerful leadership for sustainable development include Jeffrey Immelt of GE, Gary Cohen of BD Medical, Daniel Vasella and Klaus Leisinger of Novartis, and Carl-Henric Svanberg of Ericsson.

The Millennium Village Project (MVP) is the flagship demonstration of how extreme poverty can be ended in the poorest regions of rural Africa. This is a project that brings together the best of science with wonderful African leaders and committed foundations and philanthropists. It has won the support, encouragement, and guidance of the government of Japan, the Open Society Institute, with gratitude to Aryeh Neier and Julie Hayes and many other foundations, governments, philanthropists, and corporate supporters. The scientific leadership at The Earth Institute is steered by my colleagues Pedro Sanchez and Cheryl Palm, and joined by the remarkable efforts of many scientists and development specialists at The Earth Institute and the Millennium Villages. Steve Wisman and his team at Millennium Promise, including Joel Negin and Theresa Wolters, have done great work in putting into smooth operation the concepts of the project and keeping us on course. Patrick Haverman, Lamin Manneh, and Martin Fianu have all provided crucial leadership for the project at UNDP. Special thanks to Glenn Denning and Amadou Niang for skillfully leading the efforts in the East and West Africa MDG Centers of The Earth Institute, and to Suzy Blaustein and Karl Sauvant for leading the Millennium Cities Initiative. Our partners at other institutions, including president John Jenkins of Notre Dame University and Dennis Garrity of the World Agroforestry Center, greatly strengthen the project.

The Earth Institute at Columbia University is one of the world's leading centers of cross-disciplinary research, teaching, and outreach on sustainable development. Every chapter of this book depends in a vital way on the wisdom of my colleagues in agronomy, hydrology, mechanical and civil engineering, ecology, public health, climatology, economics, public management, geographic information systems, epidemiology, and more. I should like to give special thanks to three leaders of The Earth Institute, Executive Director Steve Cohen, Associate Director Peter Schlosser, and former deputy director John Mutter, for making unparalleled contributions to this novel and cutting-edge institution. I have also learned each day from Earth Institute colleagues Nirupam Bajpai, Wally Broecker, Mark Cane, James Hansen, Geoffrey Heal, Klaus Lackner, Manu Lall, Marc Levy, Vijay Modi, Mike Purdy, Cynthia Rosenzweig, Josh Ruxin, Awash Teklehaimonot, Madeleine Thomson, Elke Weber, Wing Woo, and Steve Zebiak. I also owe a debt of gratitude to Earth Institute colleagues Terry Karamanos, David Dvorak, Jennifer Genrich, Mark Inglis, and Louise Rosen. The Earth Institute Fellows, a remarkable group of postdocs engaged in research on sustainable development, have also helped to advance concepts described in this book. I would like to express my special gratitude to Matthew Bonds, Vladimir Gil, Darby Jack, Alex Mwiti, and Tobias Sigfried.

The Earth Institute is blessed with a remarkable external advisory board, which helps to steer the institute and keep it on course. I am profoundly grateful to E. O. Wilson, to whom the whole world is in debt for enlightening us and reminding us of the beauty, mystery, and vulnerability of the Creation, the natural world under so much threat from human activity. I have learned endlessly from other external advisory board members as well, and want to extend special thanks to Ken Arrow, Barry Bloom, Partha Dasgupta, Tim Palmer, Harold Varmus, and Walter Willett, all of whom are scientists of profound vision, accomplishment, and integrity who have contributed to human betterment. I have also received ample and generous informal advice from Amory Lovins and Lester Brown, both of who are of course long-standing global leaders in sustainable development.

Each day of this project I have depended on the unparalleled expertise and support of the director's office at The Earth Institute. Dr. Joanna Rubinstein is remarkable and redoubtable as chief of staff, Earth Institute strategist, and director of the Center for Global Health and Economic Development. Heidi Kleedtke, my executive assistant, keeps the complicated gears of office life turning smoothly. My personal assistants, Gordon McCord, Sam Freeman, and Annika Rosenblatt, have played a unique role in assisting me in the preparation of this book, with round-the-clock research assistance, editing, and all manner of help.

The Earth Institute reflects the vigor of Columbia University, a unique global university that combines boldness of intellectual life and commitment to the world. Columbia reflects the spirit of its remarkable president, Lee Bollinger, who again and again teaches the world about the unique values of open inquiry into the world's most pressing problems. Columbia's intellectual edge is relentlessly forwarded by Provost Alan Brinkley, Arts and Sciences vice president Nick Dirks, Research vice president David Hirsch, Columbia College dean Austin Quigley, and Executive Vice President Robert Kasdin.

From start to finish, this project was supported and guided by the tremendous literary talents at the Wylie Agency, including the legendary Andrew Wylie and my longtime wonderful editor Scott Moyers. The project was also brought to fruition by the remarkable team at the Penguin Press, including Eamon Dolan and Laura Stickney. I am grateful to all of them for guiding me with grace and skill from the very start.

As with every endeavor I have undertaken, this book could emerge only because of the unstinting, unflinching, and unmatched inspiration and support of my wife, Sonia, and our children, Lisa, Adam, and Hannah. With each succeeding book, I get to marvel and take delight in the growing technical mastery and commitments to good works of our kids. This time, Lisa read several drafts of the manuscript and made thorough, detailed, and trenchant comments and edits that greatly improved the manuscript. Adam lent a hand with his skilled edits and pointed queries and demands for tightening the writing. Hannah is our newest authority on sustainable development, and her tough questions and constant enthusiasm keep me inspired and on my toes. It is with pride and delight that I dedicate the book to these three wonderful new leaders for a better world.

List of Acronyms

BAU	business-as-usual
CBD	Convention on Biological Diversity
CCS	carbon capture and sequestration
CFCs	chlorofluorocarbons
CO_2	carbon dioxide
CTBT	Comprehensive Test Ban Treaty
EEZ	exclusive economic zone
EITI	Extractive Industries Transparency Initiative
FAO	Food and Agriculture Organization
G8	Group of Eight, the eight richest large economies. The G8 countries are: Canada, France, Germany, Italy, Japan, Russia, the United Kingdom, and the United States.
GATT	General Agreement on Tariffs and Trade
GDP	gross domestic product
GEF	global environmental facility
GFATM	Global Fund to Fight AIDS, Tuberculosis and Malaria
GNP	gross national product
GROCC	Global Roundtable on Climate Change
GWP	gross world product
HDI	Human Development Index
HIPPO	habitat destruction, invasive species, pollution, population increase, and overharvesting
ICPD	International Conference on Population and Development
IMF	International Monetary Fund
$I = P \times A \times T$	or I-PAT equation: Environmental impact = population $\times$ per capita income $\times$ the environmental impact per dollar of income

IPCC	Intergovernmental Panel on Climate Change
MDGs	Millennium Development Goals
MENA	Middle East and North Africa
MVP	Millennium Village Project
N_2O	nitrous oxide
NGO	nongovernmental organization
NRR	net reproduction rate
PAI	Population Action International
ppm	parts per million
PPP	purchasing power parity
PPPs	public private partnerships
R & D	research and development
RD & D	research, development, and demonstration
TFR	total fertility rate
UN	United Nations
UNCCD	United Nations Convention to Combat Desertification
UNDP	United Nations Development Program
UNEP	United Nations Environment Program
UNFCCC	United Nations Framework Convention on Climate Change
UNFPA	United Nations Population Fund (formerly UN Fund for Population Activities)
UNICEF	United Nations Children's Fund
USAID	United States Agency for International Development
WHO	World Health Organization
WTO	World Trade Organization

Notes

Chapter 1: Common Challenges, Common Wealth

4 **social insurance and transfer schemes:** Peter Lindert, *Growing Public: Social Spending and Economic Growth since the Eighteenth Century,* vol. 1 (New York: Cambridge University Press, 2004).

10 **"For peace is a process":** John F. Kennedy, Spring Commencement Address, American University, June 10, 1963. http://www.american.edu/media/speeches/Kennedy.htm.

10 **"And we are all mortal":** Ibid.

11 **"legacy of ashes":** Tim Weiner, *Legacy of Ashes* (New York: Random House, 2007).

13 **"ensuring universal access by 2015":** United Nations, Summary of the International Conference on Population and Development (ICPD) Program of Action. www.unfpa.org/icpd/icpd__poa.htm.

13 **G8, the eight richest large economies:** The G8 countries are: Canada, France, Germany, Italy, Japan, Russia, United Kingdom, and United States.

14 Note: The goals for the new millennium were also reflected in commitments on arms control, particularly the control of chemical weapons and nuclear arms mentioned below; this book, however, will not discuss these commitments in detail. The Chemical Weapons Convention (CWC), signed in 1993 and entered into force in 1997, outlaws the stockpiling, production, and use of chemical weapons. The Nuclear Non-Proliferation Treaty (NPT), first signed in 1968, was extended indefinitely in 1995. A year later, the Comprehensive Test Ban Treaty (CTBT) was opened for signatures. Yet these steps marked the apogee of nuclear arms control. Since the mid-1990s, three states have become nuclear powers, and the treaties themselves are threadbare if not torn asunder entirely. The United States has signed the CTBT treaty but not ratified it, while India and Pakistan have not even signed. The chance to restrain the nuclear arms race could easily disappear altogether if the NPT and CTBT are not reinforced by the political and operational support of the major powers.

15 **"reflexive practice":** Donald Schön, *The Reflective Practitioner: How Professionals Think in Action* (New York: Basic Books, 1983).

15 **new methods of training:** I am pleased to cochair the Commission on the Education of International Development Practitioners, a MacArthur Foundation initiative that is recommending a new approach to professional training in sustainable development. The commission believes that effective professional training in sustainable development should include a focus on cross-disciplinary knowledge; a combination of classroom learning and fieldwork; and skill development that includes the policy sciences, the Earth's physical systems, and management expertise.

Chapter 2: Our Crowded Planet

17 **$60 trillion of output each year:** Unless otherwise noted, I report measured national and global incomes in purchasing-power-parity (PPP) prices. This approach measures each country's na-

tional income not at the prices that prevail in that country but at common prices that are roughly benchmarked to those that prevail in the United States. Let me use an example to illustrate. Suppose there are two countries, a developing country and the United States. Each country produces haircuts and television sets. We want to compare the average income per person in the two countries. In both countries, the television sets sell for $200 each, while the haircuts are $1 in the poor country and $10 in the United States. The poor country produces 100 haircuts and 10 television sets per person per year, while the United States produces 1,000 haircuts and 100 television sets per person per year. If we use the country's own prices, the average income per person in the poor country is $2,100 (equal to [$1 × 100] × [$200 × 10]), while the U.S. average income is $30,000 (equal to [$10 × 100] + [$200 × 100]). The United States looks nearly fifteeen times richer than the poor country. In fact the "real" difference in income is only ten times, since each commodity is produced in ten times the amount per person in the United States. The developing country looks somewhat poorer than it really is, because individuals in the poor countries will earn less income but also pay less for each haircut. If we use a common set of prices to calculate the income of both countries (specifically, $10 for haircuts and $200 for television sets), the PPP-adjusted income of the developing country is now $3,000 (equal to $10 × 100 + $200 × 10) and the PPP-adjusted income of the United States is $30,000. On a PPP basis, the U.S. income is ten times that of the poor country's. The PPP-adjusted incomes provide a more accurate comparison because they offset the difference of prices of products in the two countries and keep the focus on the differences in physical outputs.

19 **gross world product:** Angus Maddison estimates that GWP rose from $5.3 trillion in 1950 to $33.7 trillion in 1998, calculated in constant 1990 U.S. dollars using purchasing-power-parity-adjusted prices. The World Bank estimates that GWP rose from $41.6 trillion in 1998 to $54.5 trillion in 2005, expressed in constant 2000 PPP-adjusted U.S. dollars. Linking these two estimates gives an 8.2-fold increase of world production between 1950 and 2005 (= 33.7/5.3 × 54.5/41.6).

20 **U.S. per capita income level:** See Robert J. Barro and Xavier Sala-i-Martin, *Economic Growth*, 2nd edition (Cambridge, Mass.: MIT Press, 2004) for a detailed discussion on convergence. There is, of course, statistical uncertainty about the "typical" rate of convergence. In the calculations in the text, I assume that a country that is at half of the income of the technological leader (assumed to be the United States) can achieve convergent growth at a rate 1.5 percentage points per year faster than the growth rate of the leader. In the statistical estimates reported by Barro and Sala-i-Martin, and in similar estimates by other researchers, the range is generally between 1 and 2 percentage points per year faster growth in the follower country (at half of the leader's income).

25 **56 percent of the world economy:** Angus Maddison, *The World Economy: A Millennial Perspective* (Paris: Development Centre of the Organization for Economic Cooperation and Development, 2001).

26 **Cities arose with:** Archeologists and anthropologists have generally assumed that urban settlements arose only with cultivation. It is possible, though, that the first cities (of course with very small populations) arose in regions of intensive hunting and gathering rather than cultivation per se. In any case, the oldest cities arose roughly ten thousand years before the present.

26 **almost all regions of the world:** See Paul Bairoch, *Cities and Economic Development: From the Dawn of History to the Present*, translated by Christopher Braider (Chicago: University of Chicago Press, 1988).

28 **global epidemic of:** For further reading see the September 2007 special issue of *Scientific American*, for a series of important articles on the new epidemic.

29 **It is useful to decompose:** The I-PAT equation is generally attributed to a series of articles and debates in the early 1970s between Barry Commoner on the one side and coauthors Paul Ehrlich and John Holdren on the other. The history of the equation is surveyed by Marion Chartow in "The IPAT Equation and Its Variants," *Journal of Industrial Ecology* 4., no. 4 (2001): 13–29. According to Chartow, the first appearance of equation in its I-PAT form is in P. Ehrlich and J. Holdren, "One-Dimensional Ecology," *Bulletin of the Atomic Scientists*, June 1972, pp. 16–27.

34 **innovations systems:** My colleague Richard Nelson has been the world's leading scholar on mapping the structure and performance of these innovation systems in many parts of the world.

For further reading see: Richard Nelson, ed., *National Innovation Systems: A Comparative Analysis* (New York: Oxford University Press, 1993).

38 **"tragedy of the commons":** Garrett Hardin, "The Tragedy of the Commons," *Science* 162 (1968): 1243–48.

38 **variety of quota systems:** J. R. Beddington et al., "Current Problems in the Management of Fisheries," *Science* 316 (June 22, 2007): 1713–16.

39 **Community-based management:** See Elinor Ostrom, *Governing the Commons: The Economics of Institutions for Collective Action* (Cambridge: Cambridge University Press, 1990) and Partha Dasgupta, "Common Property Resources: Economic Analytics," in N. S. Jodha et al., eds., *Promise, Trust, and Evolution* (New Delhi: Oxford University Press, 2007).

39 **restoration of degraded pasturelands:** Dennis Normile, "Getting at the Root of Killer Dust Storms," *Science* 317 (July 20, 2007): 314–16.

40 **megafishes project:** Richard Stone, "Aquatic Ecology: The Last of the Leviathans," *Science* 316 (June 22, 2007): 1684–88.

44 **"The global fossil":** H. H. Rogner, "An Assessment of the World Hydrocarbon Resources," *Annual Review of Energy and the Environment*, 1997.

44 **"global energy demand":** A ton of oil equivalent means an amount of a nonoil energy source, such as coal or natural gas, with the energy content equal to one ton of oil.

44 **current commercial energy use:** Total solar radiation is 174 petawatts, or 174 million gigawatts, compared with average power consumption of 15,000 gigawatts (2004), roughly 10,000 times less than solar radiation. A watt is a measure of energy use per second (specifically, joules per second), so the energy consumption in a period of time is equal to the watts multiplied by the time period. A common unit of energy consumption is kilowatt hours (1,000 watts for one hour of energy consumption).

44 **With improved technologies:** Interestingly, geothermal energy, the heat energy of the Earth's crust resulting mainly from radioactive decay in the Earth's interior, is also in vast supply, orders of magnitude larger than humanity's total commercial energy use. As with solar power, it is currently too expensive to tap commercially in most places, the exceptions being mainly in areas of active seismic activity where tectonic plates meet and thereby allow for large flows of heat from the Earth's interior to the surface. Advances in technology could enable a huge expansion in low-cost access to this vast store of heat energy. One system, known as enhanced geothermal energy, envisions drilling two very deep wells side by side down to a depth of ten kilometers (six miles) or more. At the base of these deep wells, the rock is fractured to create a connection between them. Water is pumped down one of the wells, and steam is generated by the heated water in the other well. The steam is then used to turn the turbines in a power plant. See MIT Inter-Disciplinary Panel on Geothermal Energy, *The Future of Geothermal Energy* (Cambridge, Mass.: MIT Press, 2007). Nuclear power offers another vast potential, though one that is made exceedingly, perhaps unsolvably, complicated by its intertwined links with nuclear weapons. As is well known, there are two potential forms of long-lasting nuclear energy, fission based (utilizing the energy released by splitting uranium and other radioactive materials) and fusion based (utilizing the energy released by the fusion of two hydrogen atoms into a helium atom, as happens in the sun). Only fission exists in commercial form. Fusion power is likely decades away from commercial exploitation but could be a vast source of energy in the twenty-second century and beyond. Uranium-based nuclear energy is a tried-and-true, if highly controversial, technology. It already powers roughly one sixth of the world's electricity production, including one fifth of U.S. electricity production, and around 80 percent of France's electricity. The long-term potential is vast, alongside other energy sources. The public acceptance is highly qualified, however, out of deep fears of leakages of radiation, as in the Chernobyl catastrophe; the difficulties of disposing of nuclear waste products; and the ability to convert and divert nuclear plant materials (both inputs and waste products) into weapons-grade nuclear materials. The expanded use of nuclear power is all but inevitable, notably in China, India, Japan, and several other countries. The biggest fear is that the expansion of nuclear power in some countries, especially the crisis-riven Middle East, can be a pretext for the development of a nuclear weapons industry as well. See MIT Inter-Disciplinary Panel on Nuclear Power, *The Future of Nuclear Power* (Cambridge, Mass.: MIT Press, 2003).

46 **only deepened the insecurity:** Michael Klare, *Blood and Oil: The Dangers and Consequences of America's Growing Dependency on Imported Petroleum* (New York: Metropolitan Books, 2004), and Dilip Hiro, *Blood of the Earth: The Battle for the World's Vanishing Oil Resources* (New York: Nation Books, 2006).

46 **quest for such weapons:** This book does not go into depth on global cooperation regarding weapons of mass destruction, but I mention here the success of the Nuclear Non-Proliferation Treaty (and related treaties on chemical weapons and nuclear testing) to emphasize that the pessimism regarding global cooperation is misplaced not only regarding sustainable development but also regarding the challenges of global security. While the Nuclear Non-Proliferation Treaty has not ended proliferation, it has dramatically slowed proliferation and caused dozens of countries to abandon nuclear programs. See Joseph Cirincione, *Bomb Scare: The History, Theory and Future of Nuclear Weapons* (New York: Columbia University Press, 2007). In recent years, however, the treaties have come under increasing strain partly because the United States and other nuclear powers have failed to take concrete steps toward eventual nuclear disarmament, as required by the treaty.

47 **the agreed on but unfulfilled:** Since 1970 the world community has agreed that the rich-country governments should devote 70 cents for every $100 of national income toward development aid. This 0.7 percent standard has been repeatedly reaffirmed, for example, in 2002 at the Financing for Development Summit in Monterrey, Mexico, where the world's governments, including that of the United States, pledged to "make concrete efforts toward the target of 0.7 percent of gross national product as official development assistance."

47 **"Foreign aid likely":** William Easterly, *The White Man's Burden* (New York: Penguin, 2006), p. 176.

49 **"Put the focus back":** Easterly, *The White Man's Burden*, pp. 368–69.

50 **tropical Africa:** Tropical Africa excludes South Africa; Lesotho; Namibia; and the five countries of North Africa: Algeria, Egypt, Libya, Morocco, and Tunisia.

50 **exceptions mainly in:** Botswana, 3.0; Cape Verde, 3.5; Comoros, 3.8; Gabon, 3.7; Lesotho, 3.4; Mauritius, 2.0; Namibia, 3.7; São Tomé and Principe, 3.8; Swaziland, 3.9; Seychelles, 2.1; Zimbabwe, 3.3.

50 **to just 15 percent today:** Shaohua Chen and Martin Ravallion, "How Have the World's Poor Fared since 1980?" *The World Bank Research Observer* 19, no. 2 (fall 2004): 152.

53 **There is still time:** All data in this paragraph refer to the twenty-two country members of the Development Assistance Committee (DAC) of the Organization of Economic Cooperation and Development (OECD).

Chapter 3: The Anthropocene

58 **hunter-gatherers might have totaled:** J. L. Chapman and M. J. Reiss, *Ecology* (New York and Cambridge: Cambridge University Press, 1998).

59 **hunted the large animals to extinction:** P. S. Martin and H. E. Wright, eds., *Pleistocene Extinctions: The Search for a Cause* (New Haven, Conn.: Yale University Press, 1967).

65 **Sir William Crookes, predicted:** In Crookes's presidential address to the British Association in Bristol in 1898.

66 **Figure 3.2(b):** This graph, carefully constructed by economic historian Angus Maddison, attempts to measure the level of economic production per person across many centuries and very different regions of the world. While it is a bit heroic to make such a graph, considering the difficulties of comparing the economies of the preindustrial age with those of today, there is clear evidence of its core finding of an unprecedented takeoff of economic productivity around 1800.

67 **The Nobel laureate chemist:** Paul J. Crutzen, and Eugene F. Stoermer, "The 'Anthropocene,' " *International Geosphere-Biosphere Programme Newletter* 41 (May 2000): 17–18.

68 *50 percent of the Earth's photosynthetic . . .:* Peter M. Vitousek, et al. "Human Domination of Earth's Ecosystems," *Science* 277, no. 5325, (July 25, 1997): 494–99.

72 **" fully exploited, overexploited, or depleted,":** Commission on Geosciences, Environment and Resources (CGER), *Sustaining Marine Fisheries*, Ocean Studies Board, 1999.

74 **A recent study of degradation:** H. K. Lotze et al., "Depletion, Degradation, and Recovery Potential of Estuaries and Coastal Seas," *Science* 312 (June 23, 2006): 1806–9.

74 **"Reconstructed time lines":** Ibid., p. 1806.

75 **"Our results indicate":** Ibid., p. 1808.

75 **"Although 22% of":** Ibid.

75 **But, alas, some degradation:** Ibid., p. 1806.

75 **China is currently:** MIT Inter-Disciplinary Panel on Coal, *The Future of Coal: Options for a Carbon-Constrained World* (Cambridge, Mass.: MIT Press, 2007).

76 **China's annual production is now soaring:** India's automobile sales are also rising strongly at about 15 percent per year, though at a much lower rate than in China. In 2006 sales were around 1.3 million, and are expected to rise to 2.1 million vehicles by 2010 (see *Financial Times*, September 4, 2007).

78 **could well be human forcings:** James Hansen et al., "Climate Change and Trace Gases," *Philosophical Transactions of the Royal Society A* 365 (May 2007): 1925–54.

78 **A slight rise:** James Hansen, "Climate Catastrophe," *New Scientist*, July 28, 2007.

79 **has been studied extensively by my colleague Wallace Broecker:** See Richard Alley, "Wally Was Right: Predictive Ability of the North Atlantic 'Conveyor Belt' Hypothesis for Abrupt Climate Change," *Annual Review of Earth and Planetary Sciences* 36 (2007): 241–72, for recent authoritative support for Broecker's hypothesis.

79 **a sudden abrupt cooling:** These and other abrupt-change findings and scenarios are ably described in Fred Pearce, *With Speed and Violence* (Boston: Beacon Press, 2007).

81 **"Thus, human societies":** Jared Diamond, *Collapse: How Societies Choose to Fail or Succeed* (New York: Viking, 2004), p. 38.

Chapter 4: Global Solutions for Climate Change

87 **Figure 4.2:** Figure based on P. Brohan, J. J. Kennedy, I. Harris, et al., "Uncertainty Estimates in Regional and Global Observed Temperature Changes: A New Dataset from 1850," *Journal of Geophysical Research* 111 (2006).

87 ***Stern Review on Climate Change:*** Nicholas Stern, "The Economics of Climate Change," *The Stern Review* (Cambridge: Cambridge University Press, 2007).

87 ***"Intergovernmental Panel on Climate Change":*** Intergovernmental Panel on Climate Change Fourth Round Assessment. Information available at: http://www.mnp.nl/ipcc/.

88 **Polar bears and alpine species:** Steven C. Amstrup, Bruce G. Marcot, and David C. Douglas, *Forecasting the Range-wide Status of Polar Bears at Selected Times in the 21st Century* (Virginia: U.S. Geological Survey Administrative Report, 2007).

88 **higher-latitude environments:** Carbon fertilization is the hypothesis, somewhat debated, that higher atmospheric CO_2 concentrations may "fertilize" crops and raise the productivity of photosynthesis. There are many countervailing arguments as well, so the generality of carbon fertilization as a likely effect is uncertain.

88 **interact with increased:** Recent research suggests that air pollution in Asia, caused by the burning of biomass and fossil fuels, has created a massive atmospheric brown cloud (ABM) over India. The ABM tends to create drying conditions that lower crop productivity in India. The combination of greenhouse gas emissions and the ABM have had a large adverse effect on crop yields. See Maximillian Auffhammer et al., "Integrated Model Shows That Atmospheric Brown Clouds and Greenhouse Gases Have Reduced Rice Harvests in India," *PNAS* 103, no. 52 (December 26, 2006).

91 **greenhouse gases can be reversed:** Technically, greenhouse gases are compared according to their radiative forcing, that is, how much they are warming the Earth as a result of their greenhouse effect. The radiative forcing is a result of two measures. The first is the efficiency of the greenhouse effect of the particular gas, that is, how much greenhouse effect results from a given increase in ppm of the molecule. The second is the actual increase in atmospheric concentration of the gas. The increase itself results from the balance of two forces: the emissions of the gas into the atmosphere and the natural removal of the gas from the atmosphere, for example,

through a chemical change or the uptake of the gas by the land and ocean. The radiative forcing of CO_2 is the largest of the six greenhouse gases, followed by methane, nitrous oxide, and the three fluorinated gases. The high radiative forcing of CO_2 is due to three things: the high efficiency of CO_2 as a greenhouse gas, the large human emissions of carbon dioxide, and the slow natural removal of CO_2 from the atmosphere (also called the long residence time of CO_2 in the atmosphere).

92 **Each additional 7.8 billion:** Note that there are uncertainties about the ranges of sources and sinks, and also natural year-to-year fluctuations in carbon sinks in the oceans and land.

93 **Recent evidence suggests:** S. Sitch et al., "Indirect Radiative Forcing of Climate Change Through Ozone Effects on the Land-Carbon Sink," *Nature*, August 16, 2007, pp. 791–94.

94 **brilliant analysis by my colleague James Hansen:** James Hansen, "Dangerous Human-Made Interference with Climate: A GISS ModelE Study," *Atmospheric Chemistry and Physics* 7 (2007): 2287–312.

98 **if the hybrid can be plugged:** James Kliesch and Therese Langer, *Plug-in Hybrids: An Environmental and Economic Performance Outlook*, report number T061, American Council for an Energy-Efficient Economy, September 2006; and The Institute of Electrical and Electronics Engineers, *Position Statement Plug-In Electric Hybrid Vehicles*, adopted by the board of directors June 15, 2007.

101 **This translates roughly:** Intergovernmental Panel on Climate Change (IPCC), "Special Report on Carbon Dioxide Capture and Storage." Available online at http://www.ipcc.ch/activity/srccs/index.htm.

103 **"Anything but a marginal":** Tommy Dalgaard, "Looking at Biofuels and Bioenergy," *Science* 312 (June 23, 2006): 1743.

103 **In a study published in 2005:** Klaus Lackner and Jeffrey D. Sachs, "A Robust Strategy for Sustainable Energy," *Brookings Paper on Economic Activity*, 2005.

107 **Both are needed:** International Research Institute for Climate Prediction (IRI), *Sustainable Development in Africa: Is the Climate Right?*, IRI Technical Report Number IRI-TR/05/1, 2005.

113 **In the mid-1970s:** Mario J. Molina and F. S. Rowland, "Stratospheric Sink for Chlorofluoromethanes: Chlorine Atom-Catalyzed Destruction of the Ozone," *Nature* 249 (June 28, 1974): 810–12.

113 **"a science fiction tale":** *Chemical Week*, July 16, 1975.

Chapter 5: Securing Our Water Needs

115 **Privatization of water rights:** This is the case, for example, when private landowners are all drawing water from wells that draw upon a common groundwater aquifer. In that case, each private owner will have an incentive to overexploit the aquifer. Even though the water right on their land is private, they are all drawing, in effect, on a public commons.

120 **drylands cover:** Millennium Ecosystem Assessment. Available online at http://www.millenniumassessment.org/en/index.aspx.

120 **variability of water availability:** Casey Brown and Upmanu Lall, "Water and Economic Development: The Role of Variability and Framework for Resilience," *Natural Resources Forum* 30, issue 4 (November 2006): 306–17.

122 **United Nations Development Program:** United Nations Development Program (UNDP), *Human Development Report 2006: Beyond Scarcity: Power, Poverty and the Global Water Crisis* (Macmillan Palgrave, 2006), p. 140.

125 **Recent studies:** Xuebin Zhang et al., "Detection of Human Influence on Twentieth-Century Precipitation Trends," *Nature*, July 26, 2007.

125 **Another recent study:** Fred Pearce, *When the Rivers Run Dry: Water, the Defining Crisis of the Twenty-First Century* (Boston: Beacon Press, 2006), p. 125, citing Kevin Trenberth.

126 **experience massive flooding:** T. P. Barnett, J. C. Adam, and D. P. Lettenmaier, "Potential Impacts of a Warming Climate on Water Availability in Snow-Dominated Regions," *Nature* 438 (November 2005).

126 **The Sahel:** A. Giannini, R. Saravanan, and P. Chang, "Oceanic Forcing of Sahel Rainfall on Interannual to Interdecadal Timescales," *Science* 302 (October 9, 2003): 1027–30.

127 **The Indo-Gangetic Plains:** Tushaaar Shah, *Water Policy Research Highlight: Groundwater and Human Development: Challenges and Opportunities in Livelihoods and Environment,* Water Policy Program, 2005. http://www.iwmi.org/iwmi-tata.

127 **water crisis is intersecting:** The information that follows regarding India is provided by my colleague, Columbia University hydrologist Upmanu Lall, a leading expert regarding India's water crisis.

128 **The same problems:** Richard Seager et al., "Model Projections of an Imminent Transition to a More Arid Climate in Southwestern North America," *Science* 316 (2007): 1181.

129 **"drops in rainfall":** Edward Miguel, Shanker Satyanath, and Ernest Sergent, "Economic Shocks and Civil Conflict: An Instrumental Variables Approach," *Journal of Political Economy* 112, no. 4 (2004): 725–53.

129 **"The most obvious reading":** Edward Miguel, "Poverty and Violence," in Lael Brainard and Derek Chollet, eds., *Too Poor for Peace? Global Poverty, Conflict and Security in the 21st Century* (Washington, D.C.: Brookings Institute Press, 2007), p. 55.

130 **"All told, more than":** Fred Pearce, *When the Rivers Run Dry: Water, the Defining Crisis of the Twenty-First Century* (Boston: Beacon Press, 2006), p. 178.

131 **a mere 0.03 percent:** United Nations Development Program (UNDP), *Human Development Report 2006,* p. 8.

132 **the Food and Agriculture Organization:** Food and Agriculture Organization of the United Nations, *World Agriculture: Towards 2015/2030, Summary Report,* 2003. http://www.fao.org/docrep/004/y3557e/y3557e00.HTM.

133 **Gansu Province, China:** Qiang Zhu, "The Rainwater Harvesting Projects in Mainland China," International Rainwater Catchment Systems Association. http://www.eng.warwick.ac.uk/ircsa/factsheets/ChinaRWH.pdf.

134 **and impoverished farmers:** For further discussion see J. N. Pretty et al., "Resource-Conserving Agriculture," *Environmental Science and Technology* 40, no. 4 (2006): 1114–19.

Chapter 6: A Home for All Species

139 **Millennium Ecosystem Assessment:** Millennium Ecosystem Assessment, "Ecosystems and Human Well-Being, Synthesis Report, World Resources Institute," 2005.

139 **HIPPO:** Edward O. Wilson, *The Creation: An Appeal to Save Life on Earth* (New York: W. W. Norton & Company), 2006.

140 **Recent studies:** Chris D. Thomas et al., "Extinction Risk from Climate Change," *Nature* 427 (January 8, 2004): 145–48.

141 **A recent study found:** See Boris Worm et al., "Impacts of Biodiversity Loss on Ocean Ecosystem Services," *Science* 314, no. 5800 (November 3, 2006): 787–90.

141 **Coral reefs:** See Michael Hopkin, "Oceans in Trouble as Acid Levels Rise," *Nature News,* June 30, 2005; T. P. Hughes et al., "Climate Change, Human Impacts, and the Resilience of Coral Reefs," *Science* 301 (2003): 929; John M. Pandolf, et al., "Global Trajectories of the Long-Term Decline of Coral Reef Ecosystems," *Science* 301 (2003): 955; and the Royal Society Working Group on Ocean Acidification, *Ocean Acidification Due to Increasing Atmospheric Carbon Dioxide* (London: Royal Society, June 2005).

142 **crash of amphibian populations:** See Simon Stuart et al., "Status and Trends of Amphibian Declines and Extinctions Worldwide," *Science* 306 (December 3, 2004): 1783–88; Joseph R. Mendelson III et al., "Biodiversity: Confronting Amphibian Declines and Extinctions," *Science* 313, no. 5783 (July 7, 2006): 48; and J. Alan Pounds et al., "Widespread Amphibian Extinctions from Epidemic Disease Driven by Global Warming," *Nature* 439 (January 12, 2006).

142 **Pollinators:** For an overview, see Committee on the Status of Pollinators in North America, "Status of Pollinators in America," National Research Council, 2007. For a recent account linking part of the decline to a viral infection introduced from Australia, see Erik Stolestad, "Puzzling Decline of U.S. Bees Linked to Virus from Australia," *Science* 317, no. 5843 (September 7, 2007):

1304–5. See also Diana L. Cox-Foster, et al., "A Metaelgenomic Survey of Microbes in Honey Bee Colony Collapse Disorder," *Science* 318 (October 12, 2007).

142 **Great Apes:** Alison Jolly, "The Last Great Apes?" *Science* 309, no. 5740 (September 2, 2005): 1457; and Gretchen Vogel, "Scientists Say Ebola Has Pushed Western Gorillas to the Brink," *Science* 217, (September 14, 2007): 1484.

148 **Massive vulnerability:** As just one example, New Orleans was exposed to increased damage from Hurricane Katrina in part because of the deterioration of the Mississippi Deltaic Plain (MDP), the area of natural wetlands in the Mississippi Delta. Since the Mississippi River was leveed as it emptied into the Gulf of Mexico, it no longer deposited silt into the MDP, and the MDP itself was eroded. This demonstrates one way that human activity can exacerbate natural hazards. See John W. Day Jr. et al., "Restoration of the Mississippi Delta: Lessons from Hurricanes Katrina and Rita," *Science* 315 (March 3, 2007).

150 **benefits of such practices:** J. N. Pretty et al., "Resource-Conserving Agriculture Increases Yields in Developing Countries," *Environmental Science and Technology*, 2006.

150 **agronomic techniques such as:** Anthony Trewavas, "Fertilizer: No-Till Farming Could Reduce Run-Off," *Nature* 427 (January 8, 2004): 99.

150 **This dietary transformation:** Vaclav Smil, *Feeding the World: A Challenge for the Twenty-First Century* (Boston, Mass.: MIT Press, 2000).

154 **Conservation International concluded:** E. O. Wilson, *Acting Now to Save the Earth*, School Matters Blog. http://schoolsmatter.blogspot.com/2007/04/schools-wont-matter-unless.html.

155 **A Web-based Encyclopedia of Life:** Wilson estimates that there are somewhere between 1.5 and 1.8 million cataloged species in the world, with perhaps ten to fifty times that number still waiting to be identified and studied. Wilson argues that we must make an organized push to expand our knowledge about those species, lest we allow them to be driven to extinction in our fulsome ignorance. The Encyclopedia of Life could have one expandable Web page per species, documenting all known aspects of the species: genomics, cladistics and evolution, behavior, range, abundance, ecological relations with other species, threats to survival, and so forth.

Chapter 7: Global Population Dynamics

159 **"There doesn't seem ":** "How to Deal with a Falling Population" *The Economist* 284, no. 8539 (July 28, 2007): 11.

160 **Simon Kuznets and Michael Kremer:** Michael Kremer, "Population Growth and Technological Change: One Million B.C. to 1990," *The Quarterly Journal of Economics* 108, no. 3 (August 1993): 681–716; Simon Kuznets, "Population Change and Aggregate Output," *Demographic and Economic Change in Developed Countries* (Princeton, NJ: Princeton University Press, 1960): 324–40.

177 **The standard tests have:** Robert J. Barro and Xavier Sala-i-Martin, *Economic Growth*, 2nd edition (Cambridge, Mass.: MIT Press, 2004).

177 **each country's average annual growth rate:** Initial income is expected to have a negative effect: richer countries should grow less rapidly, and poor countries more rapidly, because of the phenomenon of convergence. Educational attainment is expected to have a positive effect on growth, as are the life expectancy and the rule of law.

177 **negative effect of high fertility:** Specifically, the logarithm of TFR has a linear negative effect on the income growth rate, with a coefficient of −0.012. Here is what this means. The natural logarithm of 6 is 1.79 and of 2 is 0.69. The difference is therefore 1.10, which when multiplied by 0.012 equals 0.013, or 1.3 percentage points (= 0.013 × 100) per year of faster income growth in the low-TFR country.

178 **"That's not our business":** Arthur M. Schlesinger, *A Thousand Days: John F. Kennedy in the White House* (Boston: Houghton Mifflin, 1965), p. 601.

180 **As John C. Caldwell and coauthors:** John C. Caldwell, James F. Phillips, and Barkat-e-Khuda, "The Future of Family Planning Programs," *Issues in Family Planning* 33, no. 1 (March 2002): 1–10.

Chapter 8: Completing the Demographic Transition

186 **Correlation does not prove:** To show lower mortality causes lower fertility see Jeffrey Sachs, Dalton Conley, and Gordon C. McCord, "Africa's Lagging Demographic Transition: Evidence from Exogenous Impacts of Malaria Ecology and Agricultural Technology," NBER Working Paper 12892, February 2007. Whether the effect of reducing the fertility is greater than the effect of the mortality reduction depends not only on reducing child mortality, but also on complementary actions regarding education, family planning, and broader economic development as described in the text.

187 **Education of Girls:** Of course, the education of boys matters greatly as well. Overall higher rates of education are associated with lower fertility, but the effect of increased female education appears to be much greater.

192 **strongly pronatal:** John C. Caldwell and Pat Caldwell, "The Cultural Context of High Fertility in Sub-Saharan Africa," *Population and Development Review* 13, no. 3 (September, 1987): 409–37; and John C. Caldwell and Pat Caldwell, "Africa: The New Family Planning Frontier," *Studies in Family Planning* 33, no. 1 (March 2002): 76–86.

192 **thereby leading to an indirect:** Jeffrey D. Sachs, Dalton Conley, and Gordon C. McCord, "Africa's Lagging Demographic Transition: Evidence from Exogenous Impacts of Malaria and Agricultural Technology," NBER Working Paper Series, no. 12892, February 2007.

194 **importance of privacy to:** Caldwell and Caldwell, "Africa."

194 **seven requirements:** Ibid., p. 84.

198 **The current Bush administration:** BBC News, "China Attacks U.S. Baby Fund Cuts," July 23, 2002. http://news.bbc.co.uk3/low/americas/2146160.stm.

198 **In its 2008 budget request":** Population Action International, "Bush's Budget Slashes International Family Planning," February 12, 2007. http://www.populationaction.org/press_room/viewpoint_and_statements/2007/02_12_budget.shtml.

198 **Population Action International:** Richard Cincotta, Robert Engelman, and Daniele Anastasion, *The Security Demographic: Population and Civil Conflict After the Cold War* (Population Action International, August 2003). http://www.populationaction.org/ Publications/Reports/The__Security__Demographic/Summary.shtml.

199 **"The results of my internal":** Henrik Urdal, in Lael Brainard and Derek Chollet, eds., *Too Poor for Peace? Global Poverty, Conflict, and Security in the 21st Century* (Washington, D.C.: Brookings Institution Press, 2007), p. 96.

199 **"A recent study":** Ibid., p. 92.

199 **the youth cohort:** United Nations Population Division, *World Population Prospects: 2006 Revision*, 2007.

Chapter 9: The Strategy of Economic Development

206 **average income per person:** Angus Maddison, *The World Economy: A Millennial Perspective*, (Paris: Development Centre of the Organization for Economic Cooperation and Development, 2001). These data are in constant 1990 PPP-adjusted dollars.

208 **it must be a successful exporter:** In market terms, the importer buys foreign exchange on the market using domestic currency, while the exporter sells foreign exchange in return for domestic currency. The exchange rate balances the supply and demand for foreign currency vis-à-vis domestic currency.

213 **geography shapes economic costs:** Let me also mention two frequently noted exceptions that prove the rule. Switzerland is rich despite being landlocked, and Singapore is rich despite being tropical. These cases are much less puzzling than they might seem. Landlockedness is particularly disadvantageous for developing-country regions, where the economy's ability to export to high-income markets is paramount, and trade must generally be carried out by sea. In those circumstances, development will come first to the coastal countries and only later to the interior regions. In the case of Switzerland, however, trade with rich countries can be carried out by land just across the borders with France, Italy, Germany, and Austria. The moral of the story is that

if a country must be landlocked, it's best to be landlocked in a rich region! Singapore's case is also special. The reasons that a tropical environment is difficult for development in most places are the problems of tropical diseases and low food productivity. Singapore, however, was established in 1819 as a trading post on the most important sea lane between Europe and Asia. As a small island, it is able to control mosquito-borne diseases, and as a highly advantageous trading location, it has been able to sell trade services to the world while using the proceeds to purchase food grown elsewhere. Singapore, in other words, did not need to solve the usual problem of absorbing an impoverished peasantary.

214 **In the nineteenth century:** In a notable example, Egypt attempted textile industrialization in the 1840s and 1850s with a sound industrial strategy but was stymied by the high cost of importing coal to power the factories.

214 **resource curse:** Plentiful oil reserves may also create a curse in more subtle ways, for example, by leading to an overvalued exchange rate, which prevents the development of an internationally competitive industrial sector. The phenomenon of oil wealth leading to a strong currency and a lack of industrial competitiveness is known as the Dutch Disease. For details, see M. Humphreys, J. Sachs, and J. Stiglitz, eds., *Escaping the Resource Curse* (New York: Columbia University Press, 2007).

217 **Africa's malaria-transmitting mosquitoes:** Anthony Kiszewski et al., "A Global Index Representing the Stability of Malaria Transmission," *American Journal of Tropical Medicine and Hygiene* 70, no. 5 (2004): 486–98.

225 **population of the Middle East:** I am using the UN Population Division region of West Asia here. The region includes: Armenia, Azerbaijan, Bahrain, Cyprus, Georgia, Iraq, Israel, Jordan, Kuwait, Lebanon, Oman, Palestine, Qatar, Saudi Arabia, Syria, Turkey, United Arab Emirates, and Yemen.

226 **population is far from coasts:** Nathan Nunn and Diego Puga, "Ruggedness: The Blessing of Bad Geography in Africa," discussion paper, Center for Economic Policy Research, March 2007.

Chapter 10: Ending Poverty Traps

231 **high-yield seeds:** Note that the high-yield seeds here refer to conventional seed breeding, rather than genetically modified organisms (GMOs). Such GMOs, if successfully adapted to meet Africa's particular needs (such as drought tolerance) may well play an important role, but the use of GMOs is at best years away.

235 **77.2 percent of farms:** United States Department of Agriculture, Rural Electrification Administration, *A Brief History of Rural Electrification and Telephone Programs*, chart C-1, p. C-2, http://www.rurdev.usda.gov/rd/70th/rea-history.pdf.

237 **immediate jump in income:** See the provocative and informative book by Lant Pritchett, *Let Their People Come: Breaking the Gridlock on Global Labor Mobility* (Washington, D.C.: Center for Global Development, 2007), especially chapter 1.

237 **benefits of increased remittance:** Pritchett, *Let Their People Come*, especially chapter 4 and references.

238 **"obvious goods," such as:** William Easterly, *The White Man's Burden* (New York: Penguin, 2006), p. 368–69.

239 **ten countries:** The original ten countries are Ethiopia, Ghana, Kenya, Malawi, Mali, Nigeria, Rwanda, Senegal, Tanzania, and Uganda. New African countries joining in 2007 include Liberia, Madagascar, and Mozambique, and several others have announced their intention to join.

239 **Similar results are evident:** For further reading see Pedro Sanchez et al., *The African Millennium Villages*, Proceedings of the National Academy of Sciences Special Feature: Sustainability Science, 2007; the Millennium Village Project Web site: http://www.millenniumvillages.org/.

242 **"A good communications infrastructure":** Robert Wade, *Governing the Market: Economic Theory and the Role of Government in East Asian Industrialization* (Princeton, N.J.: Princeton University Press, 1990).

242 **"Agricultural production":** Shigera Ishikawa, *Economic Development in Asian Perspective* (Tokyo: Kinokuniya, 1967), p. 95.

243 **U.S. aid amounting to:** United States Agency for International Development, *The Greenbook.* Available online at: http://qesdb.usaid.gov/gbk/.

243 **cereal yields of 3 tons:** World Bank, World Development Indicators 2007.

244 **"I wish I were now":** Norman Borlaug, speech at India's Escort Tractor Factory, March 29, 1967. Available online at http://www.agbioworld.org/newsletter__wm/index.php?caseid=archive &newsid=2519.

244 **"[T]he developing nations":** William Gaud, "The Green Revolution: Accomplishments and Apprehensions," speech delivered before the Society for International Development, Washington, D.C., March 8, 1968.

247 **"Extreme poverty exhausts":** Lael Brainard and Derek Chollet, eds. *Too Poor for Peace? Global Poverty, Conflict, and Security in the 21st Century* (Washington, D.C.: Brookings Institution Press 2007), p. 1.

247 **I had also made this point:** Jeffrey Sachs, "The Strategic Significance of Global Inequality," (reprint) Woodrow Wilson International Center for Scholars, issue 9 (2003).

248 **the only reliable growth in Darfur:** *Encyclopedia Britannica,* The Online Encyclopedia, 2007. http://www.britannica.com/.

250 **"long-term peace":** United Nations Environmental Program (UNEP), *Sudan: Post-Conflict Environmental Assessment* 2007, p. 8, at http://www.unep.org/sudan/.

250 **"major factors in":** Ibid., p. 79.

250 **"they are generally":** Ibid., p. 77. Emphasis in original.

250 **the parties to the Darfur Peace Agreement:** See the Darfur Peace Agreement, May 2006. This agreement was signed by the government of Sudan and some of the rebel groups but not others. It was not implemented. Nonetheless, it shows the high salience put on development issues. The agreement may be found at http://allafrica.com/peaceafrica/resources/view/00010926.pdf.

Chapter 11: Economic Security in a Changing World

263 **heavy investors both in R & D:** Data on R & D expenditure, investment in knowledge, and tertiary attainment are available from the *OECD Factbook 2006: Economic and Social Statistics.*

265 **seem to be much less likely:** Alberto Alesina, Edward Glaeser, and Bruce Sacerdote, "Why Doesn't the US Have a European-Style Welfare System?" NBER Working Paper Series, no. 8524 (October 2001). Available online at http://www.nber.org/papers/w8524.

265 **"Racial discord plays":** Ibid., p. 4.

267 **the Iraq War costs:** Peter Orszag, Director of Congressional Budget Office, Statement before the Committee on the Budget of the U.S. House of Representatives on the Estimated Costs of U.S. Operations in Iraq and Afghanistan and of Other Activities Related to the War on Terrorism, October 24 2007.

267 **"Our framework of":** Jacob Hacker, *The Great Risk Shift: The Assault on American Jobs, Families, Health Care, and Retirement—And How You Can Fight Back* (Oxford and New York: Oxford University Press, 2006), p. 181.

Chapter 12: Rethinking Foreign Policy

275 ***The Utility of Force*:** Rupert Smith, *The Utility of Force: The Art of War in the Modern World* (London and New York: Allen Lane, 2005).

277 **Under much worse:** Jeffrey Sachs. "Three Years and Three Lessons since 9/11," *Facts,* September 2004.

279 **In particular, Kahl argues:** Colin H. Kahl, *States, Scarcity, and Civil Strife in the Developing World* (Princeton: Princeton University Press, 2006).

279 **It is logical:** George C. Marshal, speech at Harvard University, June 5, 1947.

280 **"Effective economic development":** *National Security Strategy 2006*, p. 33. Available online at: http://www.whitehouse.gov/nsc/nss/2006/index.html.

282 **A recent BBC-PIPA GlobeScan survey:** See Program on International Policy Attitudes (PIPA), "World View of U.S. Role Goes from Bad to Worse," January 2007.

284 **series of international health regulations:** These include reporting of cases of disease outbreaks, monitoring, provision of data to the WHO, control of border crossings, duties to consult, and other regulations agreed to in 2005 and entered into force in 2007.

288 **One Percent Doctrine:** Ron Suskind, *The One Percent Doctrine: Deep Inside America's Pursuit of Its Enemies since 9/11* (New York: Simon & Schuster, 2006).

Chapter 13: Achieving Global Goals

296 **The Green Revolution built on:** M. S. Swaminathan, ed., *Wheat Revolution: A Dialogue* (Madras, Macmillan India Ltd., 1993).

Chapter 14: The Power of One

313 **development economist Albert Hirschman:** Albert Hirschman, *The Rhetoric of Reaction: Perversity, Futility, Jeopardy,* (Cambridge, MA: The Belknap Press of Harvard University Press, 1991).

314 **"It is from numberless":** Robert F. Kennedy, Day of Affirmation Address, delivered at University of Capetown, Capetown, South Africa, June 6, 1966. Available online at http://www.mtholyoke.edu/acad/intrel/speech/rfksa.htm.

316 **"We choose to go to":** John F. Kennedy, speech at Rice University, September 12, 1962. Available online at http://www.rice.edu/fondren/woodson/speech.html.

323 **Klaus Leisinger:** Klaus M. Leisinger, "Corporate Philanthropy: The Top of the Pyramid," *Business and Society Review* 112, no. 3 (2007): 315–42.

324 **"to support improved governance":** Extractive Industries Transparency Initiative, http://www.eitransparency.org.

326 **Around 170 scientists:** Rockefeller Foundation, *Rockefeller Foundation: A History*, February 2007. Available online at http://www.rockfound.org/about__us/history/1930__1939.shtml.

327 **publication by *Forbes* magazine:** Forbes.com, "The World's Richest People," March 2007, at http://www.forbes.com/2007/03/06/billionaires-new-richest__07billionaires__cz__lk__af__0308billieintro.html.

330 **"It seems to me that":** M. S. Swaminathan, ed., *Wheat Revolution: A Dialogue* (Madras, Macmillan India Ltd., 1993), p. 98.

References

Adema, Willem, and Maxime Ladaique. "Net Social Expenditure, 2005 Edition: More Comprehensive Measures of Social Support." Organization for Economic Cooperation and Development (OECD) Social, Employment and Migration Working Papers, no. 29, 2005.

Alesina, Alberto, and George-Marios Angeletos. "Fairness and Redistribution: U.S. versus Europe." NBER Working Paper Series, no. 9502, February 2003. http://www.nber.org/papers/w9502.

Alesina, Alberto, Edward Glaeser, and Bruce Sacerdote. "Why Doesn't the U.S. Have a European-Style Welfare System?" NBER Working Paper Series, no. 8524, October 2001. http://www.nber.org/papers/w8524.

Alley, Richard. "Wally Was Right: Predictive Ability of the North Atlantic 'Conveyor Belt' Hypothesis for Abrupt Climate Change." *Annual Review of Earth and Planetary Sciences* 35 (2007): 241–72.

American Association of Port Authorities, World Port Rankings, 2005. http://www.aapa-ports.org/industry/content.cfm?itemnumber=900.

Amstrup, Steven C., Bruce G. Marcot, and David C. Douglas. *Forecasting the Rangewide Status of Polar Bears at Selected Times in the 21st Century.* Virginia: U.S. Geological Survey Administrative Report, 2007.

Angell, Norman. *The Great Illusion: A Study of the Relation of Military Power in Nations to Their Economic and Social Advantage.* London: W. Heinemann, 1911.

Attaran, Amir, and Jeffrey D. Sachs. "Defining and Refining International Donor Support for Combating the AIDS Pandemic." *The Lancet* 357 (January 6, 2001): 57–61.

Auffhammer, Maximillian, V. Ramanathan, and Jeffrey R. Vincent. "Integrated Model Shows That Atmospheric Brown Clouds and Greenhouse Gases Have Reduced Rice Harvests in India." *Proceedings of the National Academy of Sciences Special Feature: Sustainability Science*, December 8, 2006.

Axelrod, Robert. *The Evolution of Cooperation.* New York: Basic Books, 1984.

Bairoch, Paul. *Cities and Economic Development: From the Dawn of History to the Present.* Translated by Christopher Braider. Chicago: University of Chicago Press, 1988.

Barnett, T. P., J. C. Adam, and D. P. Lettenmaier. "Potential Impacts of a Warming Climate on Water Availability in Snow-Dominated Regions." *Nature* 438 (November 2005).

Barro, Robert J., and Xavier Sala-i-Martin. *Economic Growth*, 2nd edition. Cambridge, Mass.: MIT Press, 2004.

BBC World Service/PIPA/GlobeScan. "View of United States' Influence." January 2007, p. 11. http://www.globescan.com/news__archives/bbcusop/.

Beddington, J. R., et al. "Current Problems in the Management of Marine Fisheries." *Science* 316 (June 22, 2007): 1713–16.

Bloom, David, and Jeffrey D. Sachs. "Geography, Demography, and Economic Growth in Africa." *Brookings Papers on Economic Activity*, issue 2 (1998).

Borlaug, Norman. Speech at India's Escort Tractor Factory, March 29, 1967. http://www.agbioworld.org/newsletter__wm/index.php?caseid=archive&newsid=2519.

Bourguignon, François, and Christian Morrisson. *Inequality Among World Citizens: 1820–1992*. Paris: Départment et Laboratoire d'Economic Théorique et Appliquée, Ecole Normale Supérieure, 2001.

Brainard, Lael, and Derek Chollet, eds. *Too Poor for Peace? Global Poverty, Conflict, and Security in the 21st Century*. Washington, D.C.: Brookings Institution Press, 2007.

Broecker, Wallace S., M. Ewing, and B. C. Heezen. "Evidence for an Abrupt Change in Climate Close to 11,000 Years Ago." *American Journal of Science* 258, no. 429, (June 1960): 429–48.

Brohan P., J. J. Kennedy, I. Harris et al. "Uncertainty Estimates in Regional and Global Observed Temperature Changes: A New Dataset from 1850." *Journal of Geophysical Research* 111 (2006).

Brown, Casey, and Upmanu Lall. "Water and Economic Development: The Role of Variability and Framework for Resilience." *Natural Resources Forum* 30, no. 4 (November 2006): 306–17.

Brundtland, Gro Harlem, ed. *Our Common Future: The World Commission on Environment and Development*. New York and Oxford: Oxford University Press, 1987.

Bush, George W. Address to the High-Level Plenary Meeting of the United Nations, September 14, 2005. http://www.whitehouse.gov/news/releases/2005/09/20050914.html.

Caldwell, John C., and Pat Caldwell. "Africa: The New Family Planning Frontier." *Studies in Family Planning* 33, no. 1 (March 2002): 76–86.

———. "The Cultural Context of High Fertility in Sub-Saharan Africa." *Population and Development Review* 13, no. 3. (September 1987): 409–37.

Caldwell, John C., James F. Phillips, and Barkat-e-Khuda. "The Future of Family Planning Programs." *Issues in Family Planning* 33, no. 1 (March 2002): 1–10.

Center for Systemic Peace. "List of Major Episodes of Political Violence 1946–2006." http://members.aol.com/CSPmgm/narlist.htm.

Chapman, J. L., and M. J. Reiss. *Ecology*. Cambridge: Cambridge University Press, 1998.

Chemical Weekly, July 16, 1975.

Chen, Shaohua, and Martin Ravallion. "How Have the World's Poor Fared since 1980?" *The World Bank Research Observer* 19, no. 2 (Fall 2004): 152.

Christensen, Villy, et al. "Hundred-Year Decline of North Atlantic Predatory Fishes." *Fish and Fisheries* 4, no. 1 (March 2003).

Cirincione, Joseph. *Bomb Scare: The History and Future of Nuclear Weapons*. New York: Columbia University Press, 2007.

Clausewitz, Carl Von. *On War*. London: Kegan, Paul, Trench, Trübner & Co., 1908.

Commission on Geosciences, Environment and Resources (CGER). *Sustaining Marine Fisheries*. Ocean Studies Board, 1999.

Commission on Macroeconomics and Health. *Macroeconomics and Health: Investing in Health for Economic Development*. Geneva: World Health Organization, 2001.

Commoner, Barry. "The Environmental Cost of Economic Growth." In *Population, Resources and the Environment*. Washington, D.C.: Government Printing Office, 1972, pp. 339–63.

Comprehensive Nuclear Test-Ban Treaty. http://www.ctbto.org.

Conley, Dalton, Jeffrey D. Sachs, and Gordon C. McCord. "Africa's Lagging Demographic Transition: Evidence from Exogenous Impacts of Malaria and Agricultural Technology." NBER Working Paper Series, no. 12892, February 2007.

The Convention on Biological Diversity. http://www.biodiv.org.

Cox-Foster, Diana L., et al. "A Metaelgenomic Survey of Microbes in Honey Bee Colony Collapse Disorder." *Science* 318 (October 12, 2007).

Crookes, Sir William. "The Wheat Problem: Based on Remarks Made in the Presidential Address to the British Association in Bristol in 1898." New York: G. P. Putnam and Sons, 1900.

Crutzen, Paul J., and Eugene F. Stoermer. "The 'Anthropocene.' " *International Geosphere-Biosphere Programme Newsletter* 41 (May 2000): 17–18.

Dalgaard, Tommy. "Looking at Biofuels and Bioenergy." *Science* 312 (June 23, 2006): 1743.

The Darfur Peace Agreement. May 2006. http://allafrica.com/peaceafrica/resources/view/00010926.pdf.

Dasgupta, Partha. "Common Property Resources: Economic Analytics." In N. S. Jodha et al., eds., *Promise, Trust, and Evolution*. New Delhi: Oxford University Press, 2007.

Day, John W., Jr., et al. "Restoration of the Mississippi Delta: Lessons from Hurricanes Katrina and Rita." *Science* 315 (March 23, 2007).

Demurger, Sylvie, Jeffrey D. Sachs, Wing Thye Woo, Shuming Bao, Gene Chang, and Andrew Mellinger. "Geography, Economic Policy, and Regional Development in China." *Asian Economic Papers* 1, no. 1 (Winter 2002): 146–97.

Diamond, Jared. *Collapse: How Societies Choose to Fail or Succeed.* New York: Viking, 2004.

Donnelly, John. "Prevention Urged in AIDS Fight." *Boston Globe*, June 7, 2001, p. A8.

Easterly, William. *The White Man's Burden.* New York: Penguin, 2006.

Eastwood, Robert, Michael Lipton, and Andrew Newell. "Farm Size." In volume 3 of *The Handbook of Agricultural Economics.* University of Sussex, June 2004.

Ehrlich, Paul R., and John P. Holdren. "Impact of Population Growth." *Science* 171 (1971): 1212–17.

Encyclopedia Britannica, The Online Encyclopedia, 2007. http://www.britannica.com/.

Extractive Industries Transparency Initiative. www.eitransparency.org.

Faye, Michael L., Jeffrey D. Sachs, John W. McArthur, and Thomas Snow. "The Challenges Facing Landlocked Developing Countries." *Journal of Human Development* 5, no. 1 (March 2004).

Flannery, Tim. *The Weather Makers.* New York: Atlantic Monthly Press, 2006.

Food and Agriculture Organization (FAO) of the United Nations, *FAO STAT.* Rome 2007. http://fao stat.fao.org.

———. *The State of World Aquaculture 2006.* Rome: FAO, 2006. http://www.fao.org/docrep/ 009/a0874e/a0874e00.htm.

———. *World Agriculture: Towards 2015/2030, An FAO Perspective.* London and Sterling, Va.: Earthscan, 2003.

Forbes.com. "The World's Richest People." March 2007. http://www.forbes.com/2007/03/06/ billionaires-new-richest__07billionaires__cz__lk__af__0308billieintro.html.

Forslund, Anders, Daniela Froberg, and Linus Lindqvist. "The Swedish Activity Guarantee." OECD Social, Employment and Migration Working Papers 16 (January 2004).

Förster, Michael, and Marco Mira d'Ercole. "Income Distribution and Poverty in OECD Countries in the Second Half of the 1990s." OECD Social, Employment and Migration Working Papers 22 (March 2005).

Fosdick, Raymond Blaine. *Story of the Rockefeller Foundation.* New York: Harper, 1952.

Gallup, John Luke, and Jeffrey D. Sachs. "Agriculture, Climate, and Technology: Why Are the Tropics Falling Behind?" *American Journal of Agricultural Economics* 82 (August 2000): 731–77.

———. "The Economic Burden of Malaria." *American Journal of Tropical Medicine & Hygiene* 64, nos. 1, 2, supplement (January and February, 2001): 85–96.

Gallup, John Luke, Jeffrey D. Sachs, and Andrew Mellinger. "Geography and Economic Development." *International Regional Science Review* 22, no. 2 (August 1999): 179–232.

Gaud, William. "The Green Revolution: Accomplishments and Apprehensions." Speech delivered before the Society for International Development, Washington, D.C., March 8, 1968.

Giannini, A., R. Saravanan, and P. Chang. "Oceanic Forcing of Sahel Rainfall on Interannual to Interdecadal Timescales. *Science* 302 (October 9, 2003): 1027–30.

The Global Fund Against AIDS, Tuberculosis and Malaria. Progress reports available at http://www.theglobalfund.org/en/performance/results/.

The Global Roundtable on Climate Change. *The Path to Climate Sustainability: A Joint Statement by the Global Roundtable on Climate Change,* 2007. http://www.Earth.columbia.edu/grocc/grocc4__ statement.html.

Grabowsky, Mark, et al. "Distributing Insecticide-Treated Bednets During Measles Vaccination: A Low-Cost Means of Achieving High and Equitable Coverage." *Bulletin of the World Health Organization* 83, no. 3 (March 2005).

———. "Integrating Insecticide-Treated Bednets into a Measles Vaccination Campaign Achieves High, Rapid and Equitable Coverage with Direct and Voucher-Based Methods." *Tropical Medicine and International Health*, no. 11 (November 2005): 1151–60.

Hacker, Jacob. *The Great Risk Shift: The Assault on American Jobs, Families, Health Care, and Retirement—And How You Can Fight Back.* New York: Oxford University Press, 2006.

Haggett, Peter. *Geography: A Modern Synthesis*, 2nd edition.(New York: Harper & Row, 1975).

Hall-Spencer, Jason, et al. "Trawling Damage to the Northeast Atlantic Ancient Coral Reefs." *Proceedings of the Royal Society B* 269 (2002): 507–11.

Hansen, James. "Climate Catastrophe." *New Scientist*, July 28, 2007.

Hansen, James, et al. "Climate Change and Trace Gases." *Philosophical Transactions of the Royal Society A* 365 (May 2007): 1925–54.

Hansen, James, et al. "Dangerous Human-Made Interference with Climate: a GISS ModelE Study." *Atmospheric Chemistry and Physics* (2007): 2287–312.

Hardin, Garrett. "The Tragedy of the Commons." *Science* 162 (1968): 1243–48.

Hayek, Friedrich A. von. *The Road to Serfdom*. Chicago: University of Chicago Press, 1944.

Hiro, Dilip. *Blood of the Earth: The Battle for the World's Vanishing Oil Resources*. New York: Nation Books, 2006.

Hirschman, Albert. *The Rhetoric of Reaction: Perversity, Futility, Jeopardy*. Cambridge, MA: The Belknap Press of Harvard University Press, 1991.

Hopkin, Michael. "Oceans in Trouble as Acid Levels Rise." *Nature News,* June 30, 2005.

"How to Deal with a Falling Population." *The Economist*, July 26, 2007.

Hughes, T. P., et al. "Climate Change, Human Impacts, and the Resilience of Coral Reefs." *Science* 301 (2003): 929.

Humphreys, Macartan, Jeffrey D. Sachs, and Joseph Stiglitz, eds. *Escaping the Resource Curse*. New York: Columbia University Press, 2007.

The Institute of Electrical and Electronics Engineers. *Position Statement: Plug-In Electric Hybrid Vehicles*. Adopted by the Board of Directors, June 15, 2007.

Intergovernmental Panel on Climate Change. *Climate Change 2007: Fourth Assessment Report*, 2007. http://www.ipcc.ch.

———. *Carbon Dioxide Capture and Storage*, 2006. http://www.ipcc.ch/activity/srccs/index.htm.

International Conference on Population and Development, Program of Action. http://www.unfpa.org/icpd/ icpd__poa.htm.

International Conservation Union for Nature and Natural Resources. *2006 Red List of Threatened Species*, 2006. http://www.iucn.org/themes/ssc/redlist2006/redlist2006.htm.

International Energy Agency. CO_2 *Emissions from Fuel Combustion 1971–2005*. Paris: OECD, 2007.

International Monetary Fund. World Economic Outlook Database.

International Research Institute for Climate Prediction. "Sustainable Development in Africa: Is the Climate Right?" IRI Technical Report Number IRI-TR/05/1, 2005.

International Vacation Survey. Expedia.com, 2006.

Ishikawa, Shigera. *Economic Development in Asian Perspective*. Tokyo: Kinokuniya, 1967.

Jetz, Walter, Chris Carbone, Jenny Fulford, and James H. Brown. "The Scaling of Animal Space Use," *Science* 306, no. 5694 (October 8, 2004): 266–68.

Jolly, Alison. "The Last Great Apes?" *Science* no. 5740 (September 2, 2005): 1457.

Jones, E. L. *The European Miracle: Environments, Economies and Geopolitics in the History of Europe and Asia*. New York: Cambridge University Press, 1981.

Kagan, Frederick. *Finding the Target: The Transformation of American Military Policy*. New York: Encounter Books, 2006.

Kahl, Colin H. *States, Scarcity, and Civil Strife in the Developing World*. Princeton, N.J.: Princeton University Press, 2006.

Keele, Brandon F., et al. "Chimpanzee Reservoirs of Pandemic and Nonpandemic HIV." *Science* 313, no. 5786 (July 28, 2006): 523–26.

Keeling, Charles David, et al. "Atmospheric Carbon Dioxide Variations at Mauna Loa Observatory, Hawaii." *Tellus* 28 (1976): 538.

Kennedy, John F. Inaugural address, 1961. http://www.americanrhetoric.com/speeches/jfk inaugural.htm.

———. Speech at Rice University, September 12, 1962. http://www.rice.edu/fondren/ woodson/speech.html.

———. Spring commencement address at American University, June 10, 1963. http:// www.ameri-can.edu/media/speeches/Kennedy.htm.

Kennedy, Robert F. Day of Affirmation address at University of Capetown, Capetown, South Africa, June 6, 1966. http://www.americanrhetoric.com/speeches/rfkcapetown.htm.

Kiszewski, Anthony, et al., "A Global Index Representing the Stability of Malaria Transmission." *American Journal of Tropical Medicine and Hygiene* 70, no. 5 (2004) 486–98.

Klare, Michael. *Blood and Oil: The Dangers and Consequences of America's Growing Dependency on Imported Petroleum.* New York: Metropolitan Books, 2004.

Kliesch, James, and Therese Langer. "Plug-in Hybrids: An Environmental and Economic Performance Outlook." Report no. T061, American Council for an Energy-Efficient Economy, September 2006.

Kremer, Michael. "Population Growth and Technological Change: One Million B.C. to 1990." *The Quarterly Journal of Economics* 108, no. 3 (August 1993): 681–716.

Kuznets, Simon. "Population Change and Aggregate Output." *Demographic and Economic Change in Developed Countries.* Princeton, N.J.: Princeton University Press, 1960.

The Kyoto Protocol to the United Nations Framework Convention on Climate Change. http://un fccc.int/kyoto__protocol/items/2830.php.

Lackner, Klaus, and Jeffrey D. Sachs. "A Robust Strategy for Sustainable Energy." *Brookings Papers on Economic Activity,* issue 2 (2005).

Leisinger, Klaus M. "Corporate Philanthropy: The 'Top of the Pyramid.' " *Business and Society Review* 112, no. 3 (2007): 315–42.

Lindert, Peter. *Growing Public: Social Spending and Economic Growth since the Eighteenth Century,* vol. 1. New York: Cambridge University Press, 2004.

Lotze, H. K., et al. "Depletion, Degradation, and Recovery Potential of Estuaries and Coastal Seas," *Science* 312 (June 23, 2006).

McEvedy, Colin, and Richard Jones. *Atlas of World Population History.* New York: Viking Press, 1977.

McNeill, J. R. *Something New Under the Sun: An Environmental History of the Twentieth-Century World.* New York: Norton, 2006.

Maddison, Angus. *The World Economy: A Millennial Perspective.* Paris: Development Centre of the Organization for Economic Cooperation and Development, 2001.

Malthus, Thomas R. *An Essay on the Principle of Population: A View of Its Past and Present Effects on Human Happiness; with an Inquiry into Our Prospects Respecting the Future Removal or Mitigation of the Evils Which It Occasions.* 1798.

Marshall, George. Marshall Plan speech at Harvard University, June 5, 1947. http://www.georgecmar shall.org/lt/speeches/marshall__plan.cfm.

Marshall, Monty G. "Major Episodes of Political Violence 1946–2006." Center for Systemic Peace, 2007. http://members.aol.com/csprogram/warlist.htm.

Martin, P. S., and H. E. Wright, eds. *Pleistocene Extinctions: The Search for a Cause.* New Haven, Conn.: Yale University Press, 1967.

Mellinger, Andrew, Jeffrey D. Sachs, and John Luke Gallup. "Climate, Coastal Proximity, and Development." In Gordon L. Clark, Maryann P. Feldman, and Meric S. Gertler, eds., *Oxford Handbook of Economic Geography.* New York and Oxford: Oxford University Press, 2000.

Mendelson Joseph R., et al. III, "Biodiversity: Confronting Amphibian Declines and Extinctions." *Science* 313, no. 5783 (July 7, 2006).

Miguel, Edward, "Poverty and Violence: An Overview of Recent Research and Implications for Foreign Aid." In L. Brainard and D. Chollet, eds., *Too Poor For Peace?* Washington, D.C.: Brookings Institution, 2007.

Miguel, Edward, Shanker Satyanath, and Ernest Sergenti. "Economic Shocks and Civil Conflict: An Instrumental Variables Approach." *Journal of Political Economy* 112, no. 4 (2004): 725–53.

Miles, Marc A., Kim R. Holmes, Mary Anastasia O'Grady, Ana Isabel Eiras, and Anthony B. Kim. "2006 Index of Economic Freedom." Heritage Foundation, 2006.

Millennium Ecosystem Assessment. *Ecosystems and Human Well-Being: Current State and Trends.* Island Press, 2005.

———. *Ecosystems and Human Well-Being, Synthesis Report.* World Resources Institute, 2005.

The Millennium Village Project. http://www.millenniumvillages.org.

MIT Inter-Disciplinary Panel on Coal. *The Future of Coal: Options for a Carbon-Constrained World,* Cambridge, Mass.: MIT Press, 2007.

MIT Inter-Disciplinary Panel on Geothermal Energy. *The Future of Geothermal Energy.* Cambridge, Mass.: MIT Press, 2007.

MIT Inter-Disciplinary Panel on Nuclear Power. *The Future of Nuclear Power.* Cambridge, Mass.: MIT Press, 2003.

Molina, Mario J., and F. S. Rowland. "Stratospheric Sink for Chlorofluoromethanes: Chlorine Atom-Catalyzed Destruction of the Ozone." *Nature* 249 (June 28, 1974): 810–12.

The Montreal Protocol on Substances That Deplete the Ozone Layer. http://ozone.unep.org/Treaties__and__Ratification/2B__montreal__protocol.shtml.

Mora, Camilo. "Coral Reefs and the Global Network of Marine Protected Areas." *Science* 312, no. 5781 (June 23, 2006): 1750–51.

National Research Council, Committee on the Status of Pollinators in North America. "Status of Pollinators in America." 2007.

Nelson, Richard, ed., *National Innovation Systems: A Comparative Analysis.* New York: Oxford University Press, 1993.

Normile, Dennis. "Getting at the Root of Killer Dust Storms." *Science* 317 (July 20, 2007): 314–16.

Nunn, Nathan, and Diego Puga. "Ruggedness: The Blessing of Bad Geography in Africa." Discussion paper, Center for Economic Policy Research, March 2007.

Organization for Economic Co-operation and Development. *Economic Outlook* 79 (May 2006).

———. *International Development Statistics.* Paris, 2007. http://www.oecd.org/dac/stats/idsonline.

———. *OECD Factbook 2006: Economic and Social Statistics,* 2006.

———. *OECD Productivity Database,* January 2006.

———. *OECD in Figures,* 2005 edition. http://www.oecd.org/infigures/.

———. *Social Expenditure Database 1980–2001,* 2004. http://www.oecd.org/els/social/expenditure.

Orszag, Peter, Director of Congressional Budget Office, Statement before the Committee on the Budget of the U.S. House of Representatives on the Estimated Costs of U.S. Operations in Iraq and Afghanistan and of Other Activities Related to the War on Terrorism, October 24, 2007.

Ostrom, Elinor. *Governing the Commons: The Evolution of Institutions for Collective Action.* Cambridge and New York: Cambridge University Press, 1990.

Pacala, Steven, and Robert Socolow. "Stabilization Wedges: Solving the Climate with Current Technologies for the Next 50 Years." *Science* 305, no. 5686 (August 13, 2004): 968–72.

Pandolfi, John M., et al. "Global Trajectories of the Long-Term Decline of Coral Reef Ecosystems." *Science* 301 (2003): 955.

Pearce, Fred. *When the Rivers Run Dry: Water: The Defining Crisis of the Twenty-First Century.* Boston: Beacon Press, 2006.

———. *With Speed and Violence.* Boston: Beacon Press, 2007.

Pidwirny, M. *Fundamentals of Physical Geography,* 2nd Edition. 2006. http://www.physicalgeography.net/fundamentals/contents.html.

Pikitch, Ellen K., et al. "Ecosystem-Based Fisheries Management." *Science* 305, no. 5682 (July 16, 2004): 346–47.

Population Action International, "Bush's Budget Slashes International Family Planning," February 12, 2007.

———. "The Security Demographic: Population and Civil Conduct after the Cold War." August 2003. http://www.populationaction.org/publications/reports/The_Security_Demographic/summary.shtml.

———. "Trends in U.S. Population Assistance." Washington, D.C., 2007. http://www.populationaction.org/Issues/U.S._Policies/Trends_in_U.S._Population_Assistance.shtml.

Pounds, J. Alan, et al. "Widespread Amphibian Extinctions from Epidemic Disease Driven by Global Warming." *Nature,* January 12, 2006.

Pretty, J. N., et al. "Resource-Conserving Agriculture Increases Yields in Developing Countries." *Environmental Science and Technology* 40, no. 4 (2006): 1114–19.

Pritchett, Lant. *Let Their People Come: Breaking the Gridlock on Global Labor Mobility.* Washington, D.C.: Center for Global Development, 2007.

Program on International Policy Attitudes. "World View of U.S. Role Goes from Bad to Worse." January 2007.

Rappaport, Jordan, and Jeffrey D. Sachs. "The United States as a Coastal Nation." *Journal of Economic Growth* 8, no. 1 (March 2003): 5–46.

Rasmusson, R., A. Dai, and K. E. Trenberth. "Impact of Climate Change on Precipitation." In Mohamed Gad-el-Hak, ed., *Large-Scale Disasters, Prediction, Control and Mitigation.* London: Cambridge University Press, 2007, pp. 453–72.

Rhode, Robert A., Global Warming Art Project. http://www.globalwarmingart.com/wiki/image:Mauna_Loa_Carbon_Dioxide_png.

Rockefeller Foundation: A History. February 2007. http://www.rockfound.org/about__us/history/1930__1939.shtml.

Rockström, J., N. Hatibu, T. Oweis, S. Wani, J. Barron, A. Bruggeman, J. Farahani, L. Karlberg, and Z. Qiang. "Managing Water in Rainfed Agriculture." Chapter 8 in D. Molden, ed., *Water for Food, Water for Life, A Comprehensive Assessment of Water Management in Agriculture.* London: EarthScan: International Water Management Institute, 2007.

Rodriguez, Francisco, and Jeffrey D. Sachs. "Why Do Resource-Abundant Economies Grow More Slowly?" *Journal for Economic Growth* 4 (September 1999): 277–303.

Rogner, H. H. "An Assessment of the World Hydrocarbon Resources." *Annual Review of Energy and the Environment,* 1997.

Rosenzweig, Michael L. "Paradox of Enrichment: Destabilization of Exploitation Ecosystems in Ecological Time." *Science* 171 (January 29, 1971): 385–87.

Roughgarden, Jonathan, and Fraser Smith. "Why Fisheries Collapse and What to Do About It." Proceedings of the National Academy of Sciences, volume 93 (May 1996): 5078–83.

Royal Society Working Group on Ocean Acidification. *Ocean Acidification Due to Increasing Atmospheric Carbon Dioxide.* London: Royal Society, June 2005.

Sachs, Jeffrey D. *The End of Poverty.* New York: Penguin Press, 2005.

———. "A Global Fund to Fight Against AIDS." *The Washington Post,* April 7, 2001.

———. "HIV Non-Intervention: A Costly Option." Speech at the International AIDS Conference in Durban, South Africa, July 13, 2000. http://www.Earth.columbia.edu/about/director/pwrpoint/AIDSDurban.htm.

———. "The Nordic Model in Comparative Perspective." Prepared for the Venice Summer Institute, organized by CES-Ifo and the Center on Capitalism and Society, Venice International University, San Servolo, July 2006, revised October 15, 2006.

———. "The Strategic Significance of Global Inequality." (reprint) *Environmental Change and Security Project Report,* Woodrow Wilson International Center for Scholars, Issue 9 (2003).

———. "Three Years and Three Lessons since 9/11." *Facts,* September 2004. *Scientific American,* September 2007.

Sachs, Jeffrey D., John W. McArthur, Guido Schmidt-Traub, Margaret Kruk, Chandrika Bahadur, Michael Faye, and Gordon McCord. "Ending Africa's Poverty Trap." *Brookings Papers on Economic Activity,* issue 1, (2004).

Sachs, Jeffrey D., and Pia Malaney. "The Economic and Social Burden of Malaria." *Nature* 415, no. 6872 (February 7, 2002).

Sachs, Jeffrey D., and Andrew Warner. "The Big Push, Natural Resource Booms and Growth." *Journal of Development Economics* 59, no. 1 (June 1999): 43–76.

———. "The Curse of Natural Resources." *European Economic Review* 45 (May 2001).

———. "Sources of Slow Growth in African Economies." *Journal of African Economies* 6, no. 3 (1997).

Sanchez, Pedro, et al. "The African Millennium Villages." *Proceedings of the National Academy of Sciences Special Feature: Sustainability Science,* 104, no. 43 (October 23, 2007): 16775–80.

Schlesinger, Arthur M. *A Thousand Days: John F. Kennedy in the White House.* Boston: Houghton Mifflin, 1965.

Schon, Donald, *The Reflective Practitioner: How Professionals Think in Action.* New York: Basic Books, 1983.

Schumpeter, Joseph A. *Capitalism, Socialism and Democracy.* London: G. Allen & Unwin, 1947.

Scientific American, September 2007.

Seager, Richard, et al. "Model Projections of an Imminent Transition to a More Arid Climate in Southwestern North America." *Science* 316 (2007): 1181.

Sen, Amartya. *Identity and Violence: The Illusion of Destiny.* New York: W.W. Norton and Co., 2006.

Shah, Tushaaar. *Water Policy Research Highlight: Groundwater and Human Development: Challenges and Opportunities in Livelihoods and Environment.* Water Policy Program, 2005. http://www.iwmi.org/iwmi-tata.

Sitch, S., et al. "Indirect Radiative Forcing of Climate Change Through Ozone Effects on the Land-Carbon Sink." *Nature* (August 16, 2007): 791–94.

Smil, Vaclav. *Enriching the Earth: Fritz Haber, Carl Bosch, and the Transformation of World Food Production.* Cambridge, Mass.: MIT Press, 2001.

———. *Feeding the World: A Challenge for the Twenty-First Century.* Boston, Mass.: MIT Press, 2000.

———. "Improving Efficiency and Reducing Waste in Our Food System," *Environmental Sciences* 1 (2004): 17–26.

Smith, Adam. *The Wealth of Nations.* Edwin Cannan, ed. London: Methuen and Co., Ltd., 1904. Originally published in 1776.

Smith, Rupert. *The Utility of Force: The Art of War in the Modern World.* London and New York: Allen Lane, 2005.

Stern, Nicholas. *The Economics of Climate Change: The Stern Review.* Cambridge: Cambridge University Press, 2006.

Stevens, Wallace. *Collected Poems.* New York: Knopf, 1955.

Stockholm International Peace Research Institute. SIPRI Military Expenditure Database, 2007. http://first.sipri.org/non-first/milex.php.

Stone, Richard. "Aquatic Ecology: The Last of the Leviathans." *Science* 316 (June 22, 2007): 1684–88.

Stuart, Simon, et al. "Status and Trends of Amphibian Declines and Extinctions Worldwide." *Science* 306 (December 3, 2004): 1783–86.

Suskind, Ron. *The One Percent Doctrine: Deep Inside America's Pursuit of Its Enemies since 9/11.* New York: Simon and Schuster, 2006.

Swaminathan, M. S., ed. *Wheat Revolution: A Dialogue.* Madras: Macmillan India Ltd., 1993.

Teklehaimanot, Awash, Jeffrey D. Sachs, and Chris Curtis. "Malaria Control Needs Mass Distribution of Insecticidal Bednets." *The Lancet,* June 2007.

Teklehaimanot, Awash, Gordon C. McCord, and Jeffrey D. Sachs. "Scaling Up Malaria Control in Africa: An Economic and Epidemiological Assessment." *American Journal of Tropical Medicine and Hygiene.* 77 (Suppl. 6) December 2007.

Thomas, Chris D., et al. "Extinction Risk from Climate Change." *Nature* 427 (January 8, 2004).

Transparency International. *Corruption Perceptions Index (CPI)* 2006. http://www.transparency.org/policy__research/surveys__indices/cpi/2006.

Treaty on the Non-Proliferation of Nuclear Weapons. http://www.un.org/Depts/dda/WMD/treaty/.

Trewavas, Anthony. "Fertilizer: No-Till Farming Could Reduce Run-Off." *Nature* 427 (January 8, 2004): 99.

United Nations Convention to Combat Desertification. http://www.unccd.entico.com/english.

United Nations Development Program. *Human Development Report 2006: Beyond Scarcity: Power, Poverty and the Global Water Crisis.* Palgrave Macmillan, 2006.

United Nations Environment Program. *Sudan Post-Conflict Environmental Assessment,* 2007. http://www.unep.org/sudan/.

United Nations Framework Convention on Climate Change. http://www.unfccc.int.

United Nations Millennium Declaration. www.ohchr.org/english/law/millennium.htm.

United Nations Millennium Project. *Investing in Development: A Practical Plan to Achieve the Millennium Development Goals.* London: Earthscan, 2005.

———. *Public Choices, Private Decisions: Sexual and Reproductive Health and the Millennium Development Goals.* London and Sterling, Va.: Earthscan, 2006.

United Nations Population Division. *World Population in 2300.* 2003. http://www.un.org/esa/population/publications/longrange2/longrange2.htm.

———. *World Population Prospects: 2006 Revision.* New York, 2007.

———. *World Population Prospects: 1998 Revision,* New York, 1999.

United States Agency for International Development. *The Greenbook.* http://qesdb.usaid.gov/gbk/.

United States Department of Agriculture, Rural Electrification Administration. *A Brief History of the Rural Electric and Telephone Program.* 1982. http://www.rurdev.usda.gov/rd/70th/rea-history.pdf.

The United States National Security Strategy 2006. http://www.whitehouse.gov/nsc/nss/2006/index.html.

Vitousek, Peter M., et al. "Human Domination of Earth's Ecosystems." *Science* 277, no. 5325 (July 25, 1997): 494–99.

Vogel, Gretchen. "Scientists Say Ebola Has Pushed Western Gorillas to the Brink." *Science* 217, (September 14, 2007): 1484.

Vose, R. S., et al. *2007: The Global Historical Climatology Network: Long-Term Monthly Temperature, Precipitation, Sea Level Pressure, and Station Pressure Data.* ORNL/CDIAC-53, NDP-041, Carbon Dioxide Information Analysis Center, Oak Ridge National Laboratory. http://iri.columbia.edu.

Wade, Robert. *Governing the Market: Economic Theory and the Role of Government in East Asian Industrialization.* Princeton N.J.: Princeton University Press, 1990.

Weiner, Tim. *Legacy of Ashes.* New York: Random House, 2007.

White House Office of Management and Budget. *Budget of Fiscal Year 2008.* 2007. http://www.white house.gov/omb/budget/fy2008/.

Wilson, E. O. *Acting Now to Save the Earth,* School Matters Blog. http://schoolmatter.blogspot.com/2007/04/schools-wont-matter-unless.html.

———. *The Creation: An Appeal to Save Life on Earth.* New York: Norton, 2006.

———. *The Future of Life.* New York: Albert A. Knopf, 2002.

World Bank. World Development Indications. Washington D.C., 2007. http://www.worldbank.org/publications/wdi.

World Christian Database. http://worldchristiandatabase.org/wcd/.

World Economic Forum. The Global Competitiveness Report 2006–2007. Michael Porter, Klaus Schnab, Augusto Lopez-Claros, Xavier Sala-i-Martin. Palgrave Macmillan, 2006.

World Resources Institute, *Climate Analyisis Indicator Tool (CAIT),* Version 4.0, Washington D.C., 2007. http://cait.wri.org.

Worm, Boris, et al. "Impacts of Biodiversity Loss on Ocean Ecosystem Services." *Science* 314, no. 5800, (November 3, 2006): 787–90.

Yergin, Daniel. *The Prize: The Epic Quest for Oil, Money and Power.* New York: Free Press, 1993.

Yunus, Muhammad, with Alan Jolis. *Banker to the Poor: Micro-lending and the Battle Against World Poverty.* New York: Public Affairs, 1999.

Zhang, Xuebin, et al. "Detection of Human Influence on Twentieth-Century Precipitation Trends." *Nature* 448 (July 27, 2006): 461.

Zhu, Qiang. "The Rainwater Harvesting Projects in Mainland China." International Rainwater Catchment Systems Association. http://www.eng.warwick.ac.uk/ircsa/factsheets/ChinaRWH.pdf.

Index

Page references in *italics* refer to illustrations.

in economic growth, 211–12
in global problem solving, 291–92, 295
for technology investment, 208
See also business
privatization:
  of the commons, 38
  of water rights, 115–16, 131–32
problem solving, 269–339
  achieving global goals, 291–311
  achieving our goals versus costs of failure, *309*
  combining general training with specific, 15
  finding new approach for global, 7
  paralysis of global, 6
  pattern of successful, 291–95
  reactionary attitude toward, 313
  skepticism regarding, 295
public investment:
  in antiretroviral medicines for Africa, 317, 319
  in economic development, 219, 220–21, *222*, 223
  in economic growth, 211–12
  in global problem solving, 291–92, 295
  in infrastructure, 212, 221
  for saving the world, 11–12
  in subsistence economies, 209
  in technology, 208
public leadership for reducing fertility rates, 185, 190
public-private partnerships, 322–23
public transport, 99
Pugwash Conferences, 325

racism, 265–66
rainfall:
  African conflict associated with drops in, 129
  climate change will affect, 89
  in Darfur, 249, *249*
  and economic development, 119–21
  geographic variation of, 118–19
  insurance, 131, 134
  rainwater harvesting, 133
  two kinds of water from, 121–22
rain forests, 68–69, 118, 120, 149
Reagan, Ronald, 180, 198
Red Cross, 306–7
refugees, environmental, 107
regional development, 234–36
renewable energy, 30, 43
reproductive health, 180, 181–82, 188–89
research and development (R & D):
  balance of public finance and patents for, 34–35
  in carbon management, 98
  costs for sustainable development, *310*, 310–11
  federal U.S. budget for, 33
  funding for, 303–4
  in Global Roundtable on Climate Change protocol, 111
  public-private partnerships in, 322–23
  in social-welfare states, 263, *263*

of sustainable technologies, 32, 33
  at universities, 328–30
Rio Earth Summit (1992), 12–13
Rio Grande River, 123
rivers, 59, 70, 122–24, 128, 130
roads, 21, 212, 213, 231
Rockefeller Foundation, 243, 293, 302, 304, 325–27
Rotblat, Joseph, 325
Rural Electrification Administration, 235

Sahel, 11, 120, 121, 126, 248, 249, *249*
sanitation, 130, 131, 137, 209, 231
SARS, 76, 80, 147
saving, 207, 229, 262
science:
  in antiretroviral medicine development, 317
  become acquainted with, 336–37
  consensus on climate change, 109, 114
  costs of meeting Millennium Promises, *310*
  in economic development strategy, 221
  foundation support for, 303
  funding for sustainable development research, 303–4
  in global problem solving, 292–93, 295
  as nonrival, 32–33, 205–6
  organizations of scientists, 331
  versus patentable inventions, 34
  research methods as not up to challenges of sustainable development, 14–15
  Rockefeller Foundation support for, 326–27
  sharing of knowledge in, 32–33
  for sharing prosperity, 205
  in technology-based economies, 211
sea level, rise in, 28, 88, 90, 95, 107
sea otter, overhunting of, 147
seeds, 30, 33, 42, 44–45, 107, 130, 231, 239, 243–44, 293
Singapore, 215, *216*, 357n
sinks of greenhouse gases, 92, 93, 101
smallpox, 8, 46, 62, 245, 296
Smil, Vaclav, 65–66, 150, 151
snowmelt, 126
social insurance:
  in economic development strategy, 221
  in industrializing Europe, 4
  scope of, 255
  spending on, 259–60
  in United States, 267–68
social networking sites, 308, 332, 338
social security systems, 200–202
soil nutrients, 44, 65, 265
solar power:
  and fear of energy crisis, 45
  in fossil fuels, 64
  geography affects access to, 214
  in low-cost carbon management example, 104
  shift from oil to, 43, 44, 97, 99, 102
Soros, George, 326, 327